FRINGE

Page 6:
Bell and Bishop: Like Minds
Writers: Zack Whedon & Julia Cho
Artist: Tom Mandrake
Colors: Carrie Strachan

Page 17:
Bell and Bishop: Excellent Soap
Writer: Mike Johnson
Artist: Tom Mandrake
Colors: Tony Aviña
& Carrie Strachan

Page 28:
Bell and Bishop: The Escape
Writer: Alex Katsnelson
Artist: Tom Mandrake
Colors: WildStorm FX

Page 39:
Bell and Bishop: Best Laid Plans
Writer: Danielle DiSpaltro
& Alex Katsnelson
Artist: Tom Mandrake
Colors: WildStorm FX

Page 50:
Bell and Bishop:
It Runs in the Family
Writers: Alex Katsnelson
& Danielle DiSpaltro
Artist: Tom Mandrake
Colors: WildStorm FX

Page 61:
Bell and Bishop: The Visitor
Writers: Danielle DiSpaltro,
Justin Doble & Alex Katsnelson
Artist: Tom Mandrake
Colors: WildStorm FX

Page 84:
The Prisoner
Writers: Alex Katsnelson
& Danielle DiSpaltro
Pencils: Simon Coleby
Inks: Cliff Rathburn with Coleby
Colors: Jim Charalampidis

Page 96:
Strangers on a Train
Writers: Alex Katsnelson
& Matthew Pitts
Artist: Tom Mandrake
Colors: Tony Aviña

Page 108:
Run Away
Writer: Mike Johnson
Artist: Tom Mandrake
Colors: WildStorm FX

Page 120:
Space Cowboy
Writer: Kim Cavyan
Artist: Tom Mandrake
Colors: Carrie Strachan
with Darlene Royer

Page 132:
Hard Copy
Writer: Mike Johnson
Artist: Tom Mandrake
Colors: WildStorm FX

Letterer:
Wes Abbott

Story Consultants:
Athena Wickham & Dave Baronoff

Special Thanks:
Jeff Pinkner & J.H. Wyman

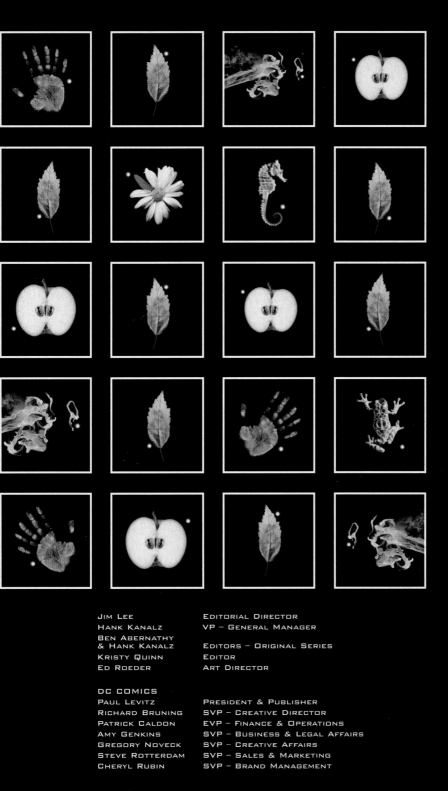

JIM LEE   EDITORIAL DIRECTOR
HANK KANALZ   VP – GENERAL MANAGER
BEN ABERNATHY
& HANK KANALZ   EDITORS – ORIGINAL SERIES
KRISTY QUINN   EDITOR
ED ROEDER   ART DIRECTOR

DC COMICS
PAUL LEVITZ   PRESIDENT & PUBLISHER
RICHARD BRUNING   SVP – CREATIVE DIRECTOR
PATRICK CALDON   EVP – FINANCE & OPERATIONS
AMY GENKINS   SVP – BUSINESS & LEGAL AFFAIRS
GREGORY NOVECK   SVP – CREATIVE AFFAIRS
STEVE ROTTERDAM   SVP – SALES & MARKETING
CHERYL RUBIN   SVP – BRAND MANAGEMENT

SUSTAINABLE FORESTRY INITIATIVE
Certified Fiber Sourcing
www.sfiprogram.org

PWC-SFICOC-260

FRINGE, published by WildStorm Productions. 888 Prospect St. #240, La Jolla, CA 92037. Cover, introduction and compilation Copyright © 2010 Warner Bros. Entertainment Inc. All Rights Reserved. Originally published in single magazine form as FRINGE #1-6 © 2008, 2009 Warner Bros. Entertainment Inc. All Rights Reserved.

FRINGE and all characters, the distinctive likenesses thereof and all related elements are trademarks of Warner Bros. Entertainment Inc. WildStorm and logo are trademarks of DC Comics. The stories, characters, and incidents mentioned in this magazine are entirely fictional. Printed on recyclable paper. WildStorm does not read or accept unsolicited submissions of ideas, stories or artwork. Printed by World Color Press, Inc, St-Romuald, QC, Canada. 11/18/09.

DC Comics, a Warner Bros. Entertainment Company.

ISBN: 978-1-4012-2491-2

Over the decades, comics have been maligned as corrupters of youth, reflections of widespread illiteracy, disrespected barnacles clinging to the underside of the mainstream. Turns out, being out of the spotlight of complete respectability has given comics a freedom to create that other media—particularly those involving expensive cameras, highly paid actors, and hardworking network executives—can't always give you. On the comics page it costs the same to draw a man crossing the street as it does to show a galaxy being born. There are no limits.

That's how we approached the FRINGE comics. Rather than just regurgitating episodes or aping the style of the show, we wanted to take advantage of the art form to tell stories that showcase how wide the world of *Fringe* is. You'll see Walter Bishop's memories—reliable or not—of his earliest experiments with William Bell, adventures that aren't constrained by special effects budgets or the fact that there is no historical proof that Hitler was actually eaten by a dinosaur.

You'll also meet characters who have never appeared on screen, but who have all been touched in some way by "The Pattern" slowly emerging across the world. Most of all we hope to give you a unique experience that you can only get from a youth-corrupting, illiteracy-spreading, disrespected medium. While this series of comics is not necessary to understanding the show on which it is based, neither is the show necessary to understand the comic. They are, however, both born of the same DNA. In a way, this series of comics have become our laboratory, where we can test ideas and imagine what might normally be impossible to produce. Devoted followers of this world will see the waves created in the comic ripple across the show.

Finally, we have to confess that we were late to the party. As kids, we were merely casual comic book readers, never imagining we would discover it as a medium we would want to work in or follow as adults. Something about the whole thing gives us that singular feeling from youth that we are somehow doing something slightly wrong, yet ultimately harmless—like playing hooky from school on your birthday.

Perhaps, then, comic books will always be on the, shall we say, fringe.

We wouldn't want it any other way.

Roberto Orci & Alex Kurtzman

Longtime collaborators and creative visionaries Alex Kurtzman and Roberto Orci began their work together as innovative storytellers in a Los Angeles-area high school. Inspired by Spielbergian action-adventure films, Kurtzman and Orci reunited after college to write for the popular television series *Hercules* and *Xena: Warrior Princess*. After working with J.J. Abrams on his hit spy series *Alias* and his directorial debut *Mission: Impossible III*, they continued with a string of blockbusters including *Transformers* and its sequel *Transformers: Revenge of the Fallen* and the summer sci-fi splash *Star Trek*. In addition to writing and producing feature films, Kurtzman and Orci are the co-creators and consulting producers on the hit Warner Bros. series *Fringe*.

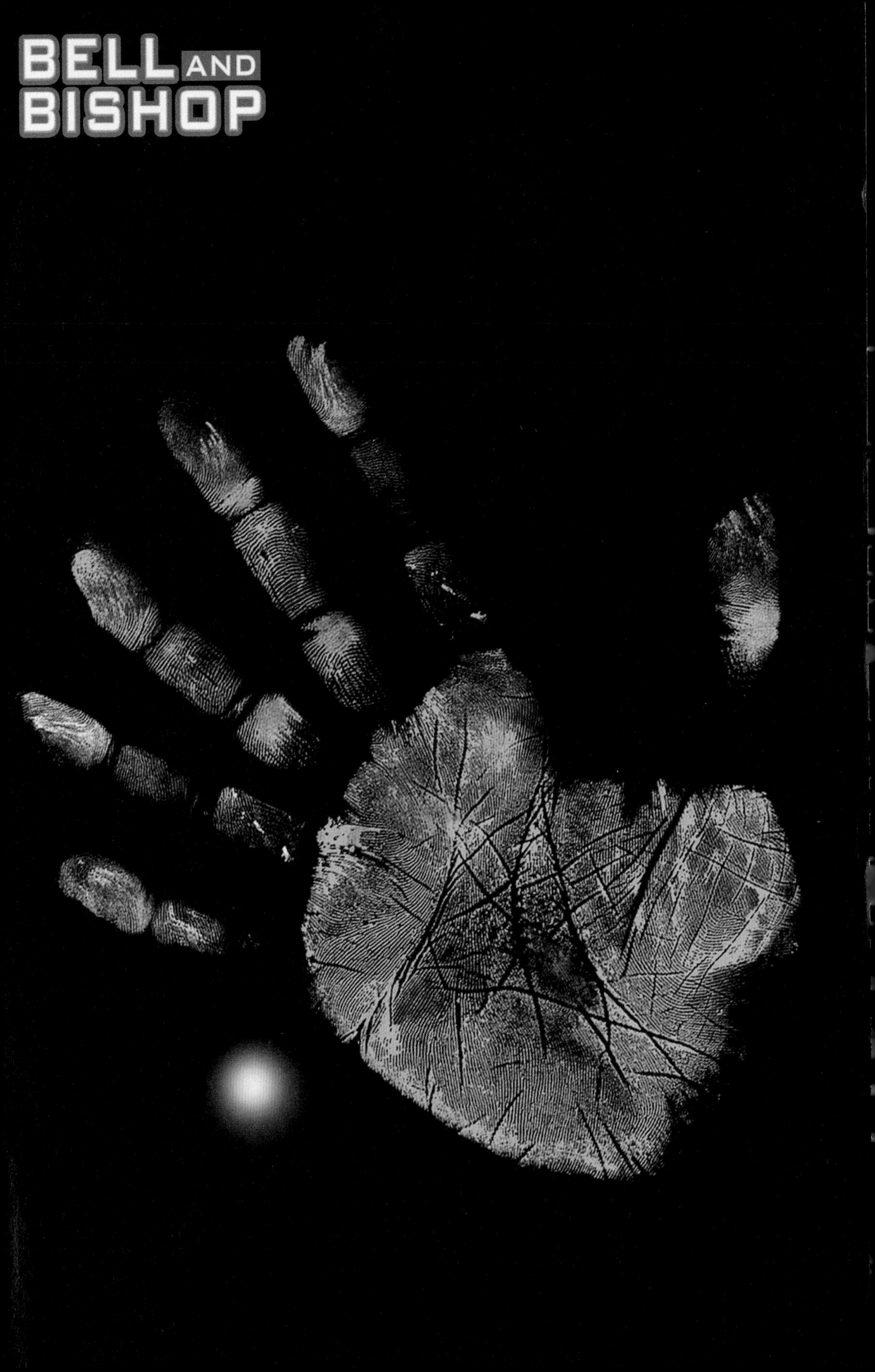
BELL AND BISHOP

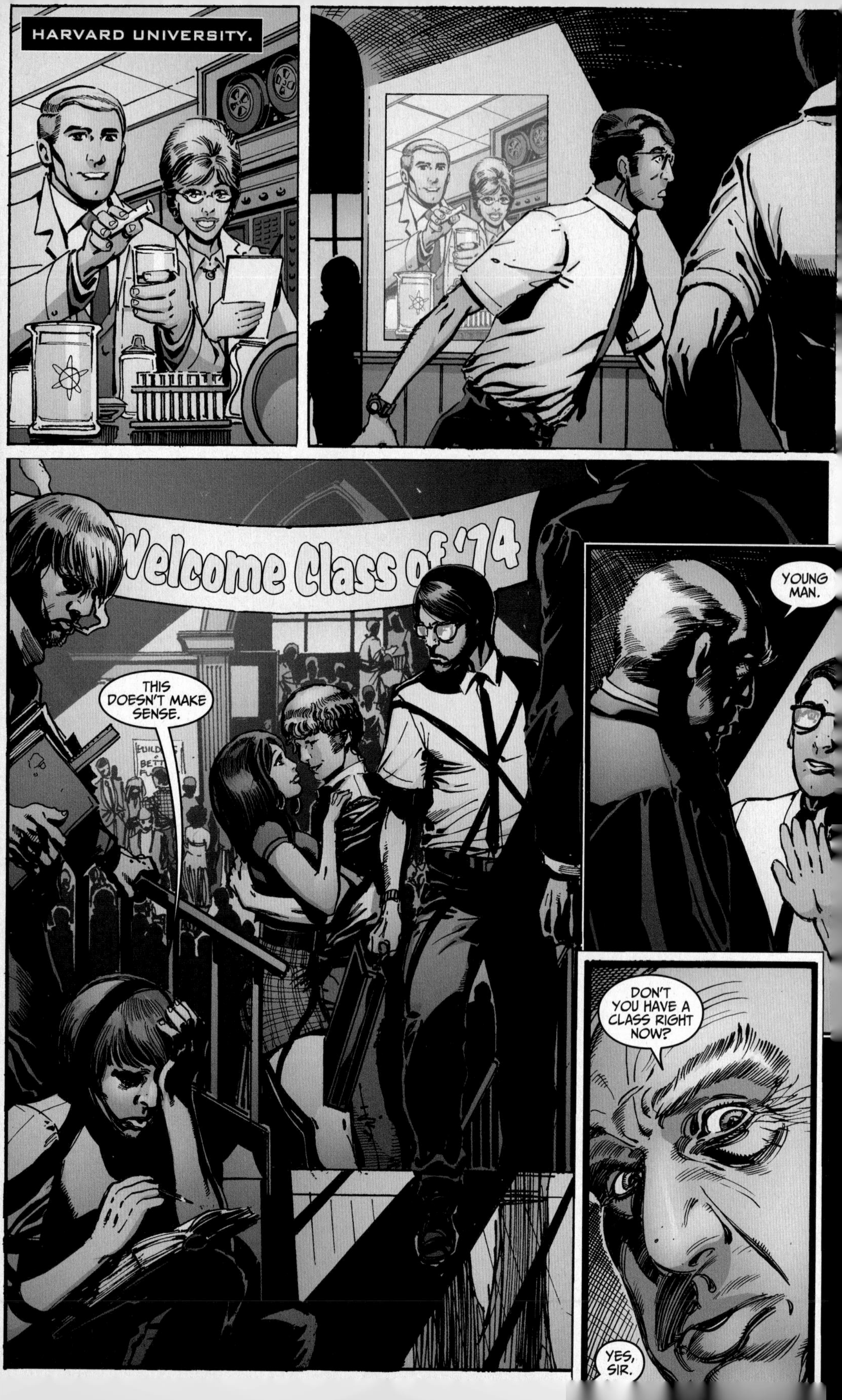
HARVARD UNIVERSITY.
Welcome Class of '74
THIS DOESN'T MAKE SENSE.
YOUNG MAN.
DON'T YOU HAVE A CLASS RIGHT NOW?
YES, SIR.

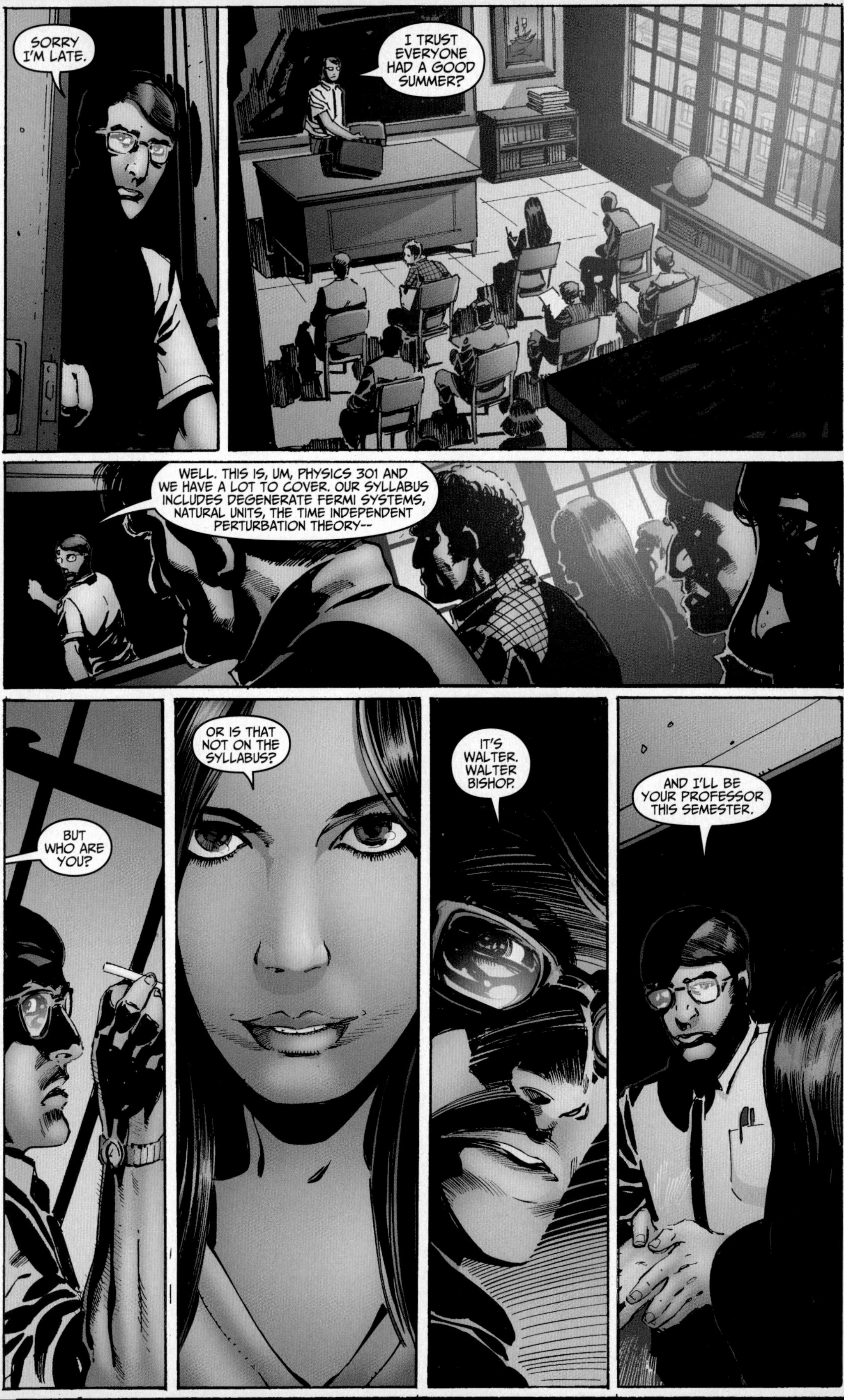
SORRY I'M LATE.
I TRUST EVERYONE HAD A GOOD SUMMER?
WELL. THIS IS, UM, PHYSICS 301 AND WE HAVE A LOT TO COVER. OUR SYLLABUS INCLUDES DEGENERATE FERMI SYSTEMS, NATURAL UNITS, THE TIME INDEPENDENT PERTURBATION THEORY--
BUT WHO ARE YOU?
OR IS THAT NOT ON THE SYLLABUS?
IT'S WALTER. WALTER BISHOP.
AND I'LL BE YOUR PROFESSOR THIS SEMESTER.

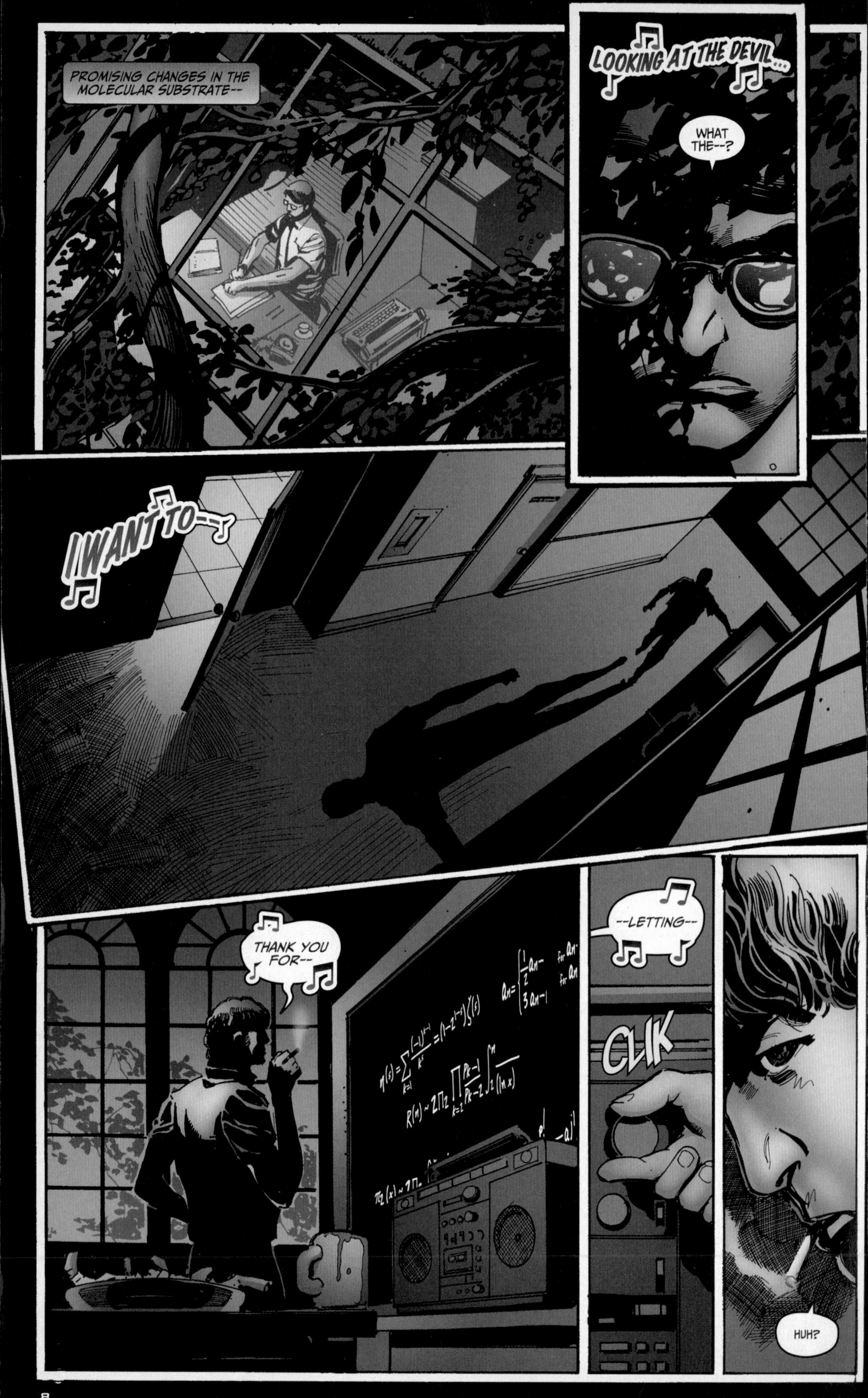
PROMISING CHANGES IN THE MOLECULAR SUBSTRATE--
LOOKING AT THE DEVIL...
WHAT THE--?
I WANT TO--
THANK YOU FOR--
--LETTING--
CLIK
HUH?

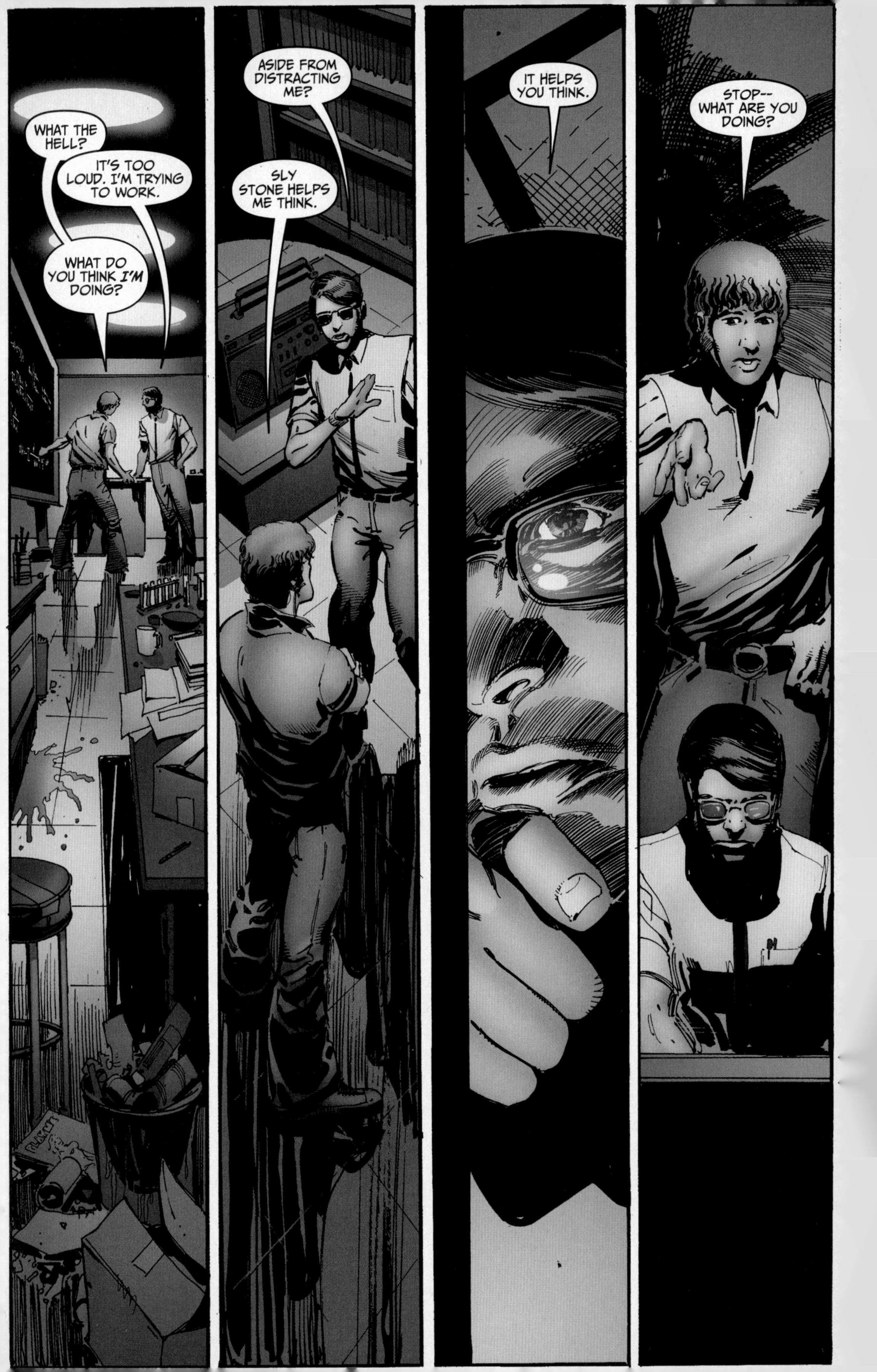
WHAT THE HELL?
IT'S TOO LOUD. I'M TRYING TO WORK.
WHAT DO YOU THINK *I'M* DOING?
ASIDE FROM DISTRACTING ME?
SLY STONE HELPS ME THINK.
IT HELPS YOU THINK.
STOP-- WHAT ARE YOU DOING?

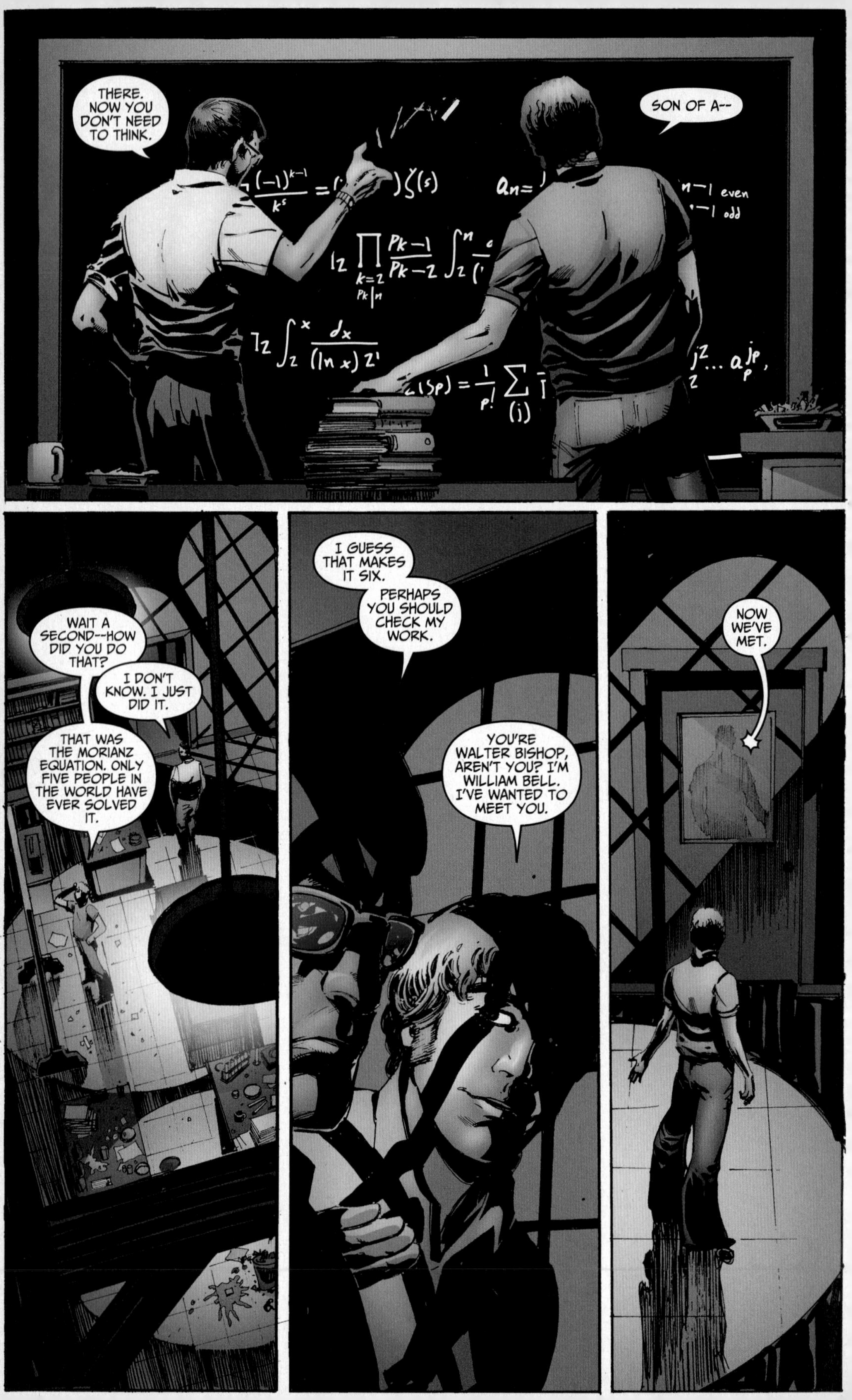
THERE. NOW YOU DON'T NEED TO THINK.
SON OF A--
WAIT A SECOND--HOW DID YOU DO THAT?
I DON'T KNOW. I JUST DID IT.
THAT WAS THE MORIANZ EQUATION. ONLY FIVE PEOPLE IN THE WORLD HAVE EVER SOLVED IT.
I GUESS THAT MAKES IT SIX.
PERHAPS YOU SHOULD CHECK MY WORK.
YOU'RE WALTER BISHOP, AREN'T YOU? I'M WILLIAM BELL. I'VE WANTED TO MEET YOU.
NOW WE'VE MET.

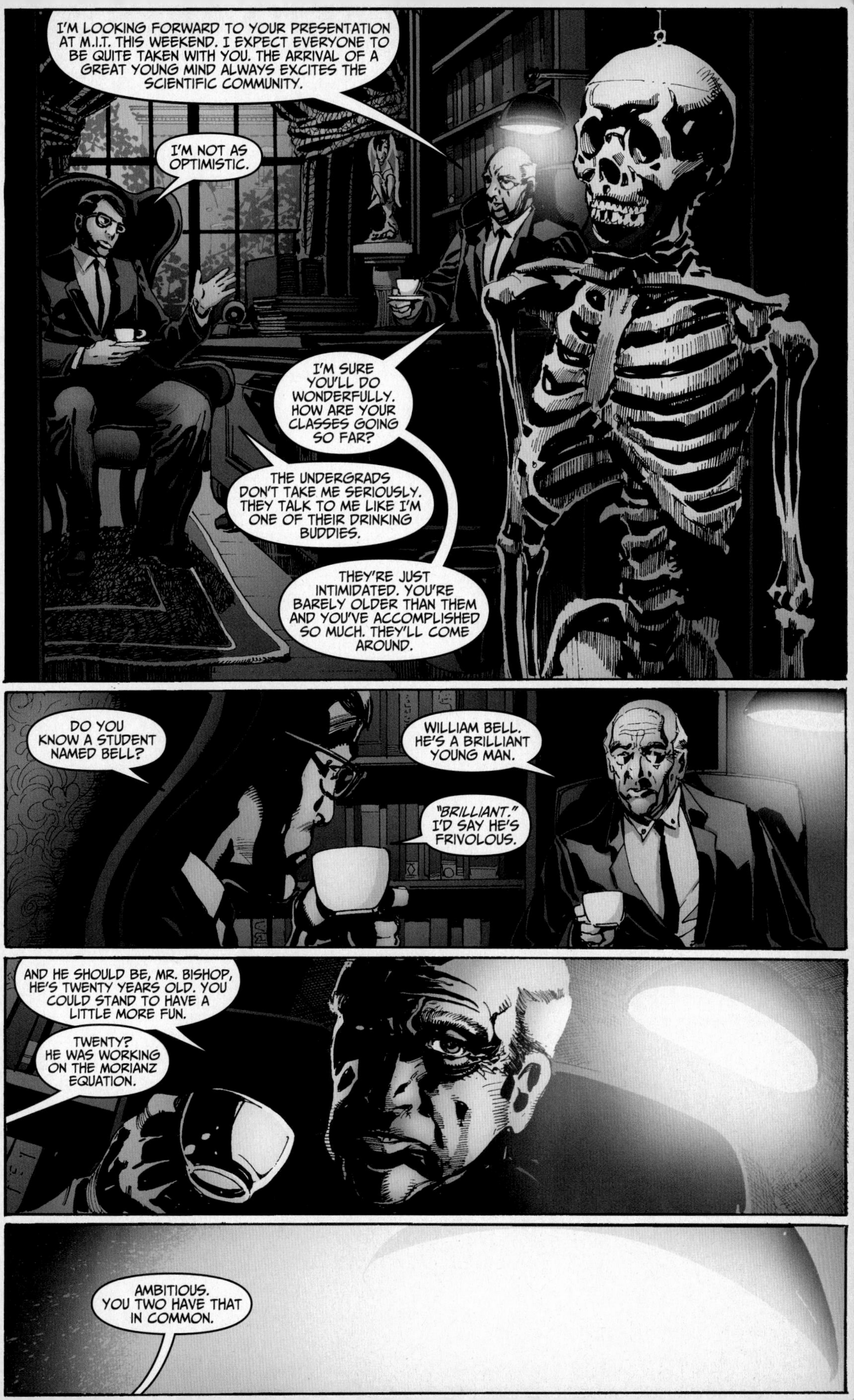
I'M LOOKING FORWARD TO YOUR PRESENTATION AT M.I.T. THIS WEEKEND. I EXPECT EVERYONE TO BE QUITE TAKEN WITH YOU. THE ARRIVAL OF A GREAT YOUNG MIND ALWAYS EXCITES THE SCIENTIFIC COMMUNITY.
I'M NOT AS OPTIMISTIC.
I'M SURE YOU'LL DO WONDERFULLY. HOW ARE YOUR CLASSES GOING SO FAR?
THE UNDERGRADS DON'T TAKE ME SERIOUSLY. THEY TALK TO ME LIKE I'M ONE OF THEIR DRINKING BUDDIES.
THEY'RE JUST INTIMIDATED. YOU'RE BARELY OLDER THAN THEM AND YOU'VE ACCOMPLISHED SO MUCH. THEY'LL COME AROUND.
DO YOU KNOW A STUDENT NAMED BELL?
WILLIAM BELL. HE'S A BRILLIANT YOUNG MAN.
"BRILLIANT." I'D SAY HE'S FRIVOLOUS.
AND HE SHOULD BE, MR. BISHOP, HE'S TWENTY YEARS OLD. YOU COULD STAND TO HAVE A LITTLE MORE FUN.
TWENTY? HE WAS WORKING ON THE MORIANZ EQUATION.
AMBITIOUS. YOU TWO HAVE THAT IN COMMON.

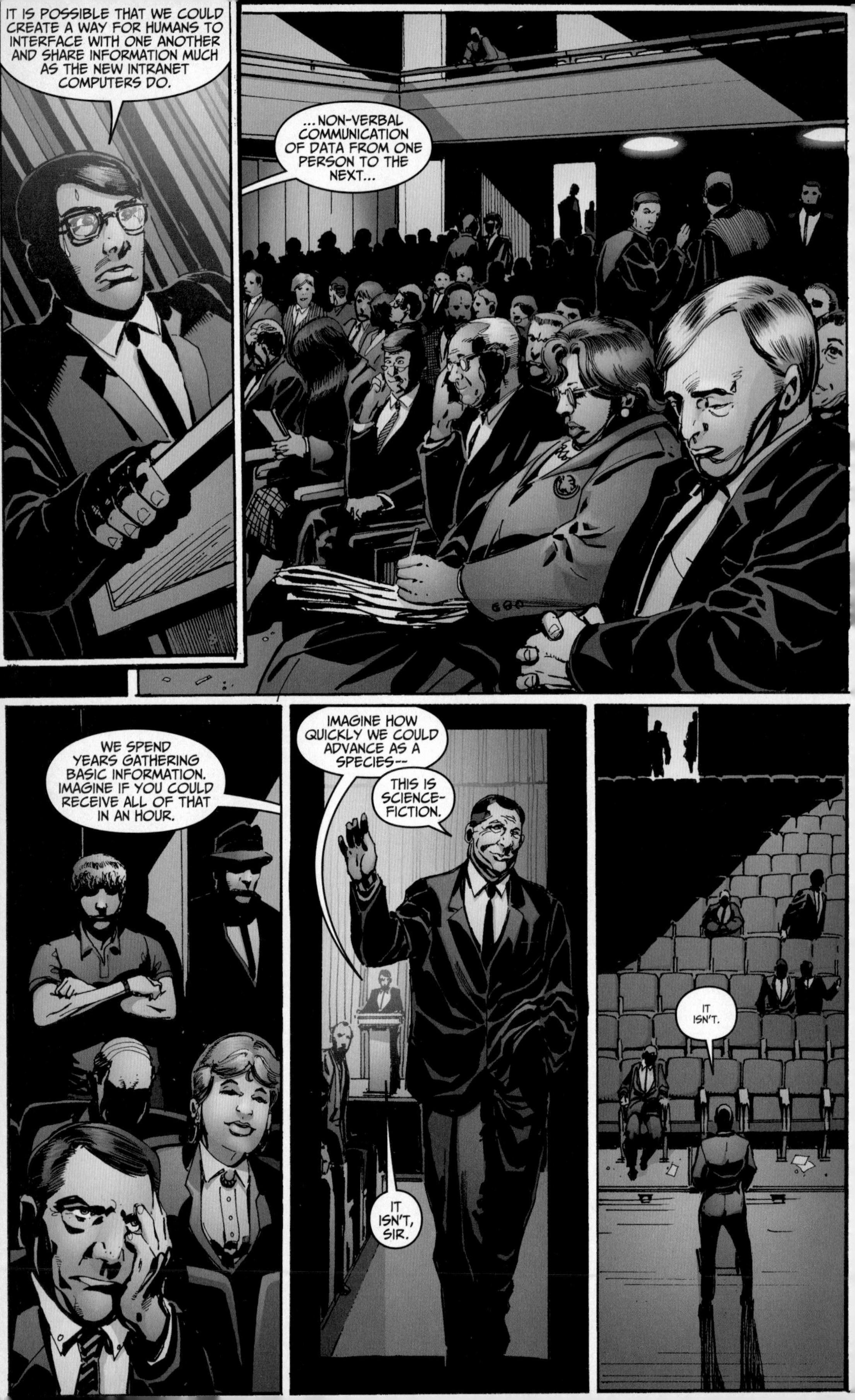

IT IS POSSIBLE THAT WE COULD CREATE A WAY FOR HUMANS TO INTERFACE WITH ONE ANOTHER AND SHARE INFORMATION MUCH AS THE NEW INTRANET COMPUTERS DO.
...NON-VERBAL COMMUNICATION OF DATA FROM ONE PERSON TO THE NEXT...
WE SPEND YEARS GATHERING BASIC INFORMATION. IMAGINE IF YOU COULD RECEIVE ALL OF THAT IN AN HOUR.
IMAGINE HOW QUICKLY WE COULD ADVANCE AS A SPECIES--
THIS IS SCIENCE-FICTION.
IT ISN'T, SIR.
IT ISN'T.

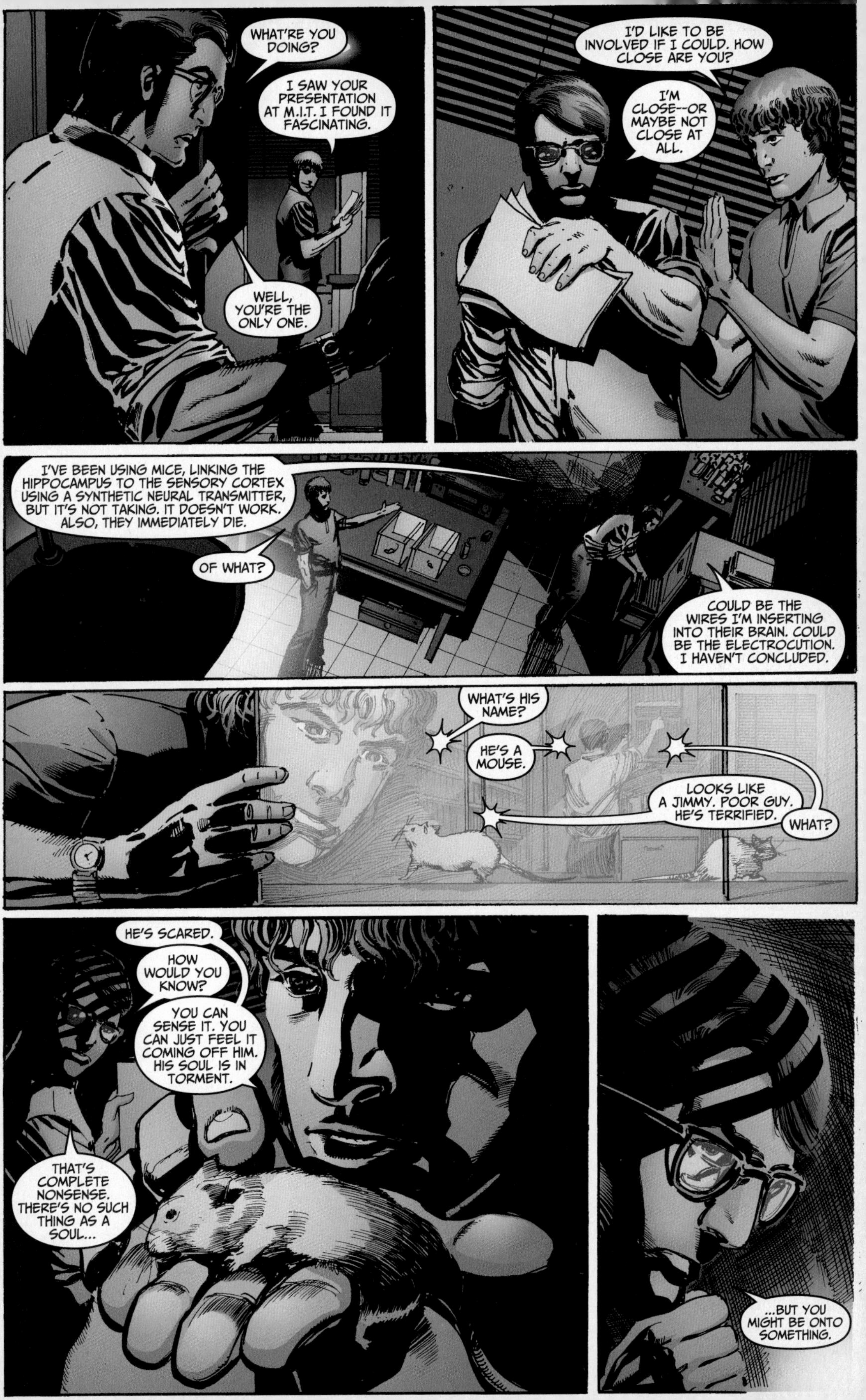
WHAT'RE YOU DOING?
I SAW YOUR PRESENTATION AT M.I.T. I FOUND IT FASCINATING.
WELL, YOU'RE THE ONLY ONE.
I'D LIKE TO BE INVOLVED IF I COULD. HOW CLOSE ARE YOU?
I'M CLOSE--OR MAYBE NOT CLOSE AT ALL.
I'VE BEEN USING MICE, LINKING THE HIPPOCAMPUS TO THE SENSORY CORTEX USING A SYNTHETIC NEURAL TRANSMITTER, BUT IT'S NOT TAKING. IT DOESN'T WORK. ALSO, THEY IMMEDIATELY DIE.
OF WHAT?
COULD BE THE WIRES I'M INSERTING INTO THEIR BRAIN. COULD BE THE ELECTROCUTION. I HAVEN'T CONCLUDED.
WHAT'S HIS NAME?
HE'S A MOUSE.
LOOKS LIKE A JIMMY. POOR GUY. HE'S TERRIFIED.
WHAT?
HE'S SCARED.
HOW WOULD YOU KNOW?
YOU CAN SENSE IT. YOU CAN JUST FEEL IT COMING OFF HIM. HIS SOUL IS IN TORMENT.
THAT'S COMPLETE NONSENSE. THERE'S NO SUCH THING AS A SOUL...
...BUT YOU MIGHT BE ONTO SOMETHING.

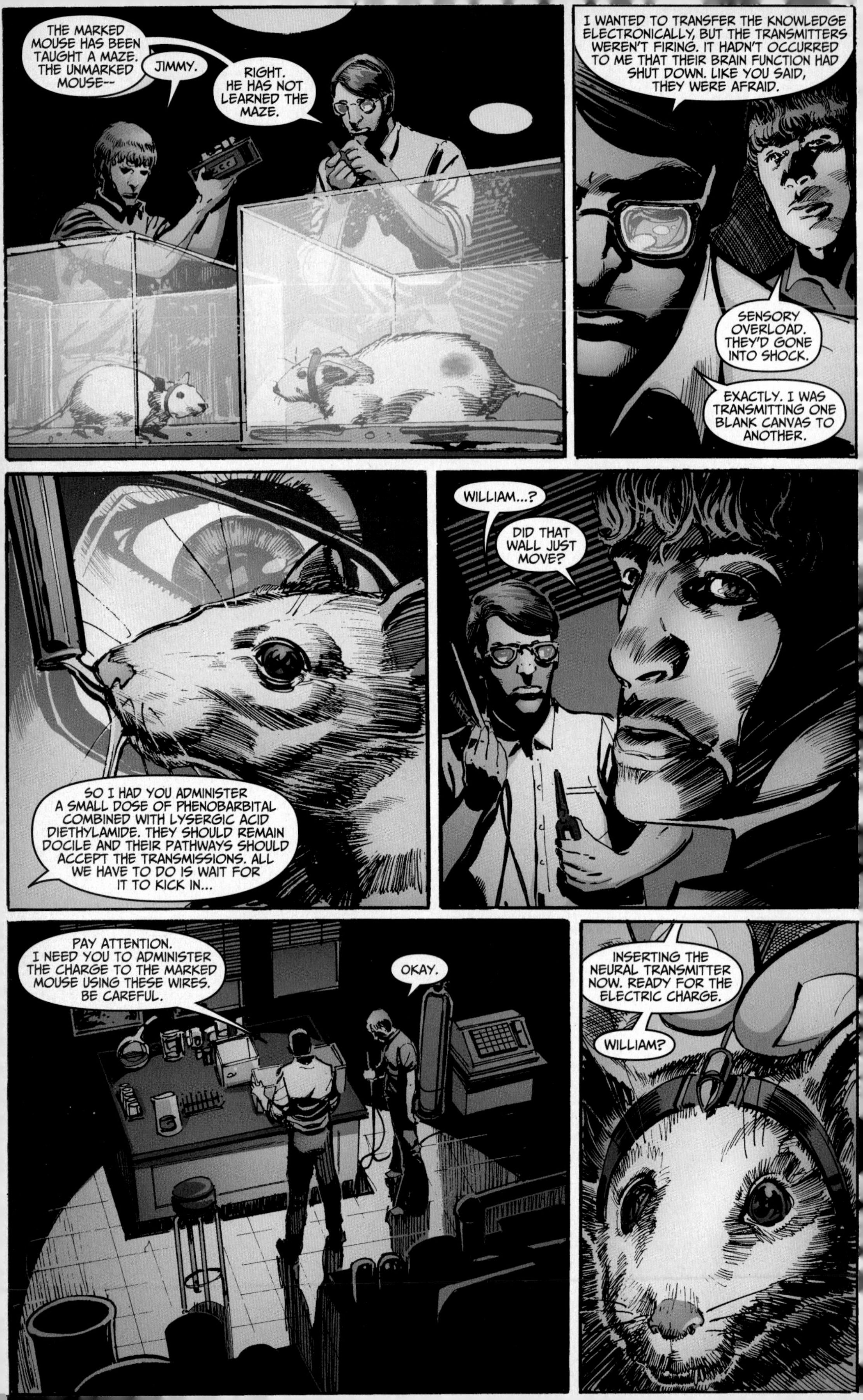
THE MARKED MOUSE HAS BEEN TAUGHT A MAZE. THE UNMARKED MOUSE--
JIMMY.
RIGHT. HE HAS NOT LEARNED THE MAZE.
I WANTED TO TRANSFER THE KNOWLEDGE ELECTRONICALLY, BUT THE TRANSMITTERS WEREN'T FIRING. IT HADN'T OCCURRED TO ME THAT THEIR BRAIN FUNCTION HAD SHUT DOWN. LIKE YOU SAID, THEY WERE AFRAID.
SENSORY OVERLOAD. THEY'D GONE INTO SHOCK.
EXACTLY. I WAS TRANSMITTING ONE BLANK CANVAS TO ANOTHER.
SO I HAD YOU ADMINISTER A SMALL DOSE OF PHENOBARBITAL COMBINED WITH LYSERGIC ACID DIETHYLAMIDE. THEY SHOULD REMAIN DOCILE AND THEIR PATHWAYS SHOULD ACCEPT THE TRANSMISSIONS. ALL WE HAVE TO DO IS WAIT FOR IT TO KICK IN...
WILLIAM...?
DID THAT WALL JUST MOVE?
PAY ATTENTION. I NEED YOU TO ADMINISTER THE CHARGE TO THE MARKED MOUSE USING THESE WIRES. BE CAREFUL.
OKAY.
INSERTING THE NEURAL TRANSMITTER NOW. READY FOR THE ELECTRIC CHARGE.
WILLIAM?

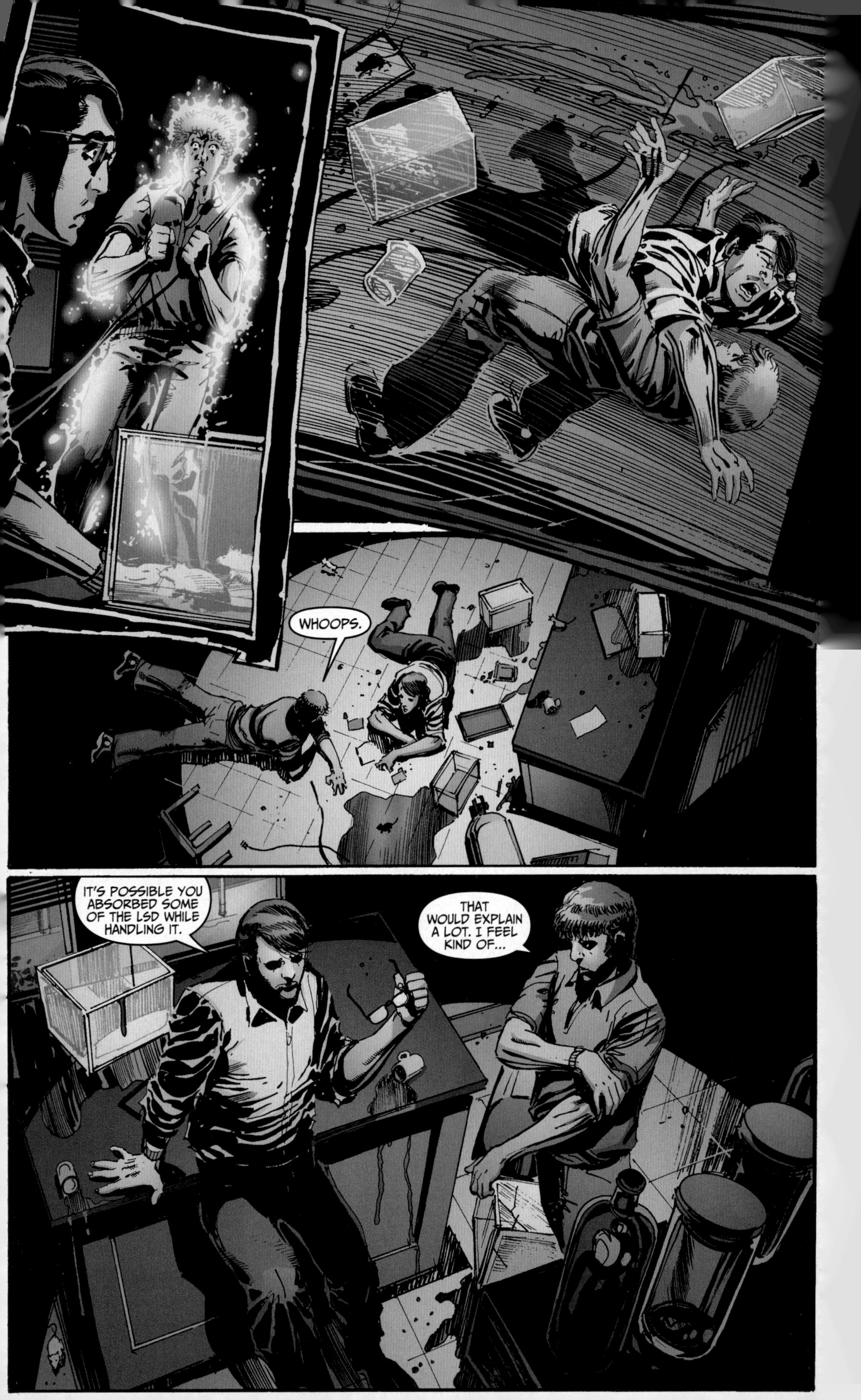
WHOOPS.
IT'S POSSIBLE YOU ABSORBED SOME OF THE LSD WHILE HANDLING IT.
THAT WOULD EXPLAIN A LOT. I FEEL KIND OF...

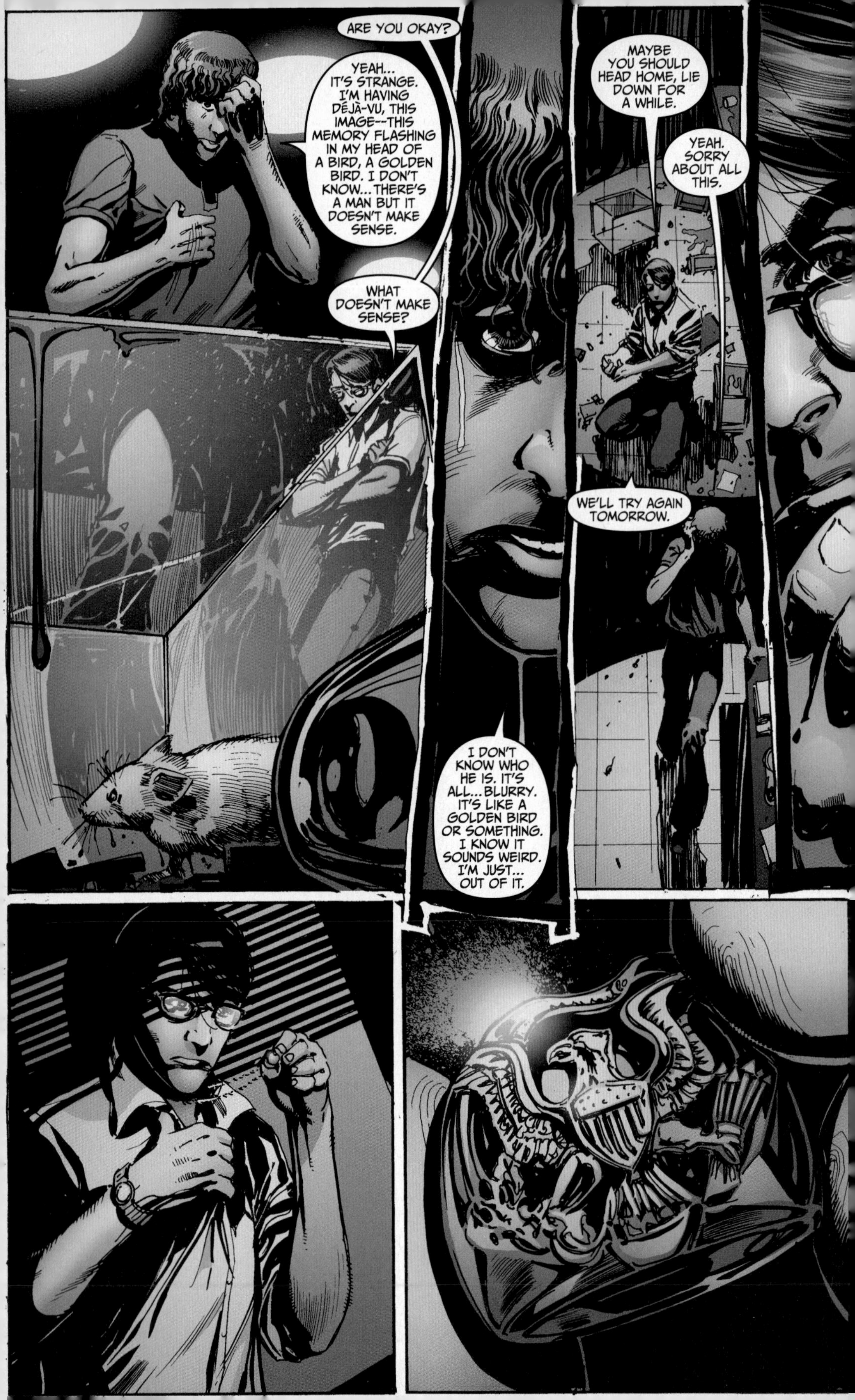
ARE YOU OKAY?
YEAH... IT'S STRANGE. I'M HAVING DÉJÀ-VU, THIS IMAGE--THIS MEMORY FLASHING IN MY HEAD OF A BIRD, A GOLDEN BIRD. I DON'T KNOW... THERE'S A MAN BUT IT DOESN'T MAKE SENSE.
WHAT DOESN'T MAKE SENSE?
I DON'T KNOW WHO HE IS. IT'S ALL... BLURRY. IT'S LIKE A GOLDEN BIRD OR SOMETHING. I KNOW IT SOUNDS WEIRD. I'M JUST... OUT OF IT.
MAYBE YOU SHOULD HEAD HOME, LIE DOWN FOR A WHILE.
YEAH. SORRY ABOUT ALL THIS.
WE'LL TRY AGAIN TOMORROW.

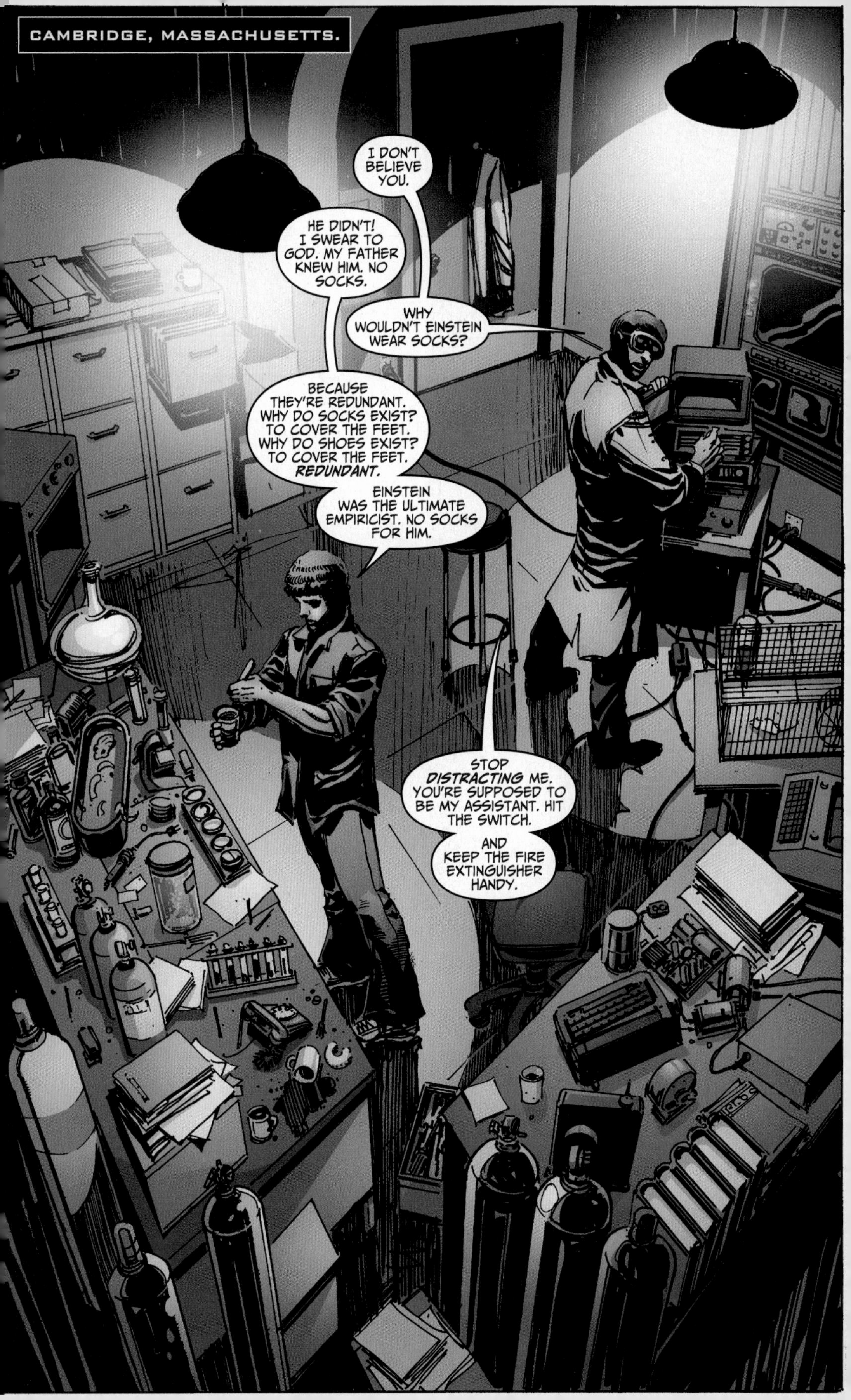
CAMBRIDGE, MASSACHUSETTS.
I DON'T BELIEVE YOU.
HE DIDN'T! I SWEAR TO GOD. MY FATHER KNEW HIM. NO SOCKS.
WHY WOULDN'T EINSTEIN WEAR SOCKS?
BECAUSE THEY'RE REDUNDANT. WHY DO SOCKS EXIST? TO COVER THE FEET. WHY DO SHOES EXIST? TO COVER THE FEET. REDUNDANT.
EINSTEIN WAS THE ULTIMATE EMPIRICIST. NO SOCKS FOR HIM.
STOP DISTRACTING ME. YOU'RE SUPPOSED TO BE MY ASSISTANT. HIT THE SWITCH.
AND KEEP THE FIRE EXTINGUISHER HANDY.

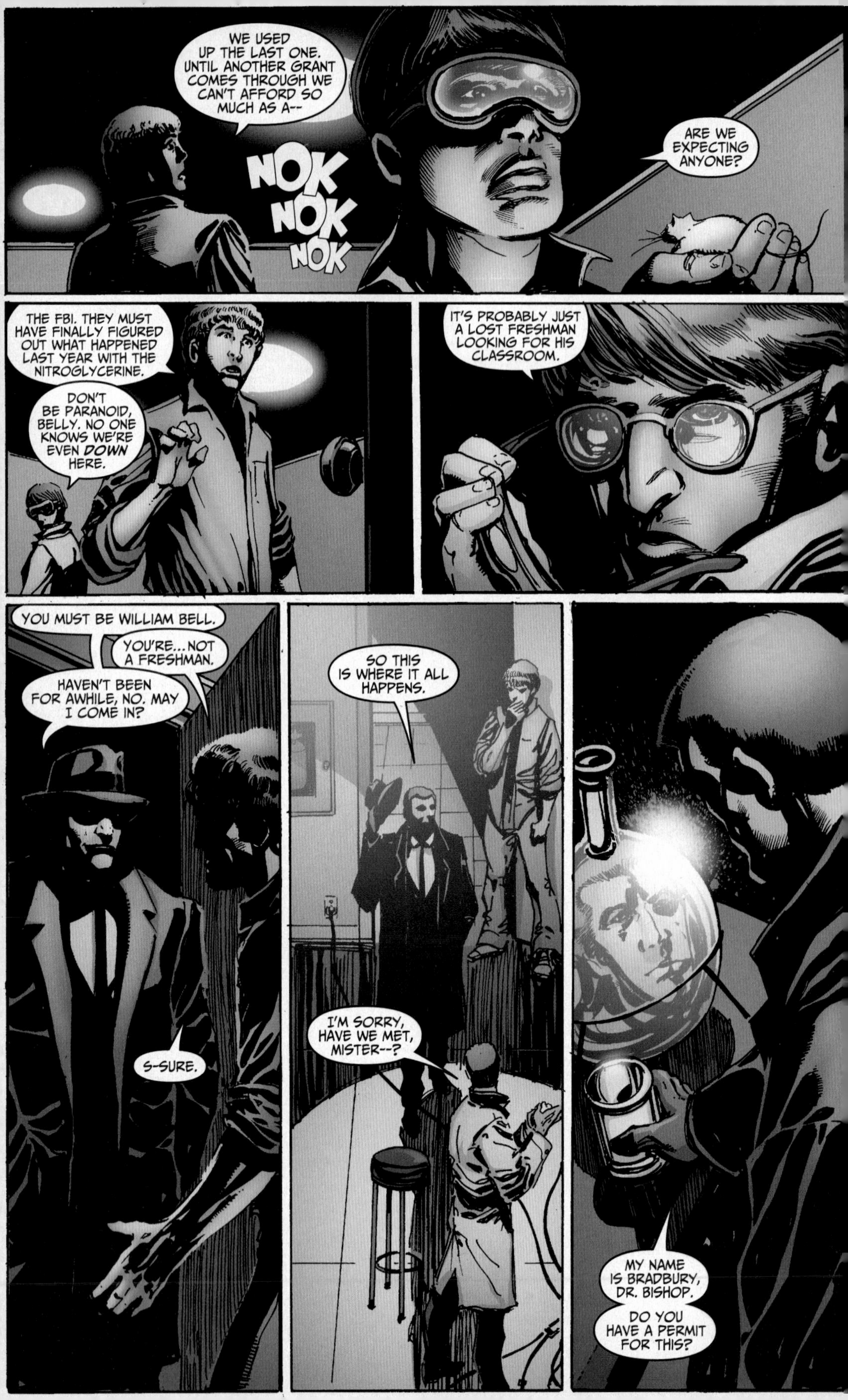
WE USED UP THE LAST ONE. UNTIL ANOTHER GRANT COMES THROUGH WE CAN'T AFFORD SO MUCH AS A--
NOK NOK NOK
ARE WE EXPECTING ANYONE?
THE FBI. THEY MUST HAVE FINALLY FIGURED OUT WHAT HAPPENED LAST YEAR WITH THE NITROGLYCERINE.
DON'T BE PARANOID, BELLY. NO ONE KNOWS WE'RE EVEN *DOWN* HERE.
IT'S PROBABLY JUST A LOST FRESHMAN LOOKING FOR HIS CLASSROOM.
YOU MUST BE WILLIAM BELL.
YOU'RE...NOT A FRESHMAN.
HAVEN'T BEEN FOR AWHILE, NO. MAY I COME IN?
S-SURE.
SO THIS IS WHERE IT ALL HAPPENS.
I'M SORRY, HAVE WE MET, MISTER--?
MY NAME IS BRADBURY, DR. BISHOP.
DO YOU HAVE A PERMIT FOR THIS?

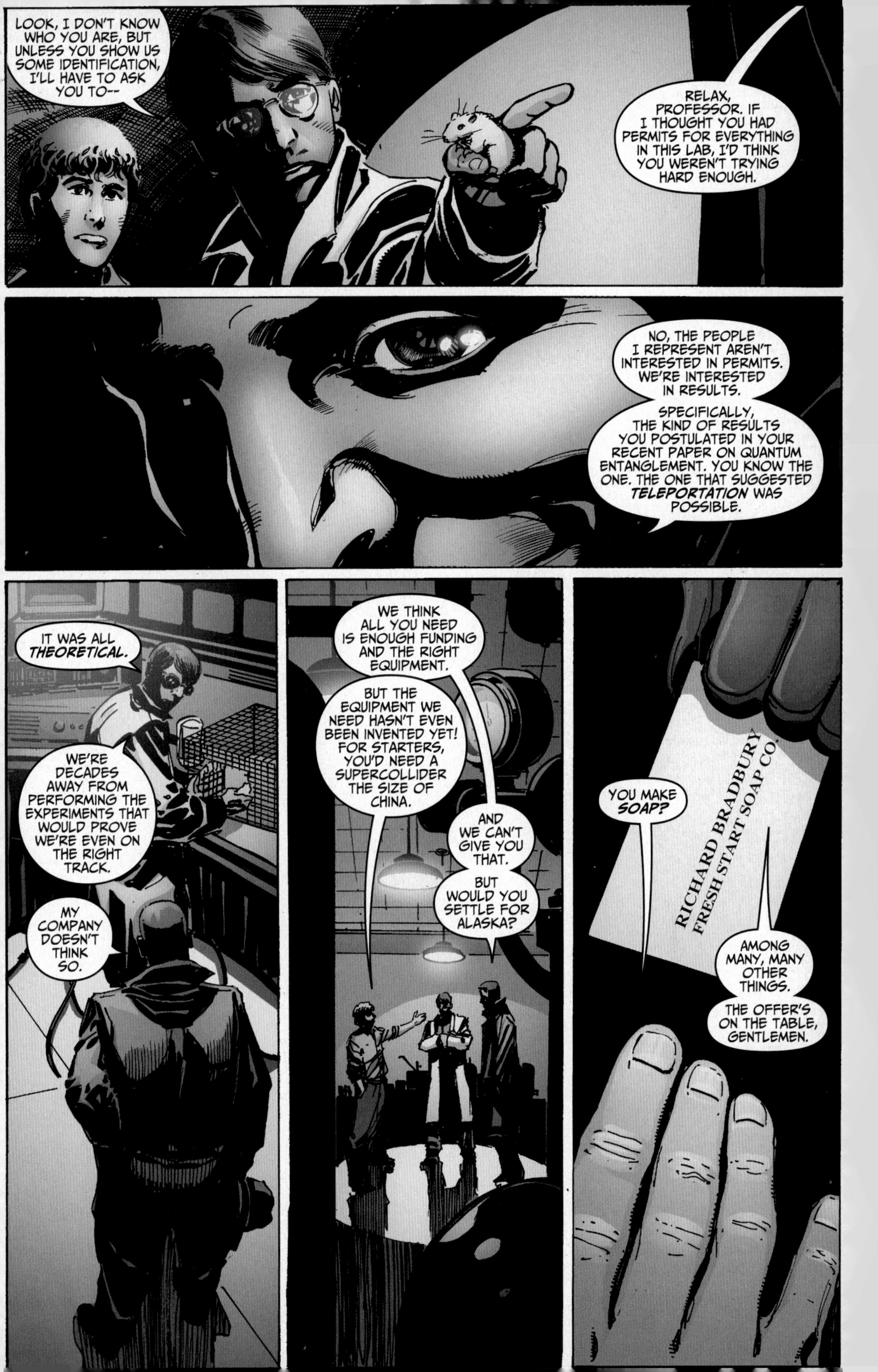
LOOK, I DON'T KNOW WHO YOU ARE, BUT UNLESS YOU SHOW US SOME IDENTIFICATION, I'LL HAVE TO ASK YOU TO--
RELAX, PROFESSOR. IF I THOUGHT YOU HAD PERMITS FOR EVERYTHING IN THIS LAB, I'D THINK YOU WEREN'T TRYING HARD ENOUGH.
NO, THE PEOPLE I REPRESENT AREN'T INTERESTED IN PERMITS. WE'RE INTERESTED IN RESULTS.
SPECIFICALLY, THE KIND OF RESULTS YOU POSTULATED IN YOUR RECENT PAPER ON QUANTUM ENTANGLEMENT. YOU KNOW THE ONE. THE ONE THAT SUGGESTED *TELEPORTATION* WAS POSSIBLE.
IT WAS ALL *THEORETICAL.*
WE'RE DECADES AWAY FROM PERFORMING THE EXPERIMENTS THAT WOULD PROVE WE'RE EVEN ON THE RIGHT TRACK.
MY COMPANY DOESN'T THINK SO.
WE THINK ALL YOU NEED IS ENOUGH FUNDING AND THE RIGHT EQUIPMENT.
BUT THE EQUIPMENT WE NEED HASN'T EVEN BEEN INVENTED YET! FOR STARTERS, YOU'D NEED A SUPERCOLLIDER THE SIZE OF CHINA.
AND WE CAN'T GIVE YOU THAT.
BUT WOULD YOU SETTLE FOR ALASKA?
RICHARD BRADBURY
FRESH START SOAP CO.
YOU MAKE *SOAP?*
AMONG MANY, MANY OTHER THINGS.
THE OFFER'S ON THE TABLE, GENTLEMEN.

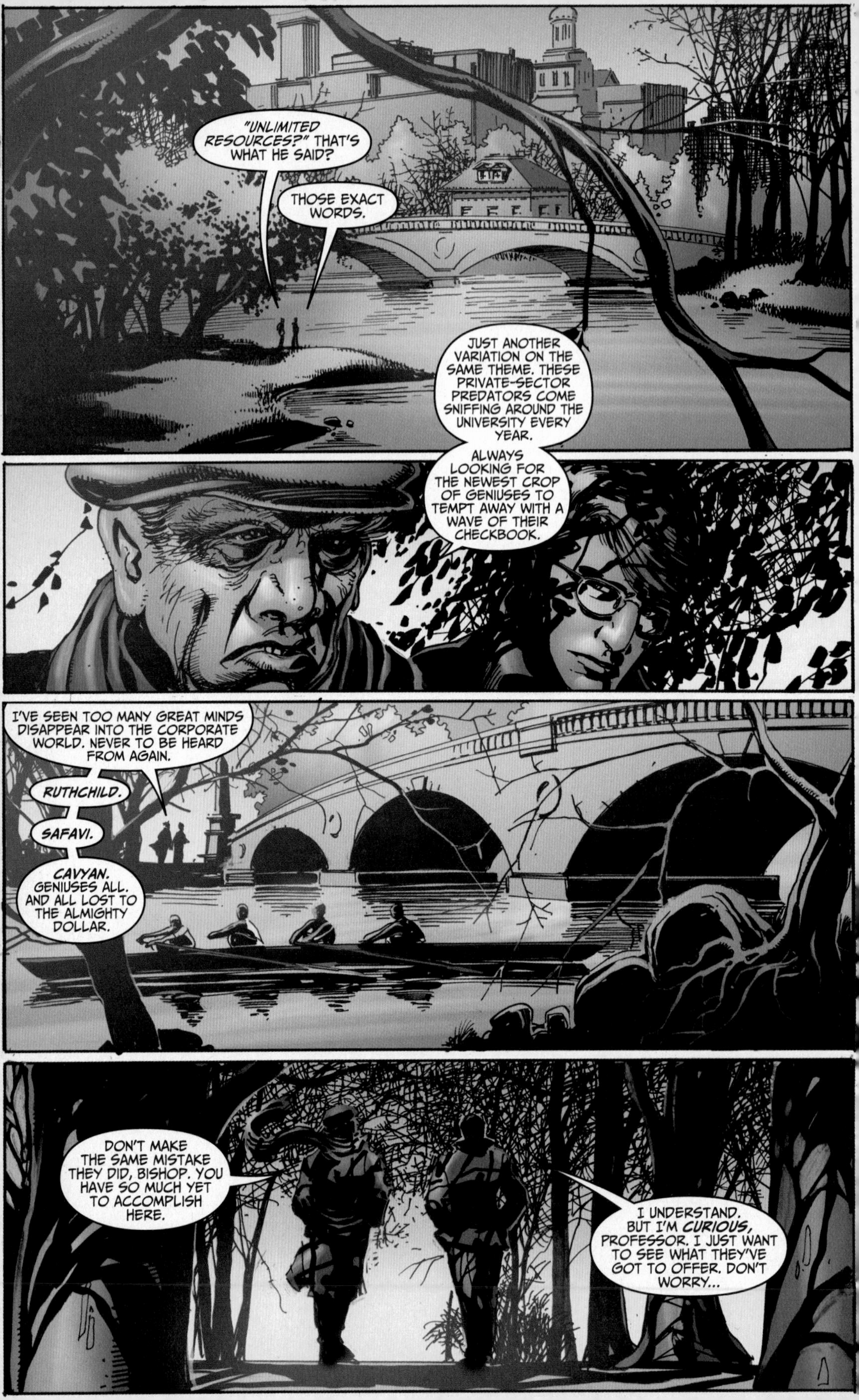
"UNLIMITED RESOURCES?" THAT'S WHAT HE SAID?
THOSE EXACT WORDS.
JUST ANOTHER VARIATION ON THE SAME THEME. THESE PRIVATE-SECTOR PREDATORS COME SNIFFING AROUND THE UNIVERSITY EVERY YEAR.
ALWAYS LOOKING FOR THE NEWEST CROP OF GENIUSES TO TEMPT AWAY WITH A WAVE OF THEIR CHECKBOOK.
I'VE SEEN TOO MANY GREAT MINDS DISAPPEAR INTO THE CORPORATE WORLD. NEVER TO BE HEARD FROM AGAIN.
RUTHCHILD.
SAFAVI.
CAVYAN. GENIUSES ALL. AND ALL LOST TO THE ALMIGHTY DOLLAR.
DON'T MAKE THE SAME MISTAKE THEY DID, BISHOP. YOU HAVE SO MUCH YET TO ACCOMPLISH HERE.
I UNDERSTAND. BUT I'M CURIOUS, PROFESSOR. I JUST WANT TO SEE WHAT THEY'VE GOT TO OFFER. DON'T WORRY...

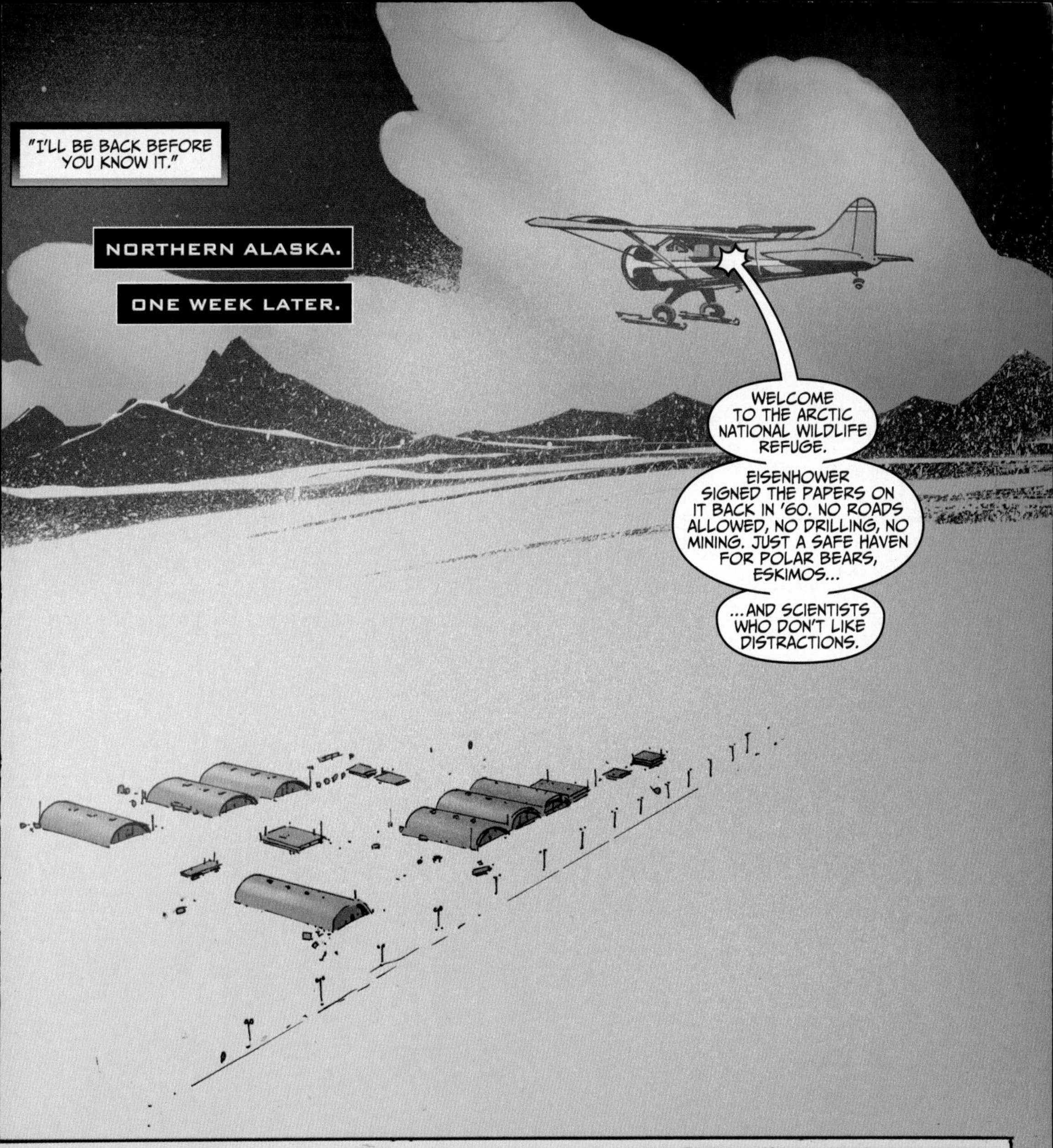
"I'LL BE BACK BEFORE YOU KNOW IT."
NORTHERN ALASKA.
ONE WEEK LATER.
WELCOME TO THE ARCTIC NATIONAL WILDLIFE REFUGE.
EISENHOWER SIGNED THE PAPERS ON IT BACK IN '60. NO ROADS ALLOWED, NO DRILLING, NO MINING. JUST A SAFE HAVEN FOR POLAR BEARS, ESKIMOS...
...AND SCIENTISTS WHO DON'T LIKE DISTRACTIONS.

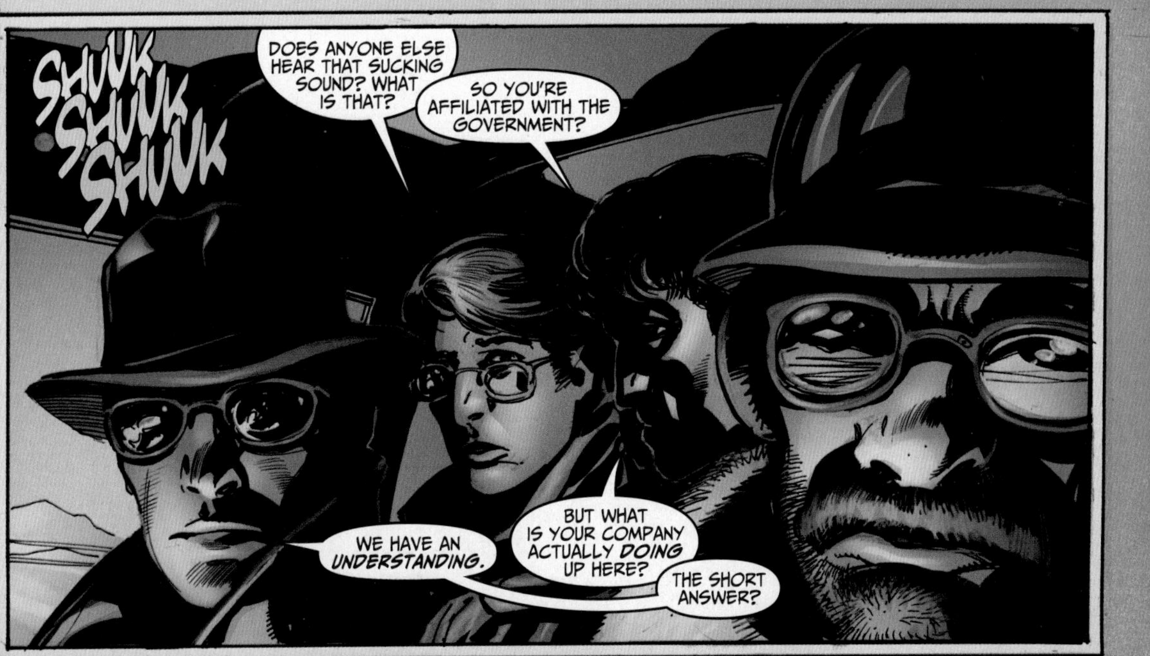
SHUUK SHUUK SHUUK
DOES ANYONE ELSE HEAR THAT SUCKING SOUND? WHAT IS THAT?
SO YOU'RE AFFILIATED WITH THE GOVERNMENT?
WE HAVE AN *UNDERSTANDING.*
BUT WHAT IS YOUR COMPANY ACTUALLY *DOING* UP HERE?
THE SHORT ANSWER?

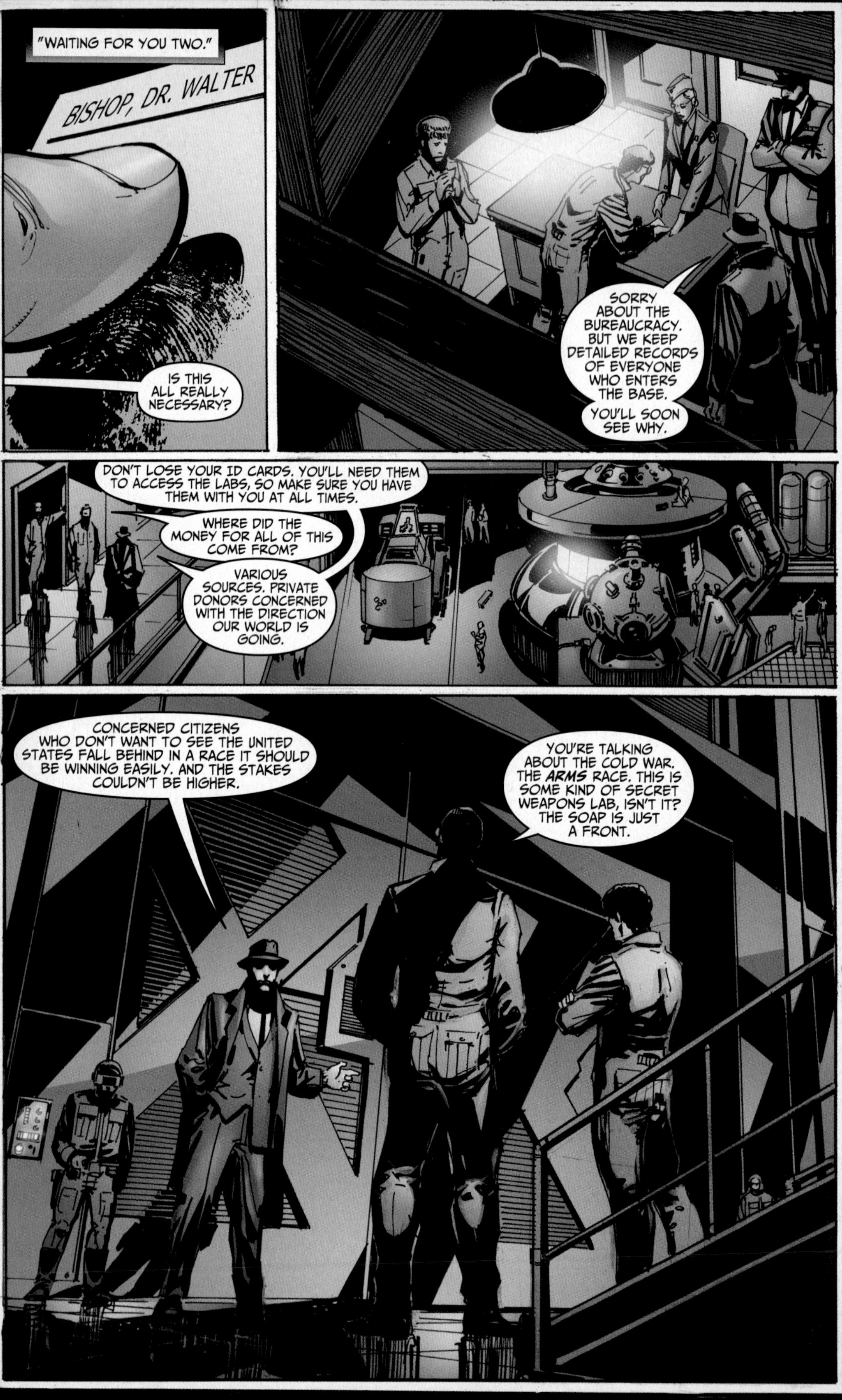

"WAITING FOR YOU TWO."
BISHOP, DR. WALTER
IS THIS ALL REALLY NECESSARY?
SORRY ABOUT THE BUREAUCRACY. BUT WE KEEP DETAILED RECORDS OF EVERYONE WHO ENTERS THE BASE.
YOU'LL SOON SEE WHY.
DON'T LOSE YOUR ID CARDS. YOU'LL NEED THEM TO ACCESS THE LABS, SO MAKE SURE YOU HAVE THEM WITH YOU AT ALL TIMES.
WHERE DID THE MONEY FOR ALL OF THIS COME FROM?
VARIOUS SOURCES. PRIVATE DONORS CONCERNED WITH THE DIRECTION OUR WORLD IS GOING.
CONCERNED CITIZENS WHO DON'T WANT TO SEE THE UNITED STATES FALL BEHIND IN A RACE IT SHOULD BE WINNING EASILY. AND THE STAKES COULDN'T BE HIGHER.
YOU'RE TALKING ABOUT THE COLD WAR. THE *ARMS* RACE. THIS IS SOME KIND OF SECRET WEAPONS LAB, ISN'T IT? THE SOAP IS JUST A FRONT.

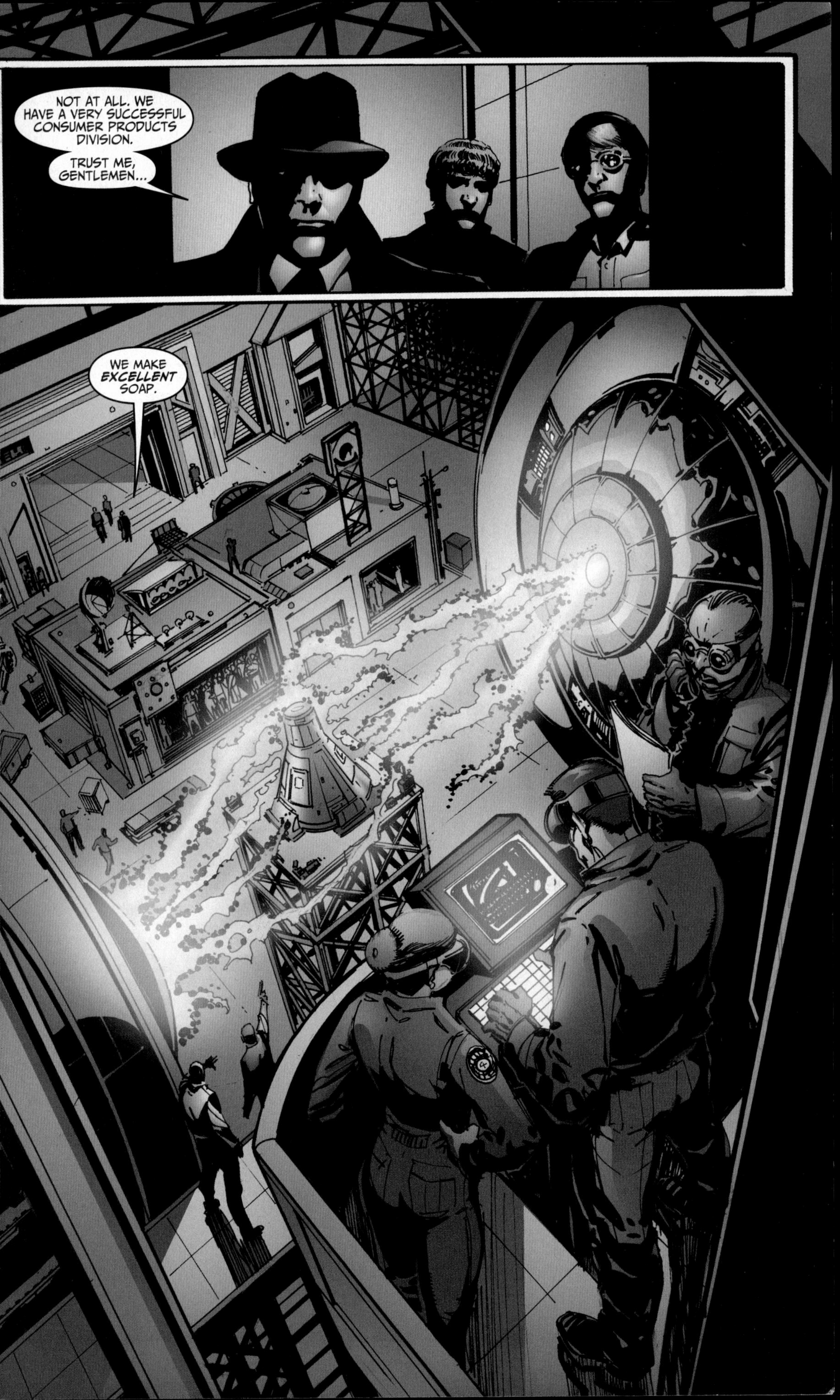
NOT AT ALL. WE HAVE A VERY SUCCESSFUL CONSUMER PRODUCTS DIVISION.
TRUST ME, GENTLEMEN...
WE MAKE *EXCELLENT* SOAP.

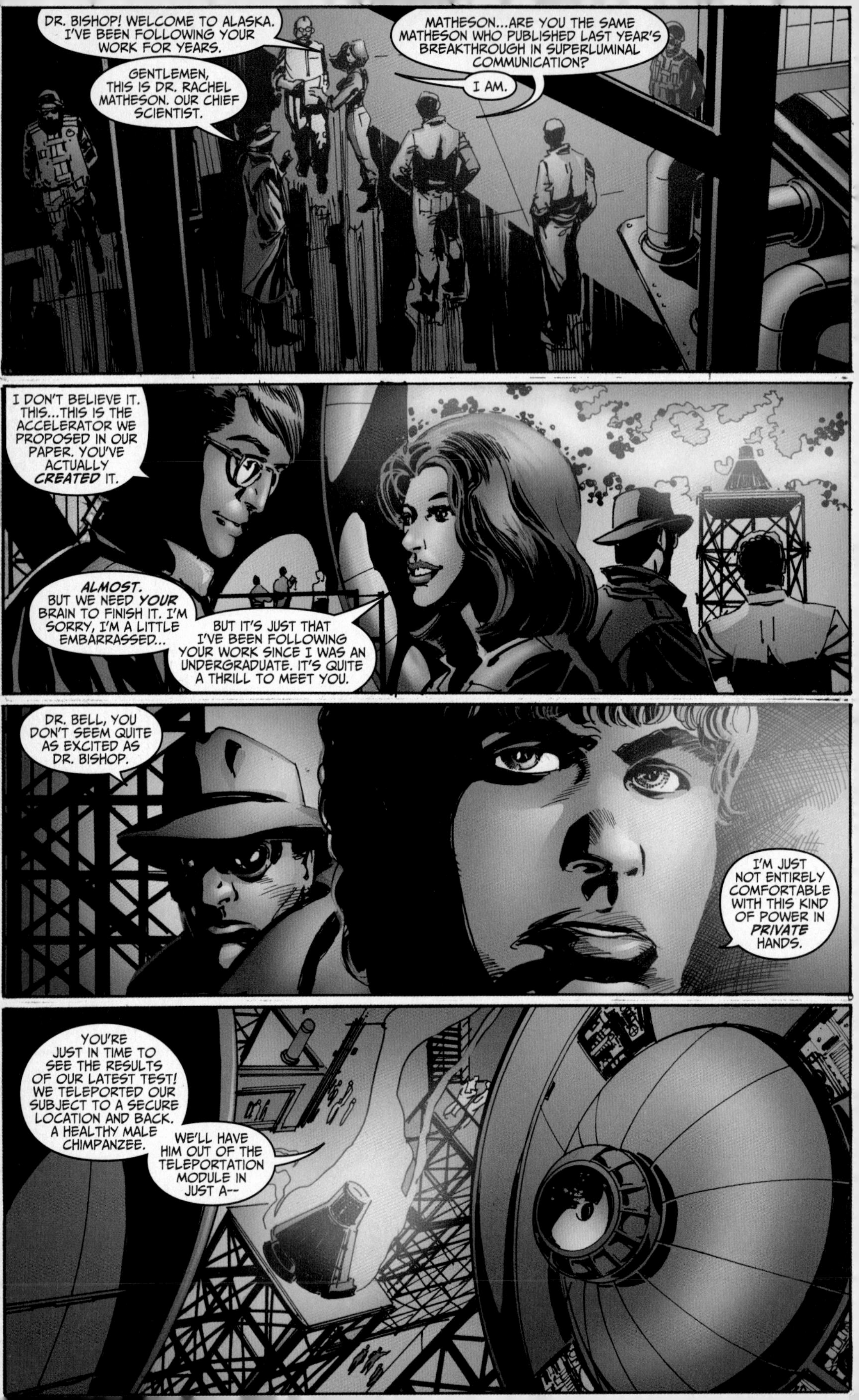
DR. BISHOP! WELCOME TO ALASKA. I'VE BEEN FOLLOWING YOUR WORK FOR YEARS.
GENTLEMEN, THIS IS DR. RACHEL MATHESON. OUR CHIEF SCIENTIST.
MATHESON...ARE YOU THE SAME MATHESON WHO PUBLISHED LAST YEAR'S BREAKTHROUGH IN SUPERLUMINAL COMMUNICATION?
I AM.
I DON'T BELIEVE IT. THIS...THIS IS THE ACCELERATOR WE PROPOSED IN OUR PAPER. YOU'VE ACTUALLY *CREATED* IT.
ALMOST. BUT WE NEED *YOUR* BRAIN TO FINISH IT. I'M SORRY, I'M A LITTLE EMBARRASSED...
BUT IT'S JUST THAT I'VE BEEN FOLLOWING YOUR WORK SINCE I WAS AN UNDERGRADUATE. IT'S QUITE A THRILL TO MEET YOU.
DR. BELL, YOU DON'T SEEM QUITE AS EXCITED AS DR. BISHOP.
I'M JUST NOT ENTIRELY COMFORTABLE WITH THIS KIND OF POWER IN *PRIVATE* HANDS.
YOU'RE JUST IN TIME TO SEE THE RESULTS OF OUR LATEST TEST! WE TELEPORTED OUR SUBJECT TO A SECURE LOCATION AND BACK. A HEALTHY MALE CHIMPANZEE.
WE'LL HAVE HIM OUT OF THE TELEPORTATION MODULE IN JUST A--

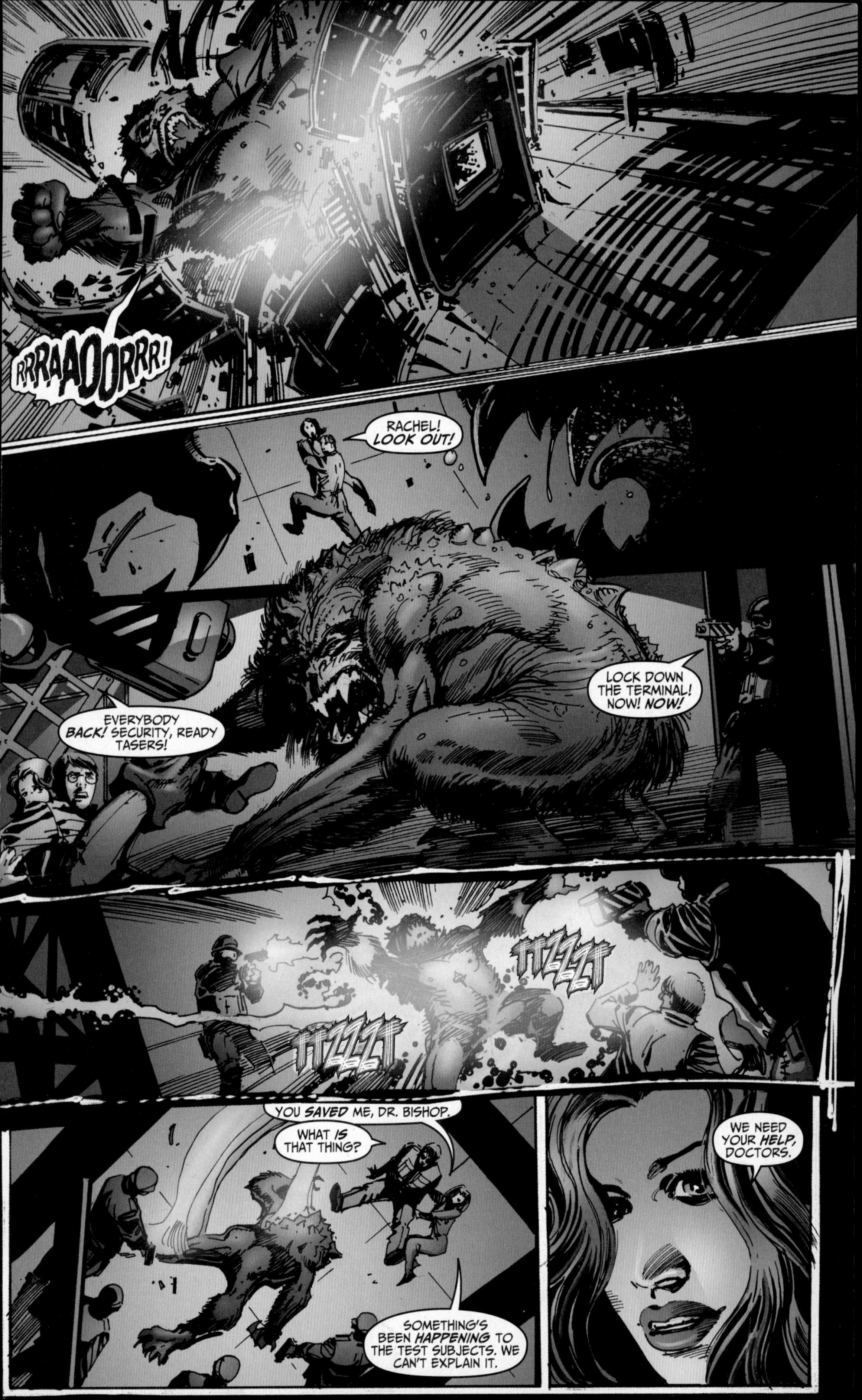
RRRAADORRR!
RACHEL! LOOK OUT!
LOCK DOWN THE TERMINAL! NOW! NOW!
EVERYBODY BACK! SECURITY, READY TASERS!
TTZZZT
TTZZZT
YOU SAVED ME, DR. BISHOP.
WHAT IS THAT THING?
SOMETHING'S BEEN HAPPENING TO THE TEST SUBJECTS. WE CAN'T EXPLAIN IT.
WE NEED YOUR HELP, DOCTORS.

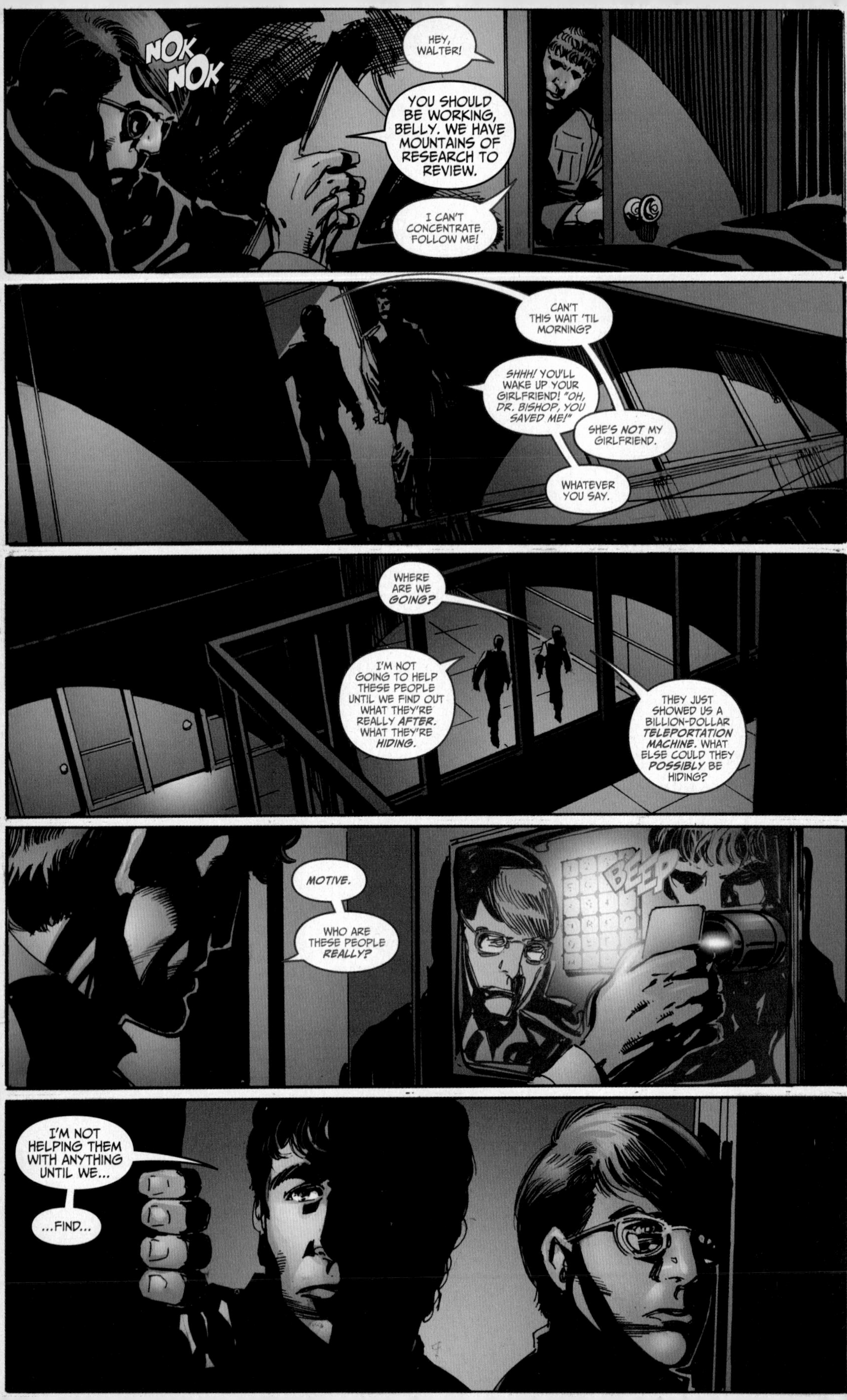
NOK NOK
HEY, WALTER!
YOU SHOULD BE WORKING, BELLY. WE HAVE MOUNTAINS OF RESEARCH TO REVIEW.
I CAN'T CONCENTRATE. FOLLOW ME!
CAN'T THIS WAIT 'TIL MORNING?
SHHH! YOU'LL WAKE UP YOUR GIRLFRIEND! "OH, DR. BISHOP, YOU SAVED ME!"
SHE'S NOT MY GIRLFRIEND.
WHATEVER YOU SAY.
WHERE ARE WE GOING?
I'M NOT GOING TO HELP THESE PEOPLE UNTIL WE FIND OUT WHAT THEY'RE REALLY AFTER. WHAT THEY'RE HIDING.
THEY JUST SHOWED US A BILLION-DOLLAR TELEPORTATION MACHINE. WHAT ELSE COULD THEY POSSIBLY BE HIDING?
MOTIVE.
WHO ARE THESE PEOPLE REALLY?
BEEP
I'M NOT HELPING THEM WITH ANYTHING UNTIL WE...
...FIND...

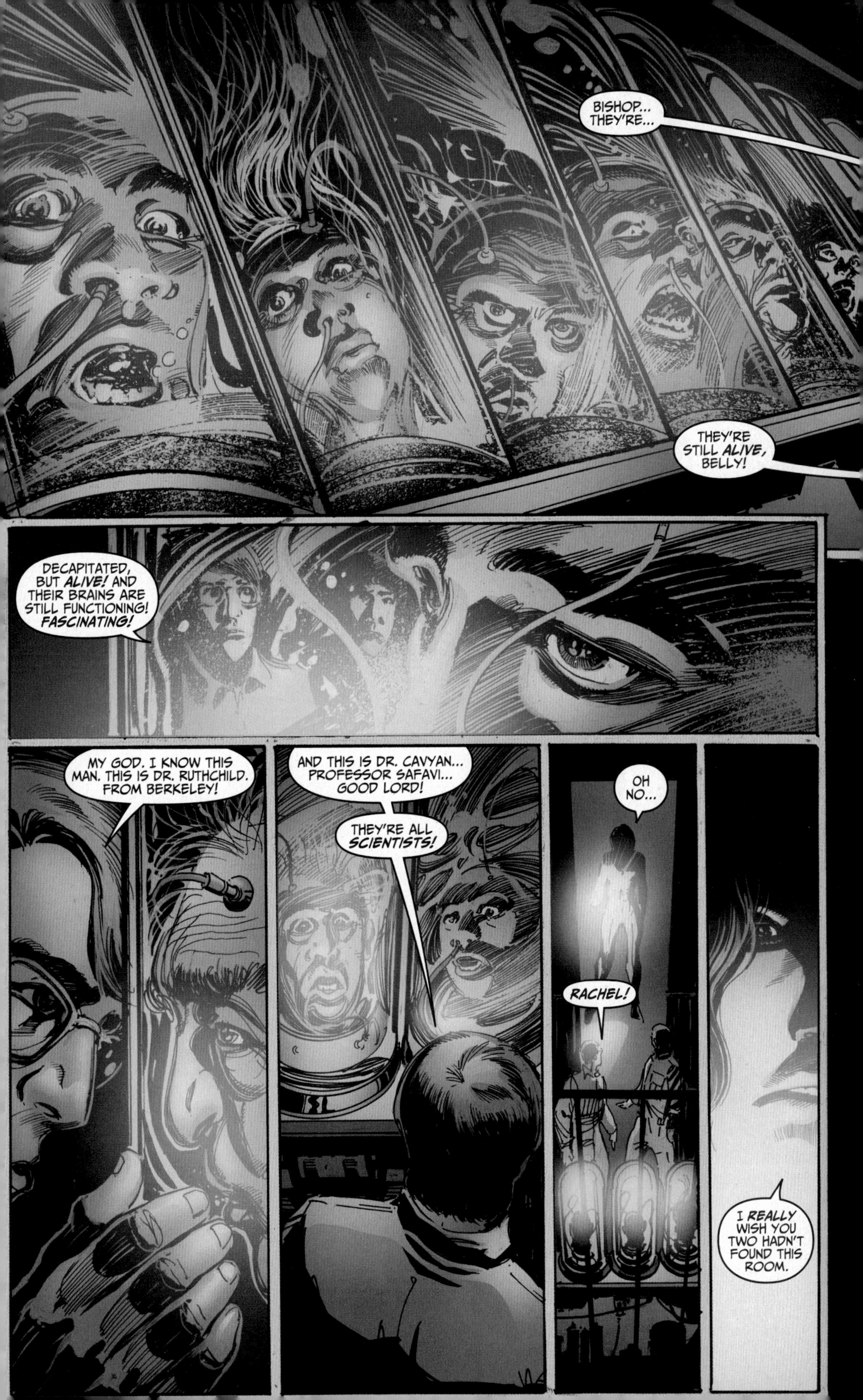
BISHOP... THEY'RE...
THEY'RE STILL ALIVE, BELLY!
DECAPITATED, BUT ALIVE! AND THEIR BRAINS ARE STILL FUNCTIONING! FASCINATING!
MY GOD. I KNOW THIS MAN. THIS IS DR. RUTHCHILD. FROM BERKELEY!
AND THIS IS DR. CAVYAN... PROFESSOR SAFAVI... GOOD LORD!
THEY'RE ALL SCIENTISTS!
OH NO...
RACHEL!
I REALLY WISH YOU TWO HADN'T FOUND THIS ROOM.

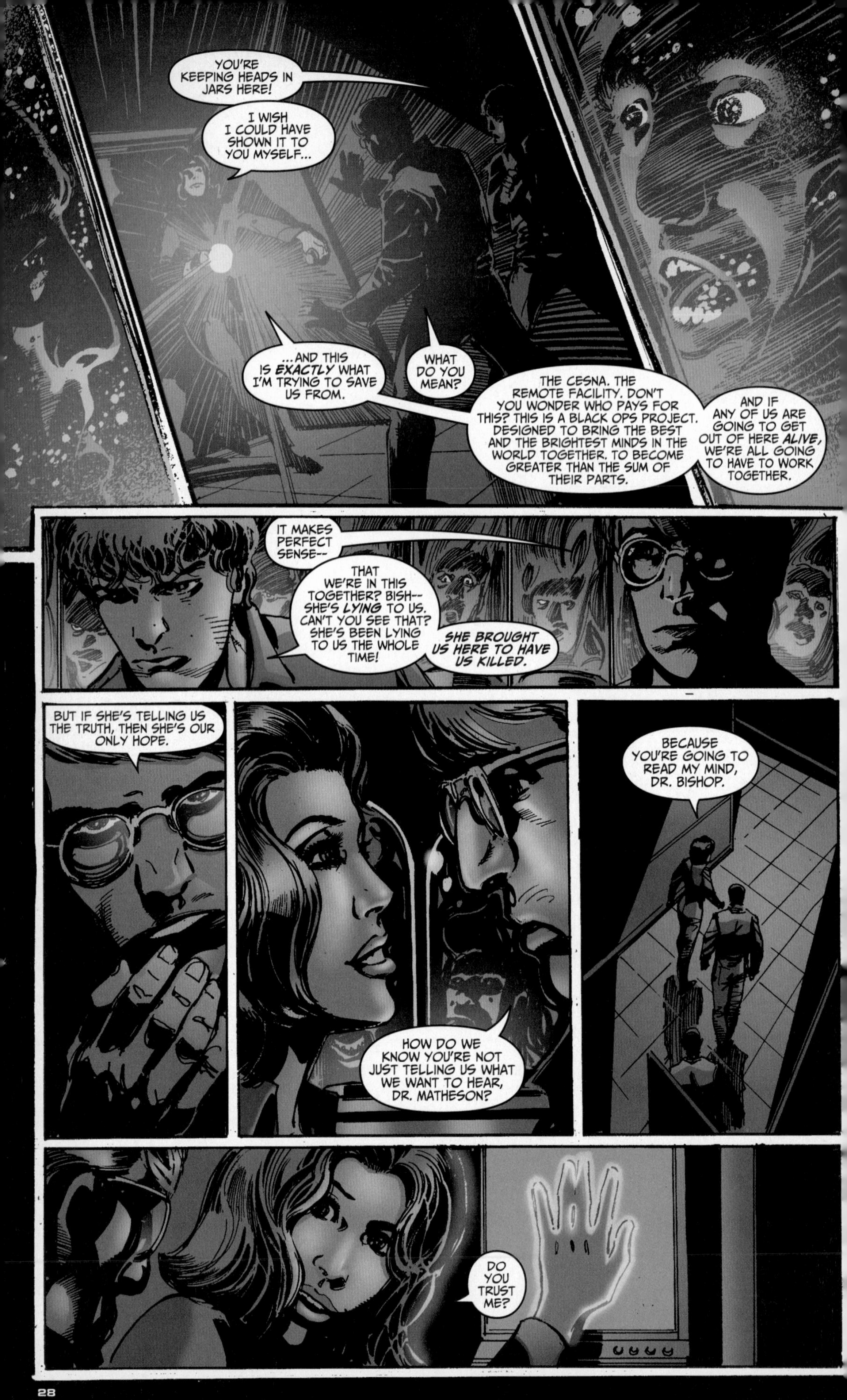

YOU'RE KEEPING HEADS IN JARS HERE!
I WISH I COULD HAVE SHOWN IT TO YOU MYSELF...
...AND THIS IS EXACTLY WHAT I'M TRYING TO SAVE US FROM.
WHAT DO YOU MEAN?
THE CESNA. THE REMOTE FACILITY. DON'T YOU WONDER WHO PAYS FOR THIS? THIS IS A BLACK OPS PROJECT. DESIGNED TO BRING THE BEST AND THE BRIGHTEST MINDS IN THE WORLD TOGETHER. TO BECOME GREATER THAN THE SUM OF THEIR PARTS.
AND IF ANY OF US ARE GOING TO GET OUT OF HERE ALIVE, WE'RE ALL GOING TO HAVE TO WORK TOGETHER.
IT MAKES PERFECT SENSE--
THAT WE'RE IN THIS TOGETHER? BISH-- SHE'S LYING TO US. CAN'T YOU SEE THAT? SHE'S BEEN LYING TO US THE WHOLE TIME!
SHE BROUGHT US HERE TO HAVE US KILLED.
BUT IF SHE'S TELLING US THE TRUTH, THEN SHE'S OUR ONLY HOPE.
HOW DO WE KNOW YOU'RE NOT JUST TELLING US WHAT WE WANT TO HEAR, DR. MATHESON?
BECAUSE YOU'RE GOING TO READ MY MIND, DR. BISHOP.
DO YOU TRUST ME?

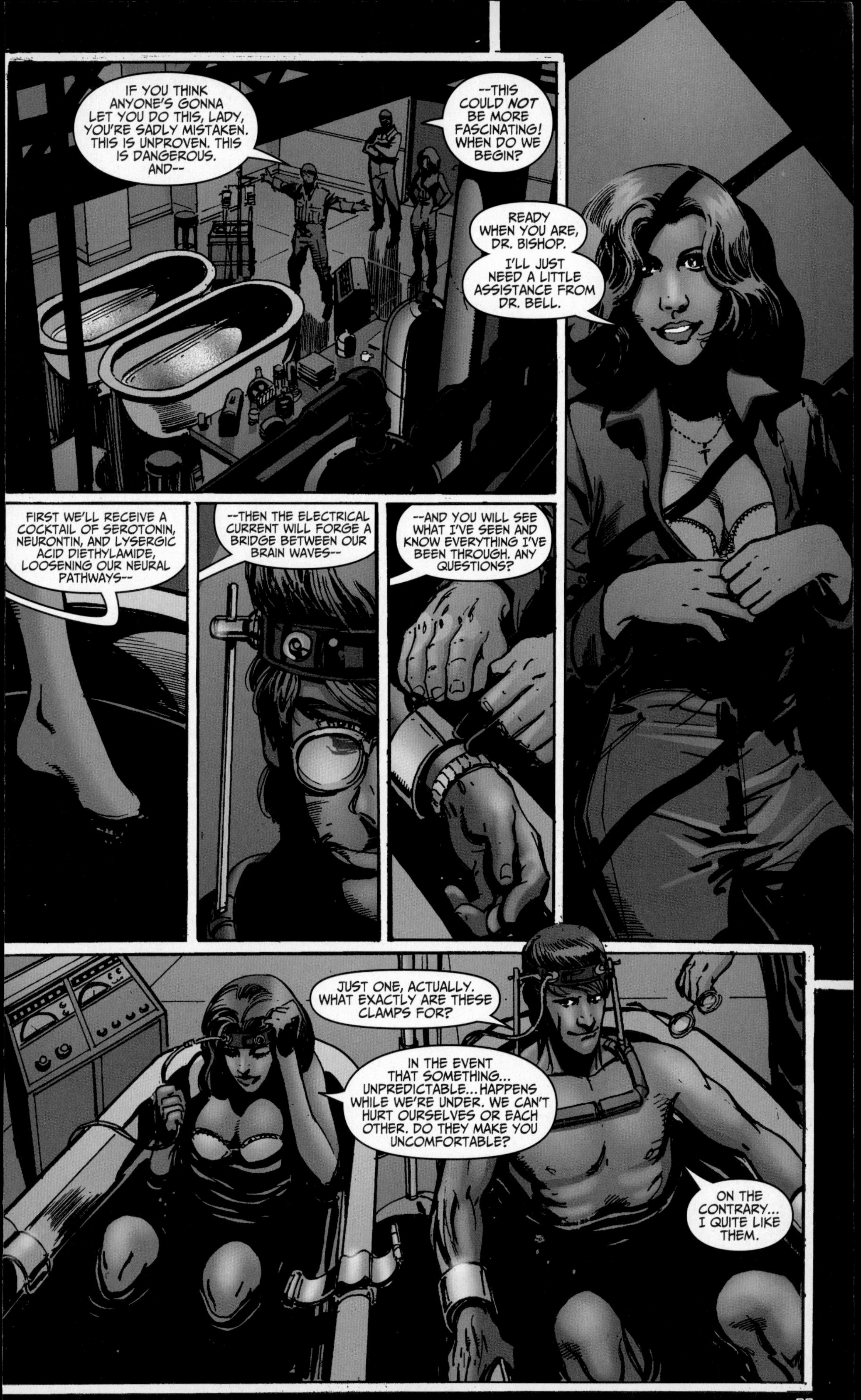

IF YOU THINK ANYONE'S GONNA LET YOU DO THIS, LADY, YOU'RE SADLY MISTAKEN. THIS IS UNPROVEN. THIS IS DANGEROUS. AND--
--THIS COULD NOT BE MORE FASCINATING! WHEN DO WE BEGIN?
READY WHEN YOU ARE, DR. BISHOP.
I'LL JUST NEED A LITTLE ASSISTANCE FROM DR. BELL.
FIRST WE'LL RECEIVE A COCKTAIL OF SEROTONIN, NEURONTIN, AND LYSERGIC ACID DIETHYLAMIDE, LOOSENING OUR NEURAL PATHWAYS--
--THEN THE ELECTRICAL CURRENT WILL FORGE A BRIDGE BETWEEN OUR BRAIN WAVES--
--AND YOU WILL SEE WHAT I'VE SEEN AND KNOW EVERYTHING I'VE BEEN THROUGH. ANY QUESTIONS?
JUST ONE, ACTUALLY. WHAT EXACTLY ARE THESE CLAMPS FOR?
IN THE EVENT THAT SOMETHING... UNPREDICTABLE... HAPPENS WHILE WE'RE UNDER. WE CAN'T HURT OURSELVES OR EACH OTHER. DO THEY MAKE YOU UNCOMFORTABLE?
ON THE CONTRARY... I QUITE LIKE THEM.

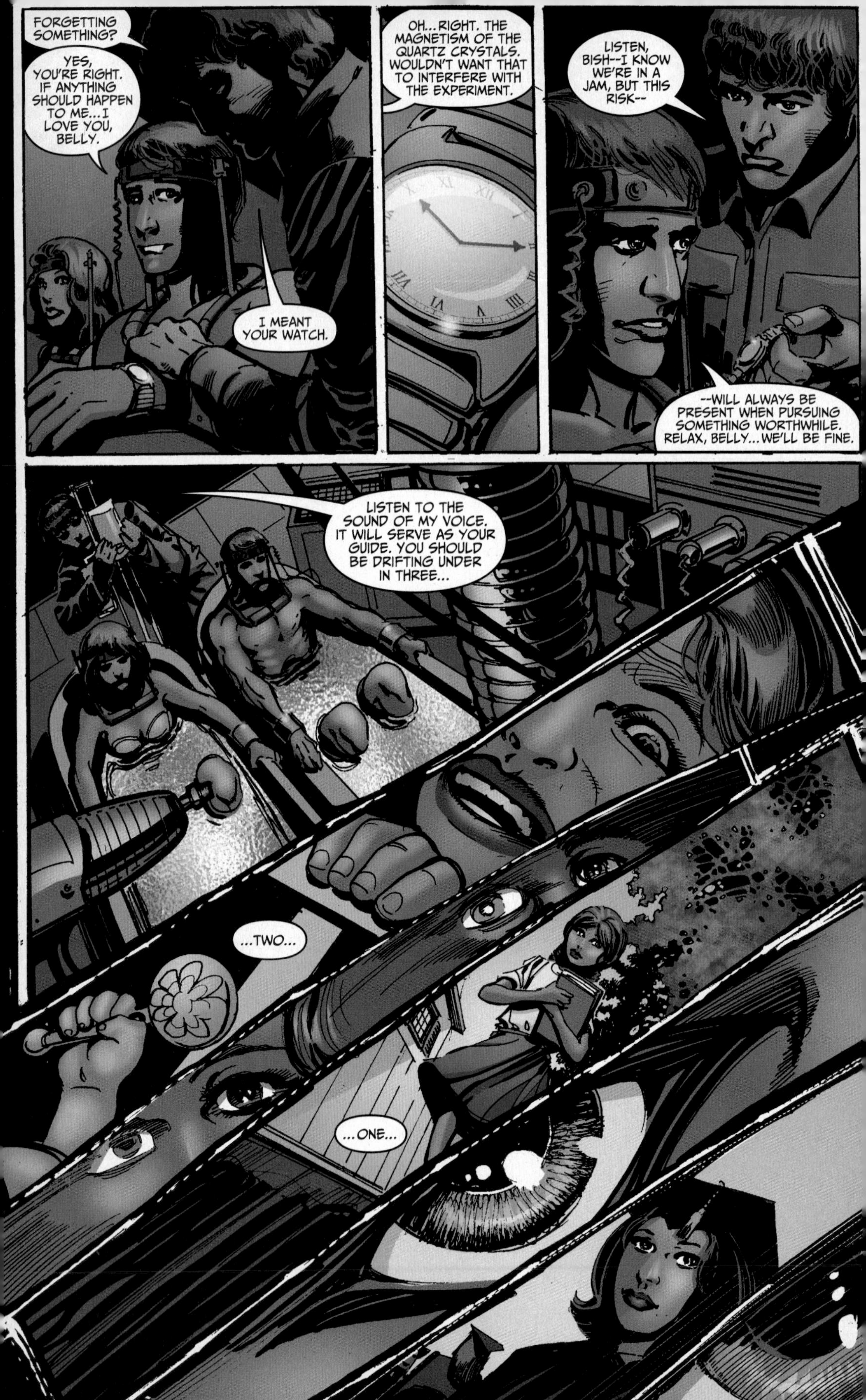
FORGETTING SOMETHING?
YES, YOU'RE RIGHT. IF ANYTHING SHOULD HAPPEN TO ME...I LOVE YOU, BELLY.
I MEANT YOUR WATCH.
OH...RIGHT. THE MAGNETISM OF THE QUARTZ CRYSTALS. WOULDN'T WANT THAT TO INTERFERE WITH THE EXPERIMENT.
LISTEN, BISH--I KNOW WE'RE IN A JAM, BUT THIS RISK--
--WILL ALWAYS BE PRESENT WHEN PURSUING SOMETHING WORTHWHILE. RELAX, BELLY...WE'LL BE FINE.
LISTEN TO THE SOUND OF MY VOICE. IT WILL SERVE AS YOUR GUIDE. YOU SHOULD BE DRIFTING UNDER IN THREE...
...TWO...
...ONE...

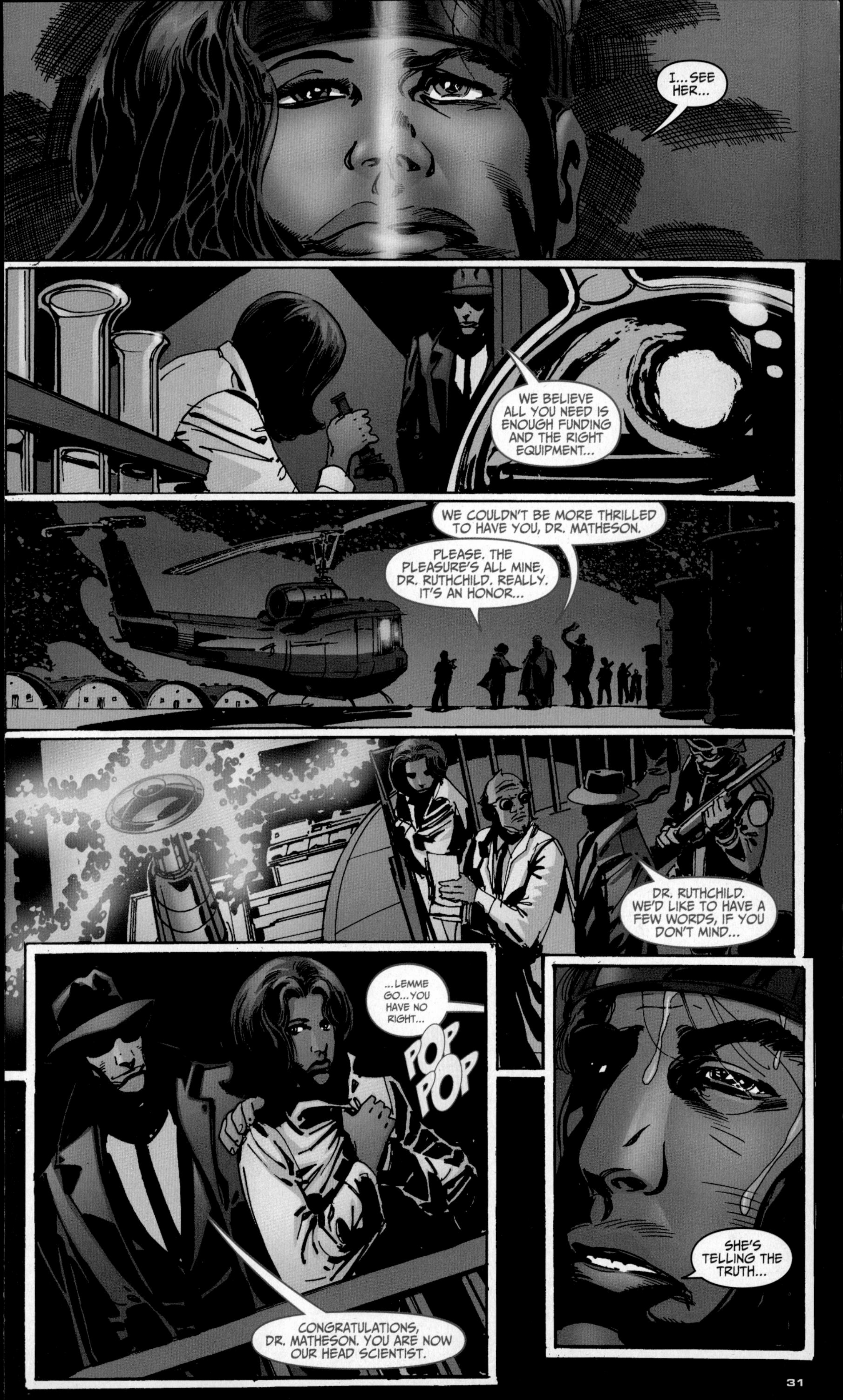
I... SEE HER...
WE BELIEVE ALL YOU NEED IS ENOUGH FUNDING AND THE RIGHT EQUIPMENT...
WE COULDN'T BE MORE THRILLED TO HAVE YOU, DR. MATHESON.
PLEASE. THE PLEASURE'S ALL MINE, DR. RUTHCHILD. REALLY. IT'S AN HONOR...
DR. RUTHCHILD. WE'D LIKE TO HAVE A FEW WORDS, IF YOU DON'T MIND...
...LEMME GO...YOU HAVE NO RIGHT...
POP POP
CONGRATULATIONS, DR. MATHESON. YOU ARE NOW OUR HEAD SCIENTIST.
SHE'S TELLING THE TRUTH...

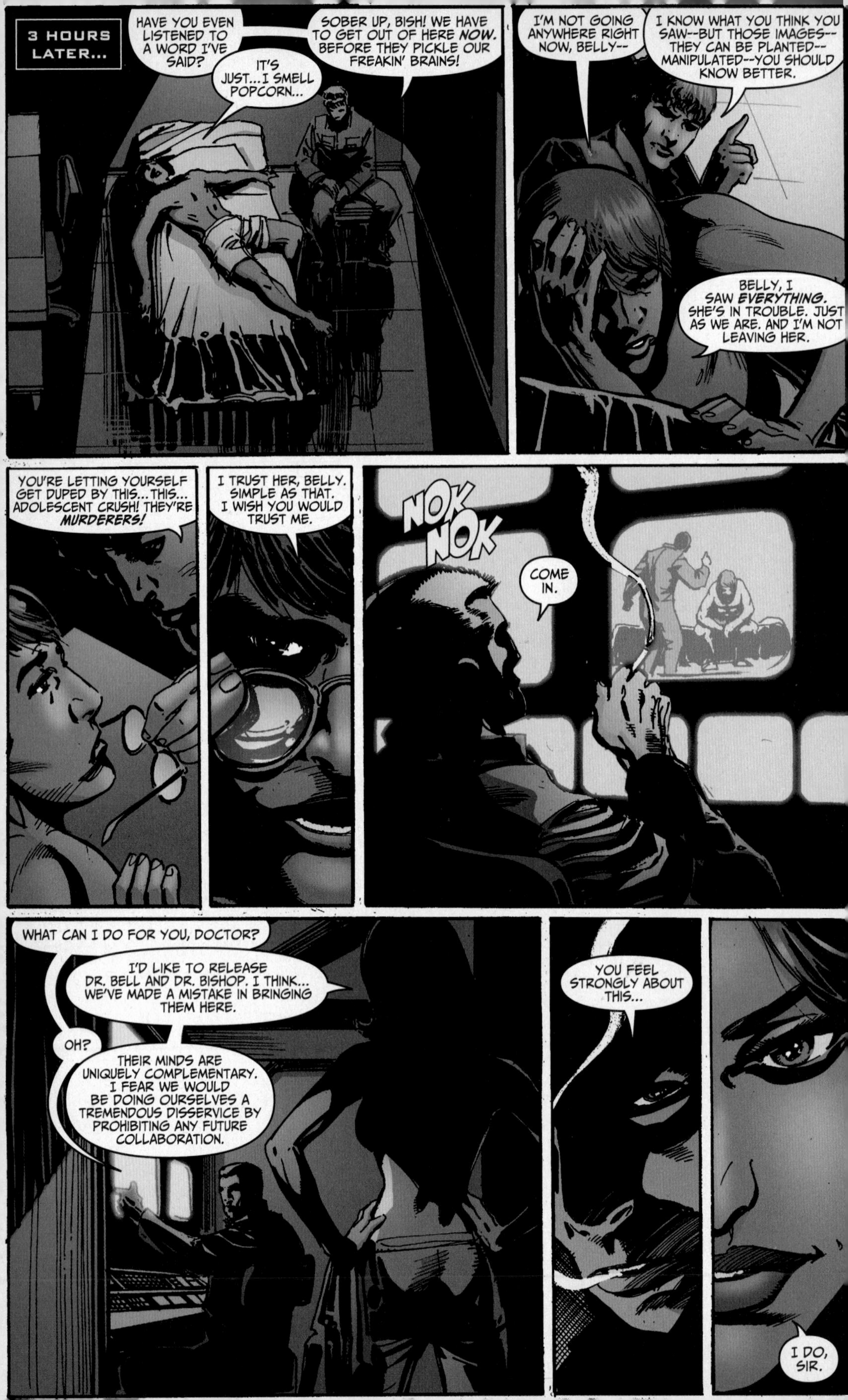
3 HOURS LATER...
HAVE YOU EVEN LISTENED TO A WORD I'VE SAID?
SOBER UP, BISH! WE HAVE TO GET OUT OF HERE NOW. BEFORE THEY PICKLE OUR FREAKIN' BRAINS!
IT'S JUST... I SMELL POPCORN...
I'M NOT GOING ANYWHERE RIGHT NOW, BELLY--
I KNOW WHAT YOU THINK YOU SAW--BUT THOSE IMAGES--THEY CAN BE PLANTED--MANIPULATED--YOU SHOULD KNOW BETTER.
BELLY, I SAW EVERYTHING. SHE'S IN TROUBLE. JUST AS WE ARE. AND I'M NOT LEAVING HER.
YOU'RE LETTING YOURSELF GET DUPED BY THIS... THIS... ADOLESCENT CRUSH! THEY'RE MURDERERS!
I TRUST HER, BELLY. SIMPLE AS THAT. I WISH YOU WOULD TRUST ME.
NOK NOK
COME IN.
WHAT CAN I DO FOR YOU, DOCTOR?
I'D LIKE TO RELEASE DR. BELL AND DR. BISHOP. I THINK... WE'VE MADE A MISTAKE IN BRINGING THEM HERE.
OH?
THEIR MINDS ARE UNIQUELY COMPLEMENTARY. I FEAR WE WOULD BE DOING OURSELVES A TREMENDOUS DISSERVICE BY PROHIBITING ANY FUTURE COLLABORATION.
YOU FEEL STRONGLY ABOUT THIS...
I DO, SIR.

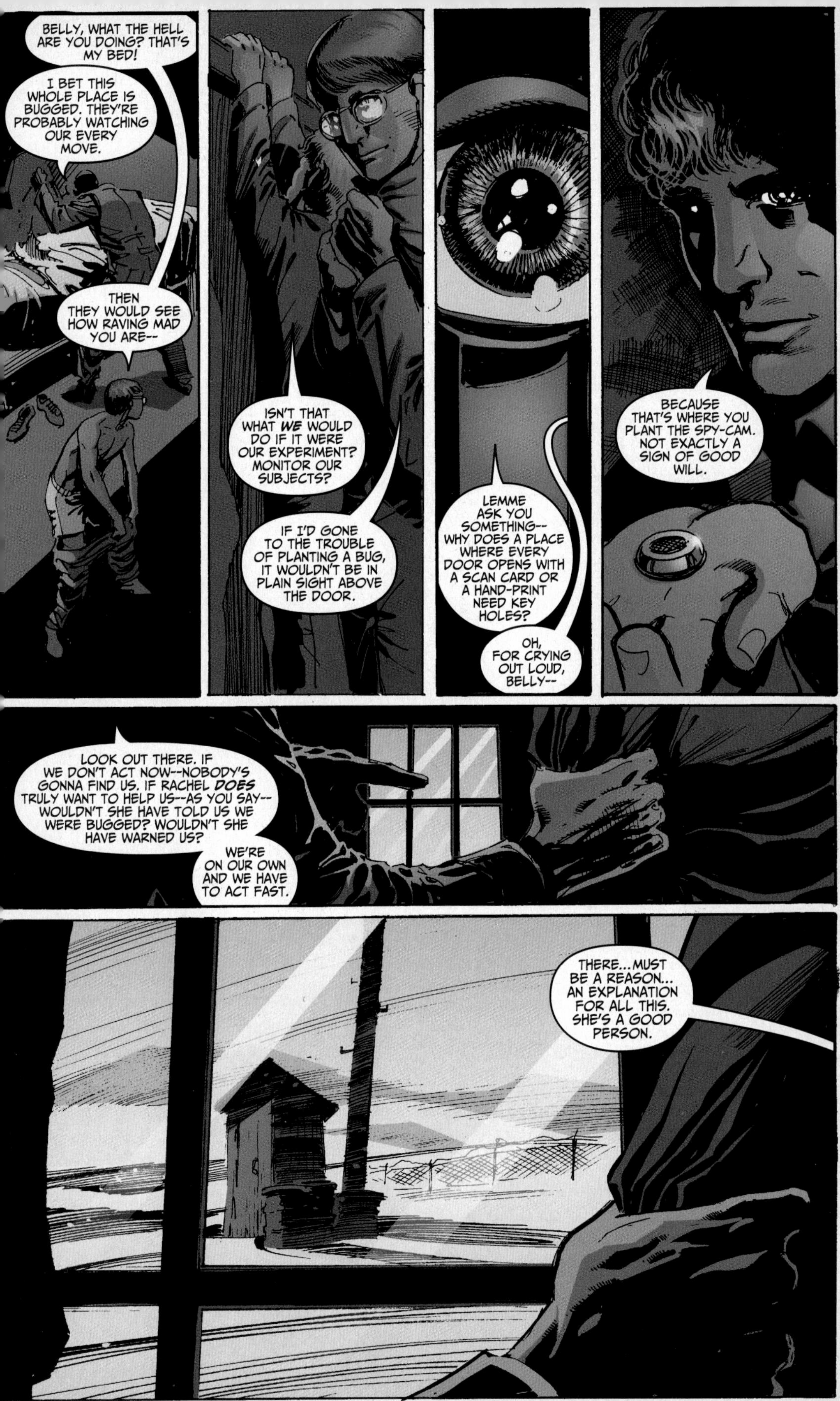
BELLY, WHAT THE HELL ARE YOU DOING? THAT'S MY BED!
I BET THIS WHOLE PLACE IS BUGGED. THEY'RE PROBABLY WATCHING OUR EVERY MOVE.
THEN THEY WOULD SEE HOW RAVING MAD YOU ARE--
ISN'T THAT WHAT *WE* WOULD DO IF IT WERE OUR EXPERIMENT? MONITOR OUR SUBJECTS?
IF I'D GONE TO THE TROUBLE OF PLANTING A BUG, IT WOULDN'T BE IN PLAIN SIGHT ABOVE THE DOOR.
LEMME ASK YOU SOMETHING-- WHY DOES A PLACE WHERE EVERY DOOR OPENS WITH A SCAN CARD OR A HAND-PRINT NEED KEY HOLES?
OH, FOR CRYING OUT LOUD, BELLY--
BECAUSE THAT'S WHERE YOU PLANT THE SPY-CAM. NOT EXACTLY A SIGN OF GOOD WILL.
LOOK OUT THERE. IF WE DON'T ACT NOW--NOBODY'S GONNA FIND US. IF RACHEL *DOES* TRULY WANT TO HELP US--AS YOU SAY-- WOULDN'T SHE HAVE TOLD US WE WERE BUGGED? WOULDN'T SHE HAVE WARNED US?
WE'RE ON OUR OWN AND WE HAVE TO ACT FAST.
THERE...MUST BE A REASON... AN EXPLANATION FOR ALL THIS. SHE'S A GOOD PERSON.

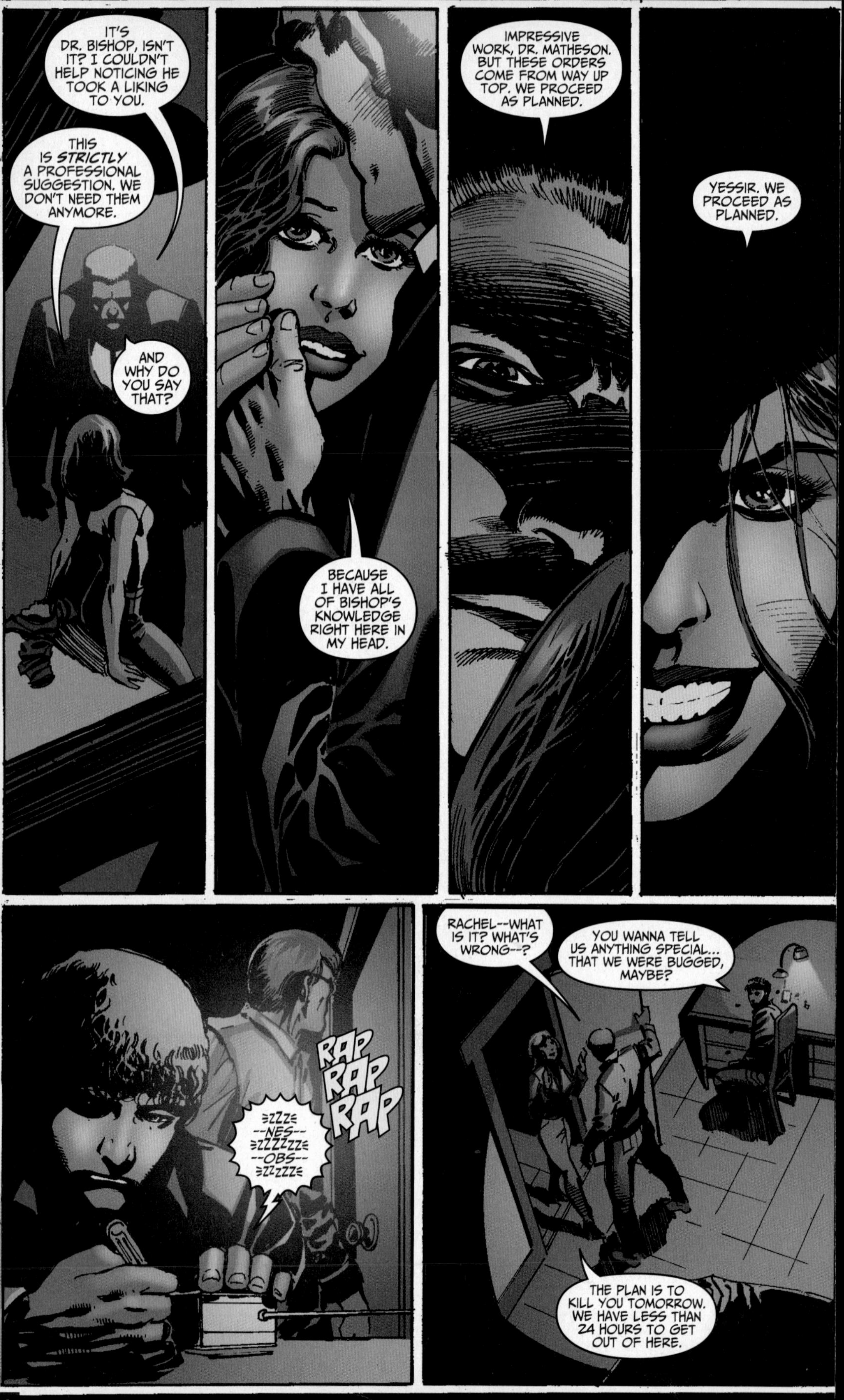
IT'S DR. BISHOP, ISN'T IT? I COULDN'T HELP NOTICING HE TOOK A LIKING TO YOU.
THIS IS *STRICTLY* A PROFESSIONAL SUGGESTION. WE DON'T NEED THEM ANYMORE.
AND WHY DO YOU SAY THAT?
BECAUSE I HAVE ALL OF BISHOP'S KNOWLEDGE RIGHT HERE IN MY HEAD.
IMPRESSIVE WORK, DR. MATHESON. BUT THESE ORDERS COME FROM WAY UP TOP. WE PROCEED AS PLANNED.
YESSIR. WE PROCEED AS PLANNED.
RAP RAP RAP
ZZZ --NES-- ZZZZZZ --OBS-- ZZZZZ
RACHEL--WHAT IS IT? WHAT'S WRONG--?
YOU WANNA TELL US ANYTHING SPECIAL... THAT WE WERE BUGGED, MAYBE?
THE PLAN IS TO KILL YOU TOMORROW. WE HAVE LESS THAN 24 HOURS TO GET OUT OF HERE.

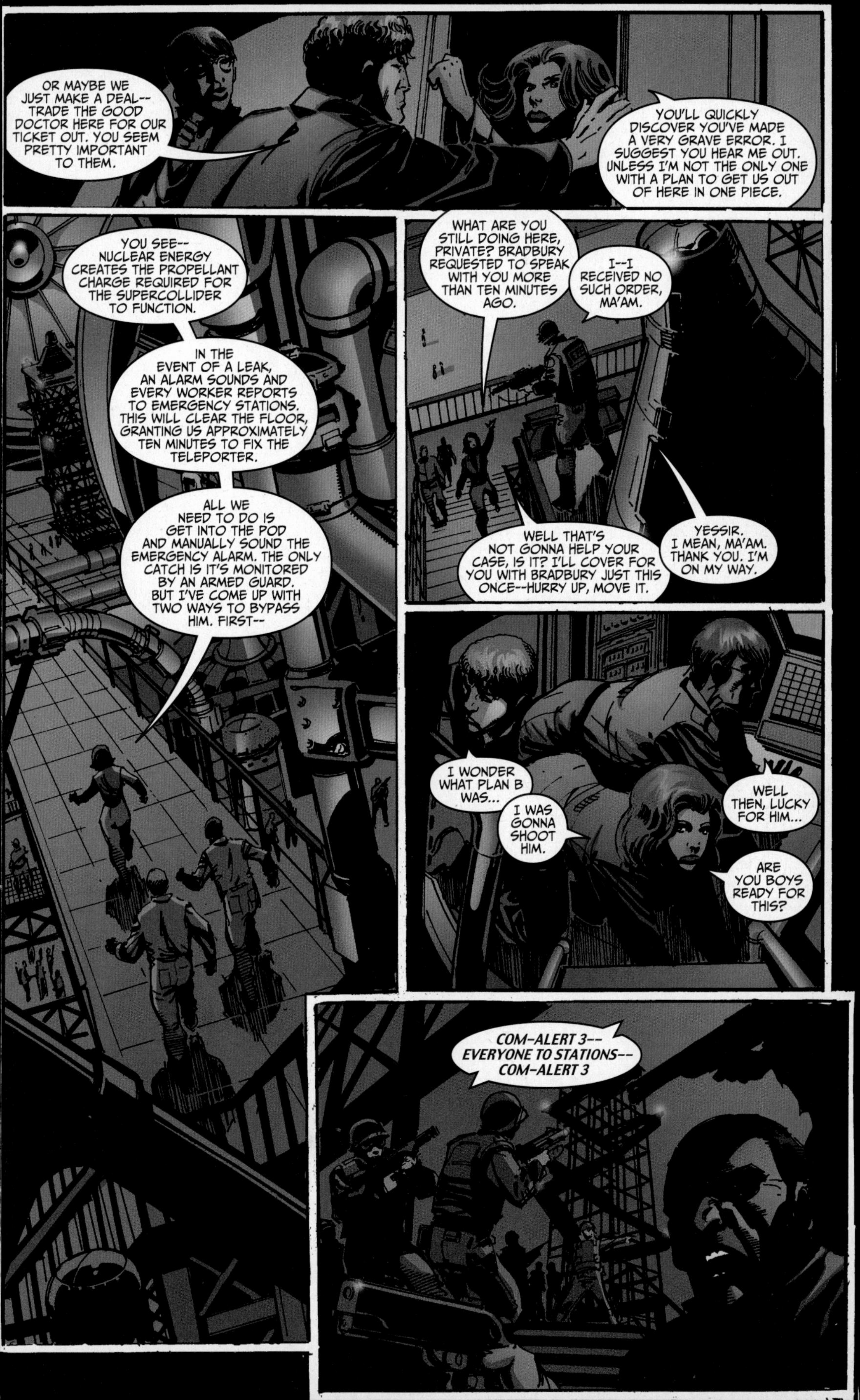
OR MAYBE WE JUST MAKE A DEAL-- TRADE THE GOOD DOCTOR HERE FOR OUR TICKET OUT. YOU SEEM PRETTY IMPORTANT TO THEM.
YOU'LL QUICKLY DISCOVER YOU'VE MADE A VERY GRAVE ERROR. I SUGGEST YOU HEAR ME OUT. UNLESS I'M NOT THE ONLY ONE WITH A PLAN TO GET US OUT OF HERE IN ONE PIECE.
YOU SEE-- NUCLEAR ENERGY CREATES THE PROPELLANT CHARGE REQUIRED FOR THE SUPERCOLLIDER TO FUNCTION.
IN THE EVENT OF A LEAK, AN ALARM SOUNDS AND EVERY WORKER REPORTS TO EMERGENCY STATIONS. THIS WILL CLEAR THE FLOOR, GRANTING US APPROXIMATELY TEN MINUTES TO FIX THE TELEPORTER.
ALL WE NEED TO DO IS GET INTO THE POD AND MANUALLY SOUND THE EMERGENCY ALARM. THE ONLY CATCH IS IT'S MONITORED BY AN ARMED GUARD. BUT I'VE COME UP WITH TWO WAYS TO BYPASS HIM. FIRST--
WHAT ARE YOU STILL DOING HERE, PRIVATE? BRADBURY REQUESTED TO SPEAK WITH YOU MORE THAN TEN MINUTES AGO.
I--I RECEIVED NO SUCH ORDER, MA'AM.
WELL THAT'S NOT GONNA HELP YOUR CASE, IS IT? I'LL COVER FOR YOU WITH BRADBURY JUST THIS ONCE--HURRY UP, MOVE IT.
YESSIR. I MEAN, MA'AM. THANK YOU. I'M ON MY WAY.
I WONDER WHAT PLAN B WAS...
I WAS GONNA SHOOT HIM.
WELL THEN, LUCKY FOR HIM...
ARE YOU BOYS READY FOR THIS?
COM-ALERT 3-- EVERYONE TO STATIONS-- COM-ALERT 3

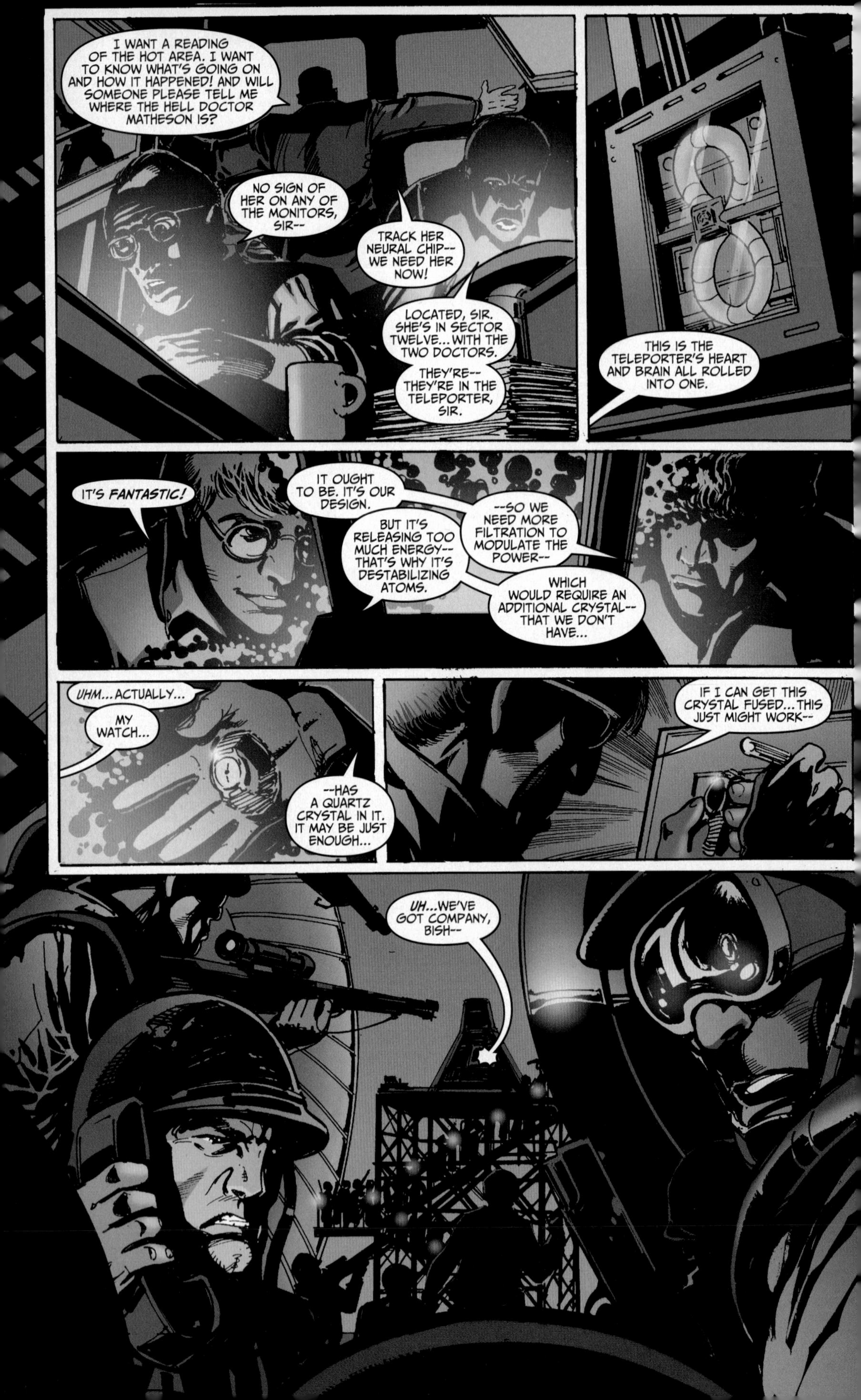
I WANT A READING OF THE HOT AREA. I WANT TO KNOW WHAT'S GOING ON AND HOW IT HAPPENED! AND WILL SOMEONE PLEASE TELL ME WHERE THE HELL DOCTOR MATHESON IS?
NO SIGN OF HER ON ANY OF THE MONITORS, SIR--
TRACK HER NEURAL CHIP-- WE NEED HER NOW!
LOCATED, SIR. SHE'S IN SECTOR TWELVE... WITH THE TWO DOCTORS.
THEY'RE-- THEY'RE IN THE TELEPORTER, SIR.
THIS IS THE TELEPORTER'S HEART AND BRAIN ALL ROLLED INTO ONE.
IT'S FANTASTIC!
IT OUGHT TO BE. IT'S OUR DESIGN.
BUT IT'S RELEASING TOO MUCH ENERGY-- THAT'S WHY IT'S DESTABILIZING ATOMS.
--SO WE NEED MORE FILTRATION TO MODULATE THE POWER--
WHICH WOULD REQUIRE AN ADDITIONAL CRYSTAL-- THAT WE DON'T HAVE...
UHM... ACTUALLY...
MY WATCH...
--HAS A QUARTZ CRYSTAL IN IT. IT MAY BE JUST ENOUGH...
IF I CAN GET THIS CRYSTAL FUSED... THIS JUST MIGHT WORK--
UH... WE'VE GOT COMPANY, BISH--

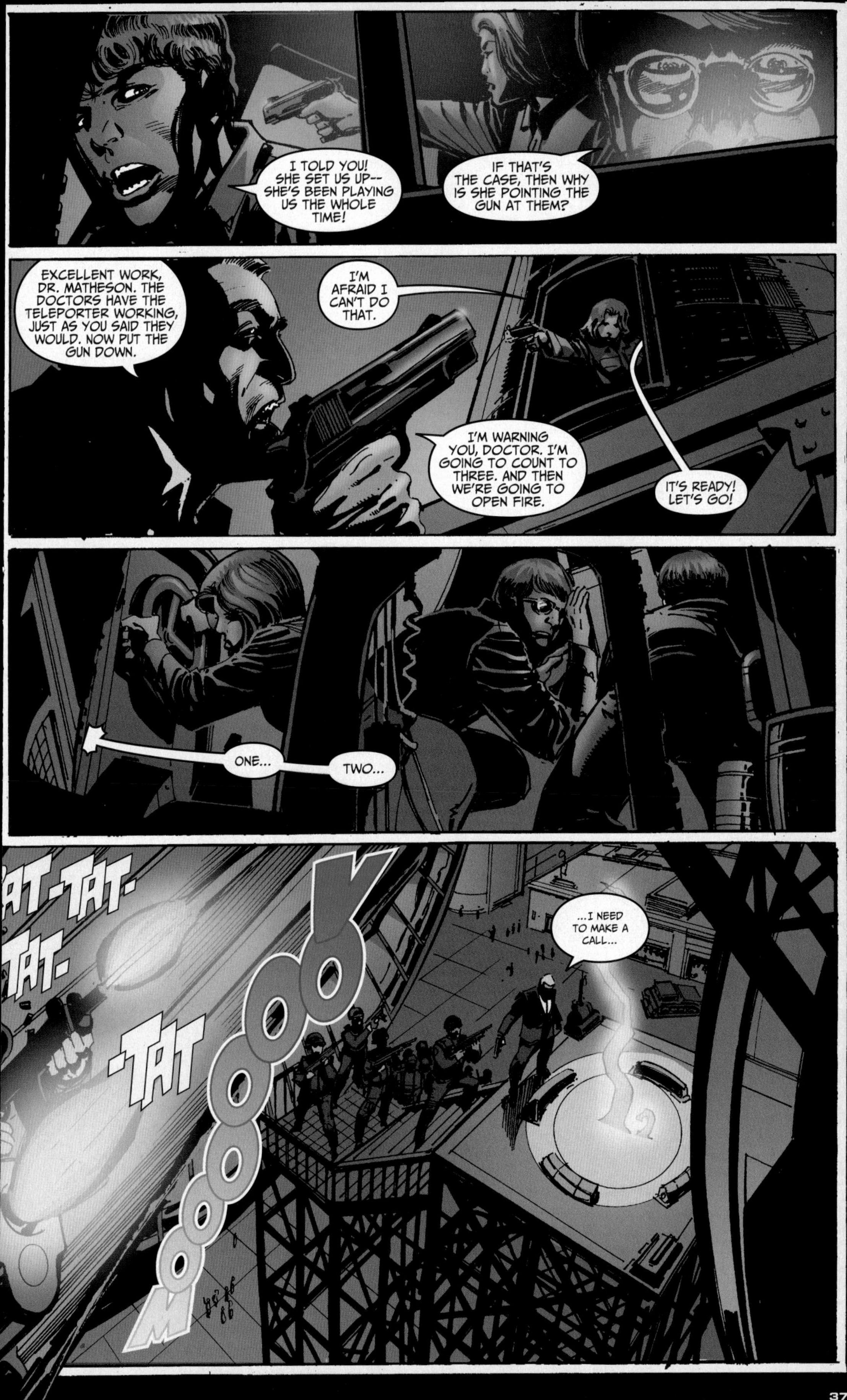
I TOLD YOU! SHE SET US UP-- SHE'S BEEN PLAYING US THE WHOLE TIME!
IF THAT'S THE CASE, THEN WHY IS SHE POINTING THE GUN AT THEM?
EXCELLENT WORK, DR. MATHESON. THE DOCTORS HAVE THE TELEPORTER WORKING, JUST AS YOU SAID THEY WOULD. NOW PUT THE GUN DOWN.
I'M AFRAID I CAN'T DO THAT.
I'M WARNING YOU, DOCTOR. I'M GOING TO COUNT TO THREE. AND THEN WE'RE GOING TO OPEN FIRE.
IT'S READY! LET'S GO!
ONE...
TWO...
-TAT-
-TAT
...I NEED TO MAKE A CALL...

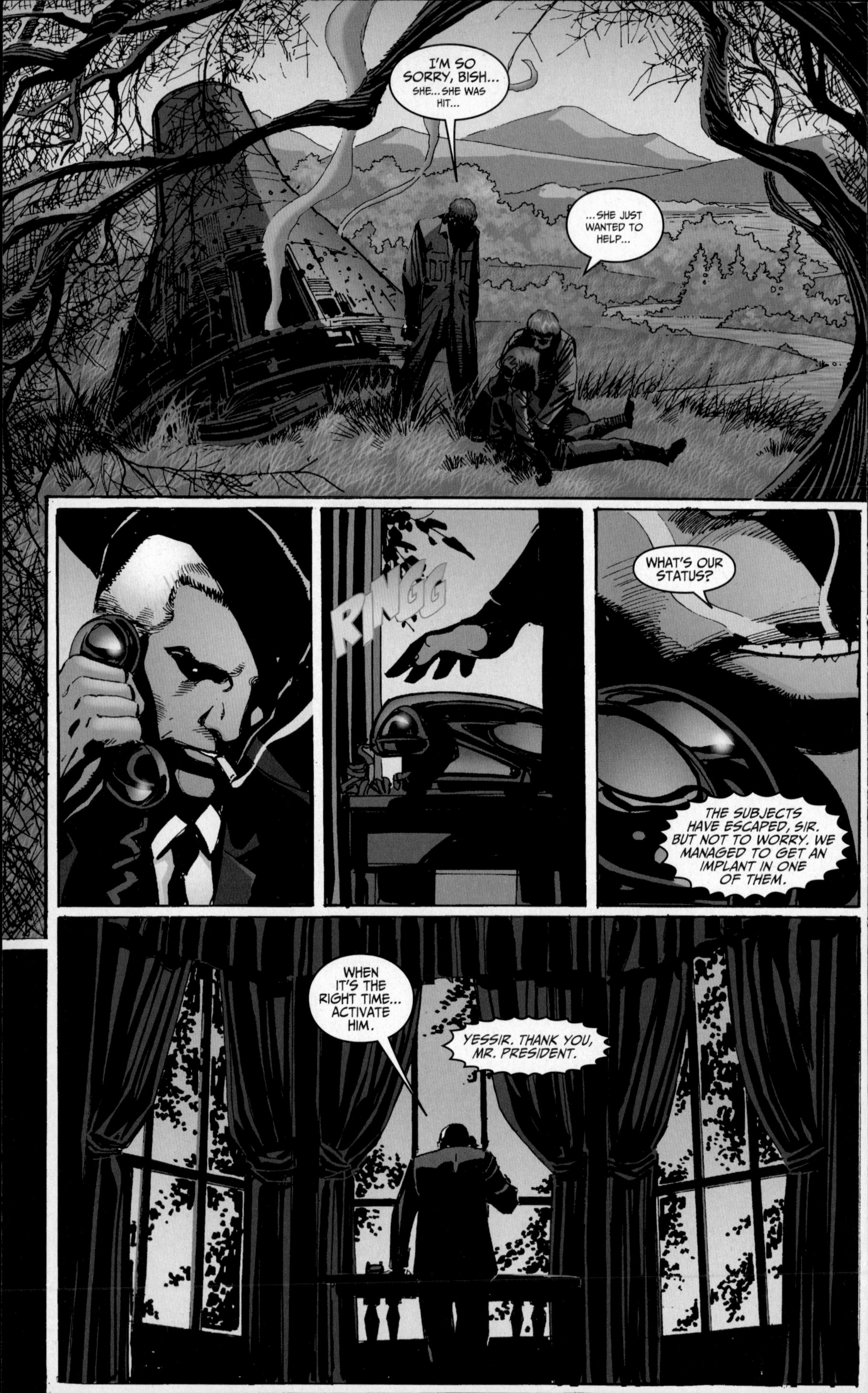
I'M SO SORRY, BISH... SHE... SHE WAS HIT...
...SHE JUST WANTED TO HELP...
RINGG
WHAT'S OUR STATUS?
THE SUBJECTS HAVE ESCAPED, SIR. BUT NOT TO WORRY. WE MANAGED TO GET AN IMPLANT IN ONE OF THEM.
WHEN IT'S THE RIGHT TIME... ACTIVATE HIM.
YESSIR. THANK YOU, MR. PRESIDENT.

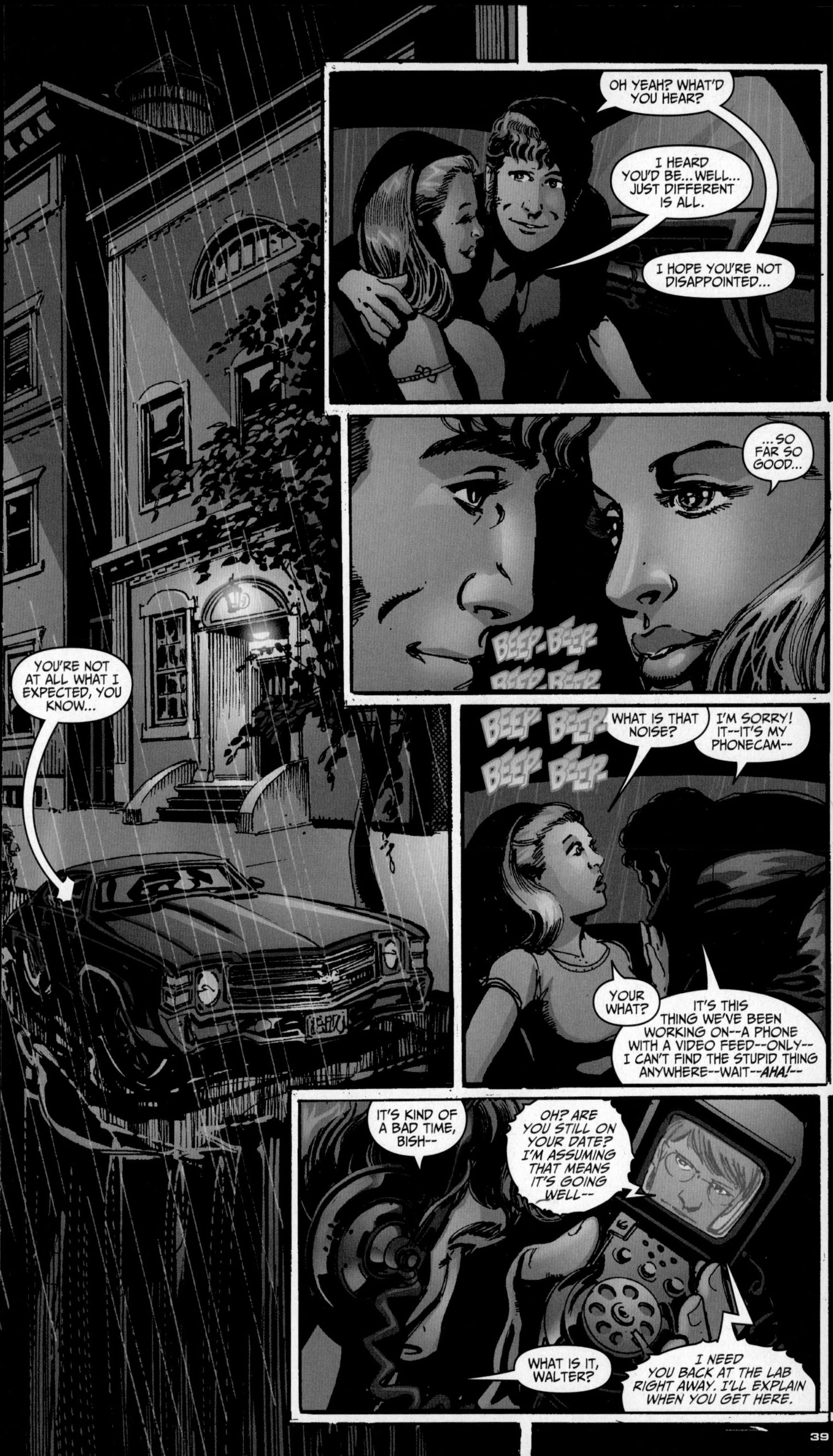
YOU'RE NOT AT ALL WHAT I EXPECTED, YOU KNOW...
OH YEAH? WHAT'D YOU HEAR?
I HEARD YOU'D BE...WELL... JUST DIFFERENT IS ALL.
I HOPE YOU'RE NOT DISAPPOINTED...
...SO FAR SO GOOD...
BEEP-BEEP
BEEP BEEP BEEP BEEP
WHAT IS THAT NOISE?
I'M SORRY! IT--IT'S MY PHONECAM--
YOUR WHAT?
IT'S THIS THING WE'VE BEEN WORKING ON--A PHONE WITH A VIDEO FEED--ONLY-- I CAN'T FIND THE STUPID THING ANYWHERE--WAIT--*AHA!*--
IT'S KIND OF A BAD TIME, BISH--
OH? ARE YOU STILL ON YOUR DATE? I'M ASSUMING THAT MEANS IT'S GOING WELL--
WHAT IS IT, WALTER?
I NEED YOU BACK AT THE LAB RIGHT AWAY. I'LL EXPLAIN WHEN YOU GET HERE.

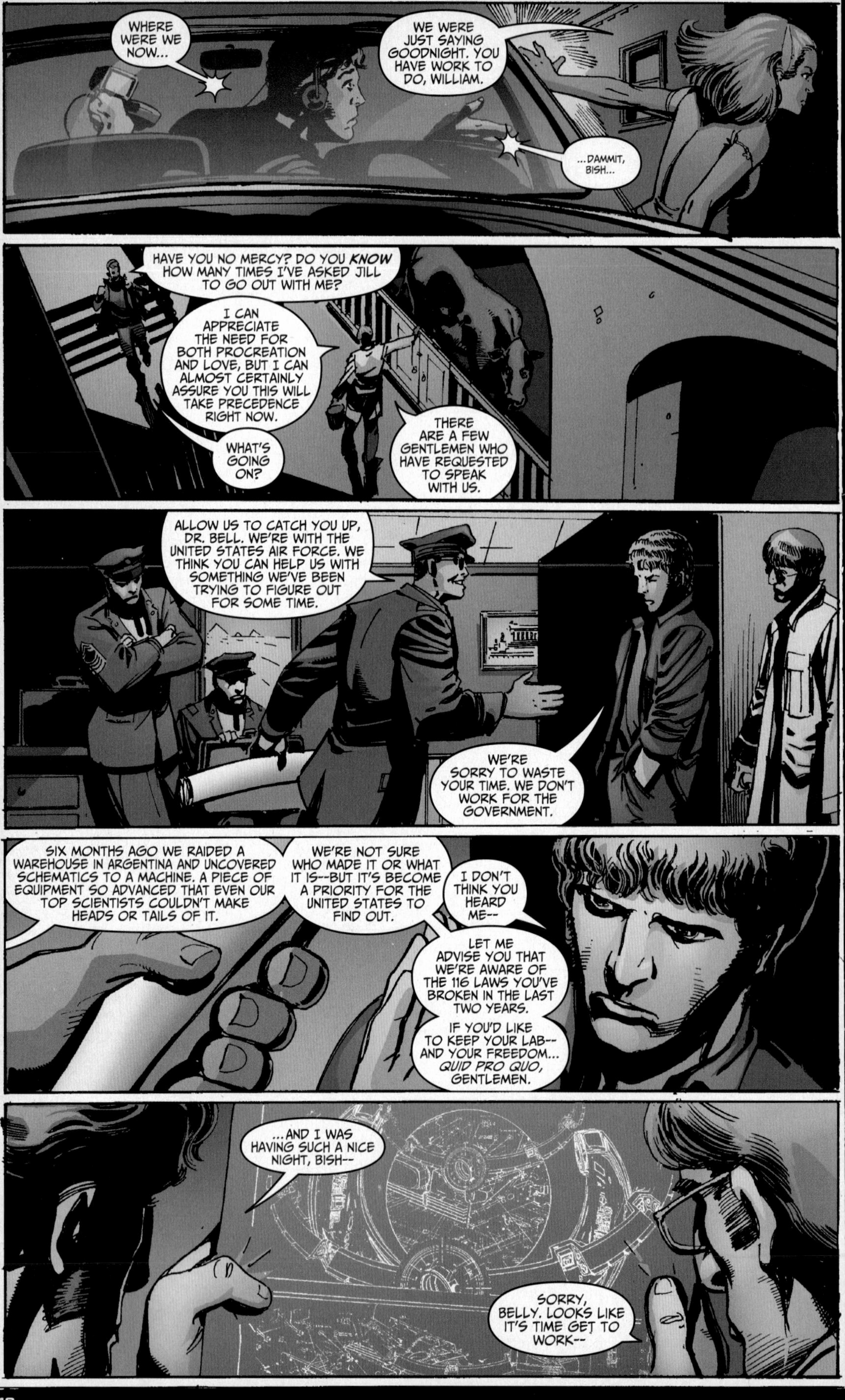
WHERE WERE WE NOW...
WE WERE JUST SAYING GOODNIGHT. YOU HAVE WORK TO DO, WILLIAM.
...DAMMIT, BISH...
HAVE YOU NO MERCY? DO YOU *KNOW* HOW MANY TIMES I'VE ASKED JILL TO GO OUT WITH ME?
I CAN APPRECIATE THE NEED FOR BOTH PROCREATION AND LOVE, BUT I CAN ALMOST CERTAINLY ASSURE YOU THIS WILL TAKE PRECEDENCE RIGHT NOW.
WHAT'S GOING ON?
THERE ARE A FEW GENTLEMEN WHO HAVE REQUESTED TO SPEAK WITH US.
ALLOW US TO CATCH YOU UP, DR. BELL. WE'RE WITH THE UNITED STATES AIR FORCE. WE THINK YOU CAN HELP US WITH SOMETHING WE'VE BEEN TRYING TO FIGURE OUT FOR SOME TIME.
WE'RE SORRY TO WASTE YOUR TIME. WE DON'T WORK FOR THE GOVERNMENT.
SIX MONTHS AGO WE RAIDED A WAREHOUSE IN ARGENTINA AND UNCOVERED SCHEMATICS TO A MACHINE. A PIECE OF EQUIPMENT SO ADVANCED THAT EVEN OUR TOP SCIENTISTS COULDN'T MAKE HEADS OR TAILS OF IT.
WE'RE NOT SURE WHO MADE IT OR WHAT IT IS--BUT IT'S BECOME A PRIORITY FOR THE UNITED STATES TO FIND OUT.
I DON'T THINK YOU HEARD ME--
LET ME ADVISE YOU THAT WE'RE AWARE OF THE 116 LAWS YOU'VE BROKEN IN THE LAST TWO YEARS.
IF YOU'D LIKE TO KEEP YOUR LAB-- AND YOUR FREEDOM... *QUID PRO QUO,* GENTLEMEN.
...AND I WAS HAVING SUCH A NICE NIGHT, BISH--
SORRY, BELLY. LOOKS LIKE IT'S TIME GET TO WORK--

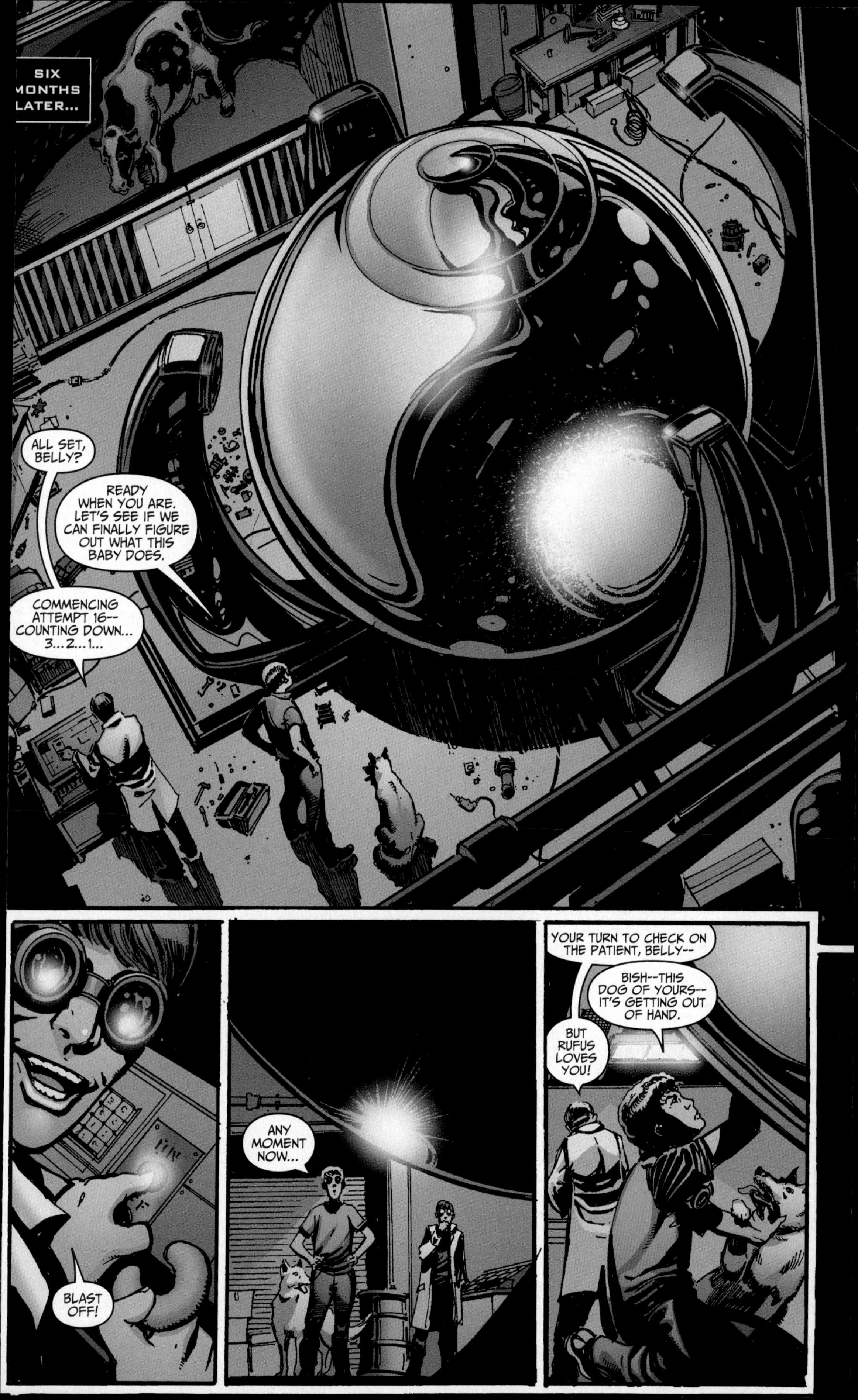
SIX MONTHS LATER...
ALL SET, BELLY?
READY WHEN YOU ARE. LET'S SEE IF WE CAN FINALLY FIGURE OUT WHAT THIS BABY DOES.
COMMENCING ATTEMPT 16-- COUNTING DOWN... 3...2...1...
BLAST OFF!
ANY MOMENT NOW...
YOUR TURN TO CHECK ON THE PATIENT, BELLY--
BISH--THIS DOG OF YOURS-- IT'S GETTING OUT OF HAND.
BUT RUFUS LOVES YOU!

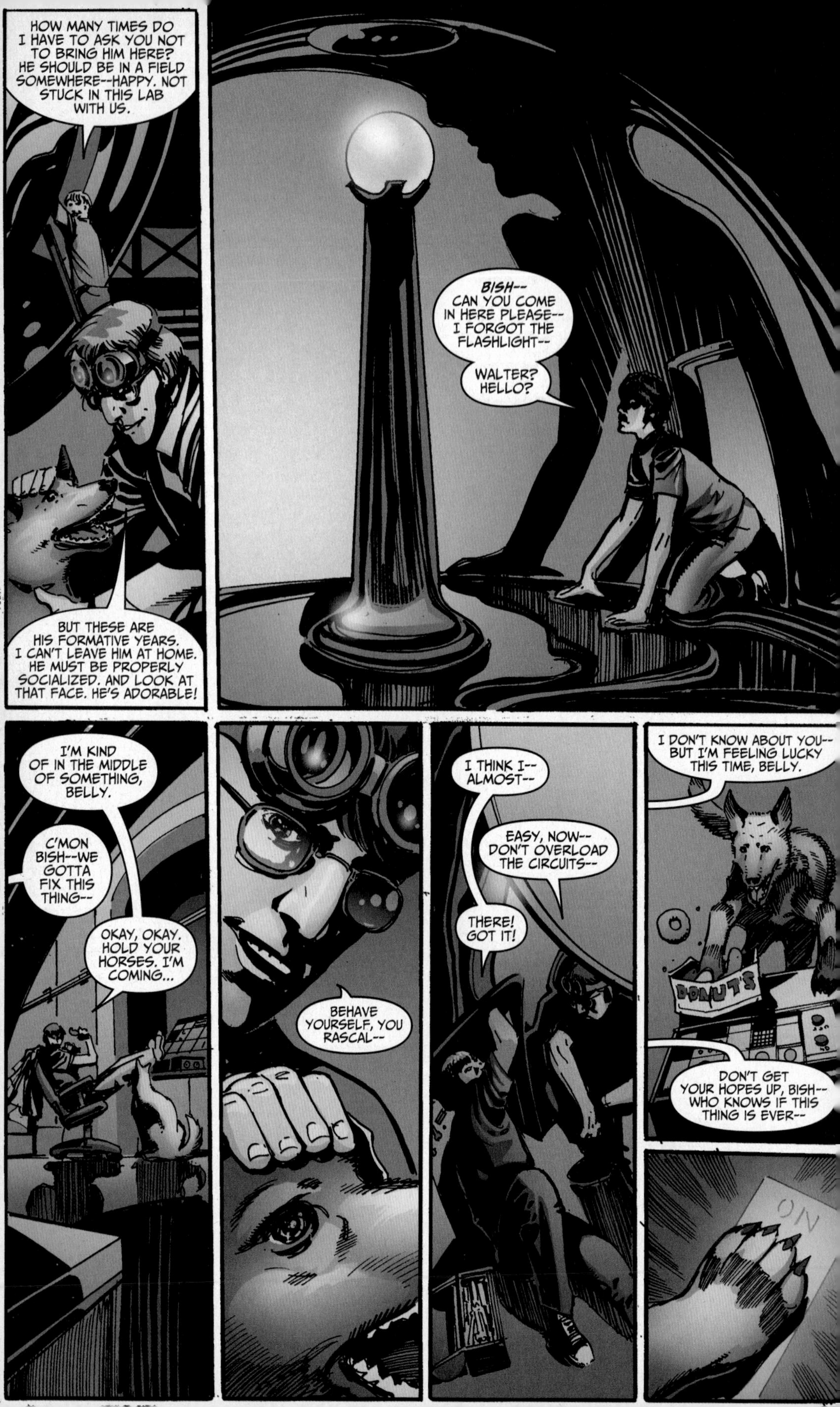
HOW MANY TIMES DO I HAVE TO ASK YOU NOT TO BRING HIM HERE? HE SHOULD BE IN A FIELD SOMEWHERE--HAPPY. NOT STUCK IN THIS LAB WITH US.
BUT THESE ARE HIS FORMATIVE YEARS. I CAN'T LEAVE HIM AT HOME. HE MUST BE PROPERLY SOCIALIZED. AND LOOK AT THAT FACE. HE'S ADORABLE!
BISH-- CAN YOU COME IN HERE PLEASE-- I FORGOT THE FLASHLIGHT--
WALTER? HELLO?
I'M KIND OF IN THE MIDDLE OF SOMETHING, BELLY.
C'MON BISH--WE GOTTA FIX THIS THING--
OKAY, OKAY. HOLD YOUR HORSES. I'M COMING...
BEHAVE YOURSELF, YOU RASCAL--
I THINK I-- ALMOST--
EASY, NOW-- DON'T OVERLOAD THE CIRCUITS--
THERE! GOT IT!
I DON'T KNOW ABOUT YOU-- BUT I'M FEELING LUCKY THIS TIME, BELLY.
DONUTS
DON'T GET YOUR HOPES UP, BISH-- WHO KNOWS IF THIS THING IS EVER--
ON

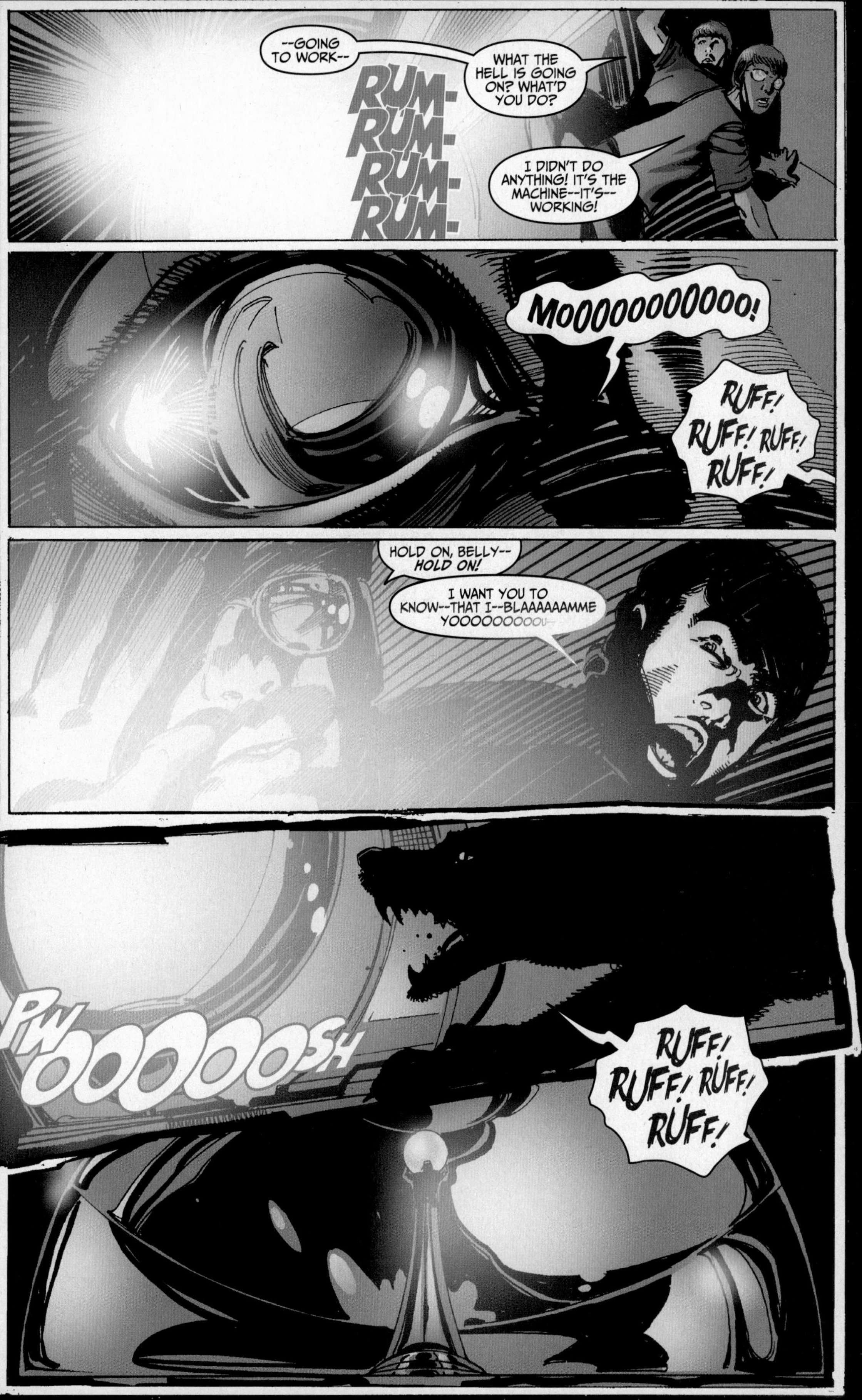
--GOING TO WORK--
RUM-RUM-RUM-RUM-
WHAT THE HELL IS GOING ON? WHAT'D YOU DO?
I DIDN'T DO ANYTHING! IT'S THE MACHINE--IT'S--WORKING!
MOOOOOOOOOOO!
RUFF! RUFF! RUFF! RUFF!
HOLD ON, BELLY-- HOLD ON!
I WANT YOU TO KNOW--THAT I--BLAAAAAAMME YOOOOOOOOOU--
PWOOOOOOSH
RUFF! RUFF! RUFF! RUFF!

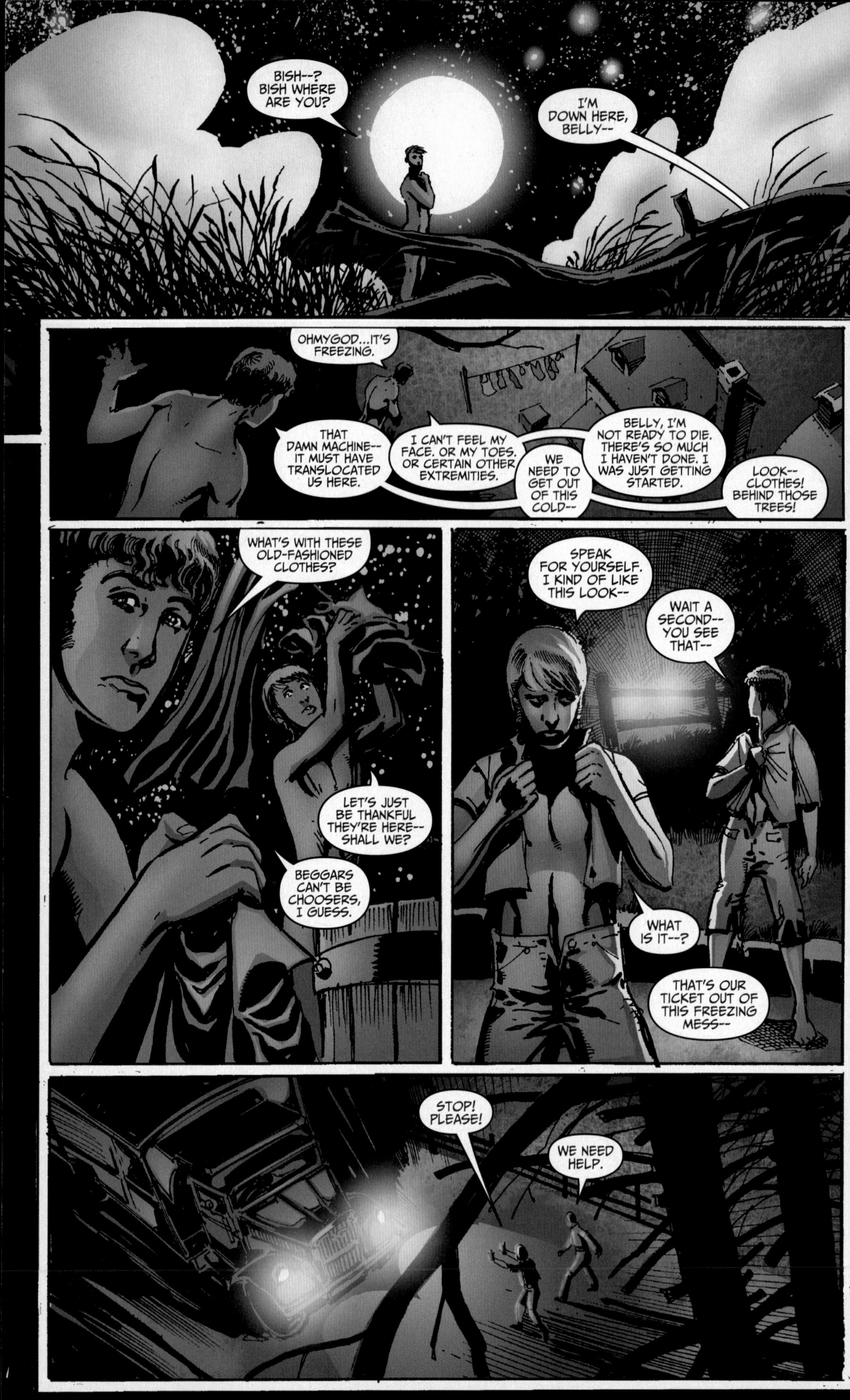
BISH--? BISH WHERE ARE YOU?
I'M DOWN HERE, BELLY--
OHMYGOD...IT'S FREEZING.
THAT DAMN MACHINE-- IT MUST HAVE TRANSLOCATED US HERE.
I CAN'T FEEL MY FACE. OR MY TOES. OR CERTAIN OTHER EXTREMITIES.
WE NEED TO GET OUT OF THIS COLD--
BELLY, I'M NOT READY TO DIE. THERE'S SO MUCH I HAVEN'T DONE. I WAS JUST GETTING STARTED.
LOOK-- CLOTHES! BEHIND THOSE TREES!
WHAT'S WITH THESE OLD-FASHIONED CLOTHES?
LET'S JUST BE THANKFUL THEY'RE HERE-- SHALL WE?
BEGGARS CAN'T BE CHOOSERS, I GUESS.
SPEAK FOR YOURSELF. I KIND OF LIKE THIS LOOK--
WAIT A SECOND-- YOU SEE THAT--
WHAT IS IT--?
THAT'S OUR TICKET OUT OF THIS FREEZING MESS--
STOP! PLEASE!
WE NEED HELP.

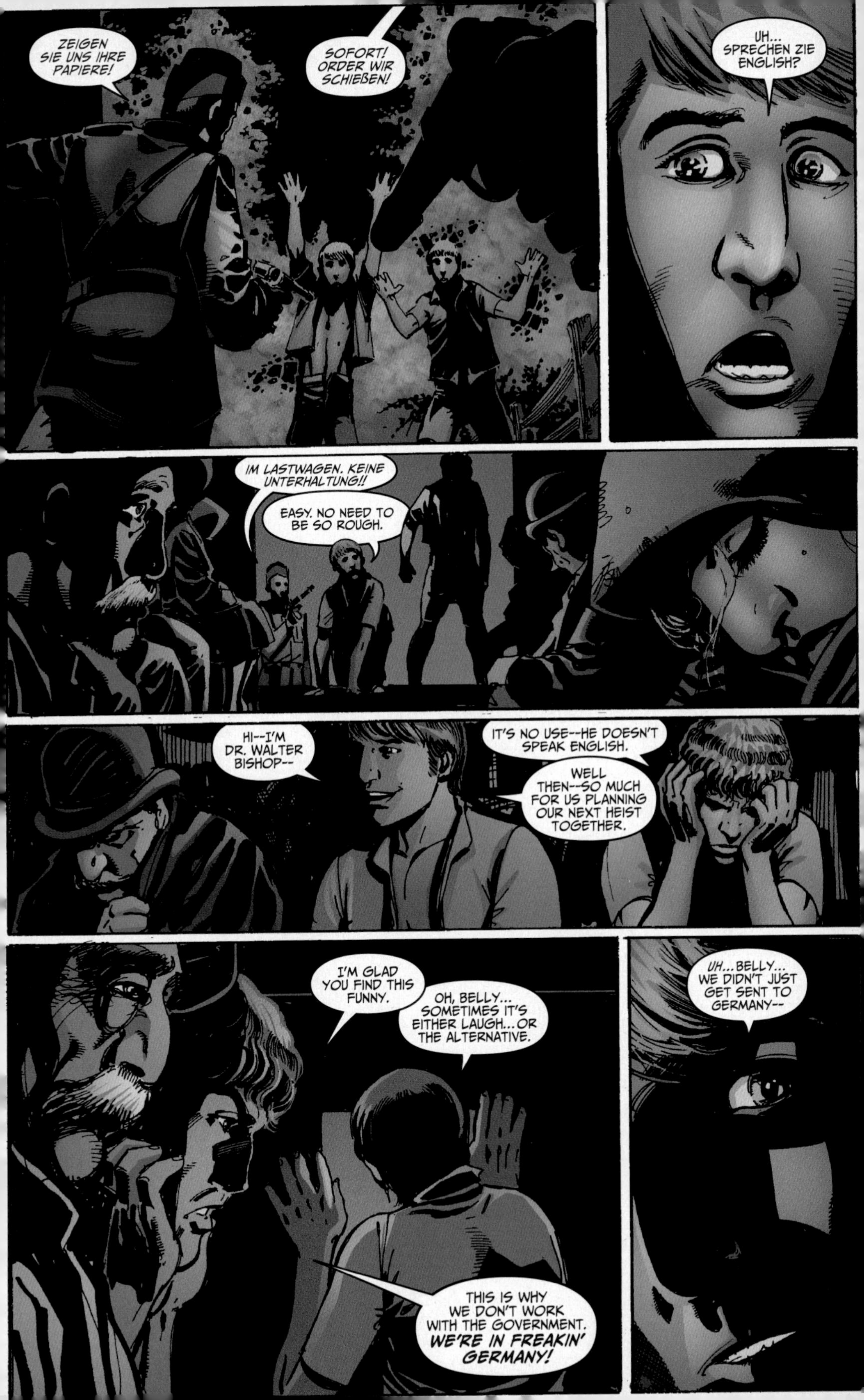
ZEIGEN SIE UNS IHRE PAPIERE!
SOFORT! ORDER WIR SCHIEßEN!
UH... SPRECHEN ZIE ENGLISH?
IM LASTWAGEN. KEINE UNTERHALTUNG!!
EASY. NO NEED TO BE SO ROUGH.
HI--I'M DR. WALTER BISHOP--
IT'S NO USE--HE DOESN'T SPEAK ENGLISH.
WELL THEN--SO MUCH FOR US PLANNING OUR NEXT HEIST TOGETHER.
I'M GLAD YOU FIND THIS FUNNY.
OH, BELLY... SOMETIMES IT'S EITHER LAUGH...OR THE ALTERNATIVE.
THIS IS WHY WE DON'T WORK WITH THE GOVERNMENT. ***WE'RE IN FREAKIN' GERMANY!***
UH...BELLY... WE DIDN'T JUST GET SENT TO GERMANY--

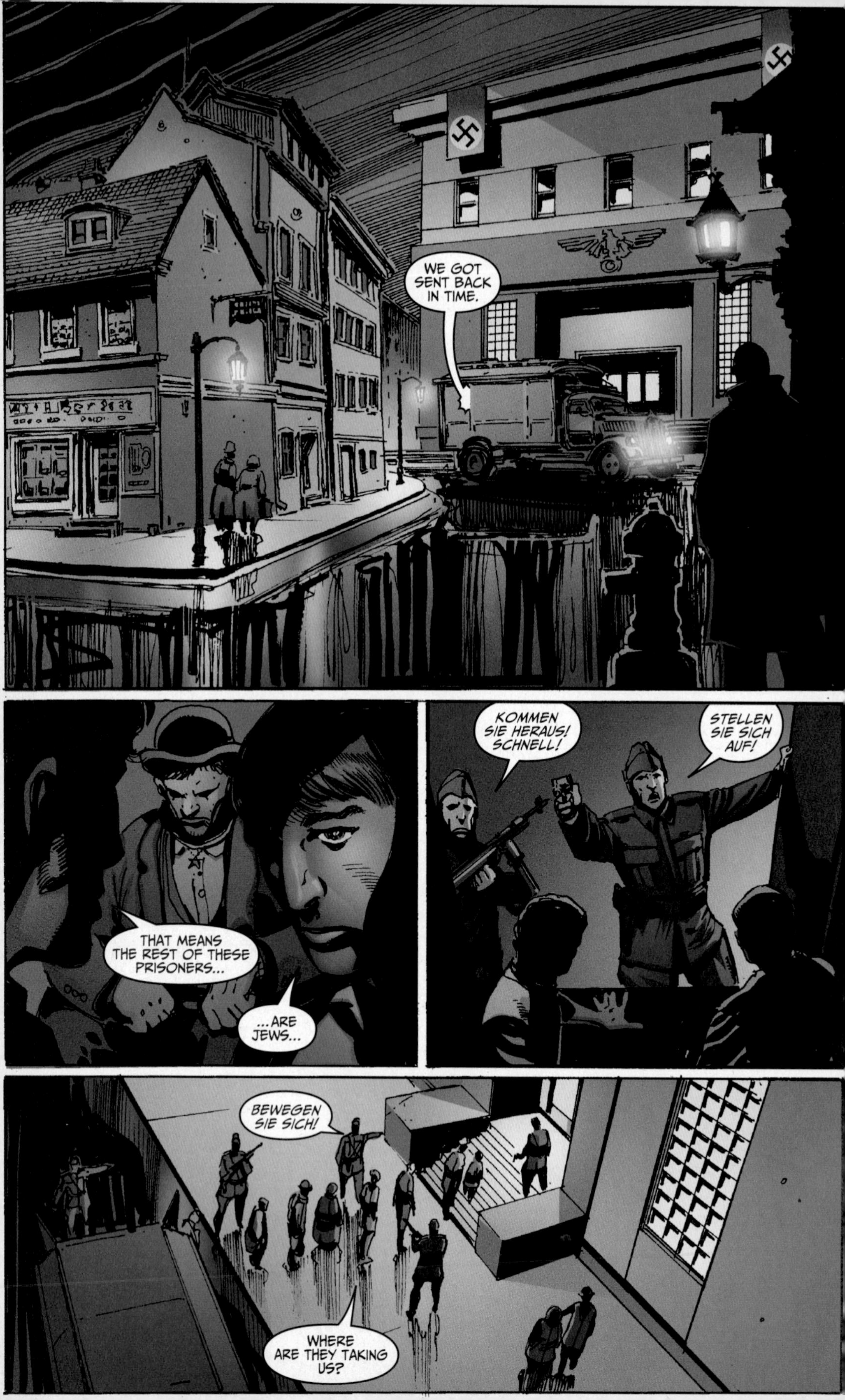
WE GOT SENT BACK IN TIME.
THAT MEANS THE REST OF THESE PRISONERS...
...ARE JEWS...
KOMMEN SIE HERAUS! SCHNELL!
STELLEN SIE SICH AUF!
BEWEGEN SIE SICH!
WHERE ARE THEY TAKING US?

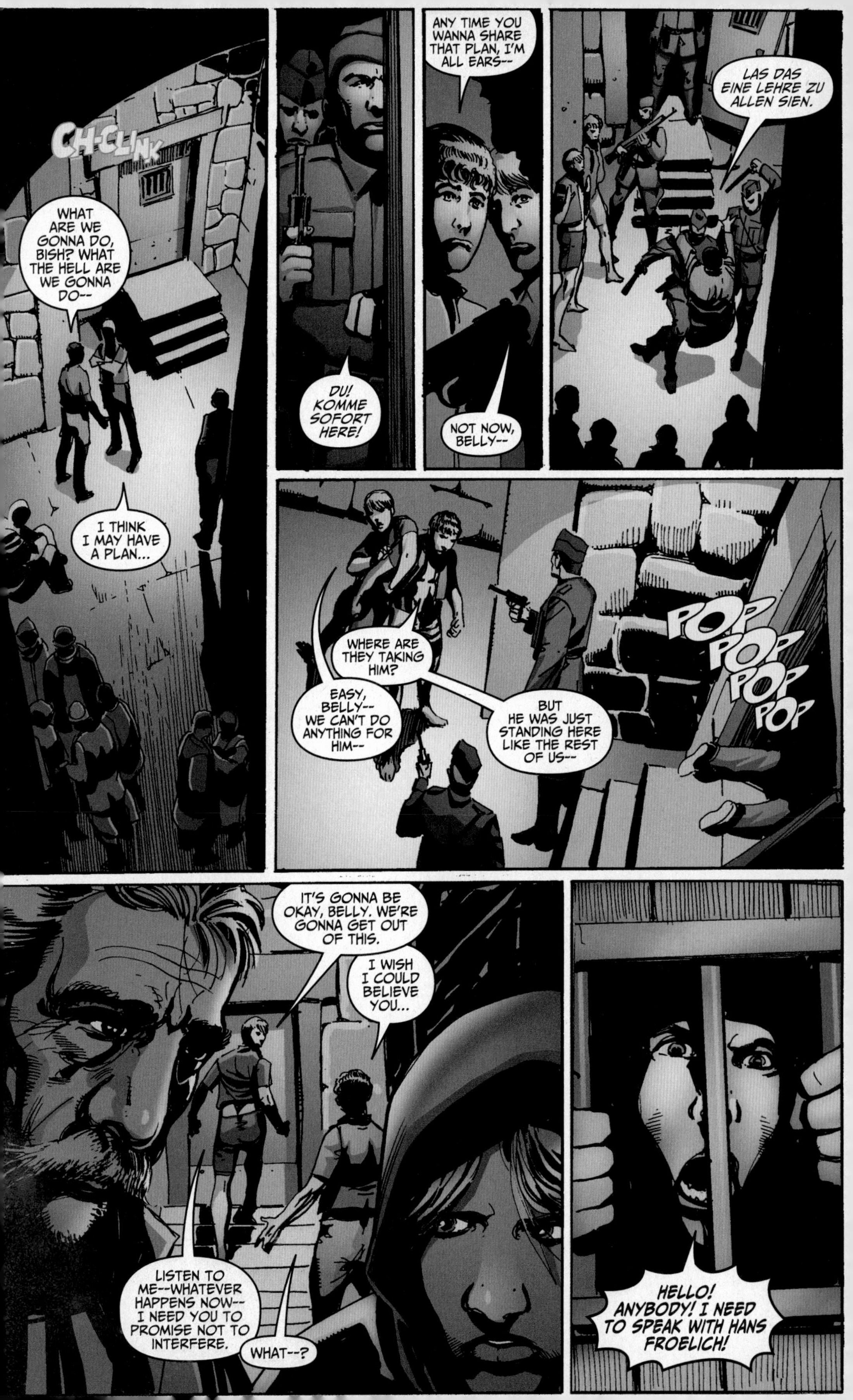
CH-CLINK
WHAT ARE WE GONNA DO, BISH? WHAT THE HELL ARE WE GONNA DO--
I THINK I MAY HAVE A PLAN...
ANY TIME YOU WANNA SHARE THAT PLAN, I'M ALL EARS--
DU! KOMME SOFORT HERE!
NOT NOW, BELLY--
LAS DAS EINE LEHRE ZU ALLEN SIEN.
WHERE ARE THEY TAKING HIM?
EASY, BELLY-- WE CAN'T DO ANYTHING FOR HIM--
BUT HE WAS JUST STANDING HERE LIKE THE REST OF US--
POP POP POP POP POP
IT'S GONNA BE OKAY, BELLY. WE'RE GONNA GET OUT OF THIS.
I WISH I COULD BELIEVE YOU...
LISTEN TO ME--WHATEVER HAPPENS NOW-- I NEED YOU TO PROMISE NOT TO INTERFERE.
WHAT--?
HELLO! ANYBODY! I NEED TO SPEAK WITH HANS FROELICH!

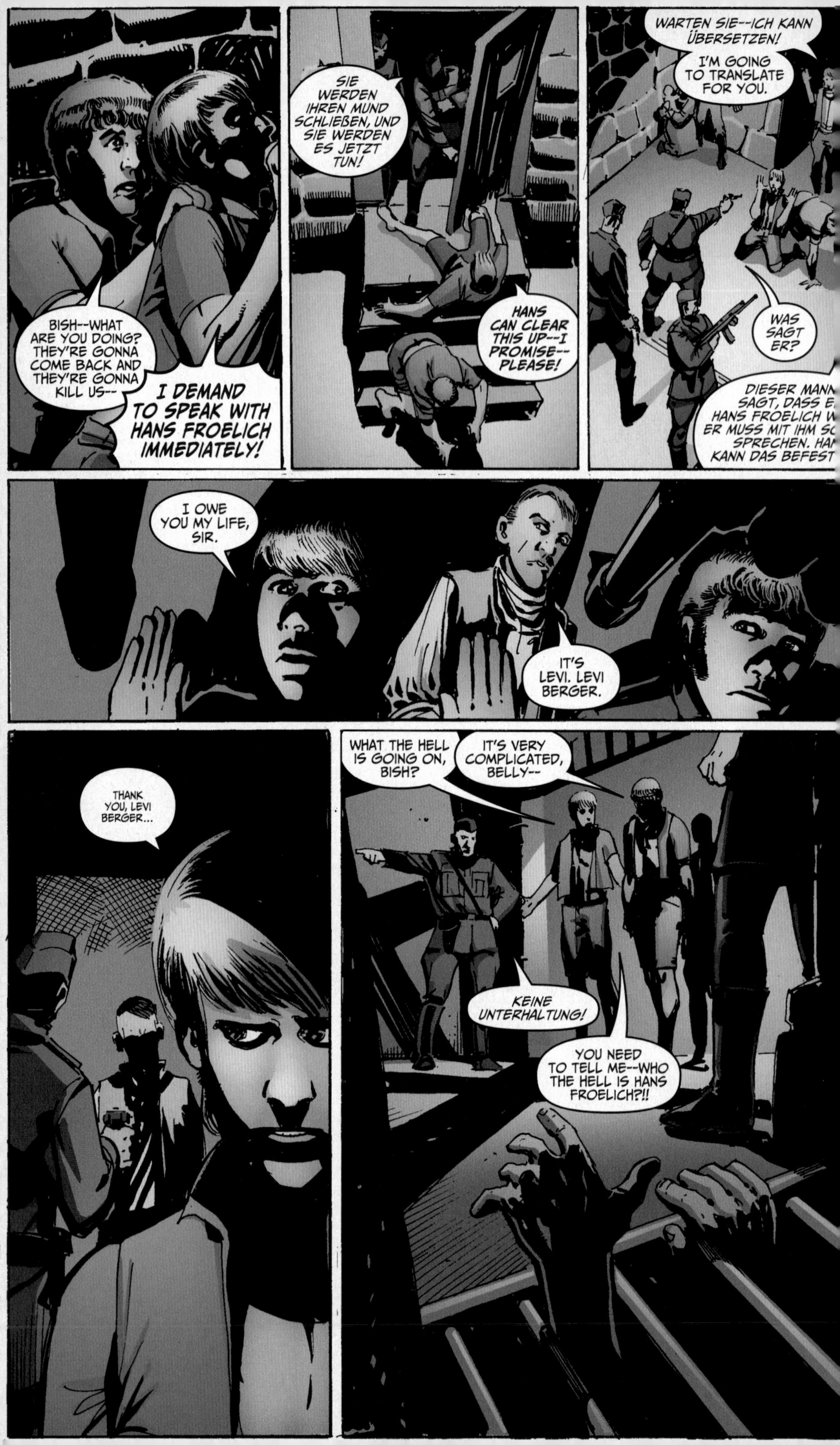
BISH--WHAT ARE YOU DOING? THEY'RE GONNA COME BACK AND THEY'RE GONNA KILL US--
I DEMAND TO SPEAK WITH HANS FROELICH IMMEDIATELY!
SIE WERDEN IHREN MUND SCHLIEßEN, UND SIE WERDEN ES JETZT TUN!
HANS CAN CLEAR THIS UP--I PROMISE--PLEASE!
WARTEN SIE--ICH KANN ÜBERSETZEN!
I'M GOING TO TRANSLATE FOR YOU.
WAS SAGT ER?
I OWE YOU MY LIFE, SIR.
IT'S LEVI. LEVI BERGER.
THANK YOU, LEVI BERGER...
WHAT THE HELL IS GOING ON, BISH?
IT'S VERY COMPLICATED, BELLY--
KEINE UNTERHALTUNG!
YOU NEED TO TELL ME--WHO THE HELL IS HANS FROELICH?!!

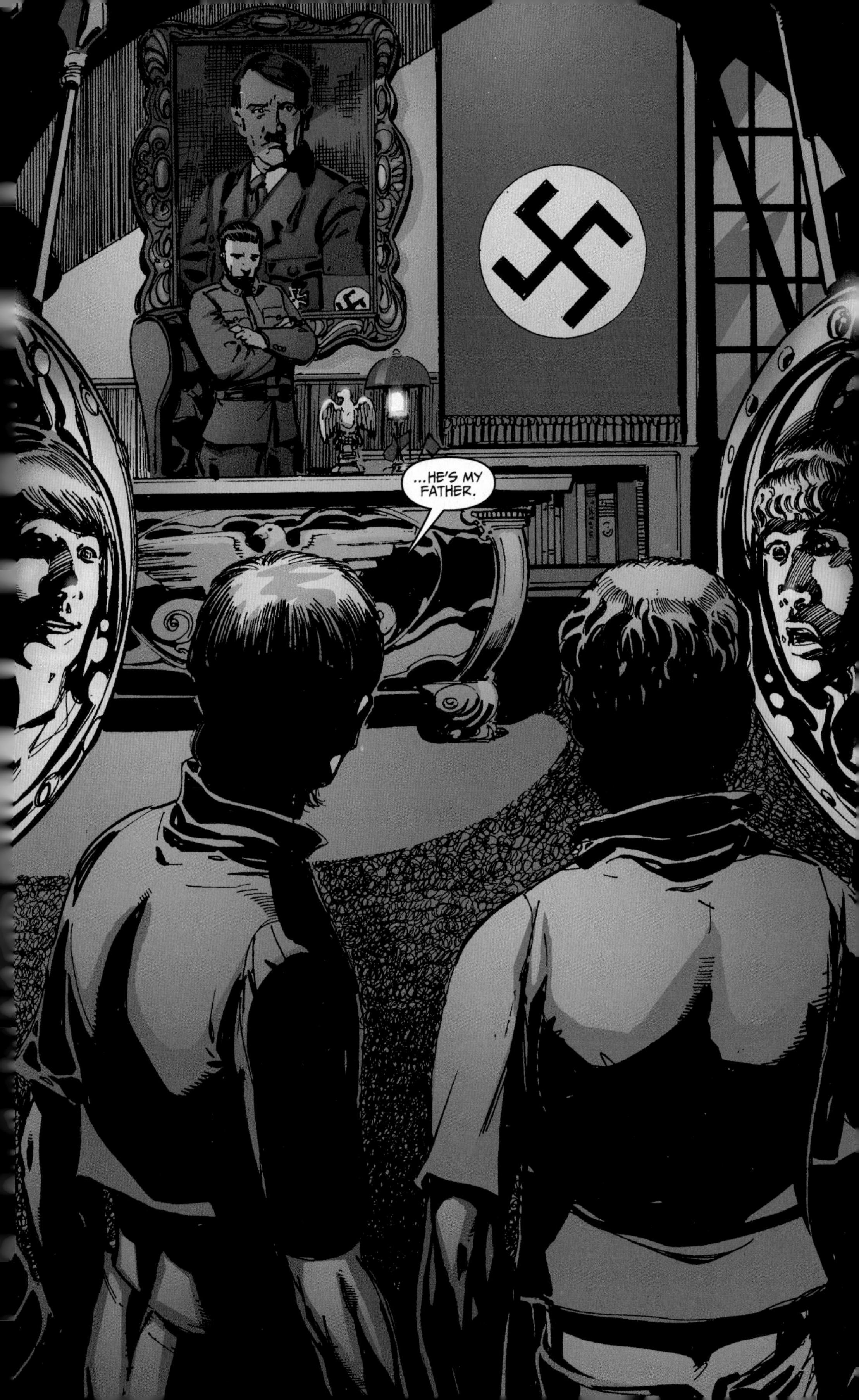
...HE'S MY FATHER.

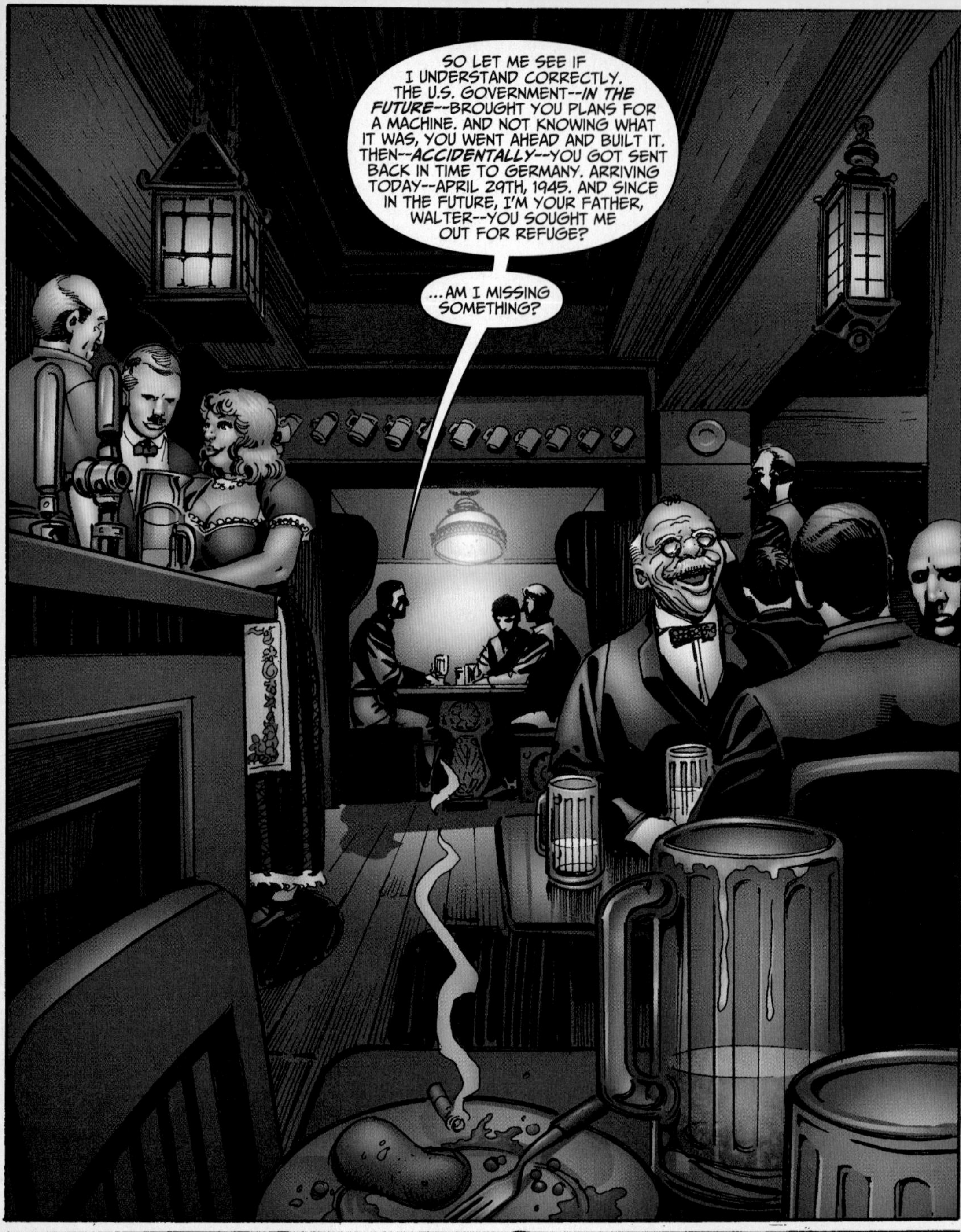
SO LET ME SEE IF I UNDERSTAND CORRECTLY. THE U.S. GOVERNMENT--*IN THE FUTURE*--BROUGHT YOU PLANS FOR A MACHINE. AND NOT KNOWING WHAT IT WAS, YOU WENT AHEAD AND BUILT IT. THEN--*ACCIDENTALLY*--YOU GOT SENT BACK IN TIME TO GERMANY. ARRIVING TODAY--APRIL 29TH, 1945. AND SINCE IN THE FUTURE, I'M YOUR FATHER, WALTER--YOU SOUGHT ME OUT FOR REFUGE?
...AM I MISSING SOMETHING?

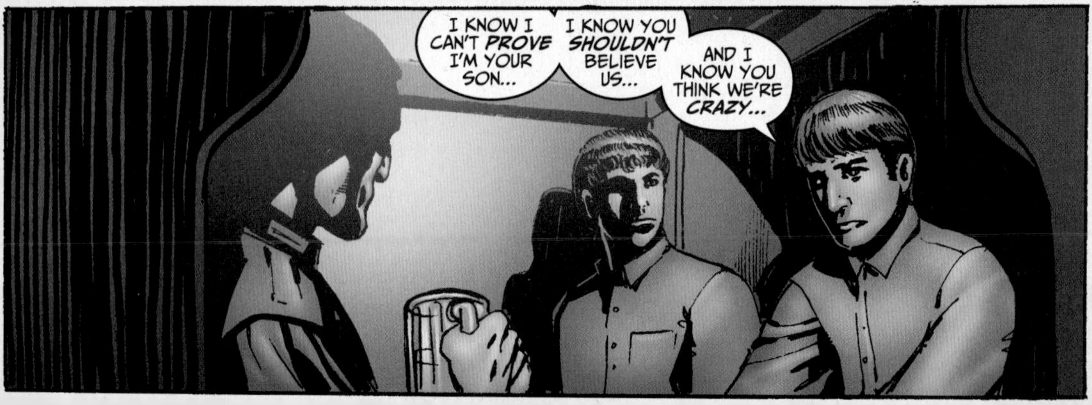
I KNOW I CAN'T *PROVE* I'M YOUR SON...
I KNOW YOU *SHOULDN'T* BELIEVE US...
AND I KNOW YOU THINK WE'RE *CRAZY*...

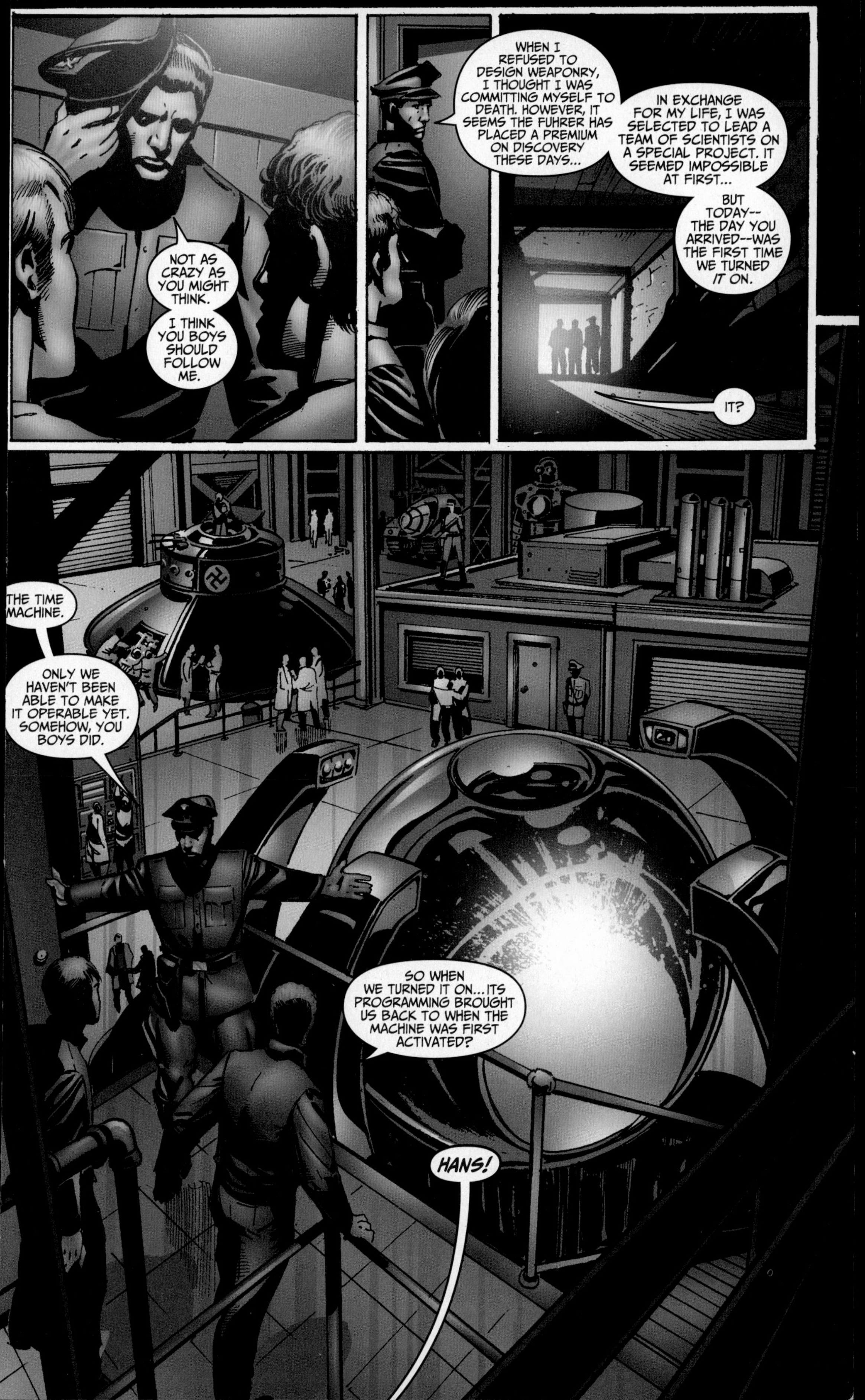
NOT AS CRAZY AS YOU MIGHT THINK.
I THINK YOU BOYS SHOULD FOLLOW ME.
WHEN I REFUSED TO DESIGN WEAPONRY, I THOUGHT I WAS COMMITTING MYSELF TO DEATH. HOWEVER, IT SEEMS THE FUHRER HAS PLACED A PREMIUM ON DISCOVERY THESE DAYS...
IN EXCHANGE FOR MY LIFE, I WAS SELECTED TO LEAD A TEAM OF SCIENTISTS ON A SPECIAL PROJECT. IT SEEMED IMPOSSIBLE AT FIRST...
BUT TODAY-- THE DAY YOU ARRIVED--WAS THE FIRST TIME WE TURNED *IT* ON.
IT?
THE TIME MACHINE.
ONLY WE HAVEN'T BEEN ABLE TO MAKE IT OPERABLE YET. SOMEHOW, YOU BOYS DID.
SO WHEN WE TURNED IT ON...ITS PROGRAMMING BROUGHT US BACK TO WHEN THE MACHINE WAS FIRST ACTIVATED?
HANS!

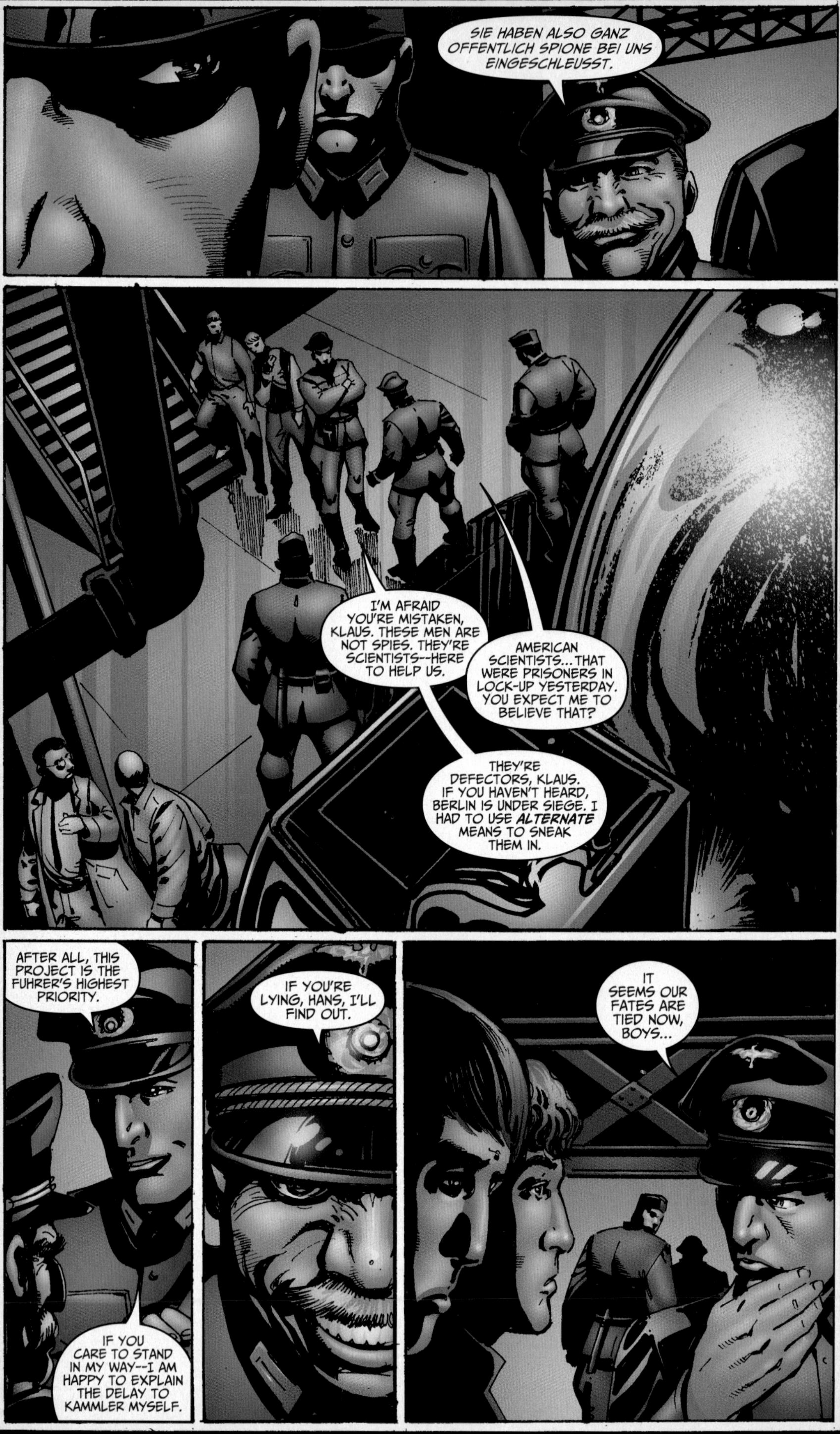
SIE HABEN ALSO GANZ OFFENTLICH SPIONE BEI UNS EINGESCHLEUSST.
I'M AFRAID YOU'RE MISTAKEN, KLAUS. THESE MEN ARE NOT SPIES. THEY'RE SCIENTISTS--HERE TO HELP US.
AMERICAN SCIENTISTS... THAT WERE PRISONERS IN LOCK-UP YESTERDAY. YOU EXPECT ME TO BELIEVE THAT?
THEY'RE DEFECTORS, KLAUS. IF YOU HAVEN'T HEARD, BERLIN IS UNDER SIEGE. I HAD TO USE ALTERNATE MEANS TO SNEAK THEM IN.
AFTER ALL, THIS PROJECT IS THE FUHRER'S HIGHEST PRIORITY.
IF YOU CARE TO STAND IN MY WAY--I AM HAPPY TO EXPLAIN THE DELAY TO KAMMLER MYSELF.
IF YOU'RE LYING, HANS, I'LL FIND OUT.
IT SEEMS OUR FATES ARE TIED NOW, BOYS...

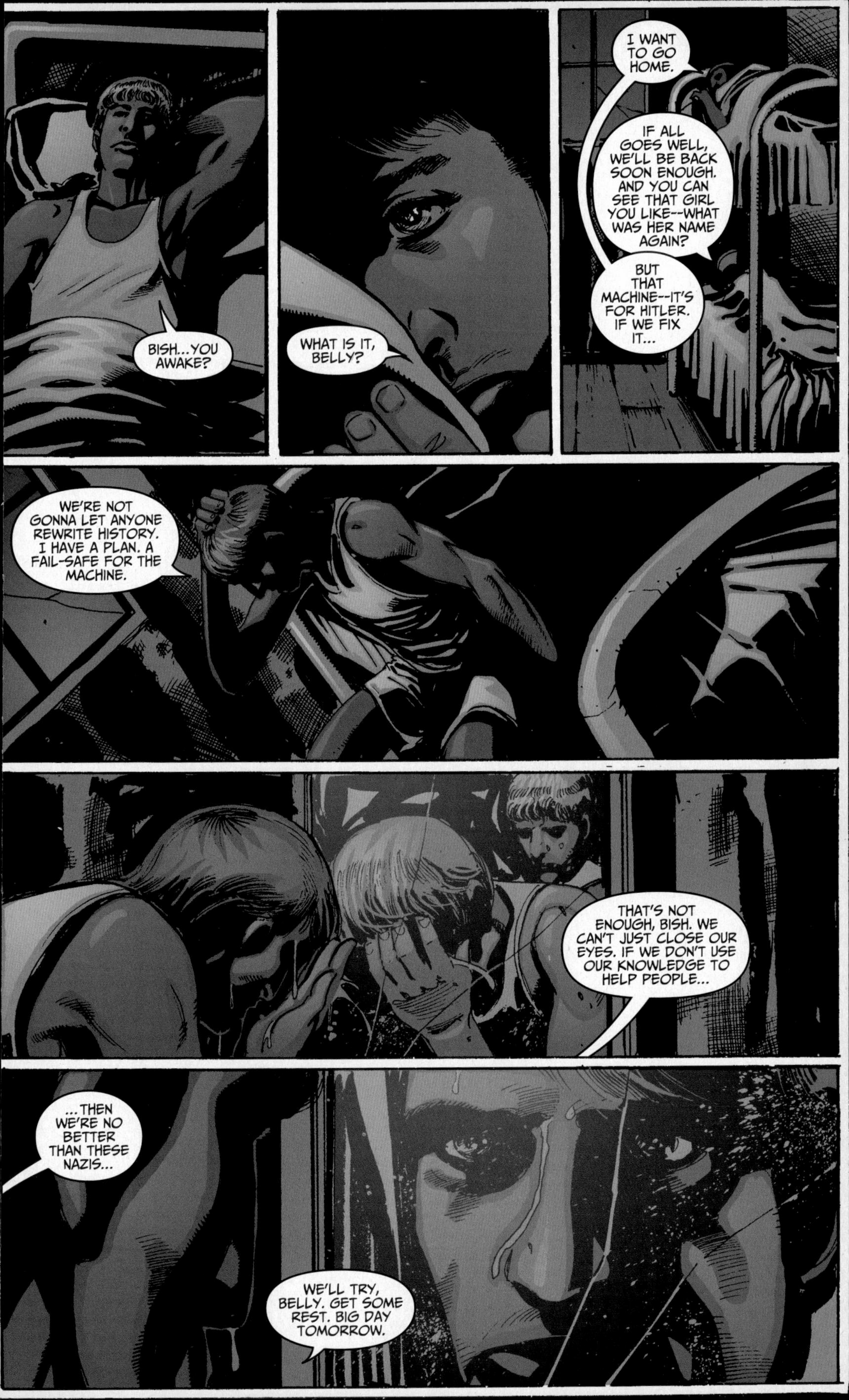

BISH...YOU AWAKE?
WHAT IS IT, BELLY?
I WANT TO GO HOME.
IF ALL GOES WELL, WE'LL BE BACK SOON ENOUGH. AND YOU CAN SEE THAT GIRL YOU LIKE--WHAT WAS HER NAME AGAIN?
BUT THAT MACHINE--IT'S FOR HITLER. IF WE FIX IT...
WE'RE NOT GONNA LET ANYONE REWRITE HISTORY. I HAVE A PLAN. A FAIL-SAFE FOR THE MACHINE.
THAT'S NOT ENOUGH, BISH. WE CAN'T JUST CLOSE OUR EYES. IF WE DON'T USE OUR KNOWLEDGE TO HELP PEOPLE...
...THEN WE'RE NO BETTER THAN THESE NAZIS...
WE'LL TRY, BELLY. GET SOME REST. BIG DAY TOMORROW.

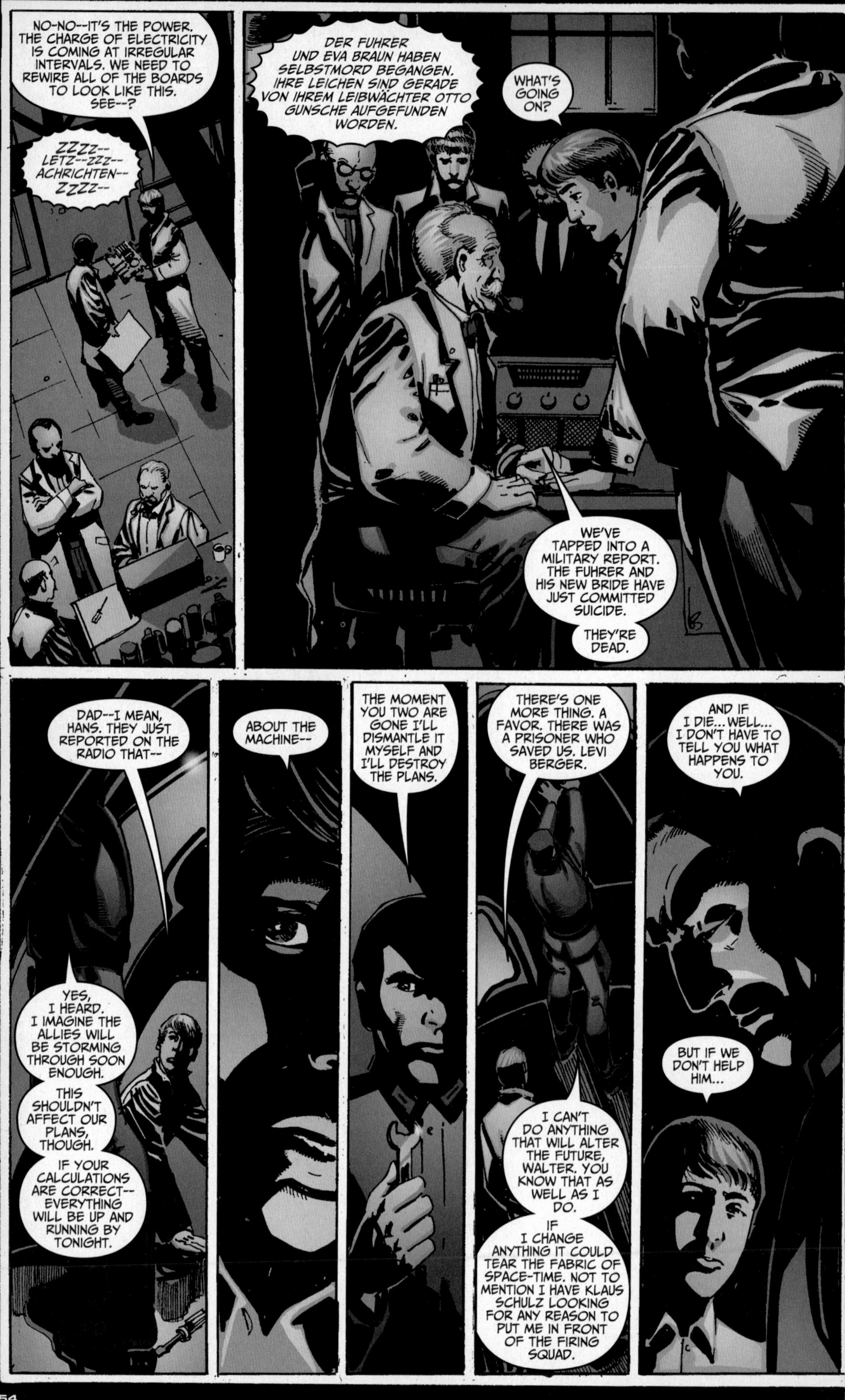
NO-NO--IT'S THE POWER. THE CHARGE OF ELECTRICITY IS COMING AT IRREGULAR INTERVALS. WE NEED TO REWIRE ALL OF THE BOARDS TO LOOK LIKE THIS. SEE--?
ZZZZ-- LETZ--ZZZ-- ACHRICHTEN-- ZZZZ--
DER FUHRER UND EVA BRAUN HABEN SELBSTMORD BEGANGEN. IHRE LEICHEN SIND GERADE VON IHREM LEIBWÄCHTER OTTO GUNSCHE AUFGEFUNDEN WORDEN.
WHAT'S GOING ON?
WE'VE TAPPED INTO A MILITARY REPORT. THE FUHRER AND HIS NEW BRIDE HAVE JUST COMMITTED SUICIDE.
THEY'RE DEAD.
DAD--I MEAN, HANS. THEY JUST REPORTED ON THE RADIO THAT--
YES, I HEARD. I IMAGINE THE ALLIES WILL BE STORMING THROUGH SOON ENOUGH.
THIS SHOULDN'T AFFECT OUR PLANS, THOUGH.
IF YOUR CALCULATIONS ARE CORRECT-- EVERYTHING WILL BE UP AND RUNNING BY TONIGHT.
ABOUT THE MACHINE--
THE MOMENT YOU TWO ARE GONE I'LL DISMANTLE IT MYSELF AND I'LL DESTROY THE PLANS.
THERE'S ONE MORE THING. A FAVOR. THERE WAS A PRISONER WHO SAVED US. LEVI BERGER.
I CAN'T DO ANYTHING THAT WILL ALTER THE FUTURE, WALTER. YOU KNOW THAT AS WELL AS I DO.
IF I CHANGE ANYTHING IT COULD TEAR THE FABRIC OF SPACE-TIME. NOT TO MENTION I HAVE KLAUS SCHULZ LOOKING FOR ANY REASON TO PUT ME IN FRONT OF THE FIRING SQUAD.
AND IF I DIE...WELL... I DON'T HAVE TO TELL YOU WHAT HAPPENS TO YOU.
BUT IF WE DON'T HELP HIM...

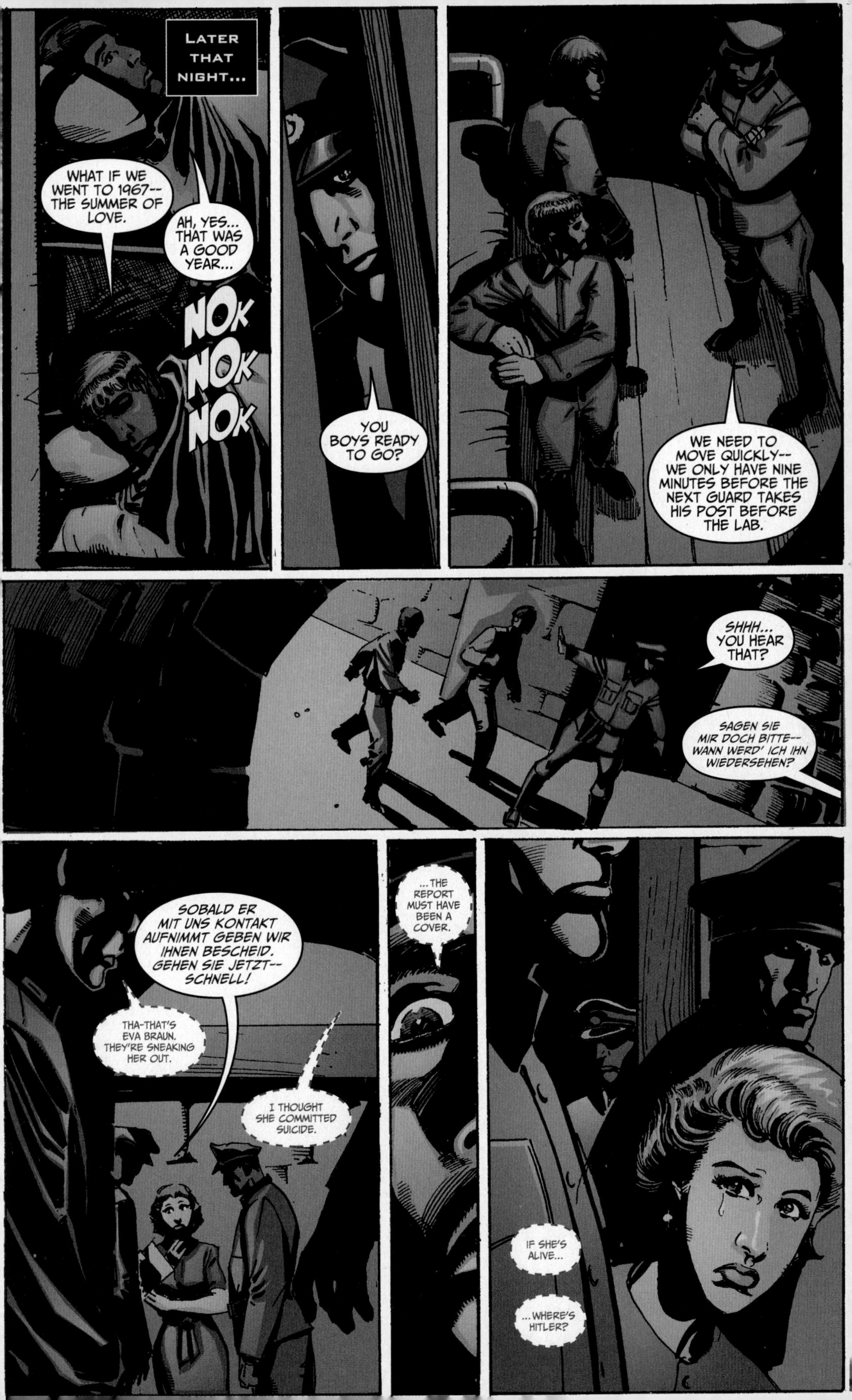
LATER THAT NIGHT...
WHAT IF WE WENT TO 1967-- THE SUMMER OF LOVE.
AH, YES... THAT WAS A GOOD YEAR...
NOK NOK NOK
YOU BOYS READY TO GO?
WE NEED TO MOVE QUICKLY-- WE ONLY HAVE NINE MINUTES BEFORE THE NEXT GUARD TAKES HIS POST BEFORE THE LAB.
SHHH... YOU HEAR THAT?
SAGEN SIE MIR DOCH BITTE-- WANN WERD' ICH IHN WIEDERSEHEN?
SOBALD ER MIT UNS KONTAKT AUFNIMMT GEBEN WIR IHNEN BESCHEID. GEHEN SIE JETZT-- SCHNELL!
THA-THAT'S EVA BRAUN. THEY'RE SNEAKING HER OUT.
I THOUGHT SHE COMMITTED SUICIDE.
...THE REPORT MUST HAVE BEEN A COVER.
IF SHE'S ALIVE...
...WHERE'S HITLER?

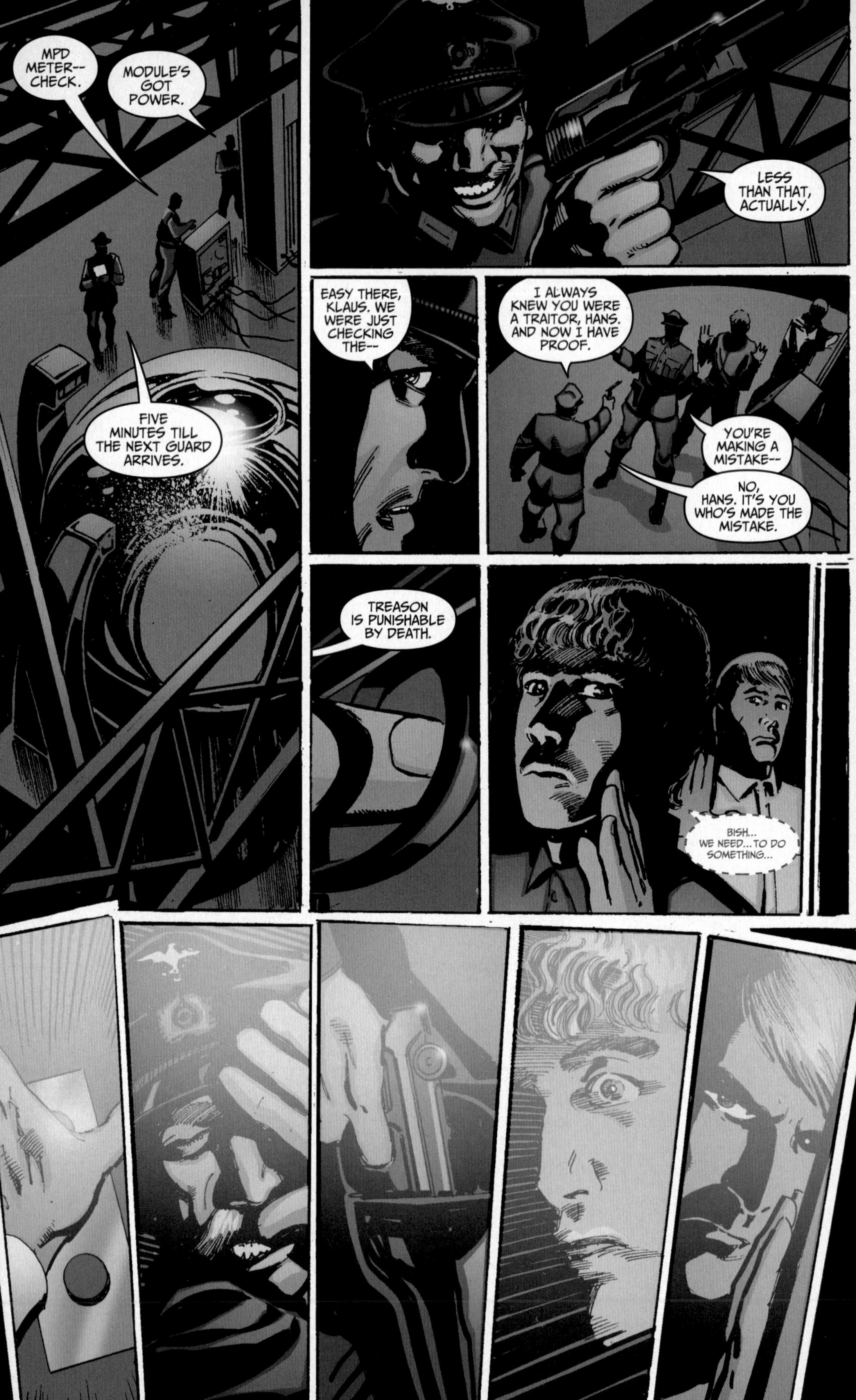
MPD METER--CHECK.
MODULE'S GOT POWER.
FIVE MINUTES TILL THE NEXT GUARD ARRIVES.
LESS THAN THAT, ACTUALLY.
EASY THERE, KLAUS. WE WERE JUST CHECKING THE--
I ALWAYS KNEW YOU WERE A TRAITOR, HANS. AND NOW I HAVE PROOF.
YOU'RE MAKING A MISTAKE--
NO, HANS. IT'S YOU WHO'S MADE THE MISTAKE.
TREASON IS PUNISHABLE BY DEATH.
BISH... WE NEED...TO DO SOMETHING...

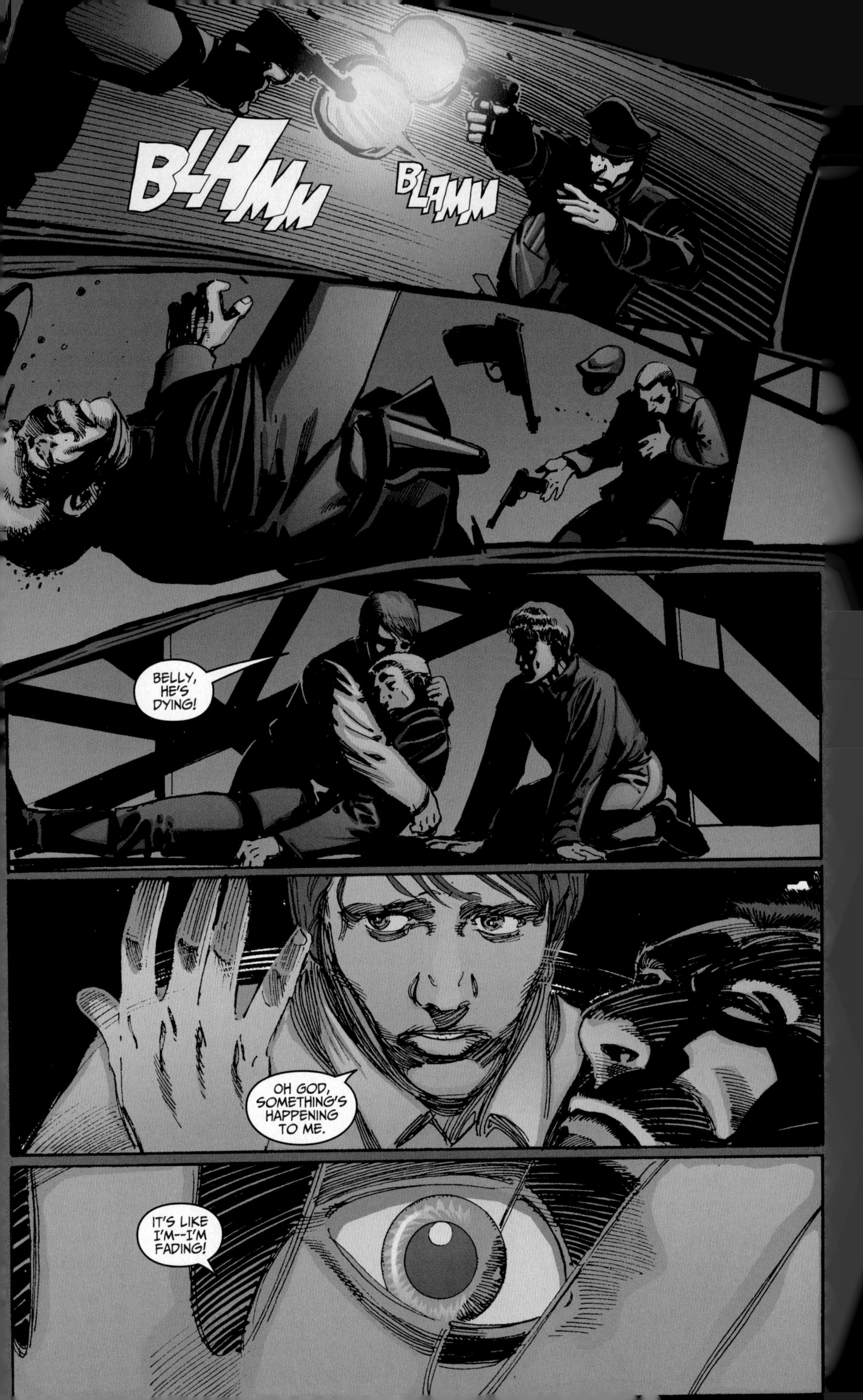
BLAMM
BLAMM
BELLY, HE'S DYING!
OH GOD, SOMETHING'S HAPPENING TO ME.
IT'S LIKE I'M--I'M FADING!

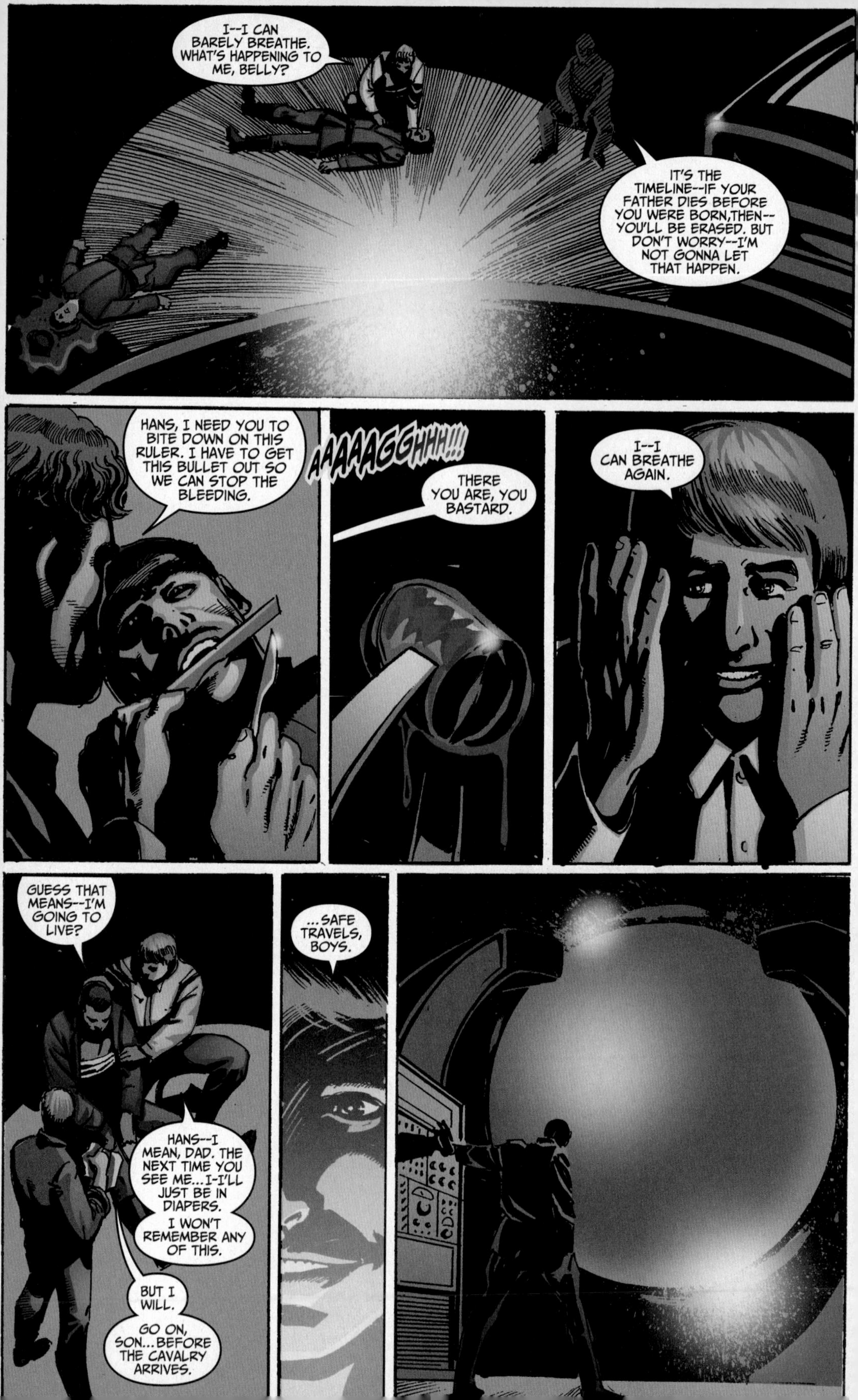
I--I CAN BARELY BREATHE. WHAT'S HAPPENING TO ME, BELLY?
IT'S THE TIMELINE--IF YOUR FATHER DIES BEFORE YOU WERE BORN,THEN--YOU'LL BE ERASED. BUT DON'T WORRY--I'M NOT GONNA LET THAT HAPPEN.
HANS, I NEED YOU TO BITE DOWN ON THIS RULER. I HAVE TO GET THIS BULLET OUT SO WE CAN STOP THE BLEEDING.
AAAAAGGHHH!!!
THERE YOU ARE, YOU BASTARD.
I--I CAN BREATHE AGAIN.
GUESS THAT MEANS--I'M GOING TO LIVE?
HANS--I MEAN, DAD. THE NEXT TIME YOU SEE ME...I-I'LL JUST BE IN DIAPERS.
I WON'T REMEMBER ANY OF THIS.
BUT I WILL.
GO ON, SON...BEFORE THE CAVALRY ARRIVES.
...SAFE TRAVELS, BOYS.

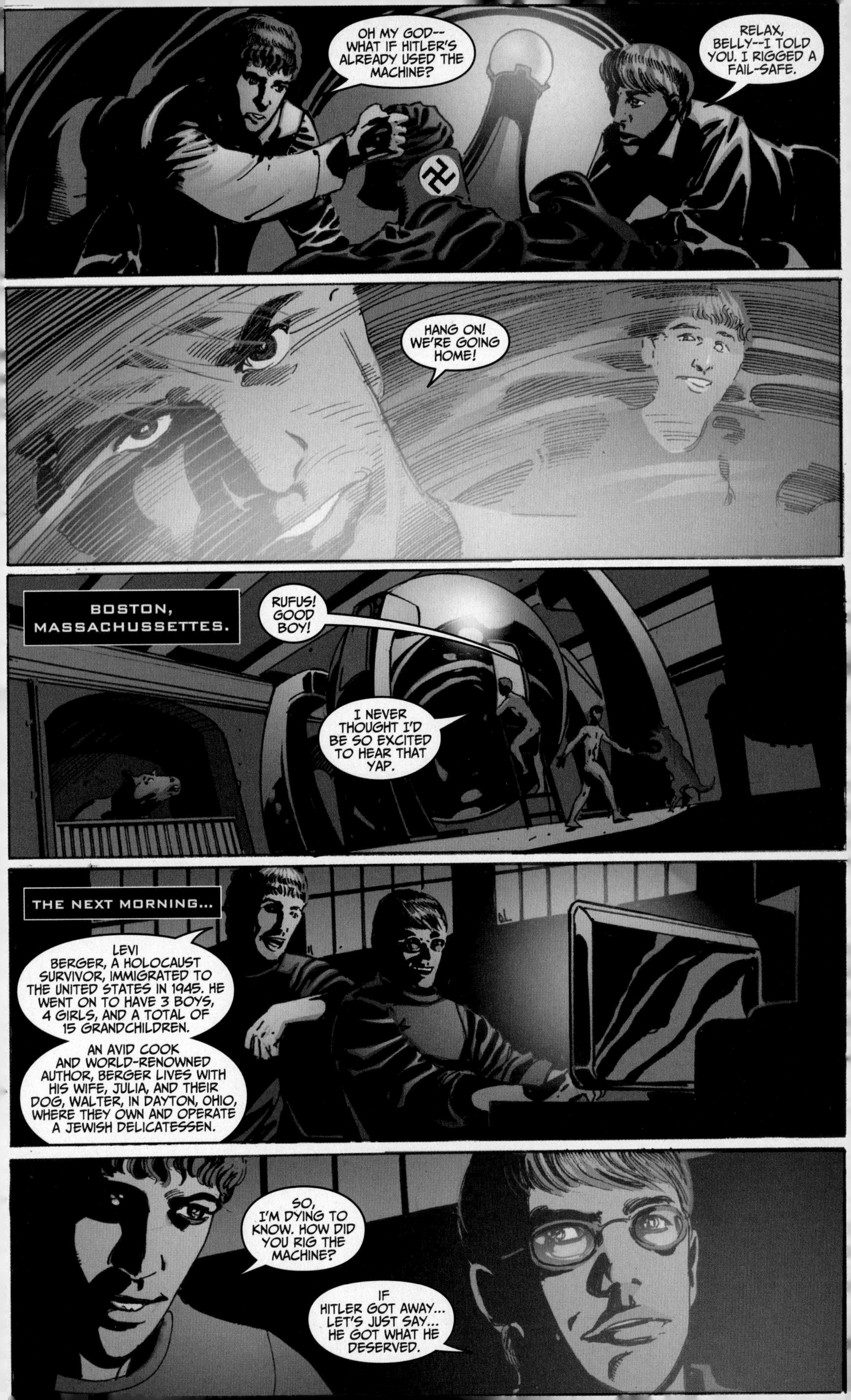
OH MY GOD-- WHAT IF HITLER'S ALREADY USED THE MACHINE?
RELAX, BELLY--I TOLD YOU. I RIGGED A FAIL-SAFE.
HANG ON! WE'RE GOING HOME!
BOSTON, MASSACHUSSETTES.
RUFUS! GOOD BOY!
I NEVER THOUGHT I'D BE SO EXCITED TO HEAR THAT YAP.
THE NEXT MORNING...
LEVI BERGER, A HOLOCAUST SURVIVOR, IMMIGRATED TO THE UNITED STATES IN 1945. HE WENT ON TO HAVE 3 BOYS, 4 GIRLS, AND A TOTAL OF 15 GRANDCHILDREN.
AN AVID COOK AND WORLD-RENOWNED AUTHOR, BERGER LIVES WITH HIS WIFE, JULIA, AND THEIR DOG, WALTER, IN DAYTON, OHIO, WHERE THEY OWN AND OPERATE A JEWISH DELICATESSEN.
SO, I'M DYING TO KNOW. HOW DID YOU RIG THE MACHINE?
IF HITLER GOT AWAY... LET'S JUST SAY... HE GOT WHAT HE DESERVED.

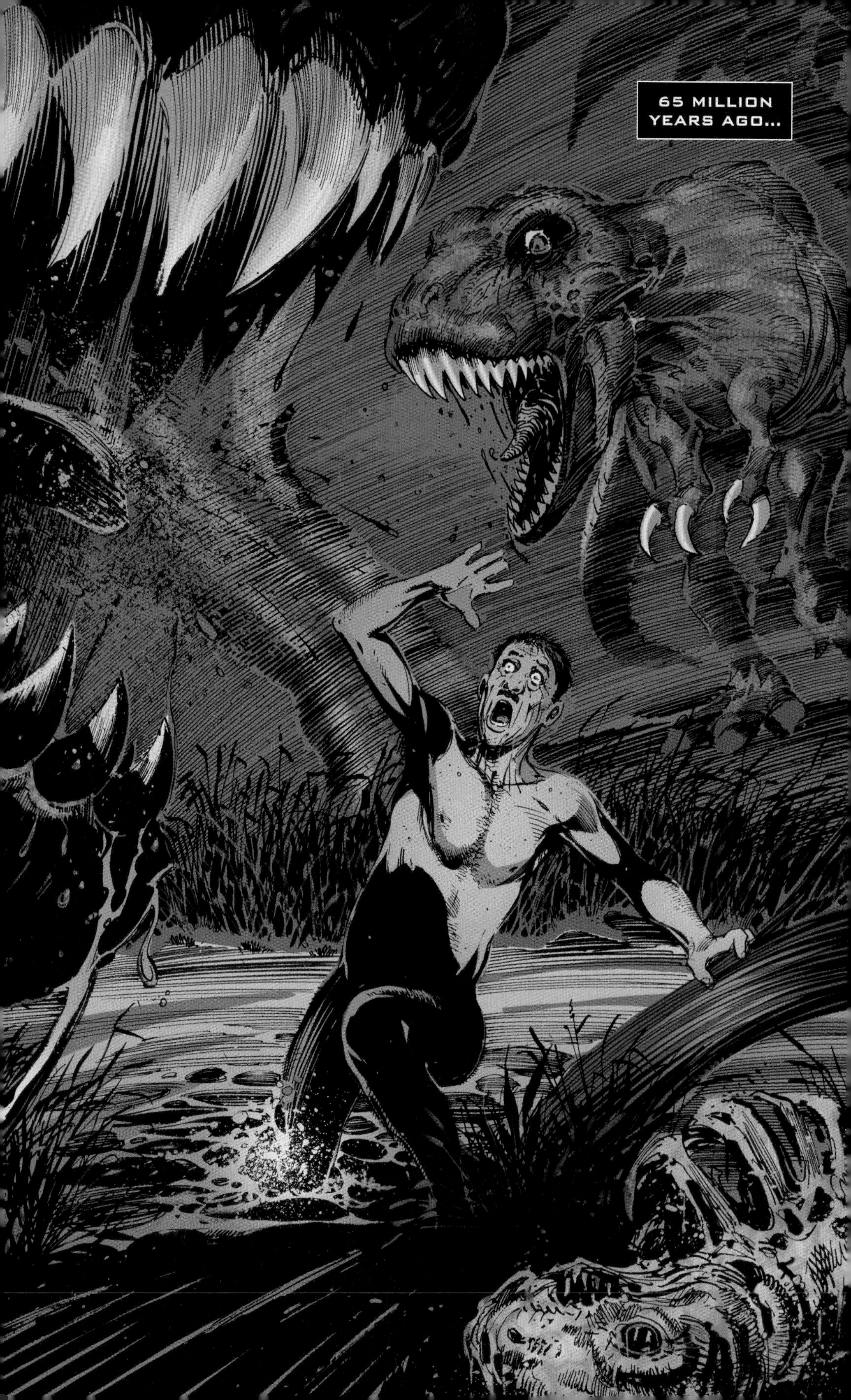
65 MILLION YEARS AGO...

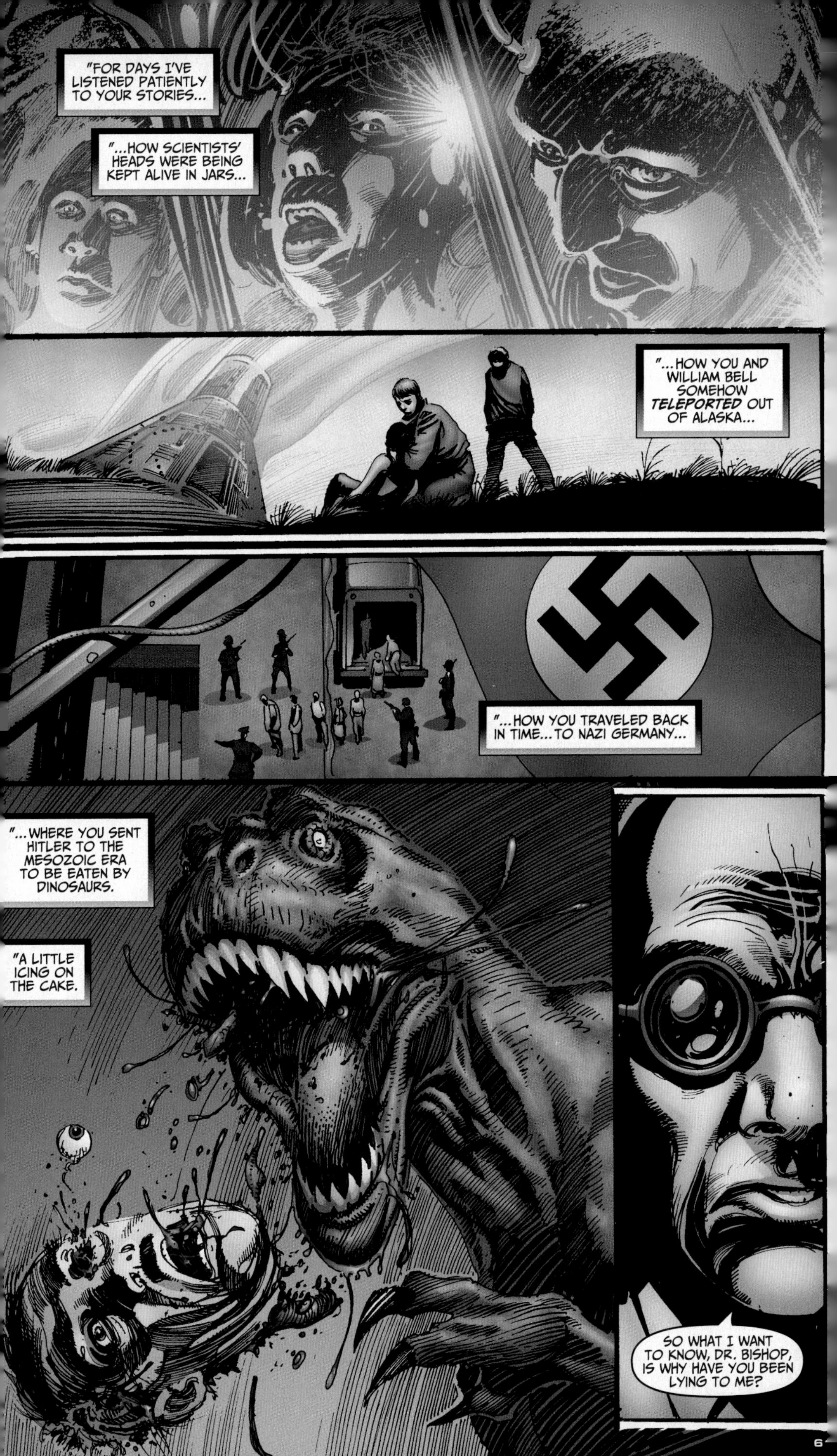
"FOR DAYS I'VE LISTENED PATIENTLY TO YOUR STORIES...
"...HOW SCIENTISTS' HEADS WERE BEING KEPT ALIVE IN JARS...
"...HOW YOU AND WILLIAM BELL SOMEHOW TELEPORTED OUT OF ALASKA...
"...HOW YOU TRAVELED BACK IN TIME...TO NAZI GERMANY...
"...WHERE YOU SENT HITLER TO THE MESOZOIC ERA TO BE EATEN BY DINOSAURS.
"A LITTLE ICING ON THE CAKE.
SO WHAT I WANT TO KNOW, DR. BISHOP, IS WHY HAVE YOU BEEN LYING TO ME?

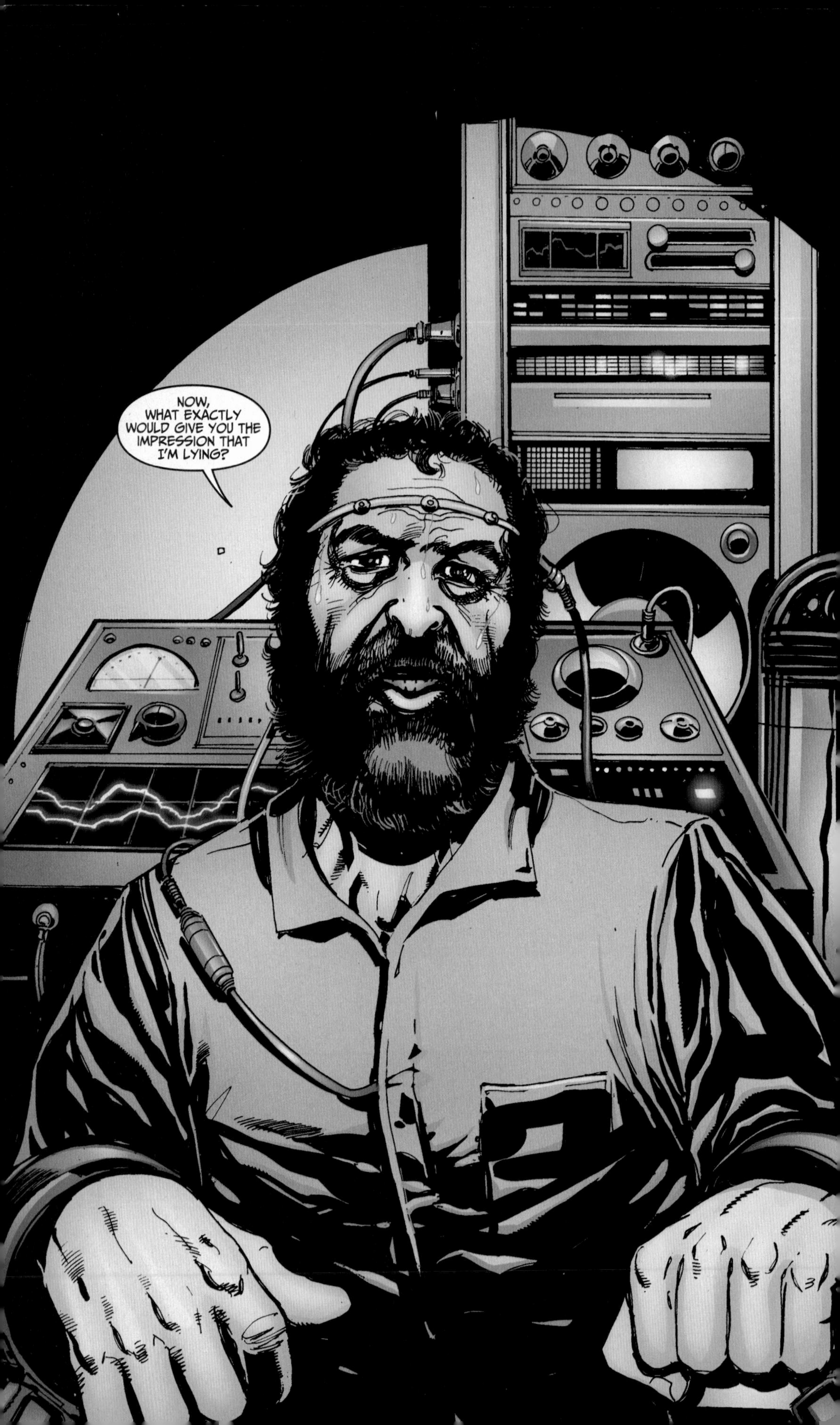
NOW, WHAT EXACTLY WOULD GIVE YOU THE IMPRESSION THAT I'M LYING?

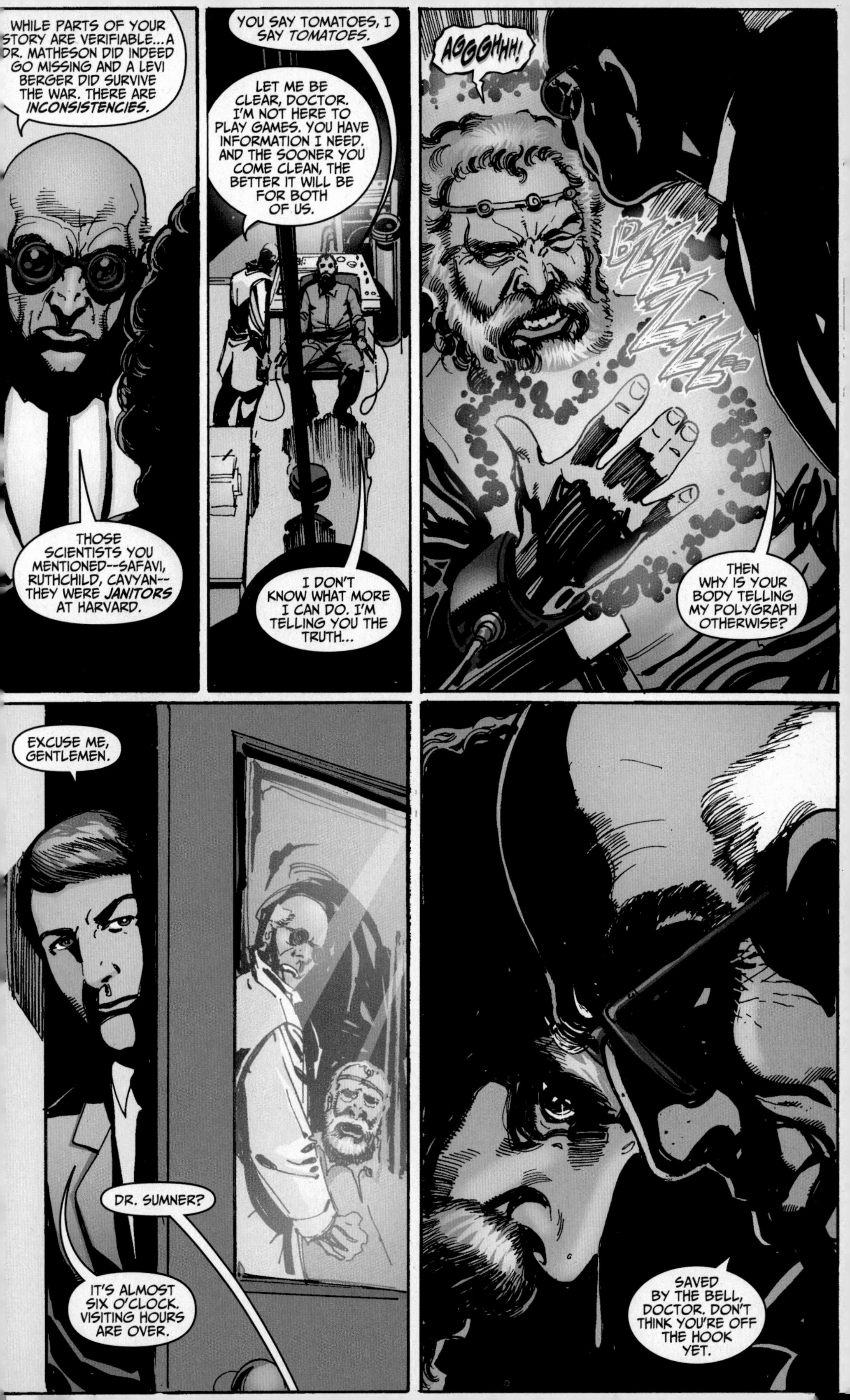
WHILE PARTS OF YOUR STORY ARE VERIFIABLE...A DR. MATHESON DID INDEED GO MISSING AND A LEVI BERGER DID SURVIVE THE WAR. THERE ARE *INCONSISTENCIES.*
THOSE SCIENTISTS YOU MENTIONED--SAFAVI, RUTHCHILD, CAVYAN--THEY WERE *JANITORS* AT HARVARD.
YOU SAY TOMATOES, I SAY *TOMATOES.*
LET ME BE CLEAR, DOCTOR. I'M NOT HERE TO PLAY GAMES. YOU HAVE INFORMATION I NEED. AND THE SOONER YOU COME CLEAN, THE BETTER IT WILL BE FOR BOTH OF US.
I DON'T KNOW WHAT MORE I CAN DO. I'M TELLING YOU THE TRUTH...
AGGGHHH!
BZZZZZ
THEN WHY IS YOUR BODY TELLING MY POLYGRAPH OTHERWISE?
EXCUSE ME, GENTLEMEN.
DR. SUMNER?
IT'S ALMOST SIX O'CLOCK. VISITING HOURS ARE OVER.
SAVED BY THE BELL, DOCTOR. DON'T THINK YOU'RE OFF THE HOOK YET.

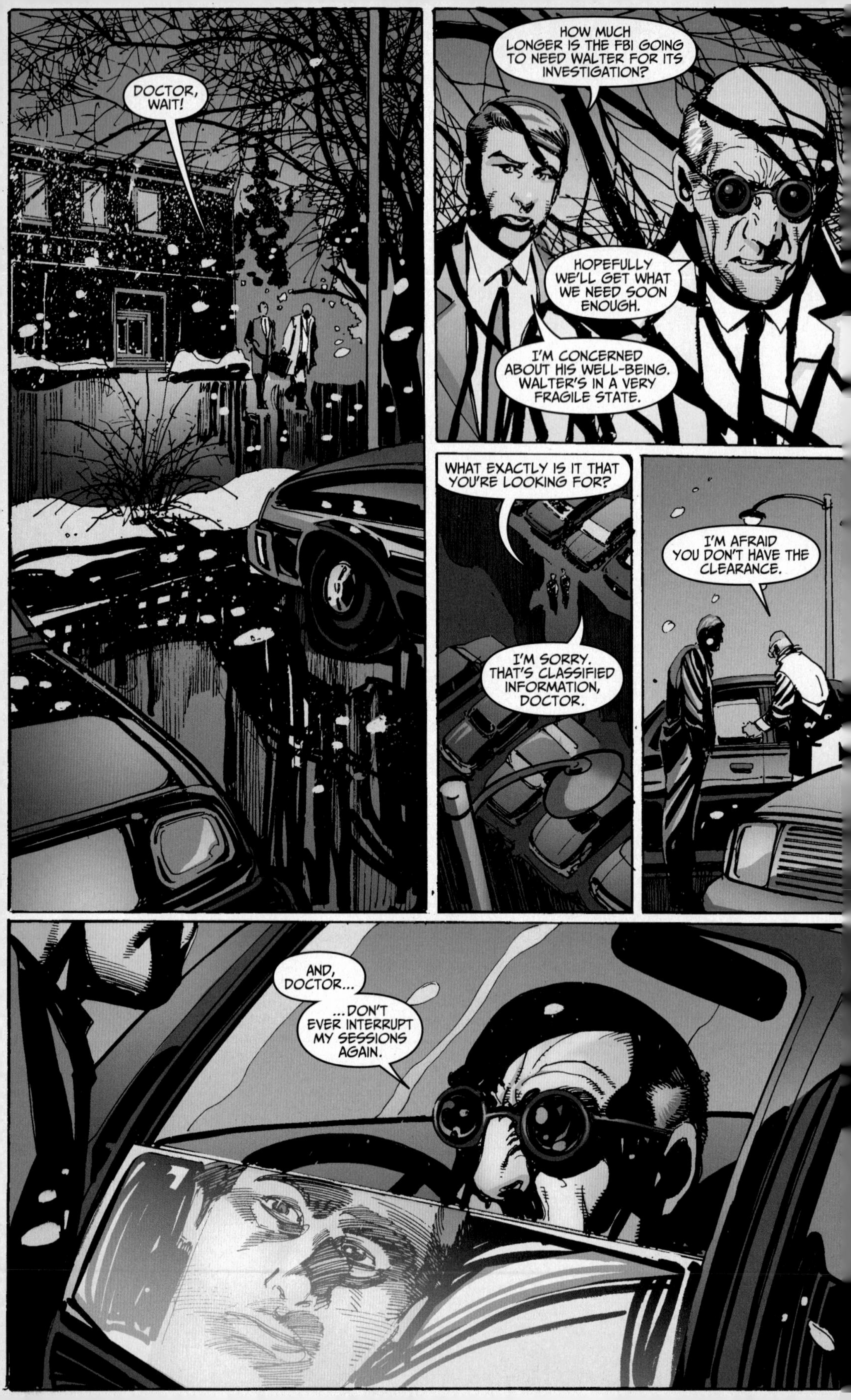
DOCTOR, WAIT!
HOW MUCH LONGER IS THE FBI GOING TO NEED WALTER FOR ITS INVESTIGATION?
HOPEFULLY WE'LL GET WHAT WE NEED SOON ENOUGH.
I'M CONCERNED ABOUT HIS WELL-BEING. WALTER'S IN A VERY FRAGILE STATE.
WHAT EXACTLY IS IT THAT YOU'RE LOOKING FOR?
I'M SORRY. THAT'S CLASSIFIED INFORMATION, DOCTOR.
I'M AFRAID YOU DON'T HAVE THE CLEARANCE.
AND, DOCTOR...
...DON'T EVER INTERRUPT MY SESSIONS AGAIN.

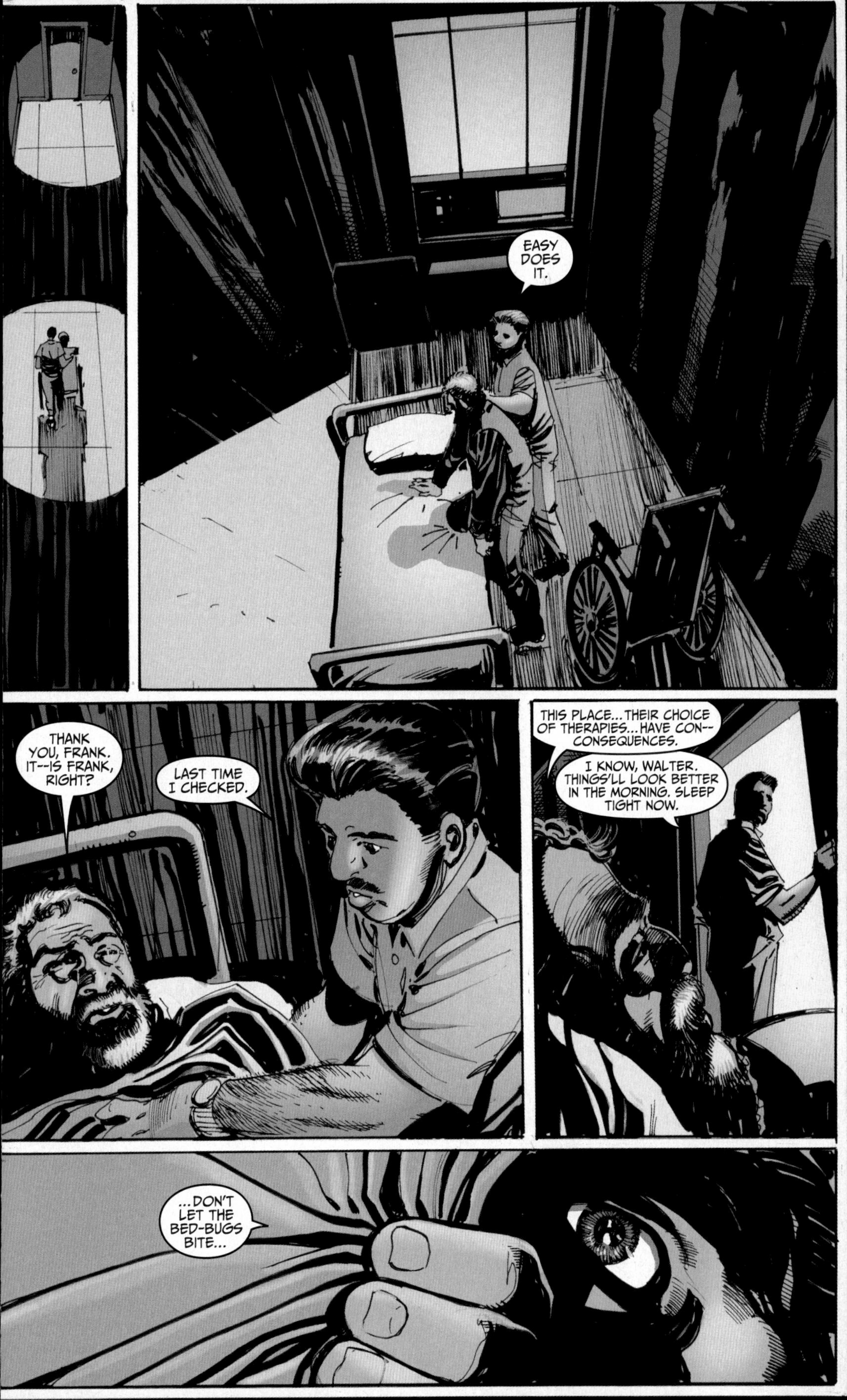
EASY DOES IT.
THANK YOU, FRANK. IT--IS FRANK, RIGHT?
LAST TIME I CHECKED.
THIS PLACE...THEIR CHOICE OF THERAPIES...HAVE CON-- CONSEQUENCES.
I KNOW, WALTER. THINGS'LL LOOK BETTER IN THE MORNING. SLEEP TIGHT NOW.
...DON'T LET THE BED-BUGS BITE...

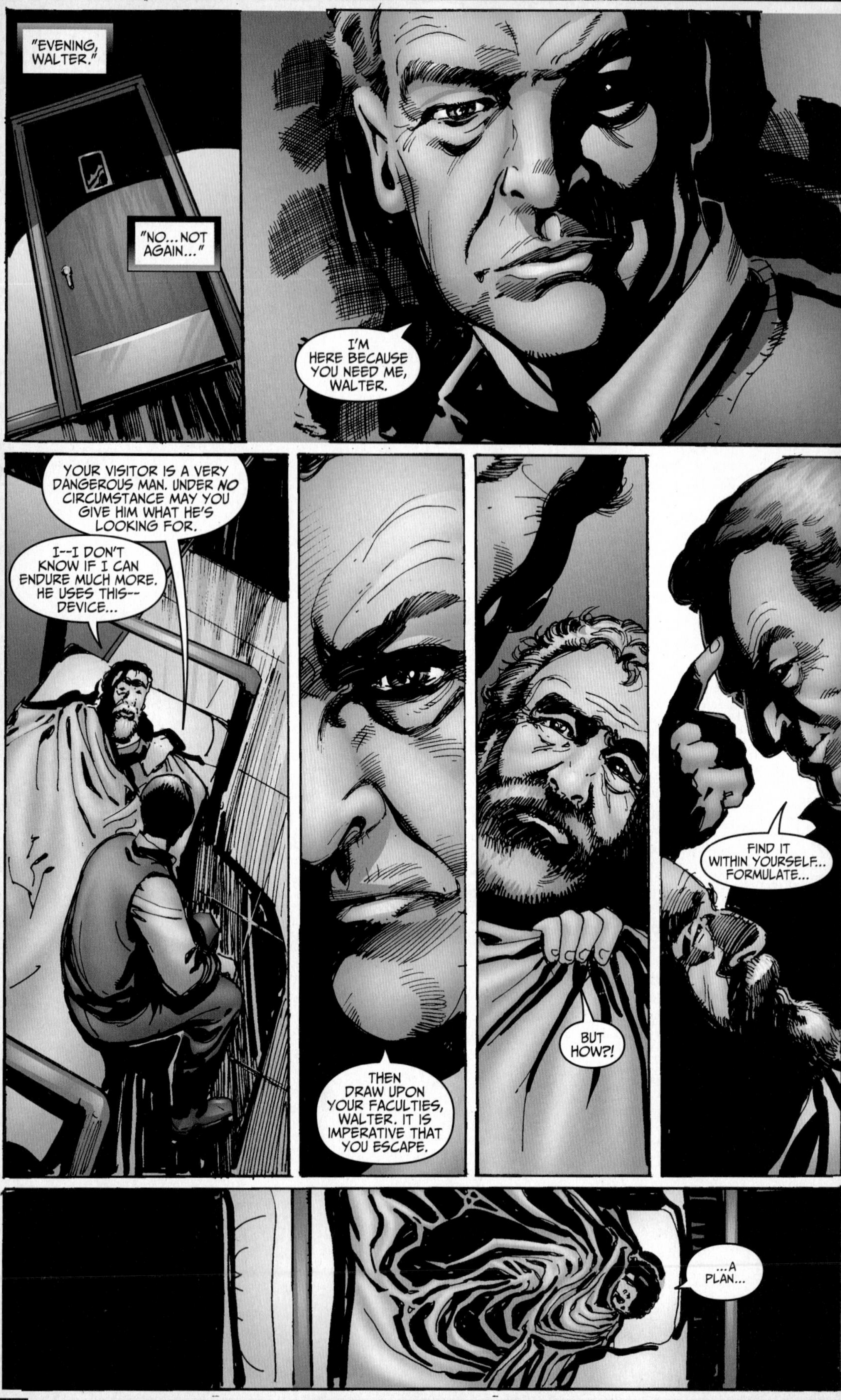
"EVENING, WALTER."
"NO...NOT AGAIN..."
I'M HERE BECAUSE YOU NEED ME, WALTER.
YOUR VISITOR IS A VERY DANGEROUS MAN. UNDER NO CIRCUMSTANCE MAY YOU GIVE HIM WHAT HE'S LOOKING FOR.
I--I DON'T KNOW IF I CAN ENDURE MUCH MORE. HE USES THIS-- DEVICE...
THEN DRAW UPON YOUR FACULTIES, WALTER. IT IS IMPERATIVE THAT YOU ESCAPE.
BUT HOW?!
FIND IT WITHIN YOURSELF... FORMULATE...
...A PLAN...

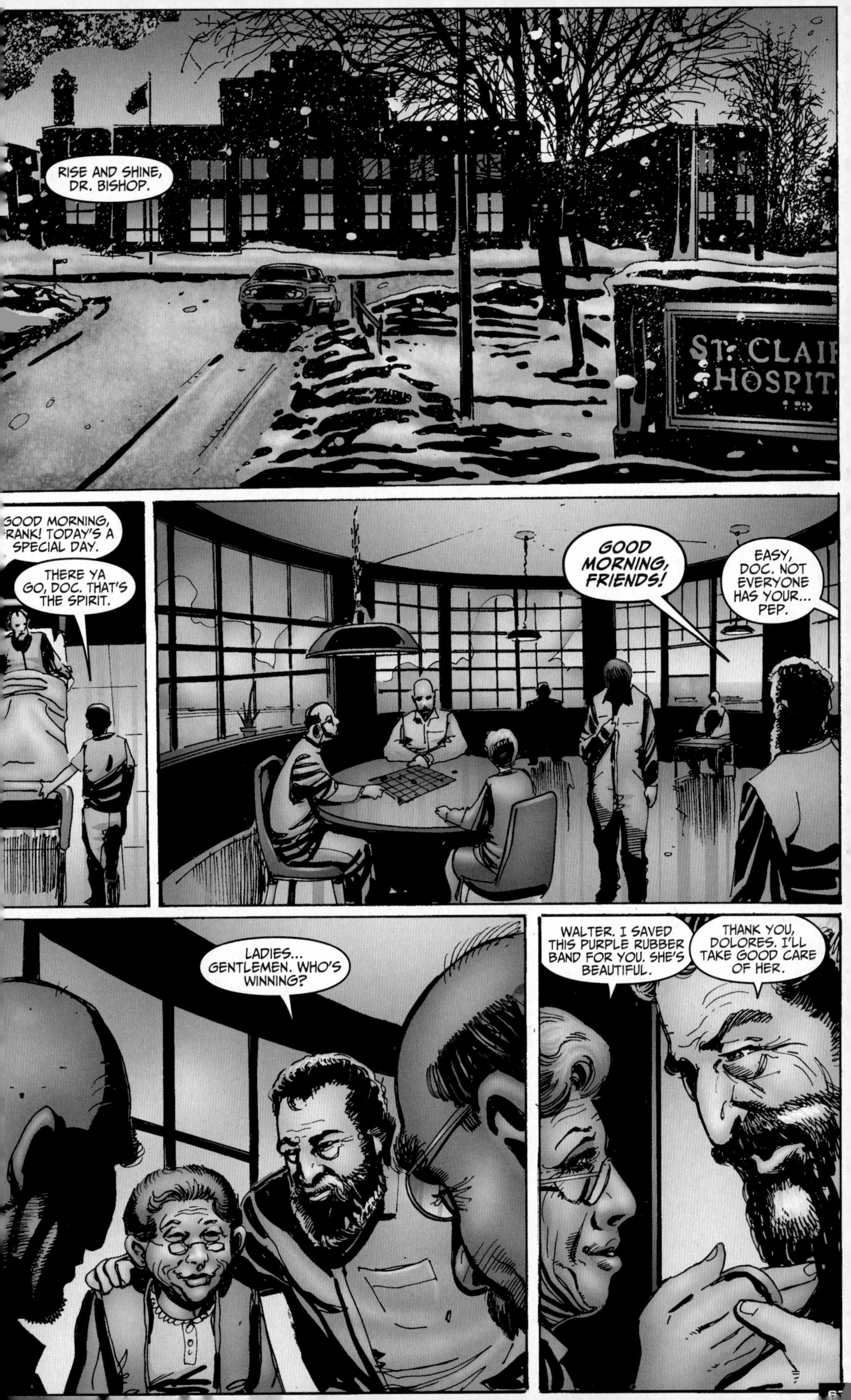

RISE AND SHINE, DR. BISHOP.
ST. CLAIR HOSPIT
GOOD MORNING, FRANK! TODAY'S A SPECIAL DAY.
THERE YA GO, DOC. THAT'S THE SPIRIT.
GOOD MORNING, FRIENDS!
EASY, DOC. NOT EVERYONE HAS YOUR... PEP.
LADIES... GENTLEMEN. WHO'S WINNING?
WALTER. I SAVED THIS PURPLE RUBBER BAND FOR YOU. SHE'S BEAUTIFUL.
THANK YOU, DOLORES. I'LL TAKE GOOD CARE OF HER.

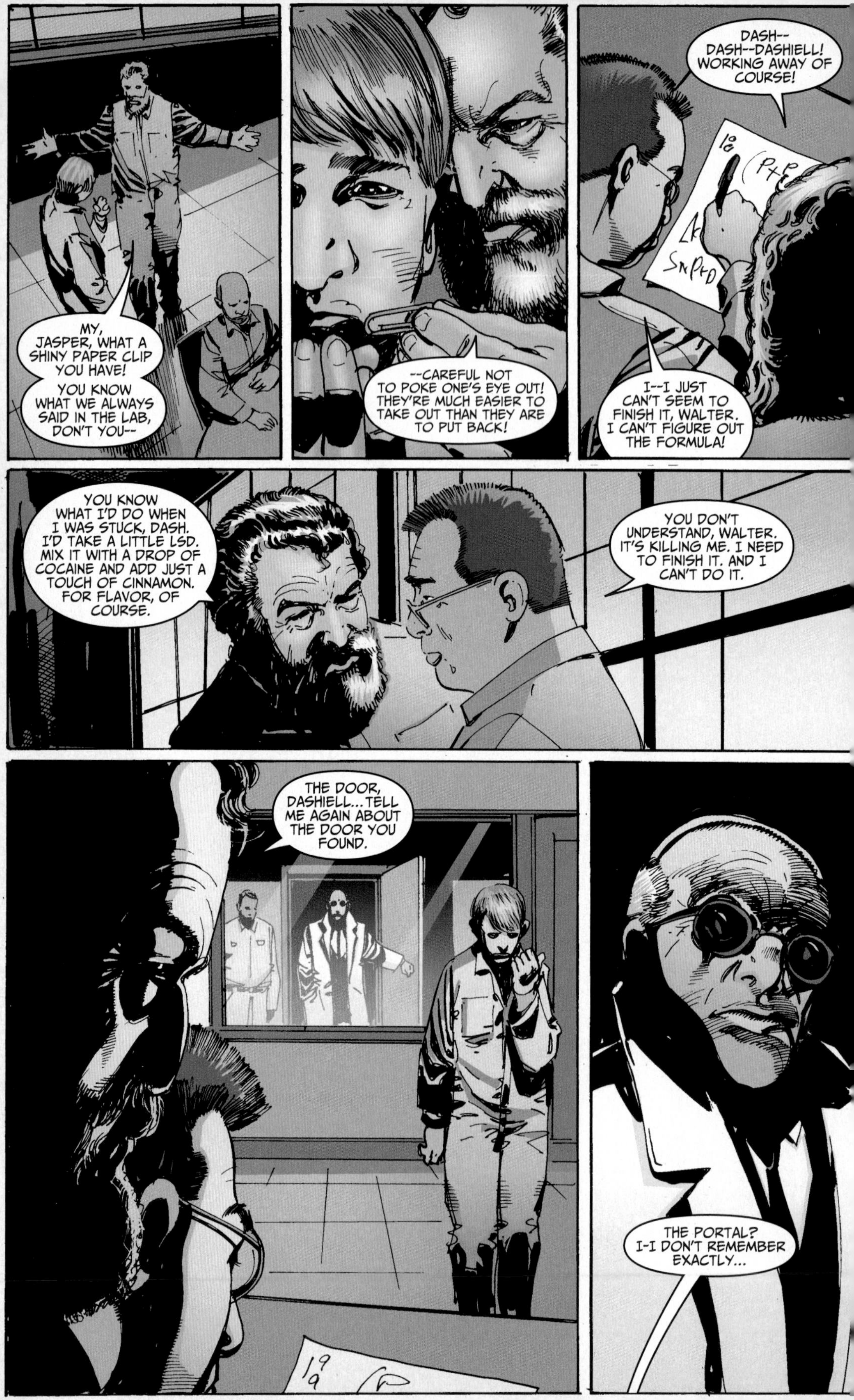
MY, JASPER, WHAT A SHINY PAPER CLIP YOU HAVE!
YOU KNOW WHAT WE ALWAYS SAID IN THE LAB, DON'T YOU--
--CAREFUL NOT TO POKE ONE'S EYE OUT! THEY'RE MUCH EASIER TO TAKE OUT THAN THEY ARE TO PUT BACK!
DASH-- DASH--DASHIELL! WORKING AWAY OF COURSE!
I--I JUST CAN'T SEEM TO FINISH IT, WALTER. I CAN'T FIGURE OUT THE FORMULA!
YOU KNOW WHAT I'D DO WHEN I WAS STUCK, DASH. I'D TAKE A LITTLE LSD. MIX IT WITH A DROP OF COCAINE AND ADD JUST A TOUCH OF CINNAMON. FOR FLAVOR, OF COURSE.
YOU DON'T UNDERSTAND, WALTER. IT'S KILLING ME. I NEED TO FINISH IT. AND I CAN'T DO IT.
THE DOOR, DASHIELL... TELL ME AGAIN ABOUT THE DOOR YOU FOUND.
THE PORTAL? I-I DON'T REMEMBER EXACTLY...

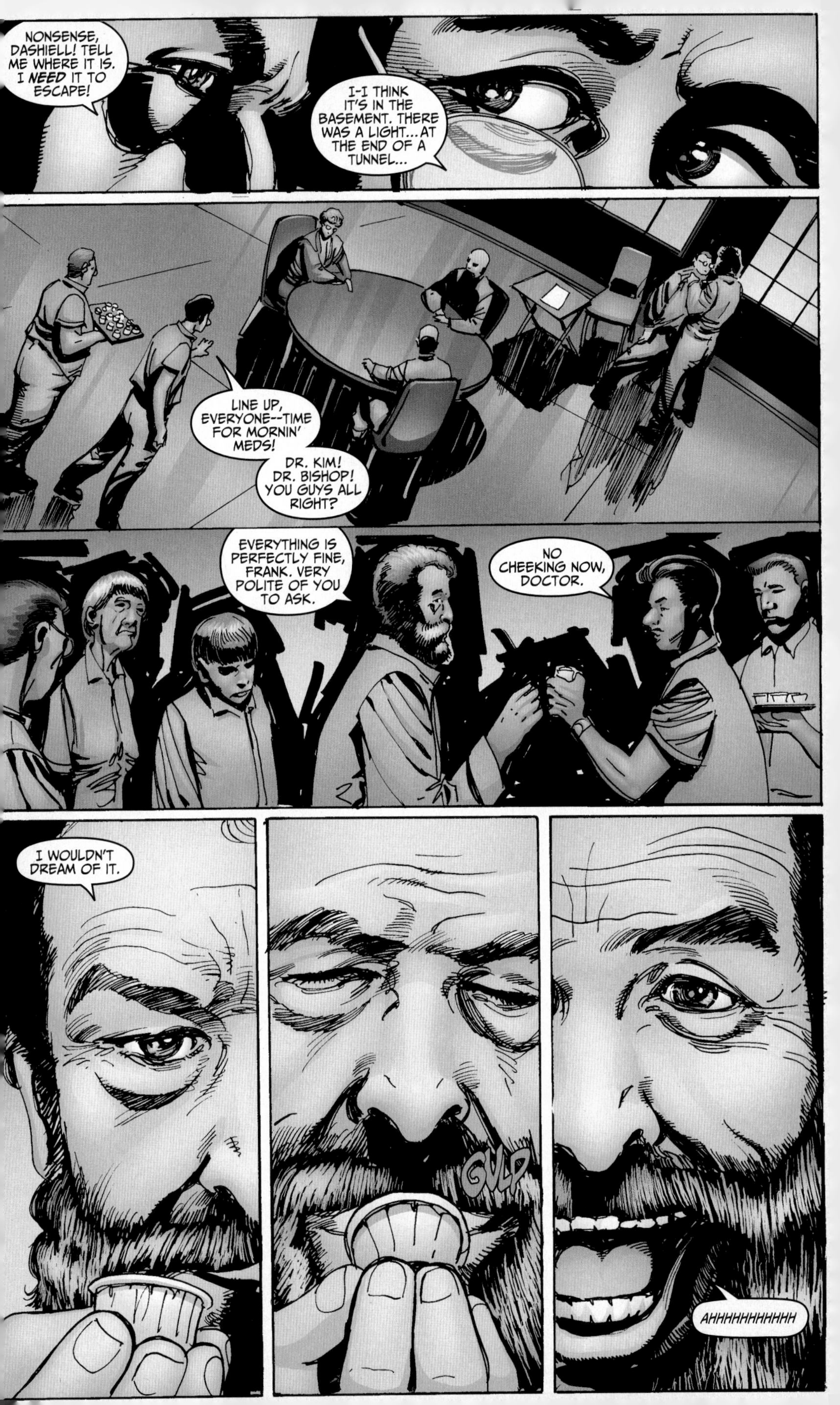
NONSENSE, DASHIELL! TELL ME WHERE IT IS. I *NEED* IT TO ESCAPE!
I-I THINK IT'S IN THE BASEMENT. THERE WAS A LIGHT... AT THE END OF A TUNNEL...
LINE UP, EVERYONE--TIME FOR MORNIN' MEDS!
DR. KIM! DR. BISHOP! YOU GUYS ALL RIGHT?
EVERYTHING IS PERFECTLY FINE, FRANK. VERY POLITE OF YOU TO ASK.
NO CHEEKING NOW, DOCTOR.
I WOULDN'T DREAM OF IT.
GULP
AHHHHHHHHHHHH

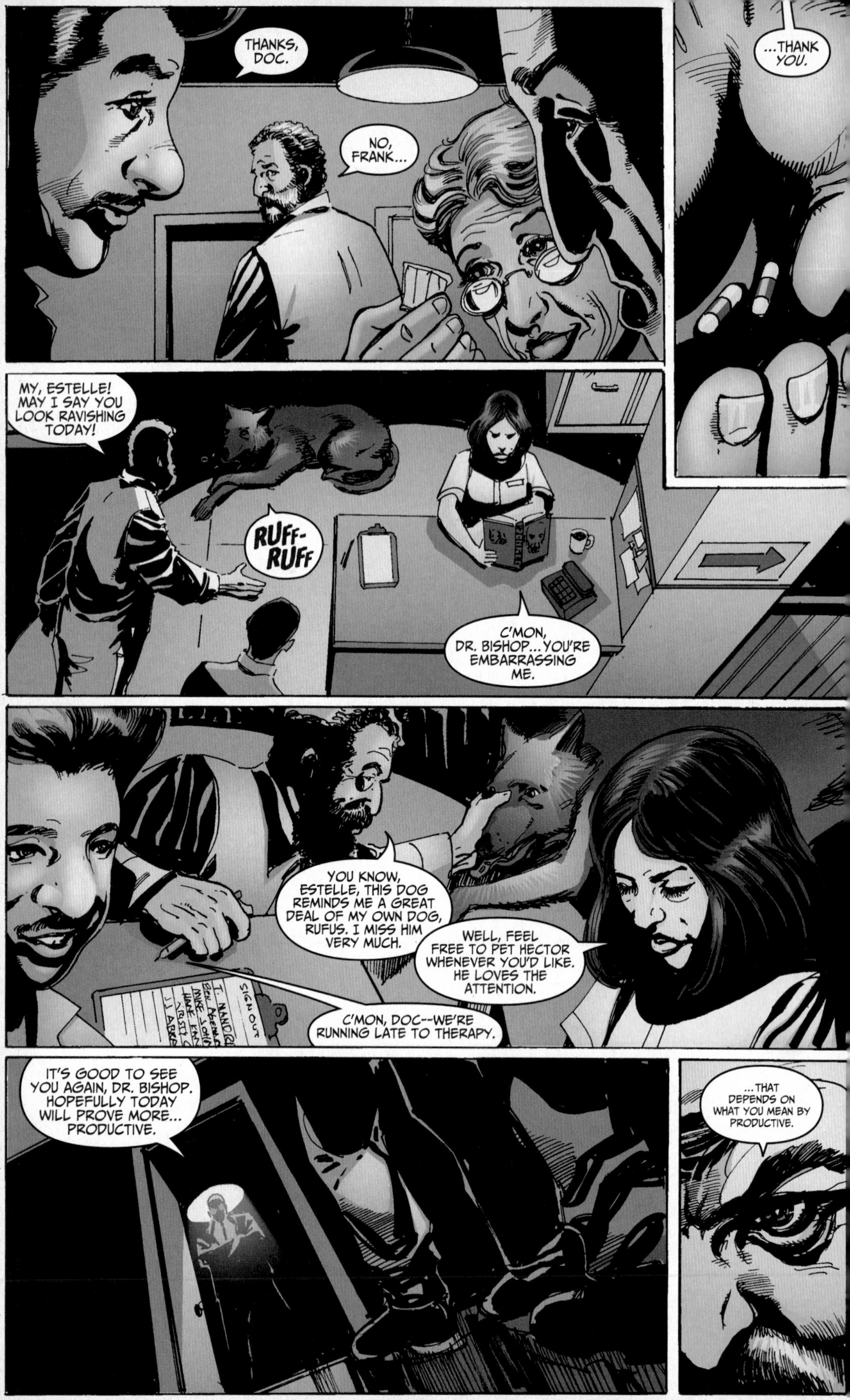
THANKS, DOC.
NO, FRANK...
...THANK YOU.
MY, ESTELLE! MAY I SAY YOU LOOK RAVISHING TODAY!
RUFF-RUFF
C'MON, DR. BISHOP...YOU'RE EMBARRASSING ME.
YOU KNOW, ESTELLE, THIS DOG REMINDS ME A GREAT DEAL OF MY OWN DOG, RUFUS. I MISS HIM VERY MUCH.
WELL, FEEL FREE TO PET HECTOR WHENEVER YOU'D LIKE. HE LOVES THE ATTENTION.
SIGN OUT
C'MON, DOC--WE'RE RUNNING LATE TO THERAPY.
IT'S GOOD TO SEE YOU AGAIN, DR. BISHOP. HOPEFULLY TODAY WILL PROVE MORE... PRODUCTIVE.
...THAT DEPENDS ON WHAT YOU MEAN BY PRODUCTIVE.

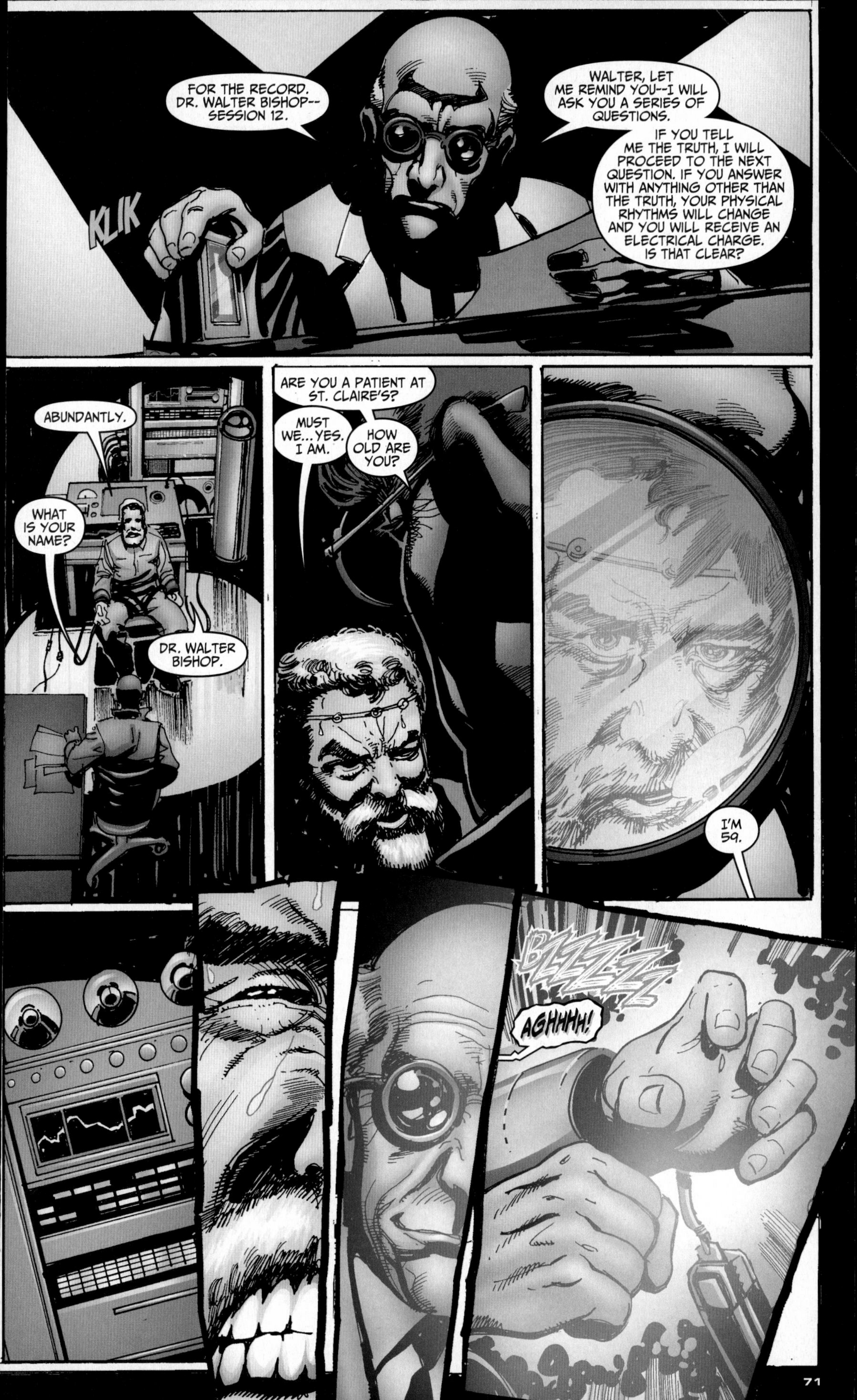
FOR THE RECORD. DR. WALTER BISHOP--SESSION 12.
KLIK
WALTER, LET ME REMIND YOU--I WILL ASK YOU A SERIES OF QUESTIONS.
IF YOU TELL ME THE TRUTH, I WILL PROCEED TO THE NEXT QUESTION. IF YOU ANSWER WITH ANYTHING OTHER THAN THE TRUTH, YOUR PHYSICAL RHYTHMS WILL CHANGE AND YOU WILL RECEIVE AN ELECTRICAL CHARGE. IS THAT CLEAR?
ABUNDANTLY.
WHAT IS YOUR NAME?
DR. WALTER BISHOP.
ARE YOU A PATIENT AT ST. CLAIRE'S?
MUST WE...YES. I AM.
HOW OLD ARE YOU?
I'M 59.
AGHHHH!

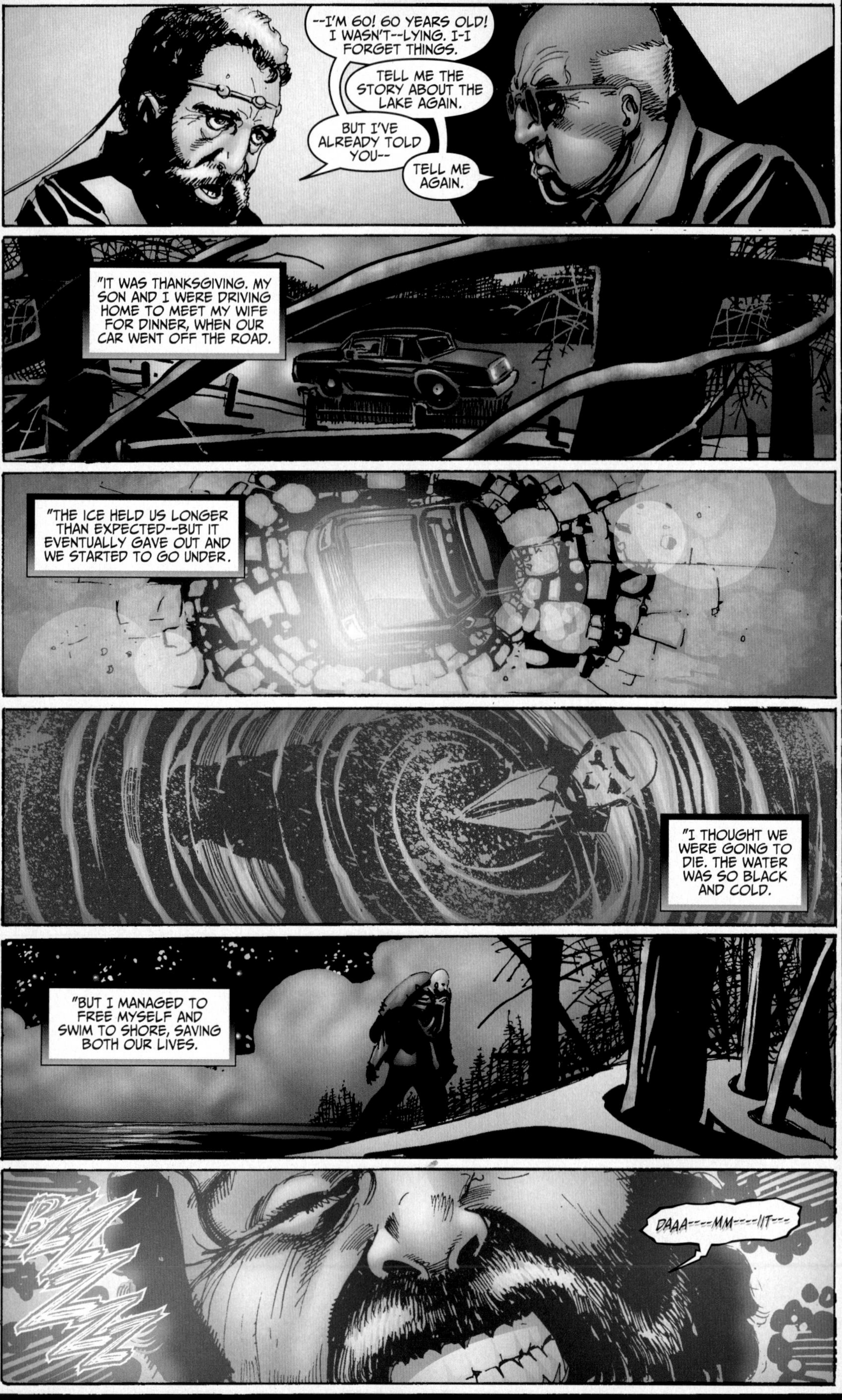
--I'M 60! 60 YEARS OLD! I WASN'T--LYING. I-I FORGET THINGS.
TELL ME THE STORY ABOUT THE LAKE AGAIN.
BUT I'VE ALREADY TOLD YOU--
TELL ME AGAIN.
"IT WAS THANKSGIVING. MY SON AND I WERE DRIVING HOME TO MEET MY WIFE FOR DINNER, WHEN OUR CAR WENT OFF THE ROAD.
"THE ICE HELD US LONGER THAN EXPECTED--BUT IT EVENTUALLY GAVE OUT AND WE STARTED TO GO UNDER.
"I THOUGHT WE WERE GOING TO DIE. THE WATER WAS SO BLACK AND COLD.
"BUT I MANAGED TO FREE MYSELF AND SWIM TO SHORE, SAVING BOTH OUR LIVES.
DAAA----MM----IIT---

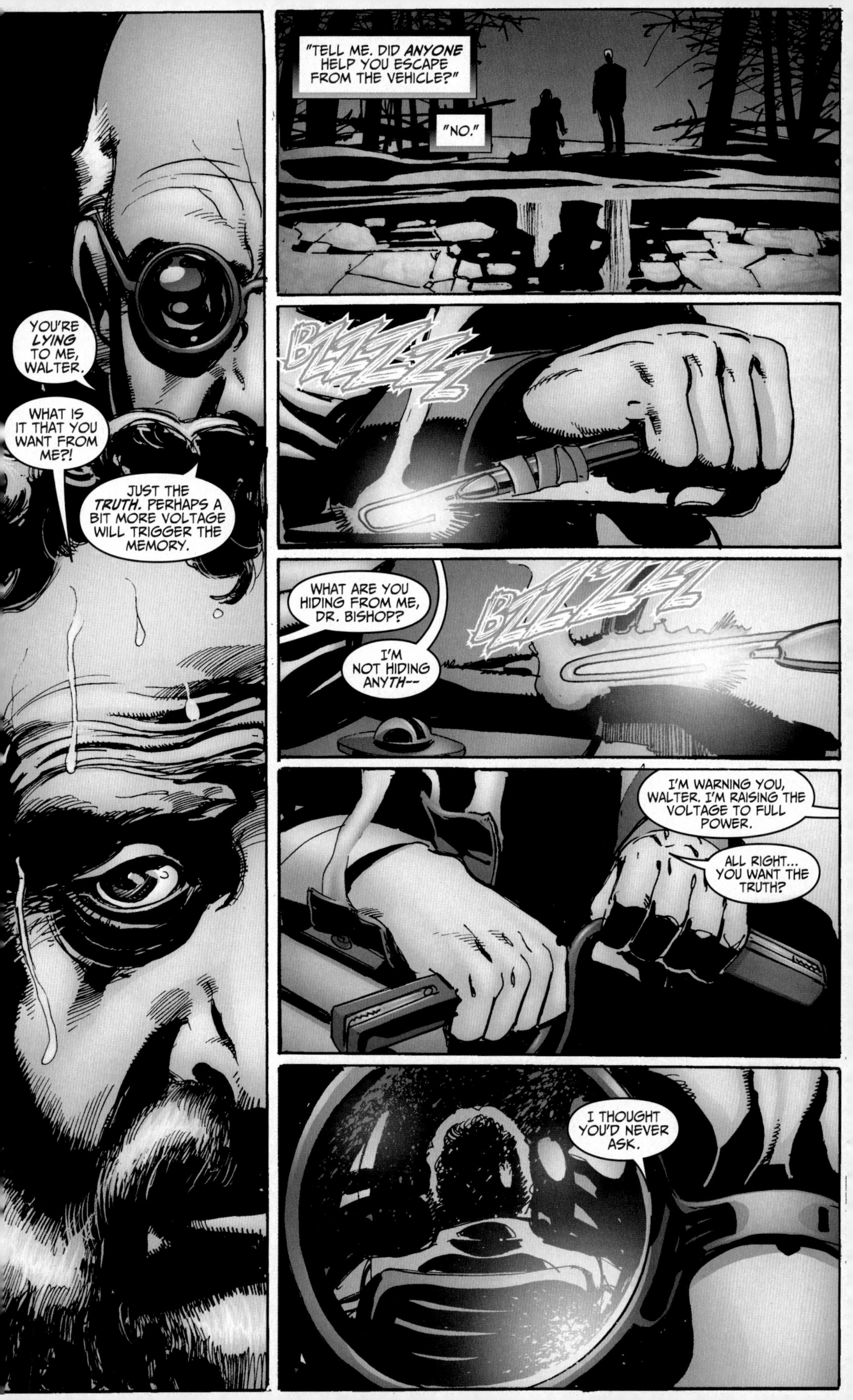
"TELL ME. DID ANYONE HELP YOU ESCAPE FROM THE VEHICLE?"
"NO."
YOU'RE LYING TO ME, WALTER.
WHAT IS IT THAT YOU WANT FROM ME?!
JUST THE TRUTH. PERHAPS A BIT MORE VOLTAGE WILL TRIGGER THE MEMORY.
BZZZZZ
WHAT ARE YOU HIDING FROM ME, DR. BISHOP?
I'M NOT HIDING ANYTH--
BZZZZ
I'M WARNING YOU, WALTER. I'M RAISING THE VOLTAGE TO FULL POWER.
ALL RIGHT... YOU WANT THE TRUTH?
I THOUGHT YOU'D NEVER ASK.

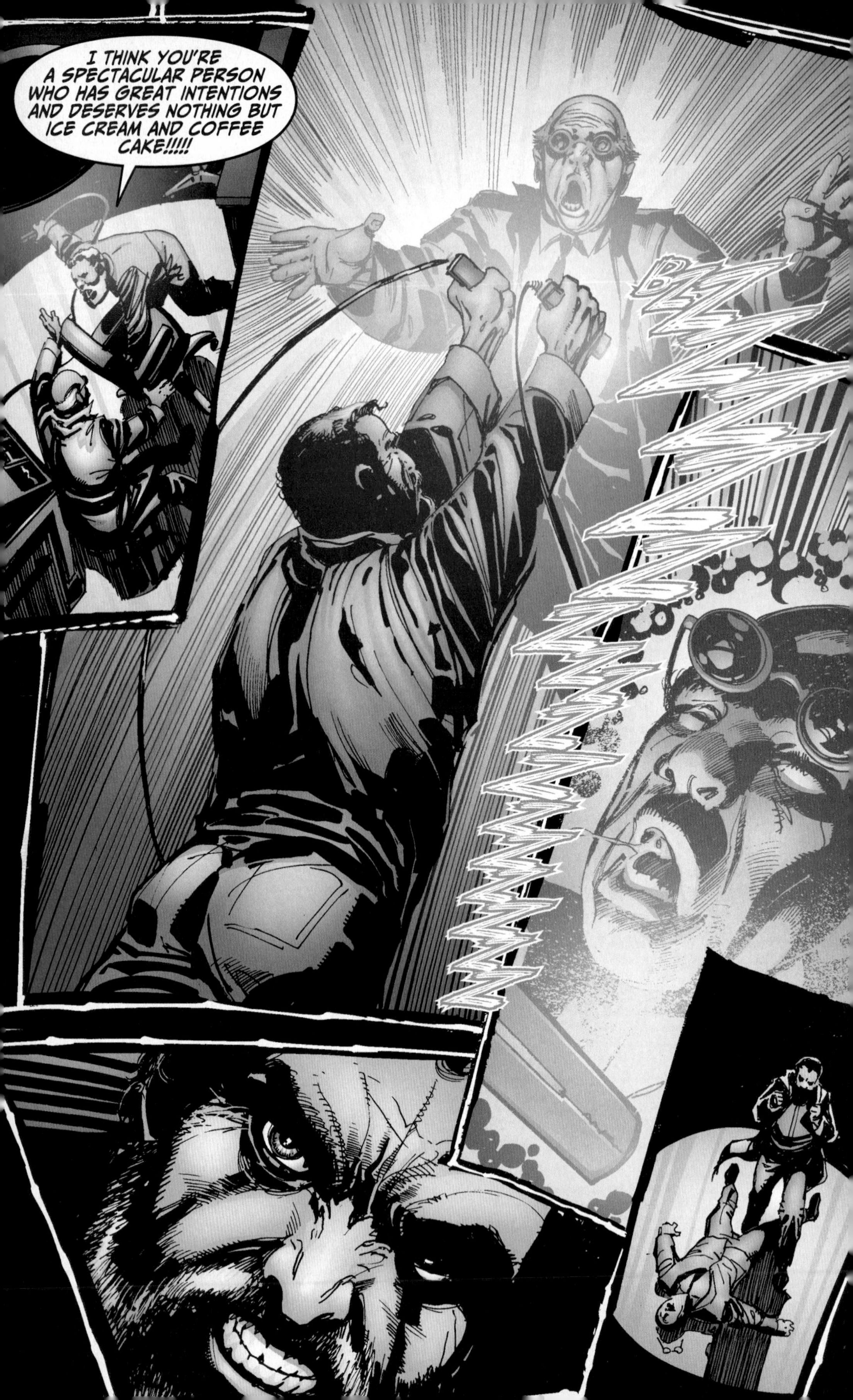
I THINK YOU'RE A SPECTACULAR PERSON WHO HAS GREAT INTENTIONS AND DESERVES NOTHING BUT ICE CREAM AND COFFEE CAKE!!!!!

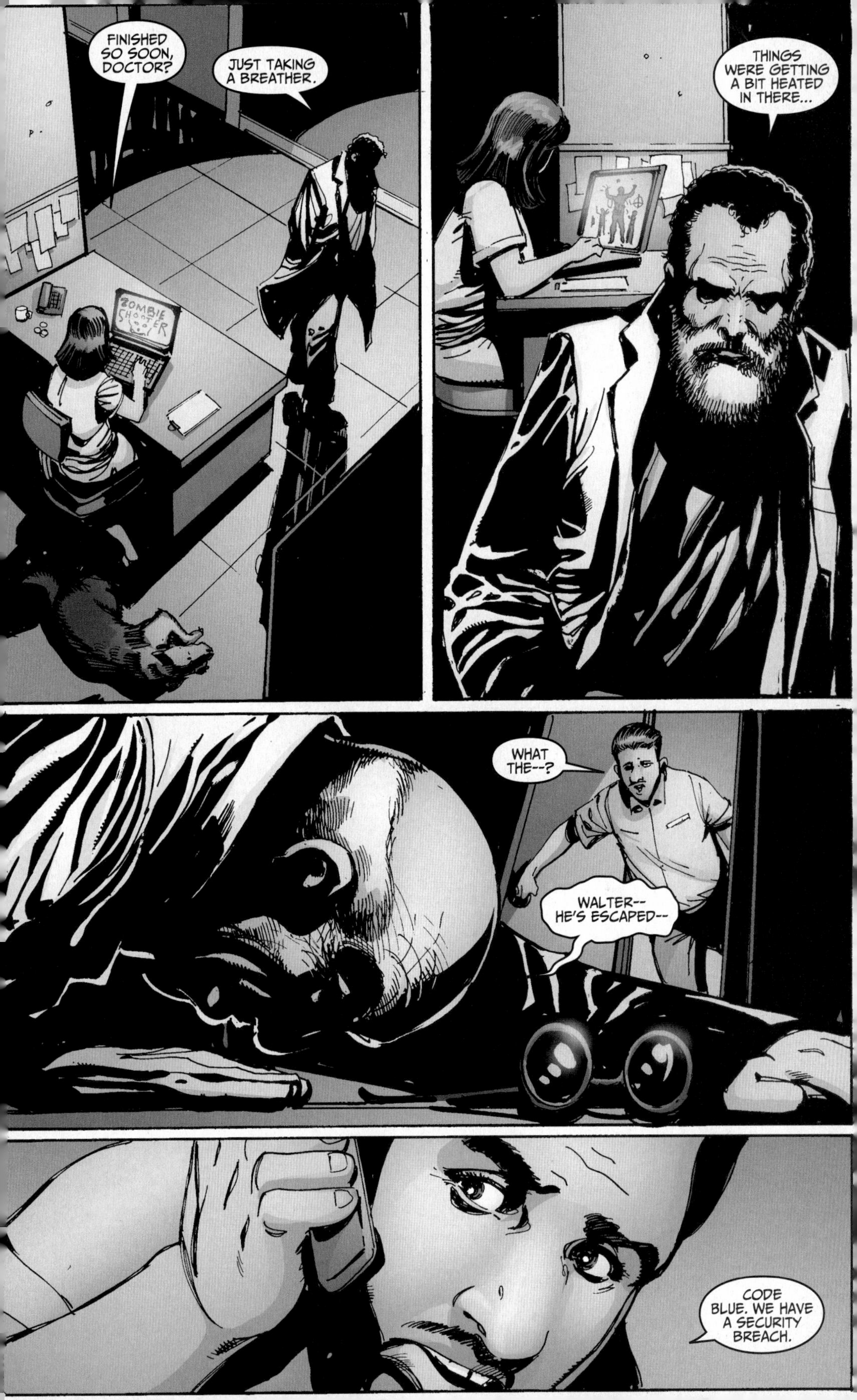
FINISHED SO SOON, DOCTOR?
JUST TAKING A BREATHER.
ZOMBIE SHOOTER
THINGS WERE GETTING A BIT HEATED IN THERE...
WHAT THE--?
WALTER-- HE'S ESCAPED--
CODE BLUE. WE HAVE A SECURITY BREACH.

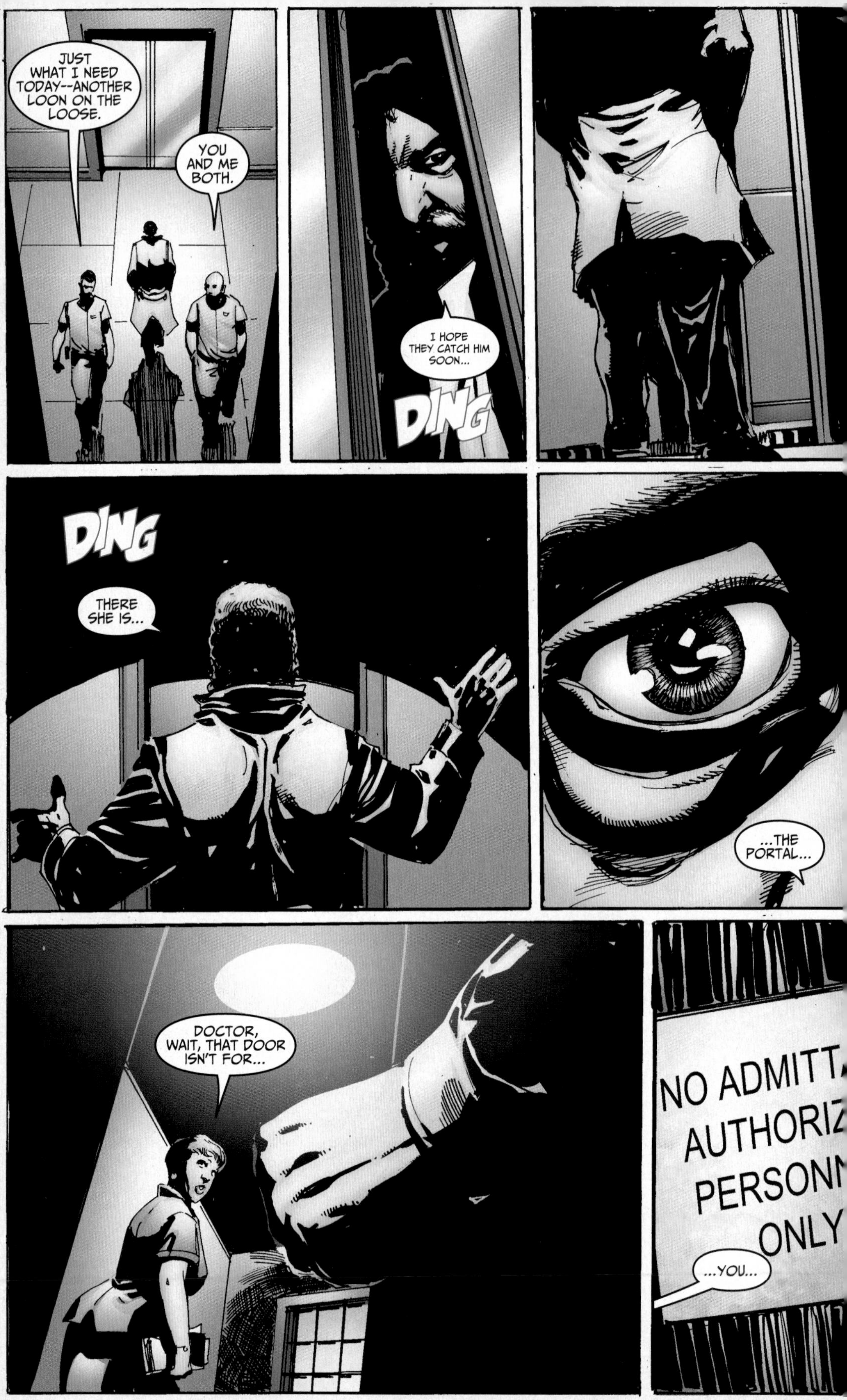
JUST WHAT I NEED TODAY--ANOTHER LOON ON THE LOOSE.
YOU AND ME BOTH.
I HOPE THEY CATCH HIM SOON...
DING
DING
THERE SHE IS...
...THE PORTAL...
DOCTOR, WAIT, THAT DOOR ISN'T FOR...
NO ADMITT
AUTHORIZ
PERSONN
ONLY
...YOU...

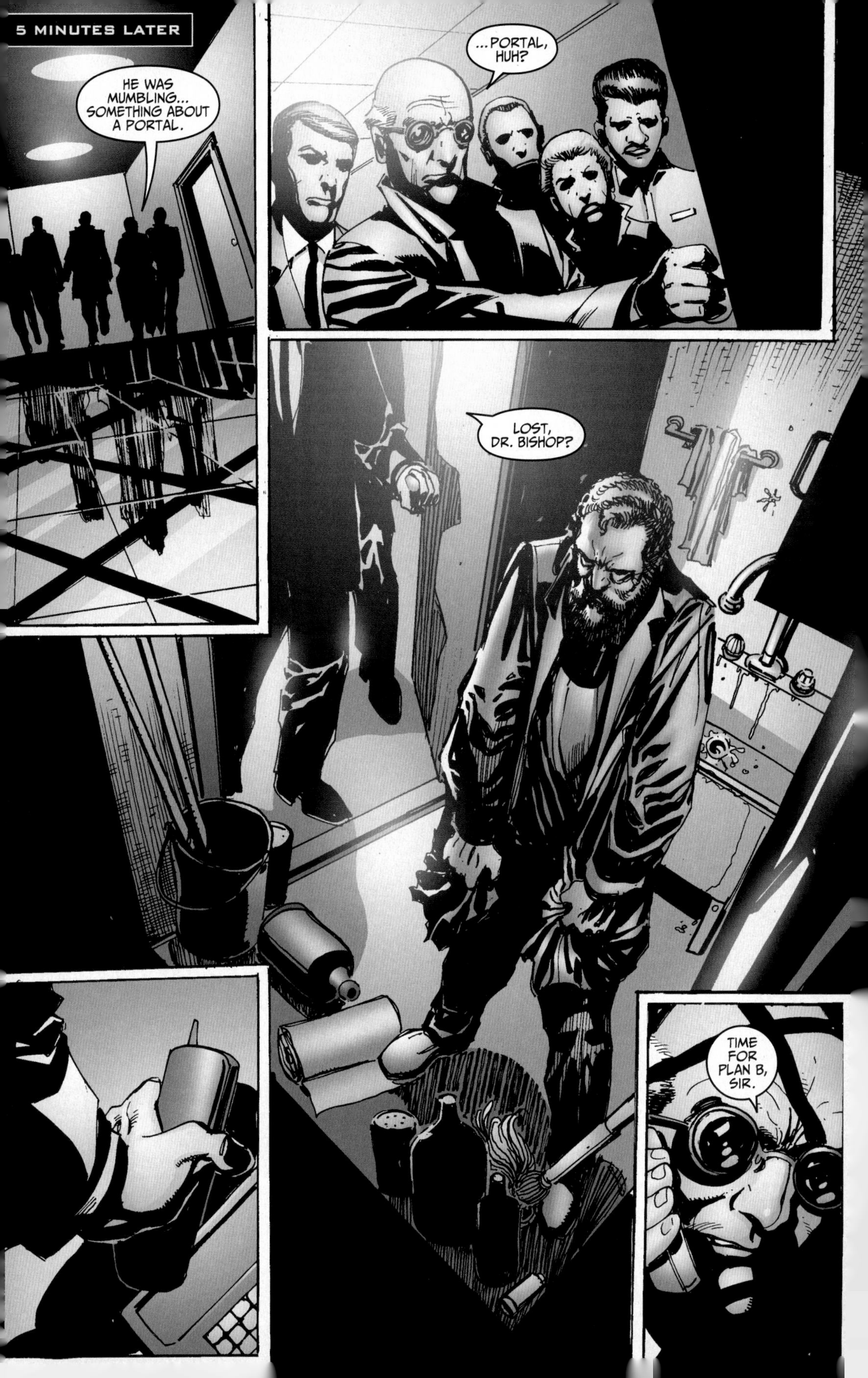
5 MINUTES LATER
HE WAS MUMBLING... SOMETHING ABOUT A PORTAL.
...PORTAL, HUH?
LOST, DR. BISHOP?
TIME FOR PLAN B, SIR.

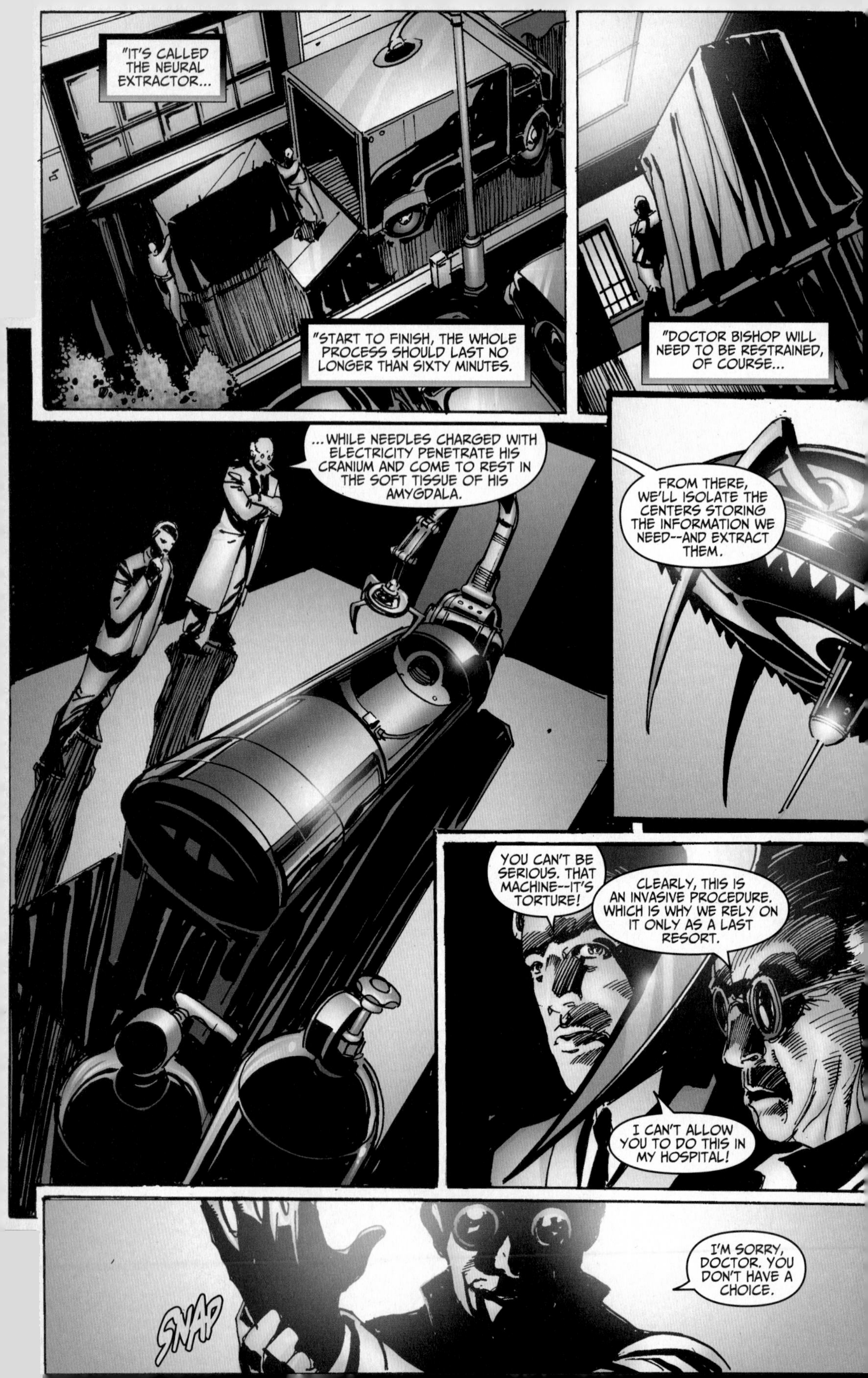
"IT'S CALLED THE NEURAL EXTRACTOR...
"START TO FINISH, THE WHOLE PROCESS SHOULD LAST NO LONGER THAN SIXTY MINUTES.
"DOCTOR BISHOP WILL NEED TO BE RESTRAINED, OF COURSE...
...WHILE NEEDLES CHARGED WITH ELECTRICITY PENETRATE HIS CRANIUM AND COME TO REST IN THE SOFT TISSUE OF HIS AMYGDALA.
FROM THERE, WE'LL ISOLATE THE CENTERS STORING THE INFORMATION WE NEED--AND EXTRACT THEM.
YOU CAN'T BE SERIOUS. THAT MACHINE--IT'S TORTURE!
CLEARLY, THIS IS AN INVASIVE PROCEDURE. WHICH IS WHY WE RELY ON IT ONLY AS A LAST RESORT.
I CAN'T ALLOW YOU TO DO THIS IN MY HOSPITAL!
I'M SORRY, DOCTOR. YOU DON'T HAVE A CHOICE.
SNAP

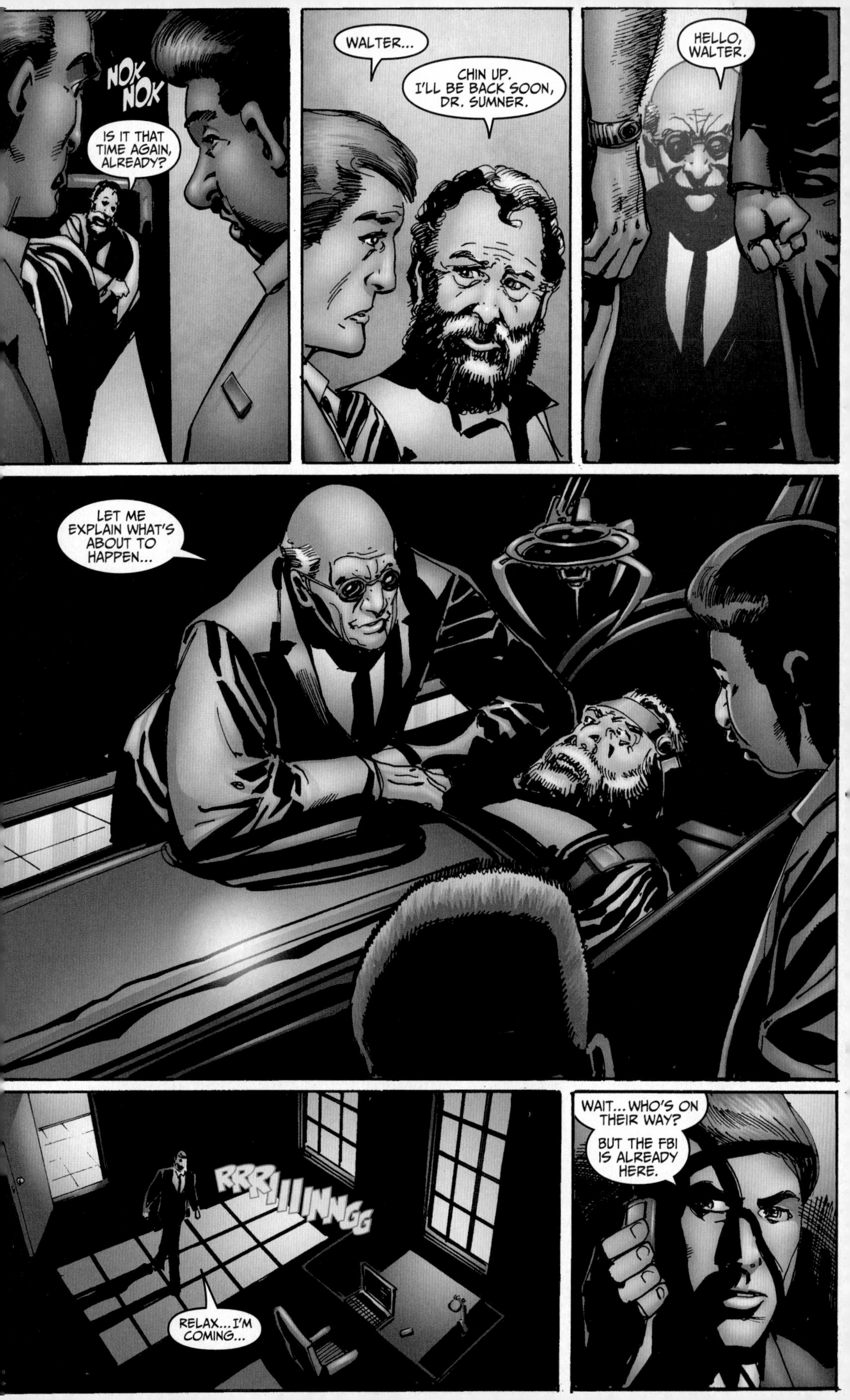
NOK NOK
IS IT THAT TIME AGAIN, ALREADY?
WALTER...
CHIN UP. I'LL BE BACK SOON, DR. SUMNER.
HELLO, WALTER.
LET ME EXPLAIN WHAT'S ABOUT TO HAPPEN...
RRRIIIINNGG
RELAX...I'M COMING...
WAIT...WHO'S ON THEIR WAY?
BUT THE FBI IS ALREADY HERE.

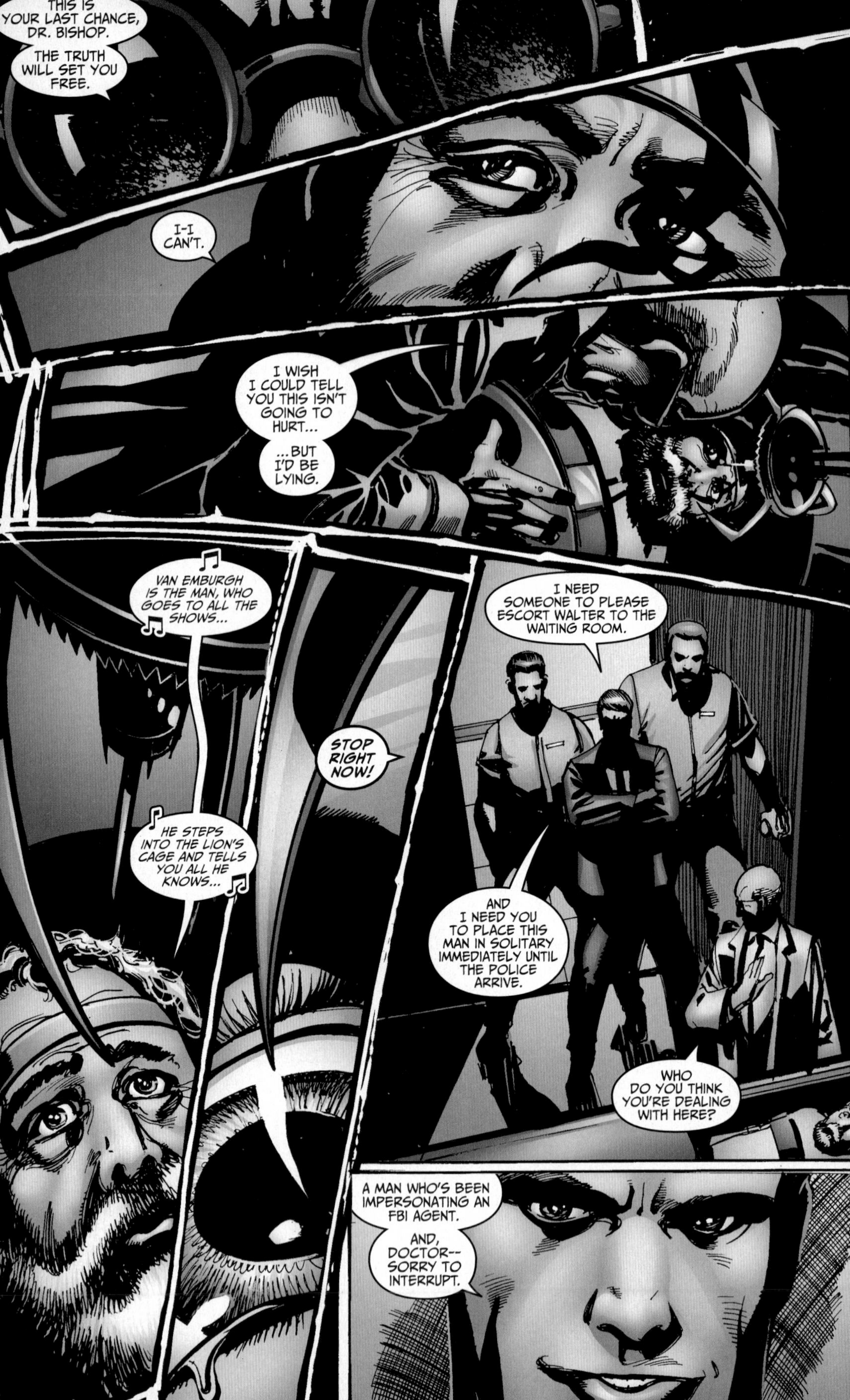
THIS IS YOUR LAST CHANCE, DR. BISHOP.
THE TRUTH WILL SET YOU FREE.
I-I CAN'T.
I WISH I COULD TELL YOU THIS ISN'T GOING TO HURT...
...BUT I'D BE LYING.
VAN EMBURGH IS THE MAN, WHO GOES TO ALL THE SHOWS...
HE STEPS INTO THE LION'S CAGE AND TELLS YOU ALL HE KNOWS...
STOP RIGHT NOW!
I NEED SOMEONE TO PLEASE ESCORT WALTER TO THE WAITING ROOM.
AND I NEED YOU TO PLACE THIS MAN IN SOLITARY IMMEDIATELY UNTIL THE POLICE ARRIVE.
WHO DO YOU THINK YOU'RE DEALING WITH HERE?
A MAN WHO'S BEEN IMPERSONATING AN FBI AGENT.
AND, DOCTOR-- SORRY TO INTERRUPT.

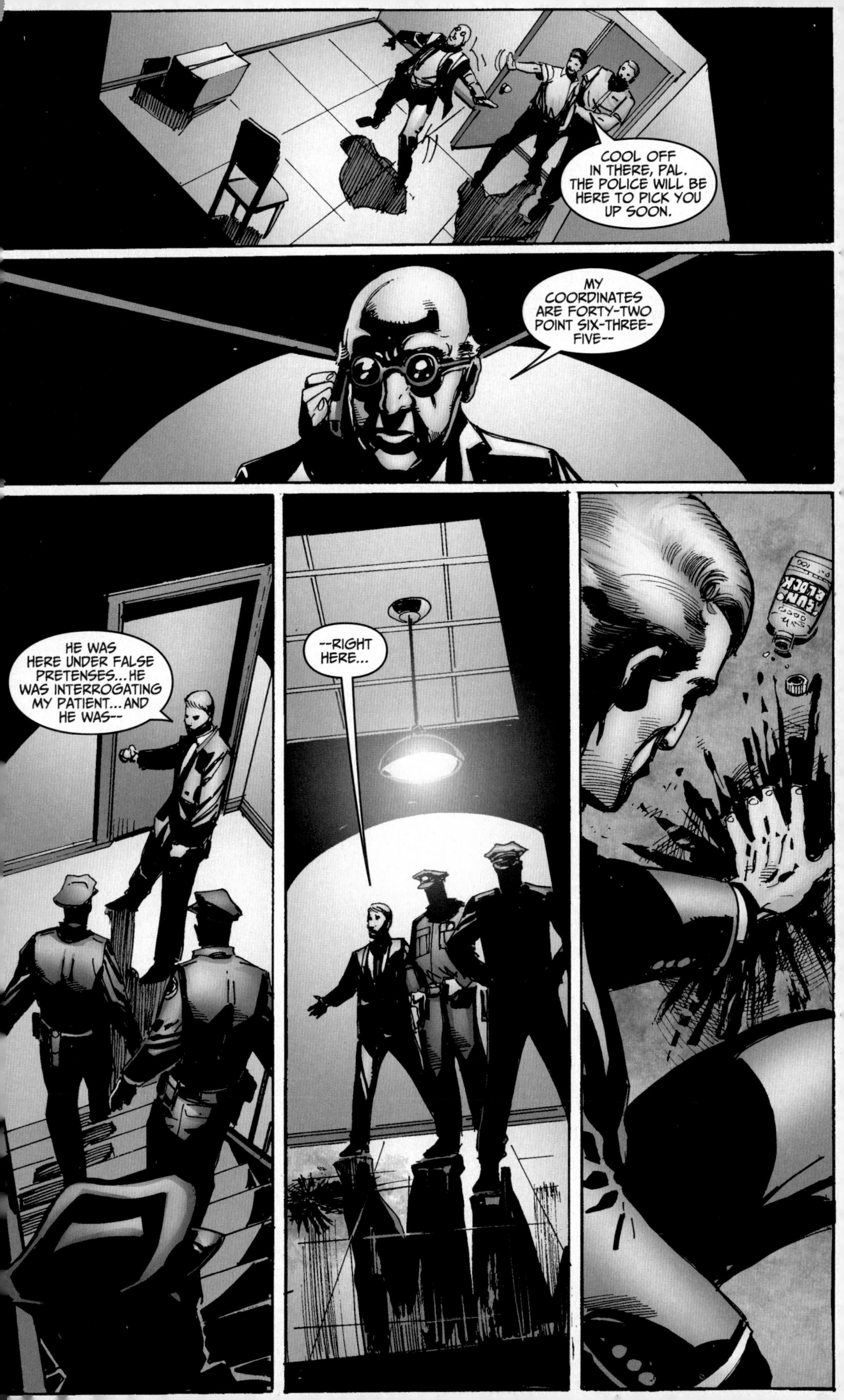
COOL OFF IN THERE, PAL. THE POLICE WILL BE HERE TO PICK YOU UP SOON.
MY COORDINATES ARE FORTY-TWO POINT SIX-THREE-FIVE--
HE WAS HERE UNDER FALSE PRETENSES...HE WAS INTERROGATING MY PATIENT...AND HE WAS--
--RIGHT HERE...

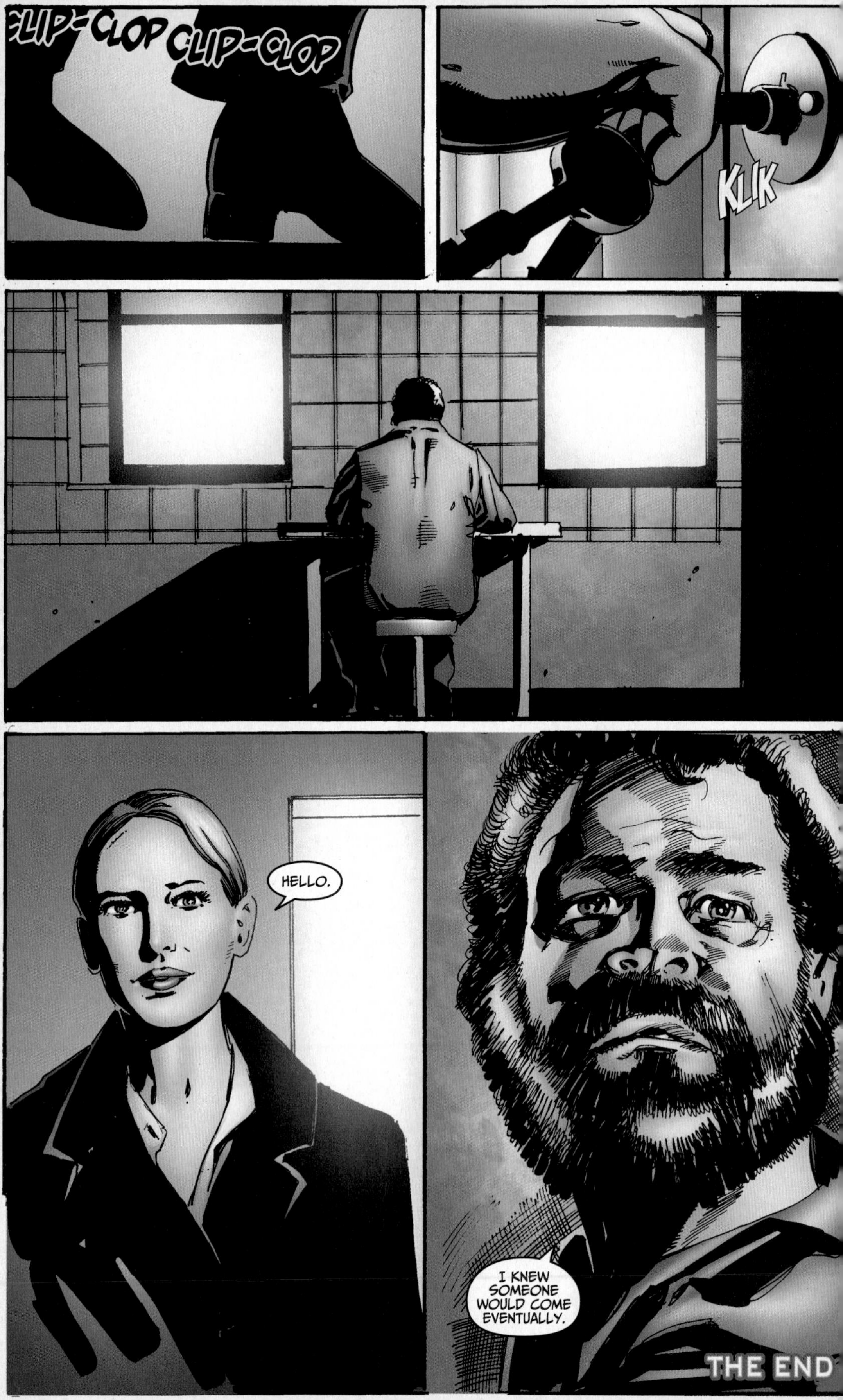
CLIP-CLOP CLIP-CLOP
KLIK
HELLO.
I KNEW SOMEONE WOULD COME EVENTUALLY.
THE END

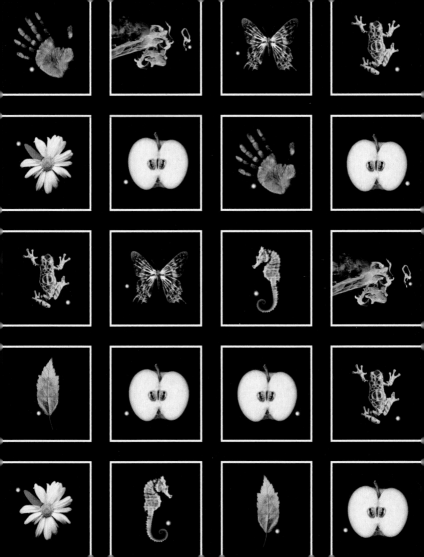

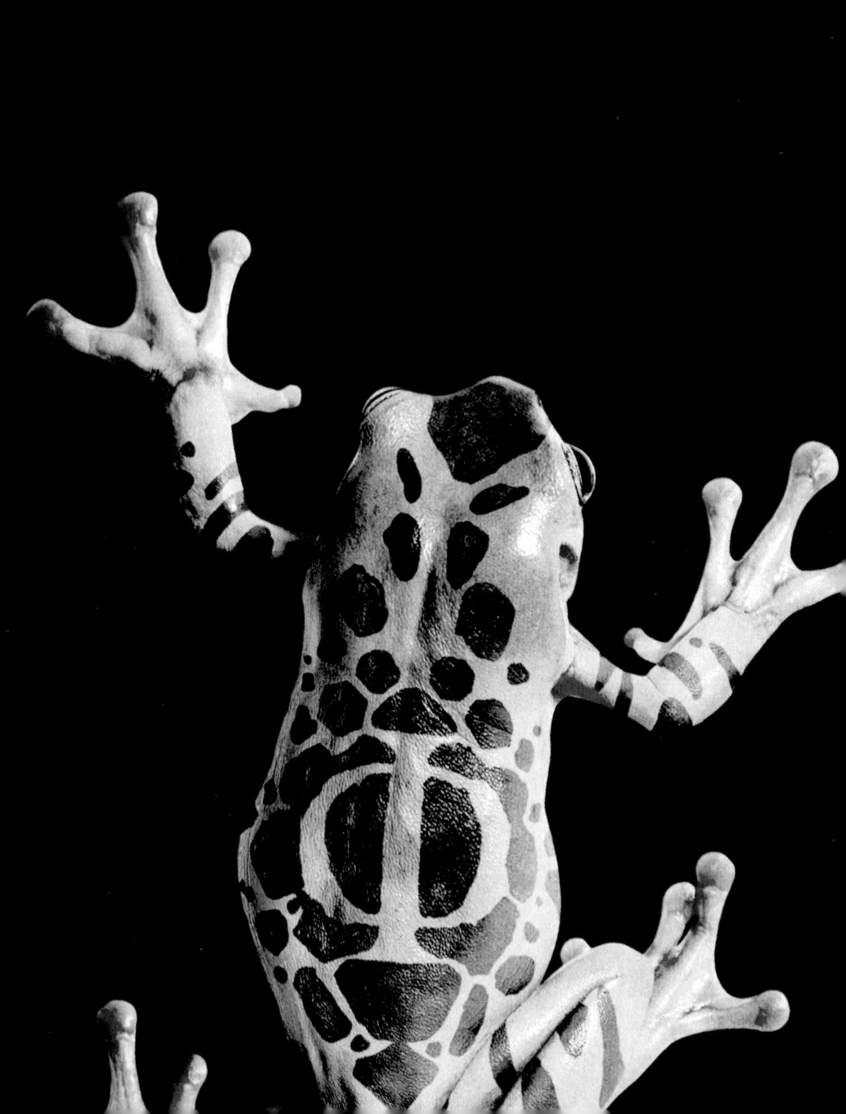

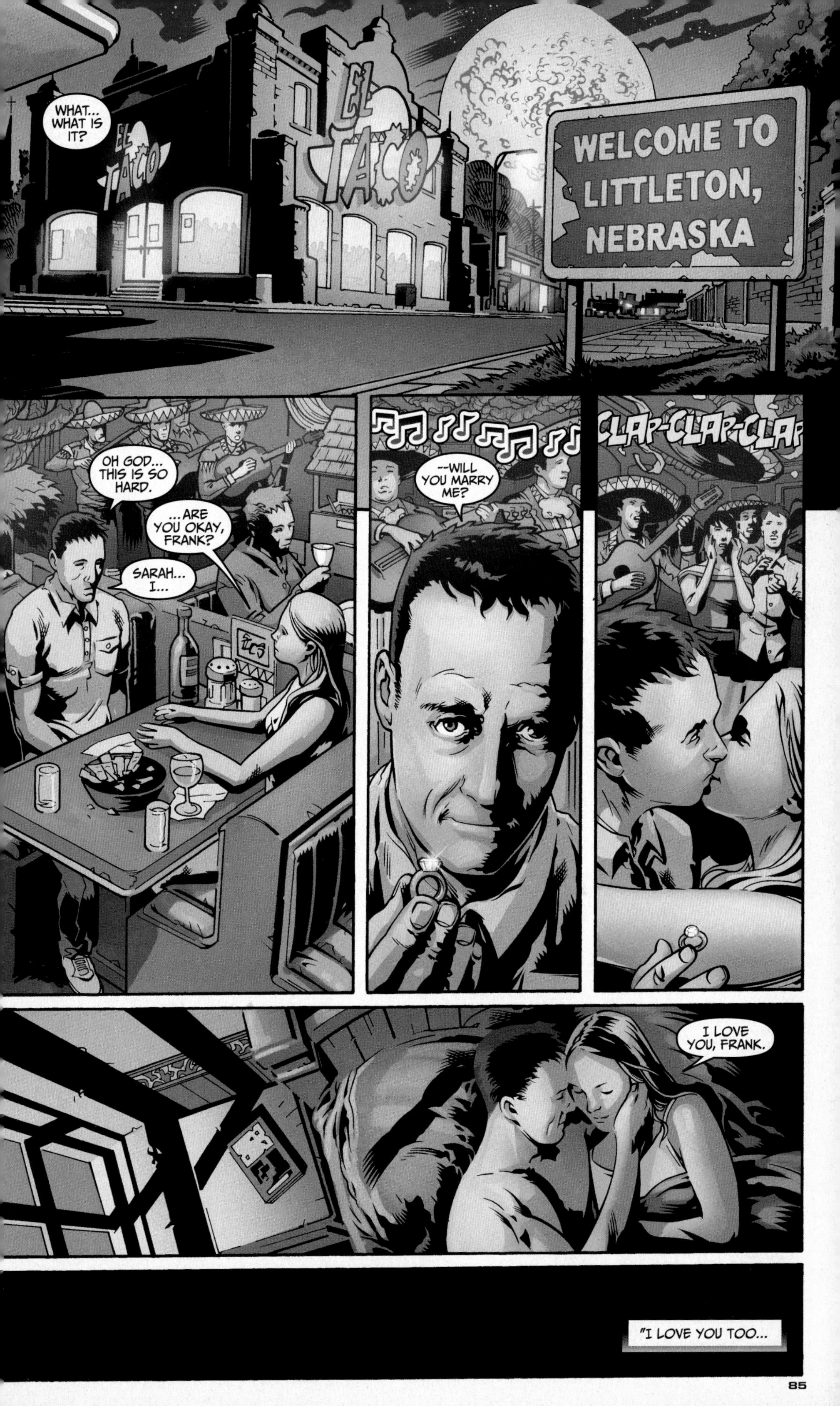
WHAT... WHAT IS IT?
EL TACO
WELCOME TO LITTLETON, NEBRASKA
OH GOD... THIS IS SO HARD.
...ARE YOU OKAY, FRANK?
SARAH... I...
--WILL YOU MARRY ME?
CLAP-CLAP-CLAP
I LOVE YOU, FRANK.
"I LOVE YOU TOO...

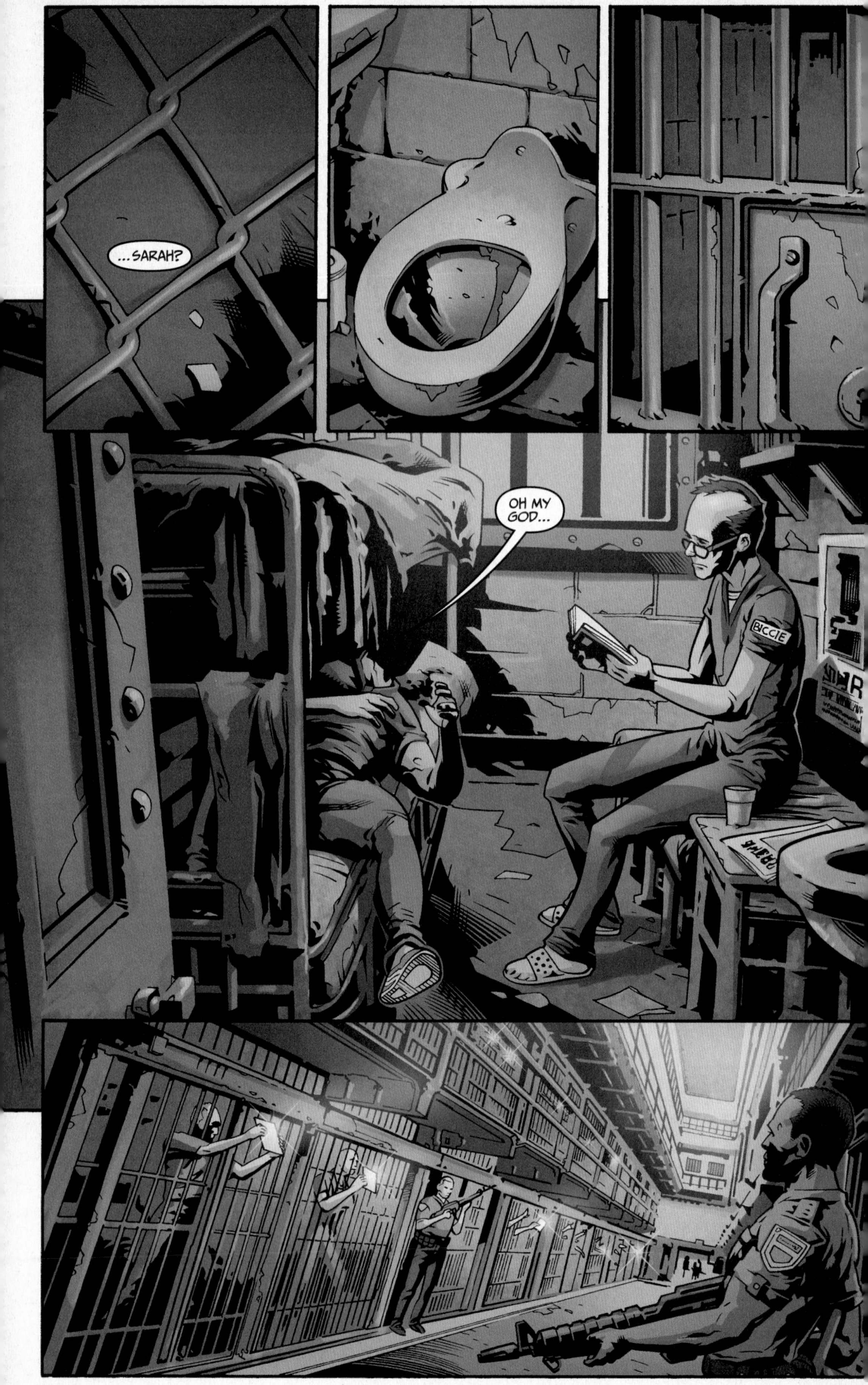
...SARAH?
OH MY GOD...
BIGGIE

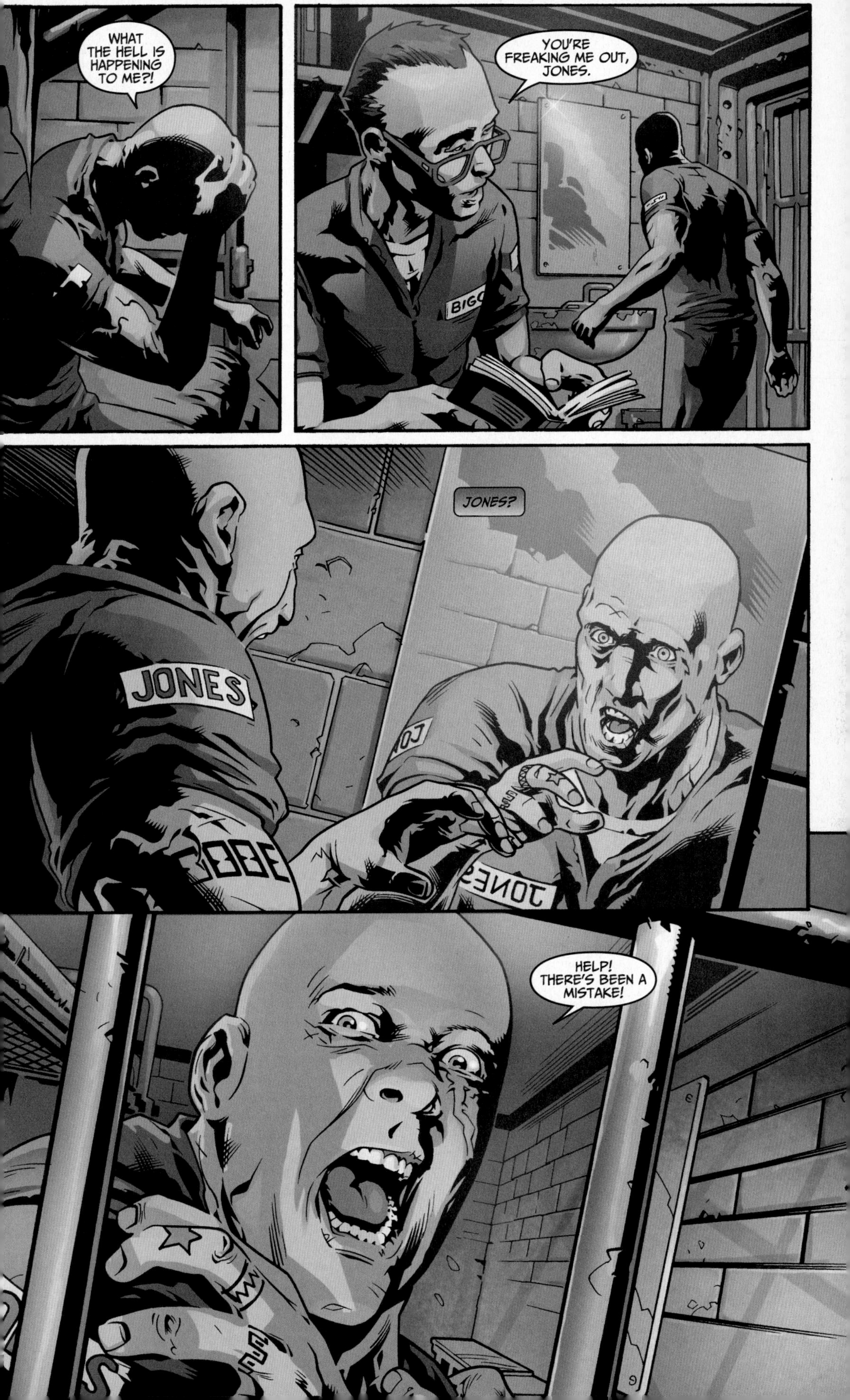
WHAT THE HELL IS HAPPENING TO ME?!
YOU'RE FREAKING ME OUT, JONES.
BIGG
JONES?
JONES
HELP! THERE'S BEEN A MISTAKE!

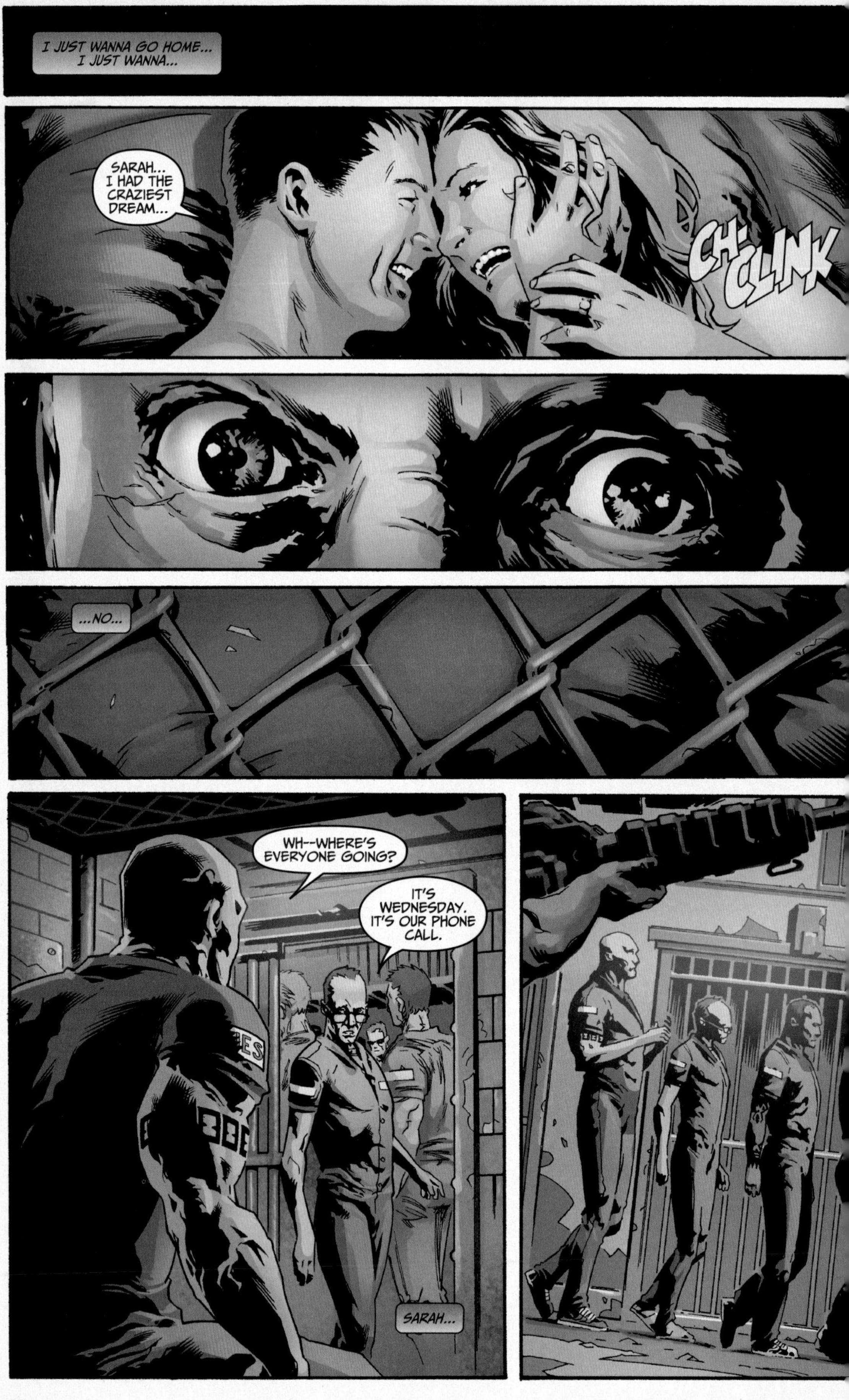

I JUST WANNA GO HOME...
I JUST WANNA...
SARAH... I HAD THE CRAZIEST DREAM...
CH-CLINK
...NO...
WH--WHERE'S EVERYONE GOING?
IT'S WEDNESDAY. IT'S OUR PHONE CALL.
SARAH...

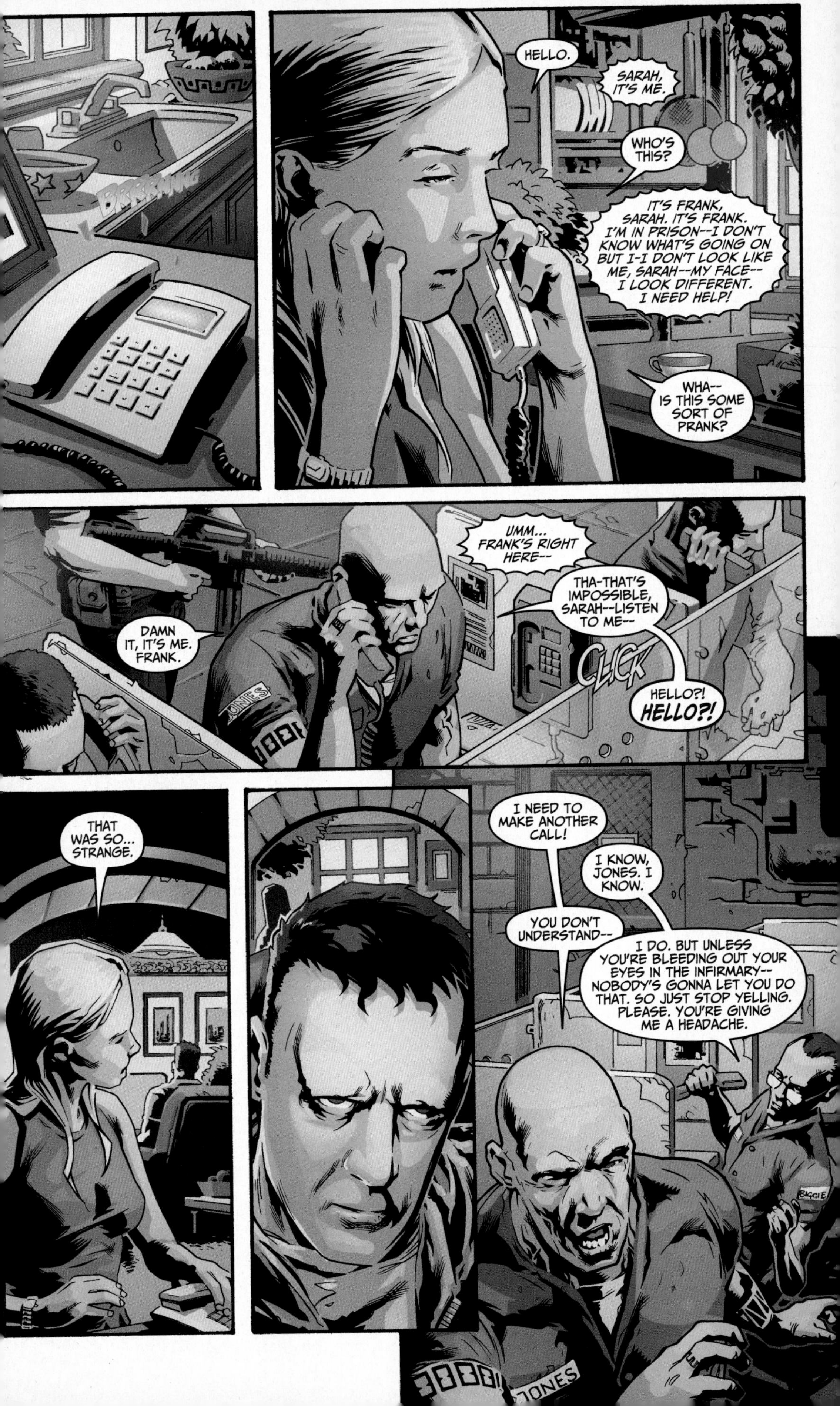
BRRRANNG
HELLO.
SARAH, IT'S ME.
WHO'S THIS?
IT'S FRANK, SARAH. IT'S FRANK. I'M IN PRISON--I DON'T KNOW WHAT'S GOING ON BUT I-I DON'T LOOK LIKE ME, SARAH--MY FACE--I LOOK DIFFERENT. I NEED HELP!
WHA--IS THIS SOME SORT OF PRANK?
UMM... FRANK'S RIGHT HERE--
DAMN IT, IT'S ME. FRANK.
THA-THAT'S IMPOSSIBLE, SARAH--LISTEN TO ME--
CLICK
HELLO?! HELLO?!
JONES
THAT WAS SO... STRANGE.
I NEED TO MAKE ANOTHER CALL!
I KNOW, JONES. I KNOW.
YOU DON'T UNDERSTAND--
I DO. BUT UNLESS YOU'RE BLEEDING OUT YOUR EYES IN THE INFIRMARY--NOBODY'S GONNA LET YOU DO THAT. SO JUST STOP YELLING. PLEASE. YOU'RE GIVING ME A HEADACHE.
BIGGIE
JONES

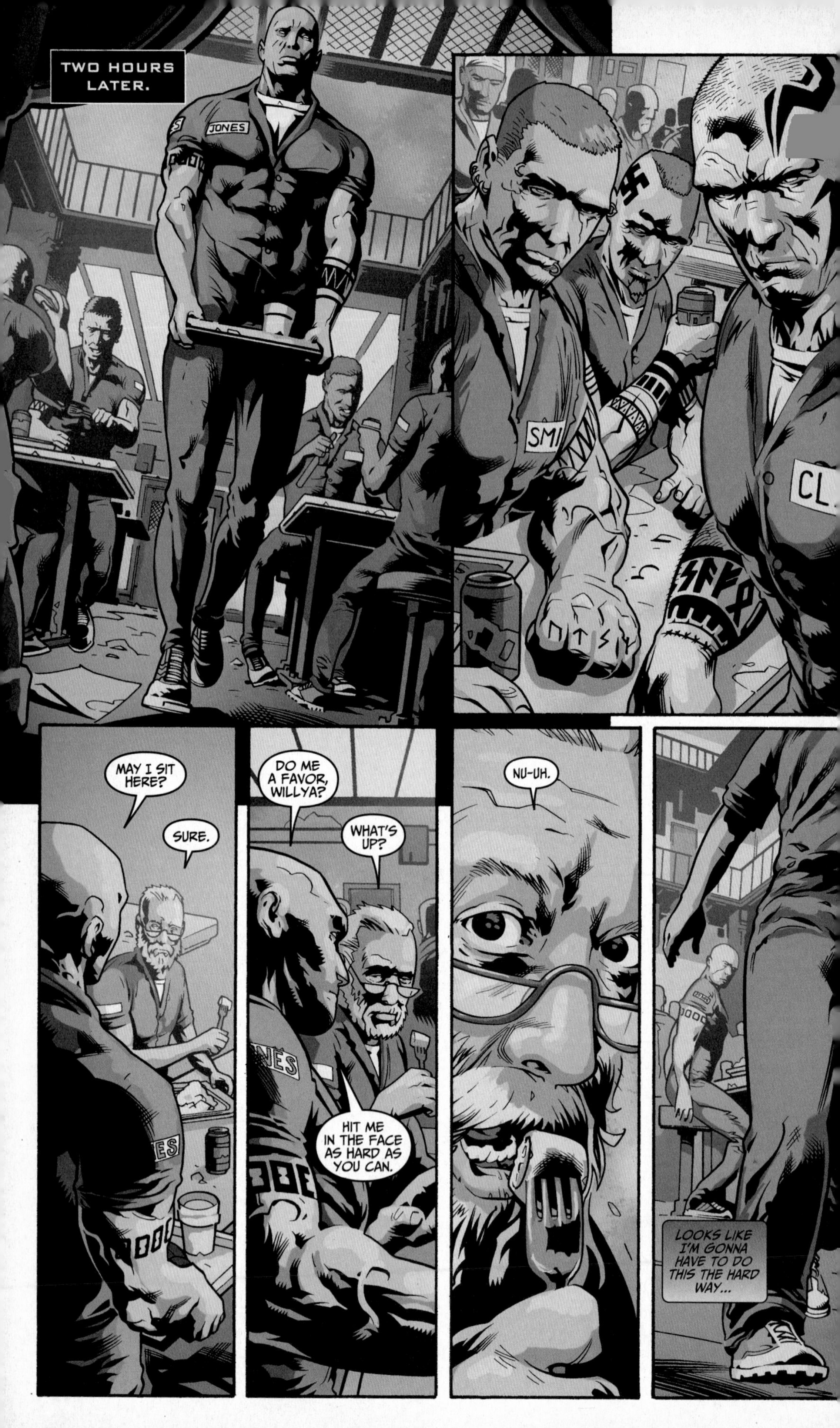
TWO HOURS LATER.
JONES
SMI
CL
MAY I SIT HERE?
SURE.
DO ME A FAVOR, WILLYA?
WHAT'S UP?
HIT ME IN THE FACE AS HARD AS YOU CAN.
NU-UH.
LOOKS LIKE I'M GONNA HAVE TO DO THIS THE HARD WAY...

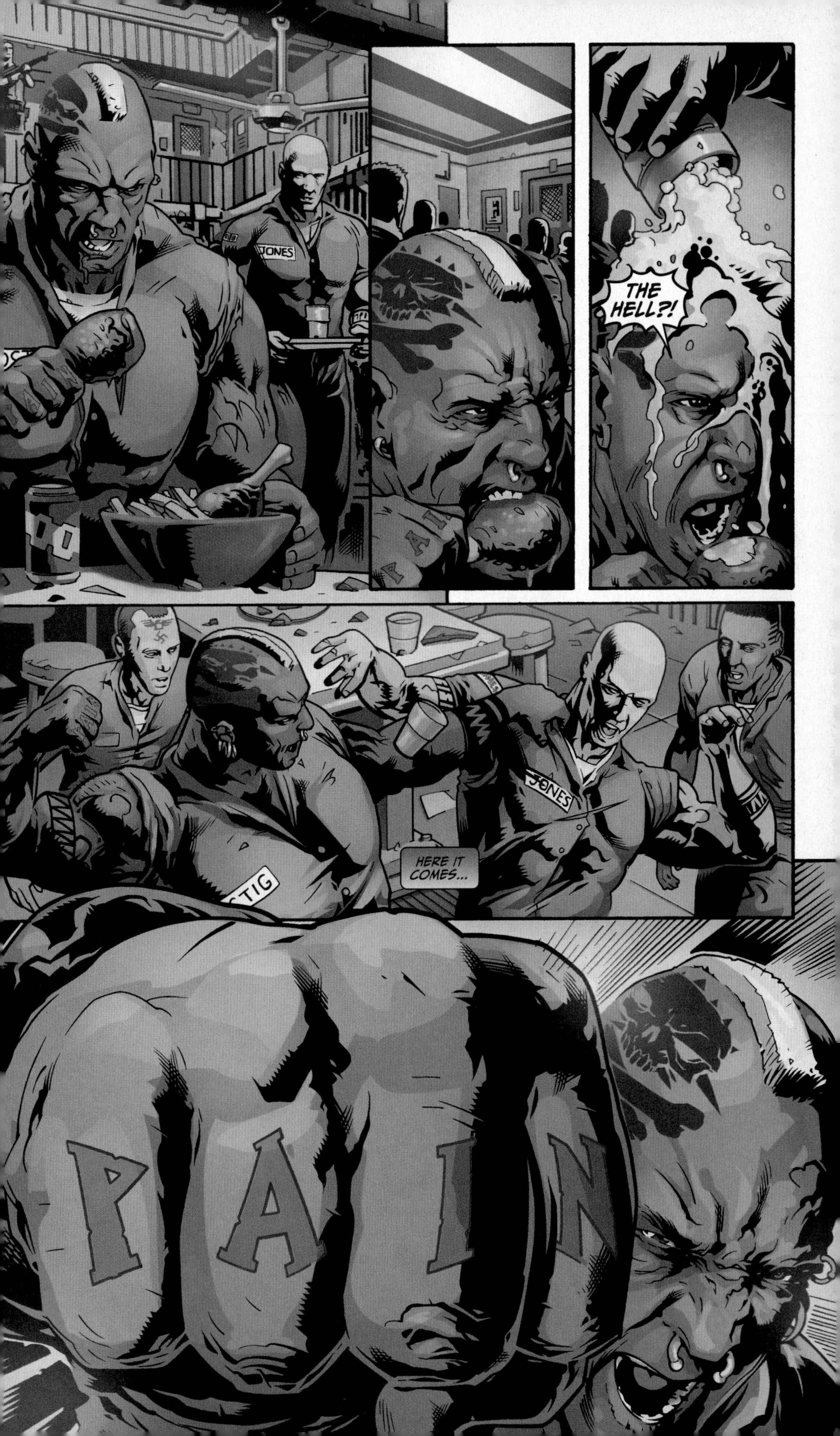
THE HELL?!
HERE IT COMES...

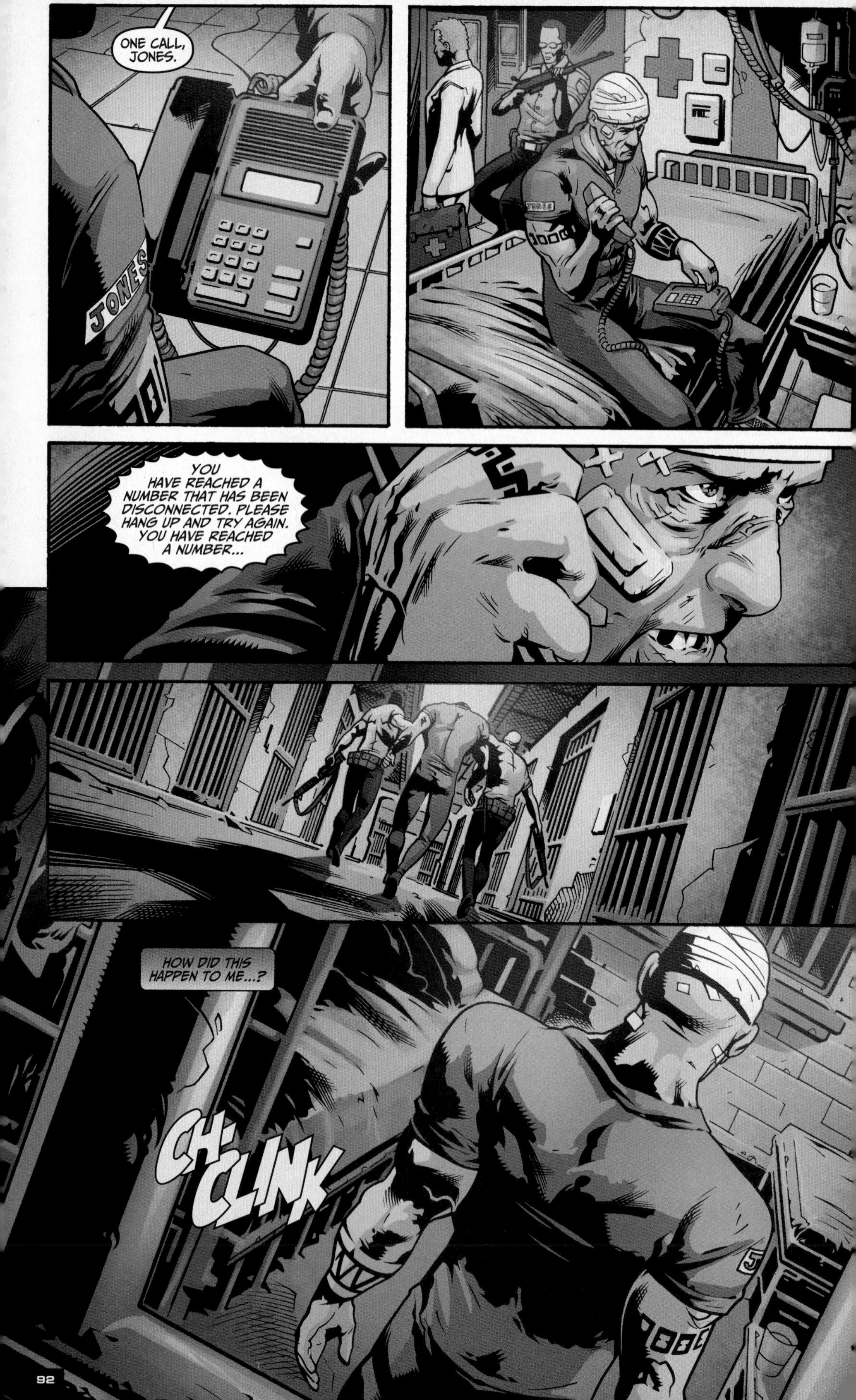

ONE CALL, JONES.
YOU HAVE REACHED A NUMBER THAT HAS BEEN DISCONNECTED. PLEASE HANG UP AND TRY AGAIN. YOU HAVE REACHED A NUMBER...
HOW DID THIS HAPPEN TO ME...?
CH-CLINK

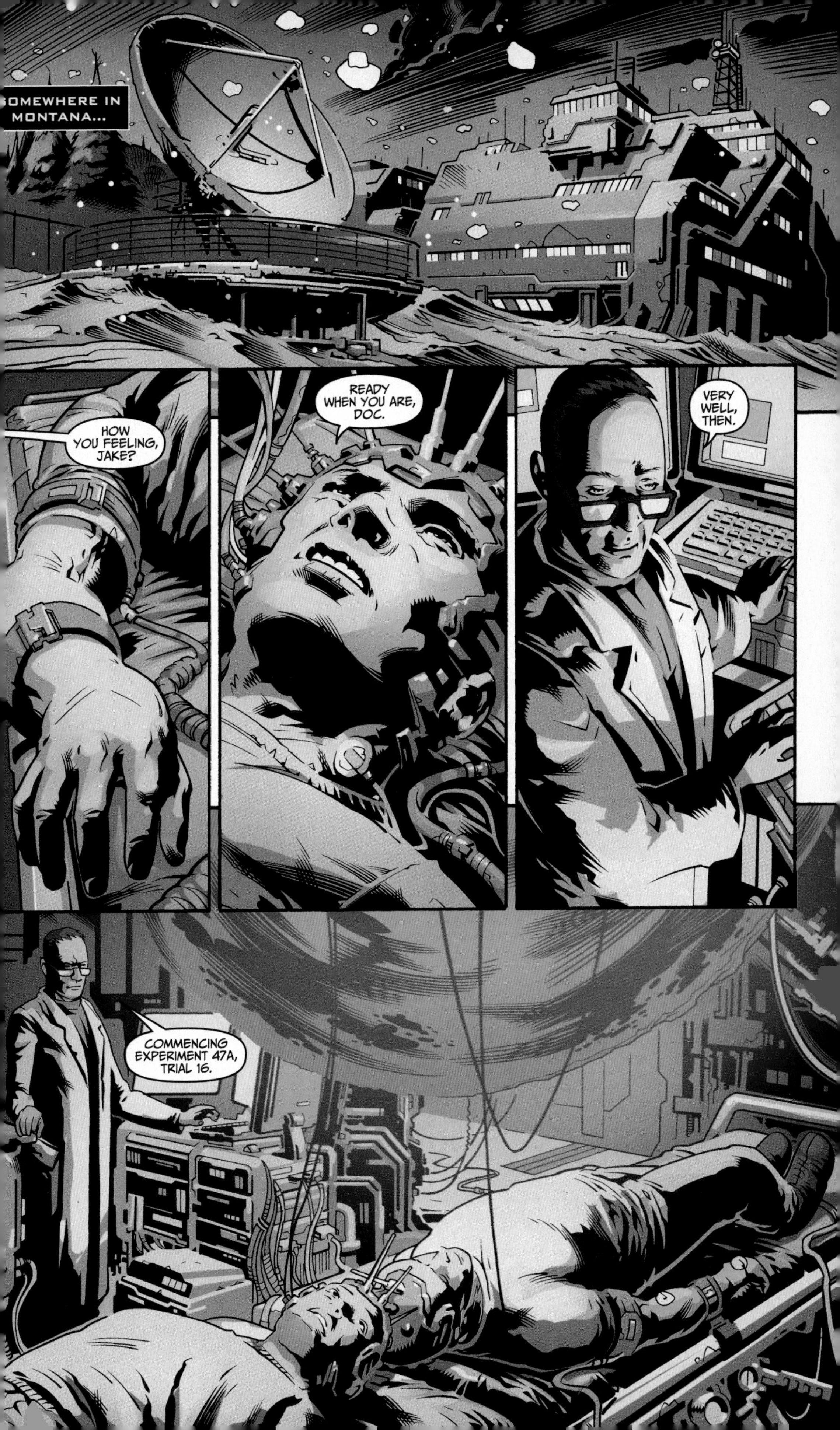
OMEWHERE IN MONTANA...
HOW YOU FEELING, JAKE?
READY WHEN YOU ARE, DOC.
VERY WELL, THEN.
COMMENCING EXPERIMENT 47A, TRIAL 16.

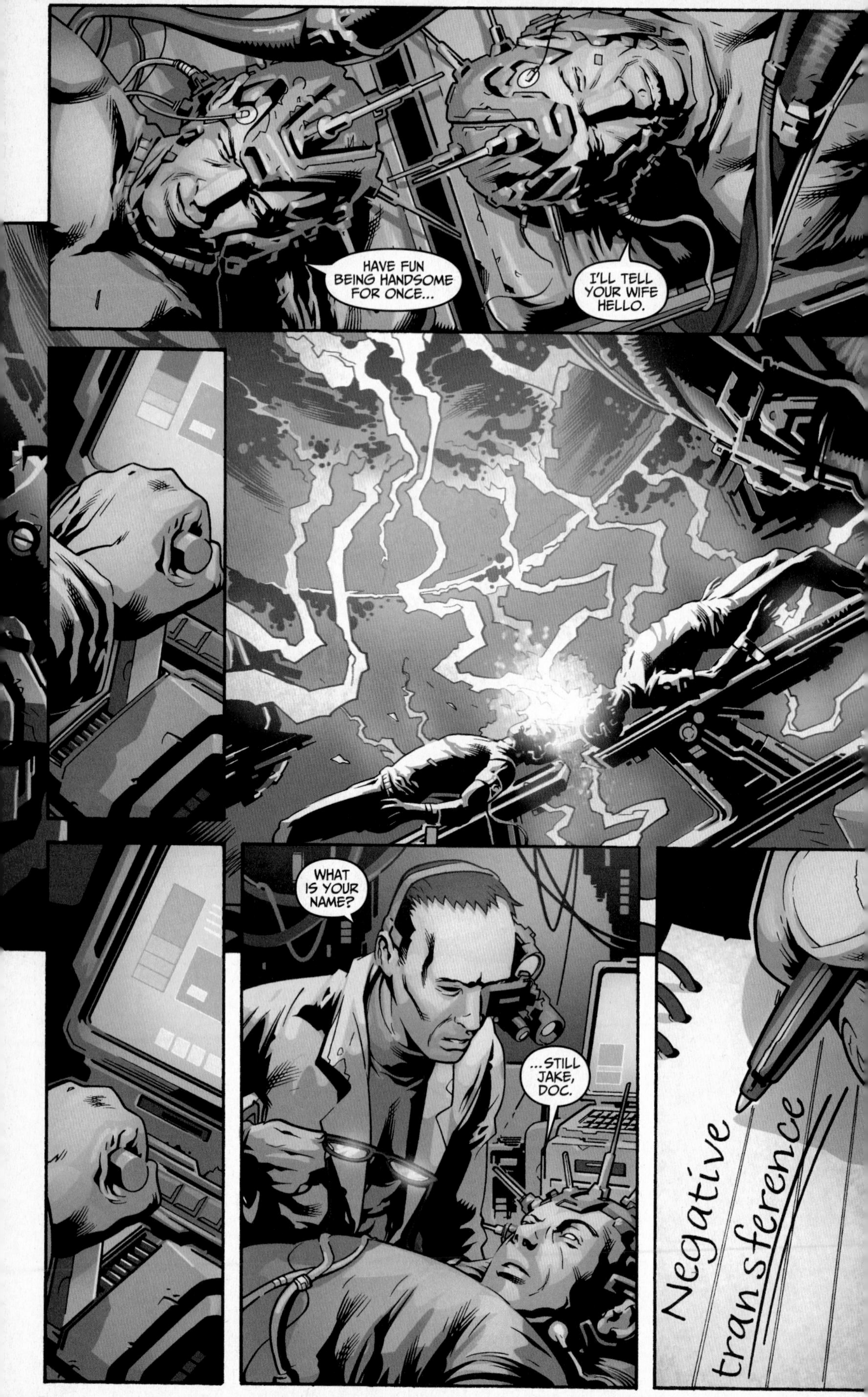
HAVE FUN BEING HANDSOME FOR ONCE...
I'LL TELL YOUR WIFE HELLO.
WHAT IS YOUR NAME?
...STILL JAKE, DOC.
Negative transference

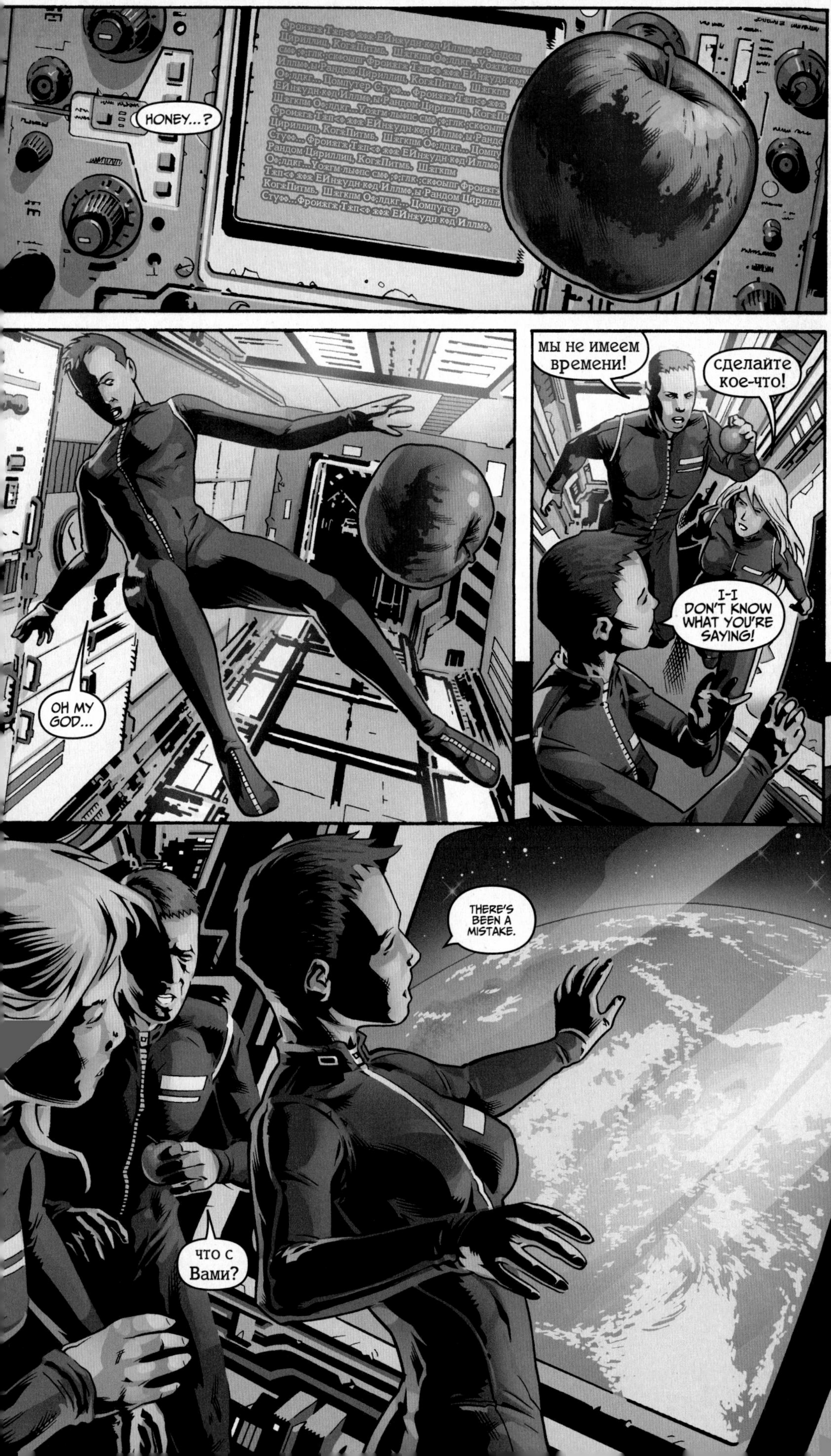
HONEY...?
OH MY GOD...
мы не имеем времени!
сделайте кое-что!
I-I DON'T KNOW WHAT YOU'RE SAYING!
THERE'S BEEN A MISTAKE.
что с Вами?

STRANGERS
ON A TRAIN

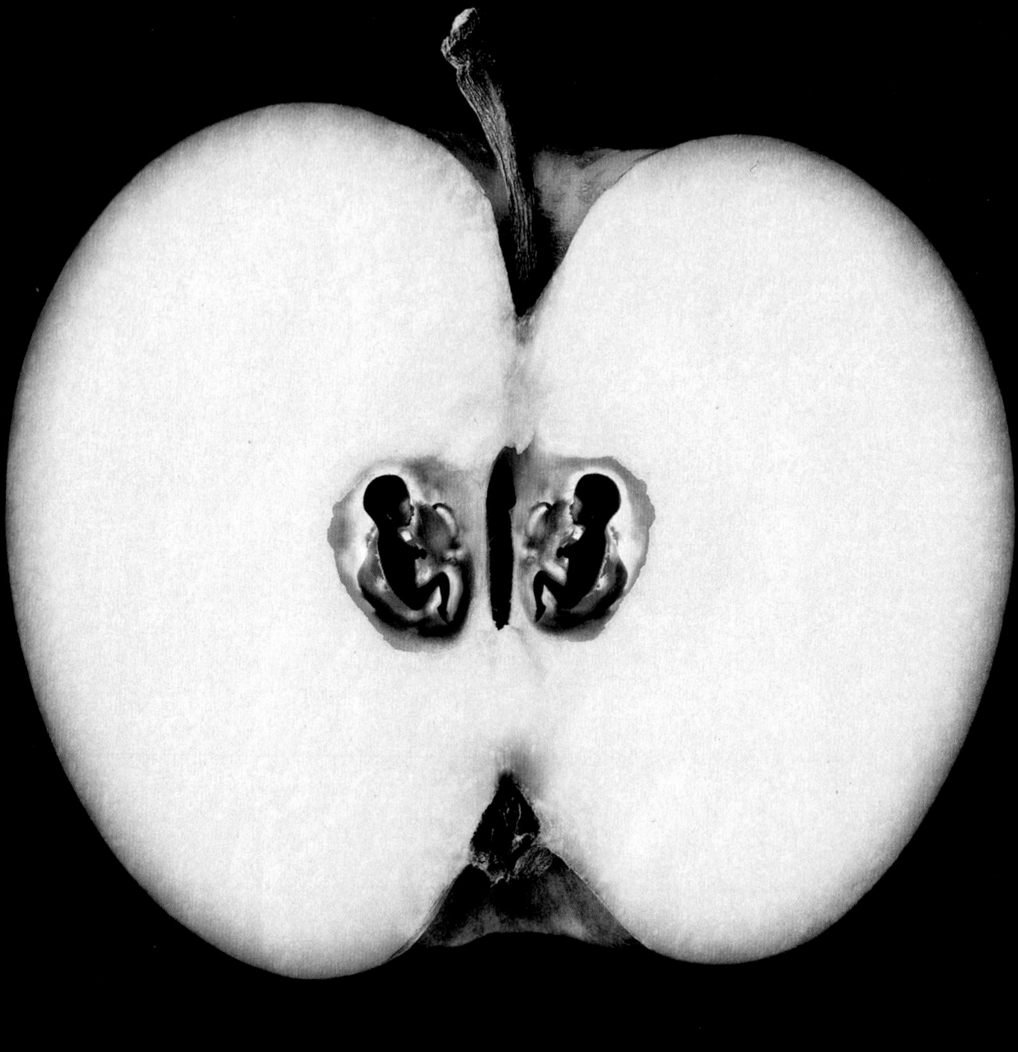

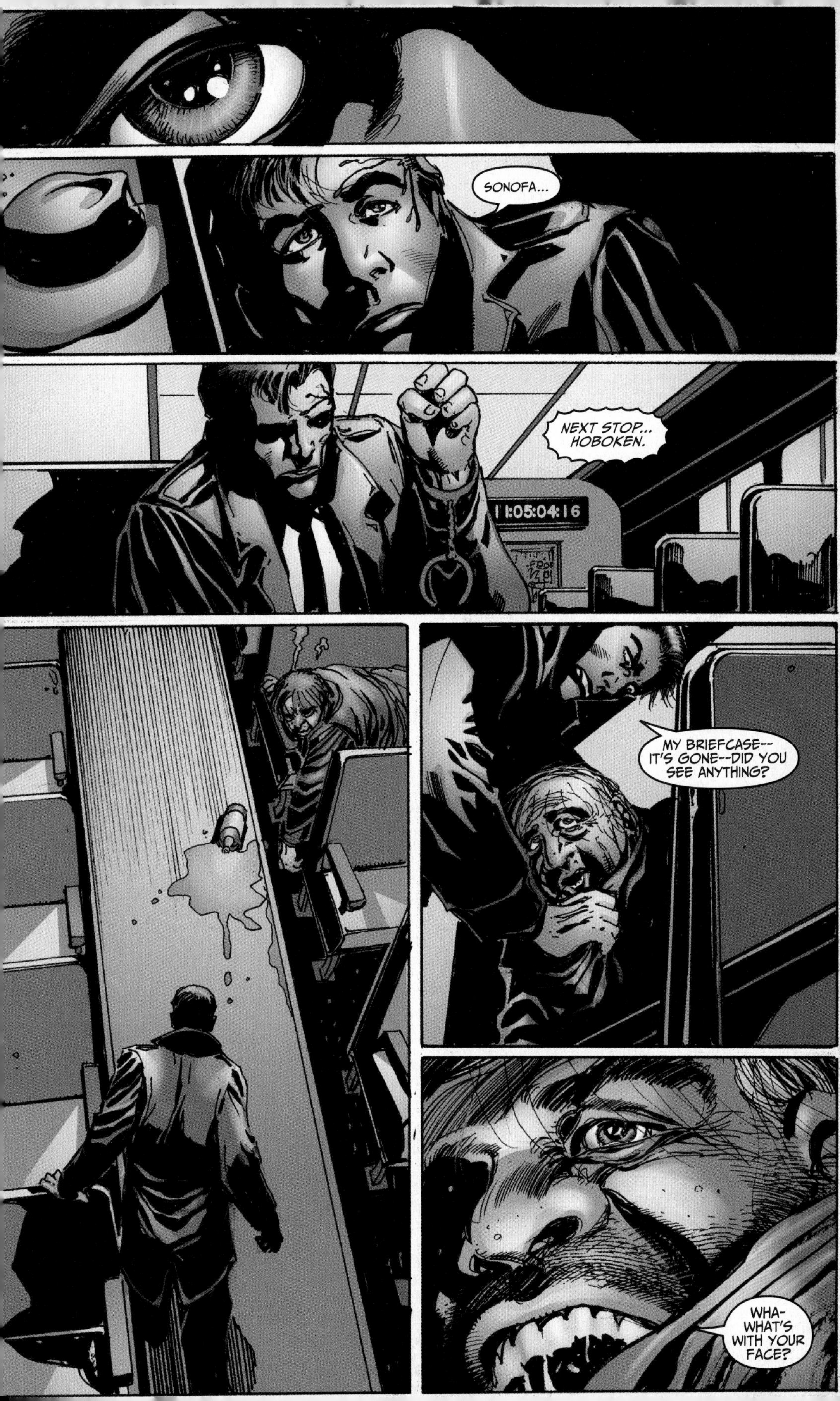
SONOFA...
NEXT STOP... HOBOKEN.
11:05:04:16
MY BRIEFCASE-- IT'S GONE--DID YOU SEE ANYTHING?
WHA- WHAT'S WITH YOUR FACE?

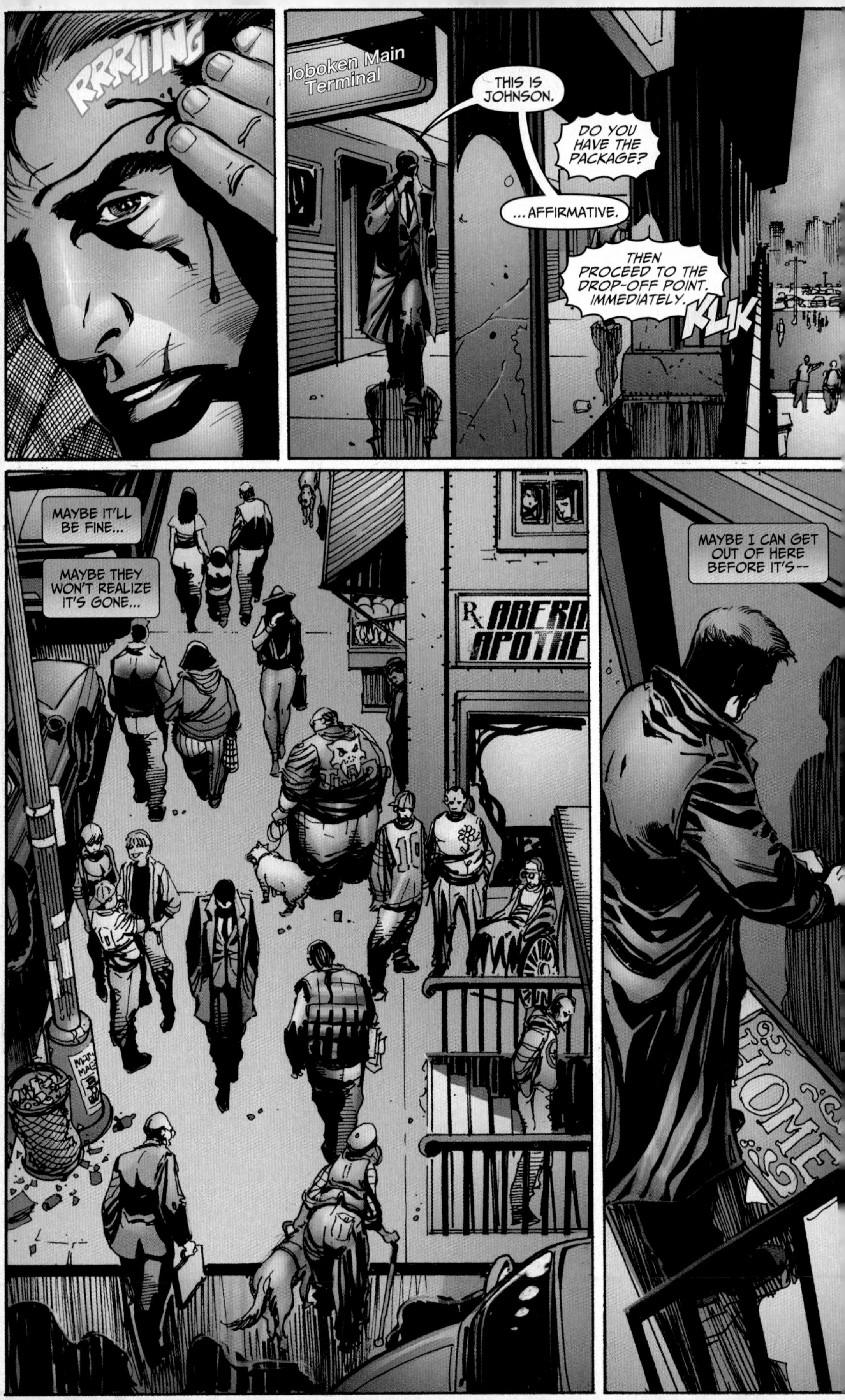
RRRIIING
Hoboken Main Terminal
THIS IS JOHNSON.
DO YOU HAVE THE PACKAGE?
...AFFIRMATIVE.
THEN PROCEED TO THE DROP-OFF POINT. IMMEDIATELY.
KLIK
MAYBE IT'LL BE FINE...
MAYBE THEY WON'T REALIZE IT'S GONE...
MAYBE I CAN GET OUT OF HERE BEFORE IT'S--

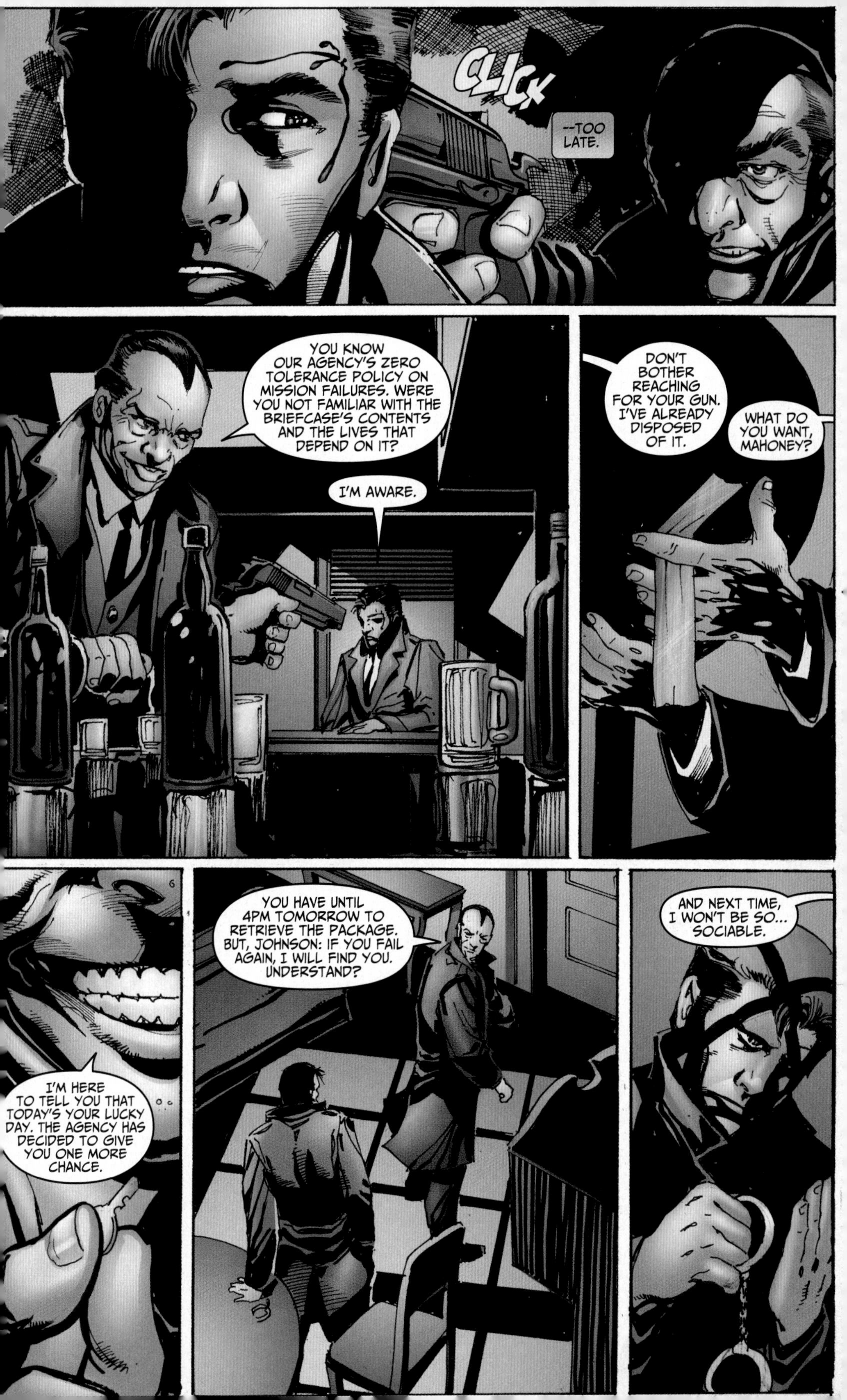
CLICK
--TOO LATE.
YOU KNOW OUR AGENCY'S ZERO TOLERANCE POLICY ON MISSION FAILURES. WERE YOU NOT FAMILIAR WITH THE BRIEFCASE'S CONTENTS AND THE LIVES THAT DEPEND ON IT?
I'M AWARE.
DON'T BOTHER REACHING FOR YOUR GUN. I'VE ALREADY DISPOSED OF IT.
WHAT DO YOU WANT, MAHONEY?
I'M HERE TO TELL YOU THAT TODAY'S YOUR LUCKY DAY. THE AGENCY HAS DECIDED TO GIVE YOU ONE MORE CHANCE.
YOU HAVE UNTIL 4PM TOMORROW TO RETRIEVE THE PACKAGE. BUT, JOHNSON: IF YOU FAIL AGAIN, I WILL FIND YOU. UNDERSTAND?
AND NEXT TIME, I WON'T BE SO... SOCIABLE.

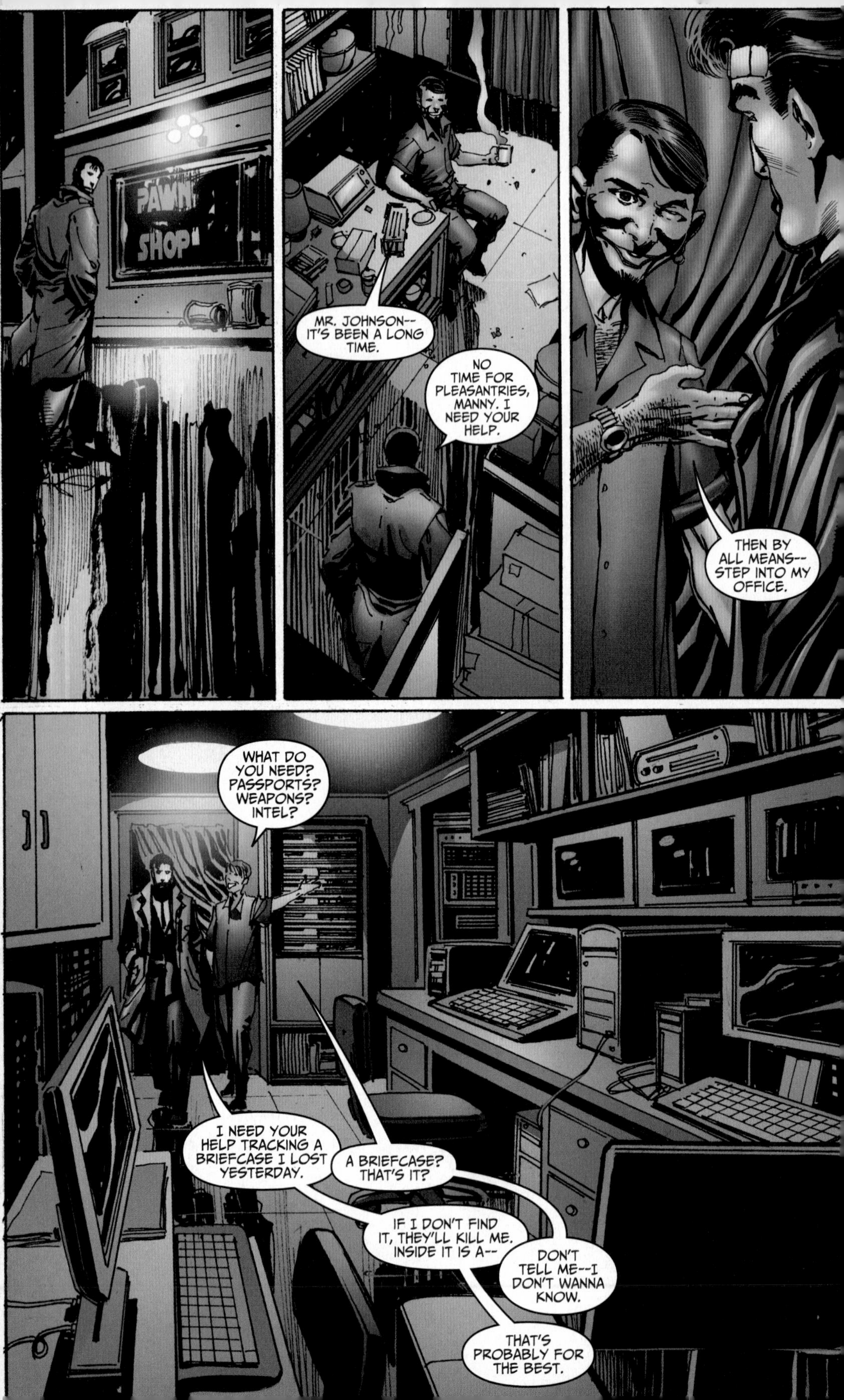
PAWN SHOP
MR. JOHNSON-- IT'S BEEN A LONG TIME.
NO TIME FOR PLEASANTRIES, MANNY. I NEED YOUR HELP.
THEN BY ALL MEANS-- STEP INTO MY OFFICE.
WHAT DO YOU NEED? PASSPORTS? WEAPONS? INTEL?
I NEED YOUR HELP TRACKING A BRIEFCASE I LOST YESTERDAY.
A BRIEFCASE? THAT'S IT?
IF I DON'T FIND IT, THEY'LL KILL ME. INSIDE IT IS A--
DON'T TELL ME--I DON'T WANNA KNOW.
THAT'S PROBABLY FOR THE BEST.

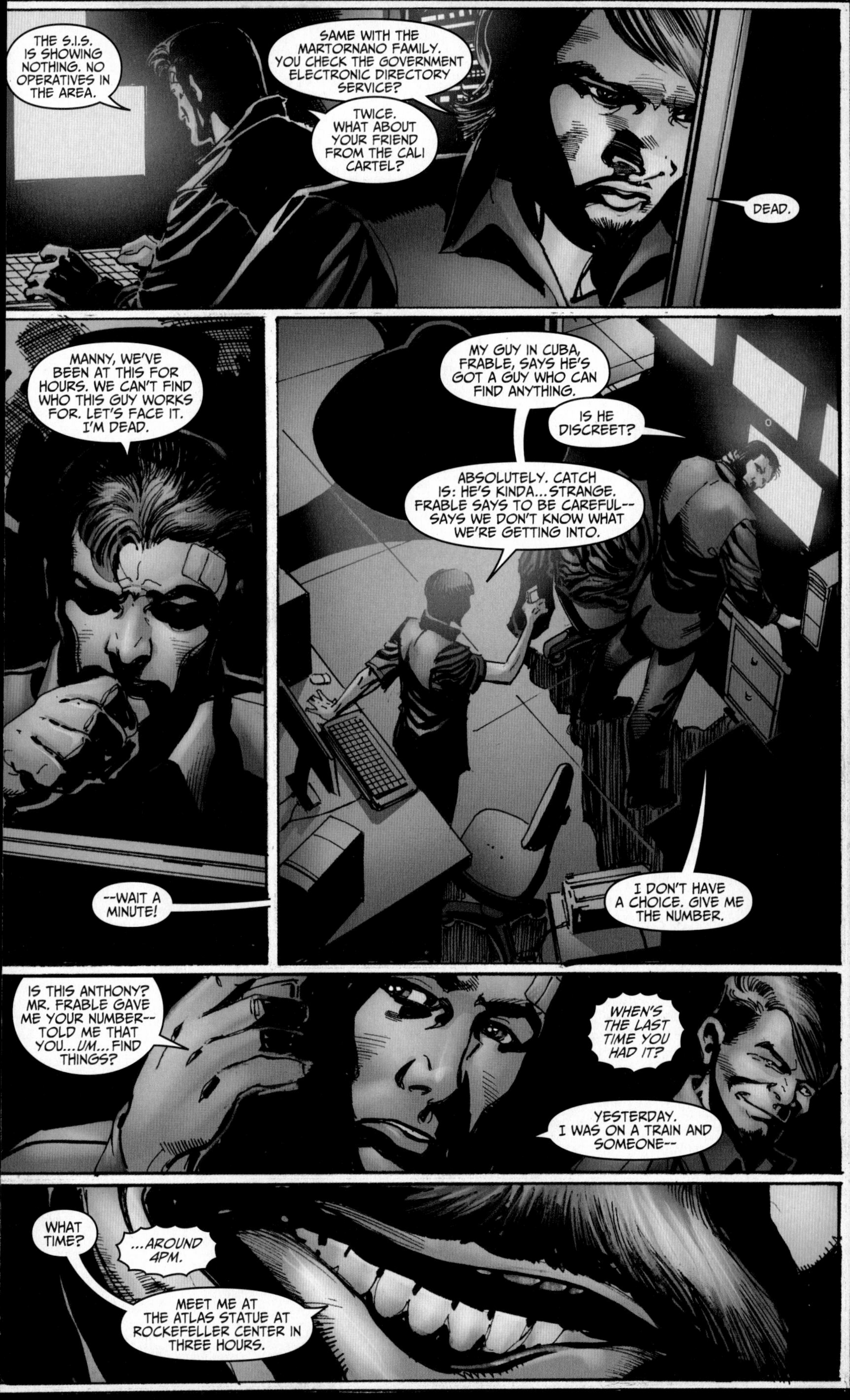

THE S.I.S. IS SHOWING NOTHING. NO OPERATIVES IN THE AREA.
SAME WITH THE MARTORNANO FAMILY. YOU CHECK THE GOVERNMENT ELECTRONIC DIRECTORY SERVICE?
TWICE. WHAT ABOUT YOUR FRIEND FROM THE CALI CARTEL?
DEAD.
MANNY, WE'VE BEEN AT THIS FOR HOURS. WE CAN'T FIND WHO THIS GUY WORKS FOR. LET'S FACE IT. I'M DEAD.
--WAIT A MINUTE!
MY GUY IN CUBA, FRABLE, SAYS HE'S GOT A GUY WHO CAN FIND ANYTHING.
IS HE DISCREET?
ABSOLUTELY. CATCH IS: HE'S KINDA... STRANGE. FRABLE SAYS TO BE CAREFUL-- SAYS WE DON'T KNOW WHAT WE'RE GETTING INTO.
I DON'T HAVE A CHOICE. GIVE ME THE NUMBER.
IS THIS ANTHONY? MR. FRABLE GAVE ME YOUR NUMBER-- TOLD ME THAT YOU...UM...FIND THINGS?
WHEN'S THE LAST TIME YOU HAD IT?
YESTERDAY. I WAS ON A TRAIN AND SOMEONE--
WHAT TIME?
...AROUND 4PM.
MEET ME AT THE ATLAS STATUE AT ROCKEFELLER CENTER IN THREE HOURS.

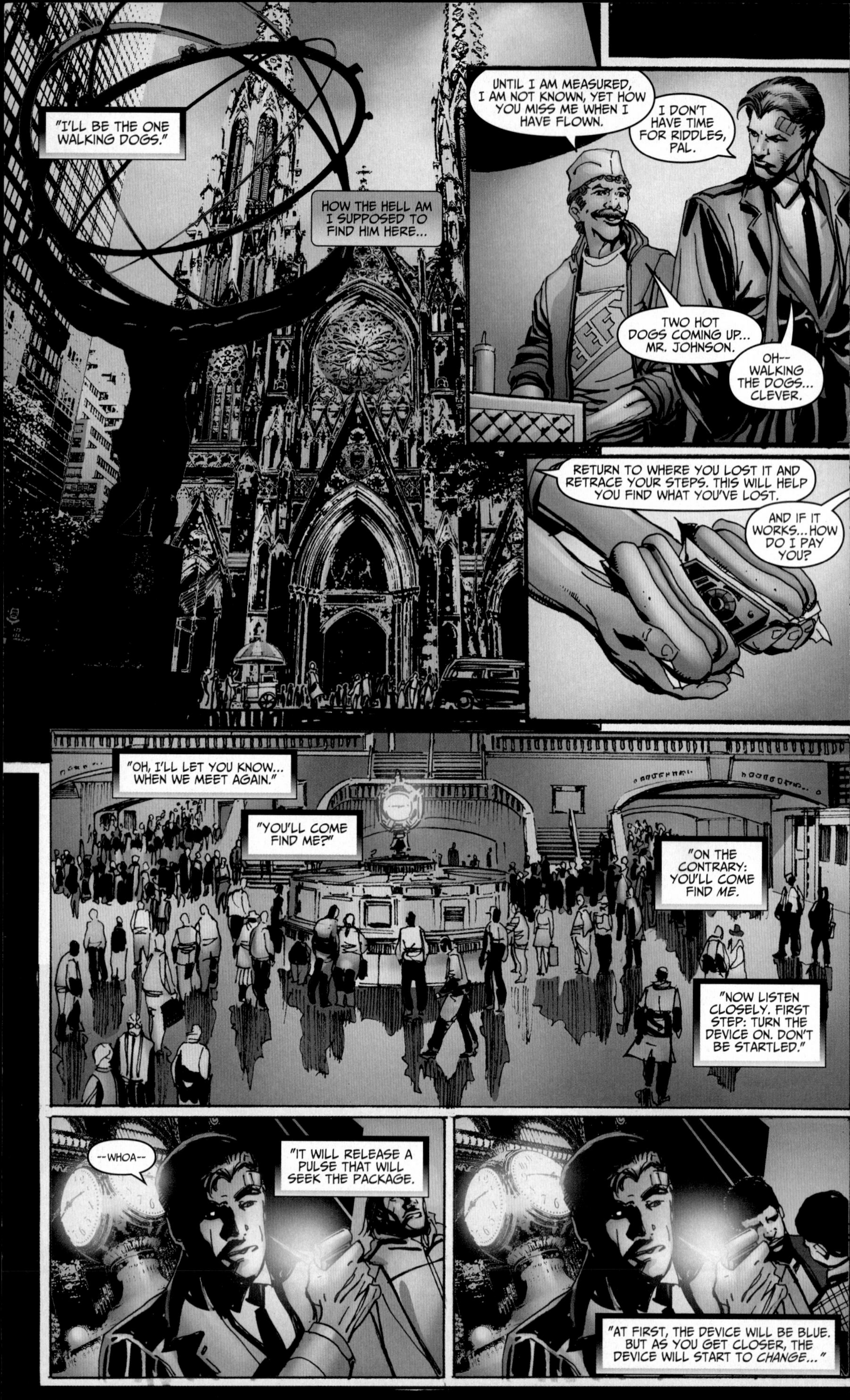
"I'LL BE THE ONE WALKING DOGS."
HOW THE HELL AM I SUPPOSED TO FIND HIM HERE...
UNTIL I AM MEASURED, I AM NOT KNOWN, YET HOW YOU MISS ME WHEN I HAVE FLOWN.
I DON'T HAVE TIME FOR RIDDLES, PAL.
TWO HOT DOGS COMING UP... MR. JOHNSON.
OH-- WALKING THE DOGS... CLEVER.
RETURN TO WHERE YOU LOST IT AND RETRACE YOUR STEPS. THIS WILL HELP YOU FIND WHAT YOU'VE LOST.
AND IF IT WORKS...HOW DO I PAY YOU?
"OH, I'LL LET YOU KNOW... WHEN WE MEET AGAIN."
"YOU'LL COME FIND ME?"
"ON THE CONTRARY: YOU'LL COME FIND *ME*.
"NOW LISTEN CLOSELY. FIRST STEP: TURN THE DEVICE ON. DON'T BE STARTLED."
--WHOA--
"IT WILL RELEASE A PULSE THAT WILL SEEK THE PACKAGE.
"AT FIRST, THE DEVICE WILL BE BLUE. BUT AS YOU GET CLOSER, THE DEVICE WILL START TO *CHANGE*..."

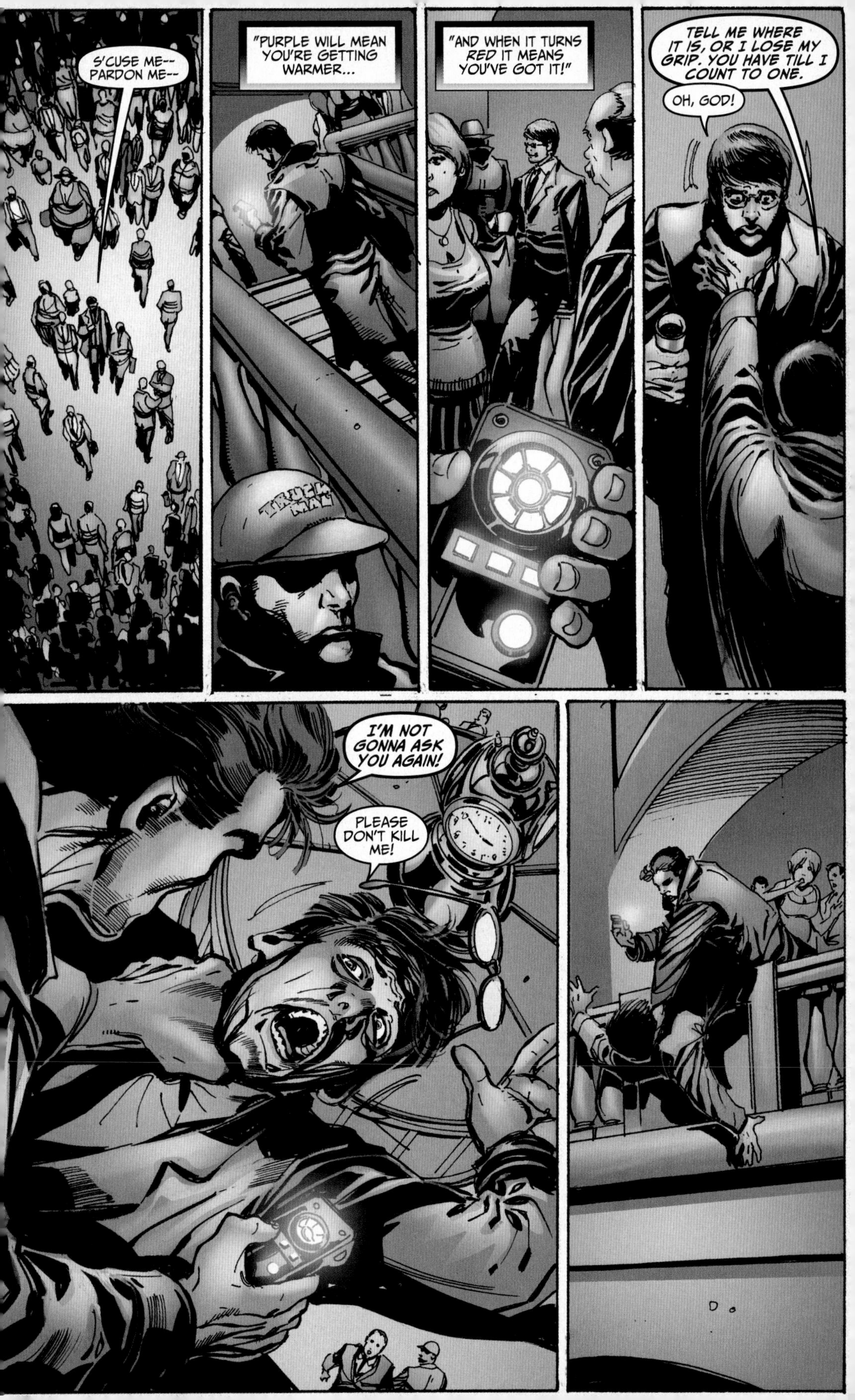
S'CUSE ME--
PARDON ME--
"PURPLE WILL MEAN YOU'RE GETTING WARMER...
"AND WHEN IT TURNS RED IT MEANS YOU'VE GOT IT!"
TELL ME WHERE IT IS, OR I LOSE MY GRIP. YOU HAVE TILL I COUNT TO ONE.
OH, GOD!
I'M NOT GONNA ASK YOU AGAIN!
PLEASE DON'T KILL ME!

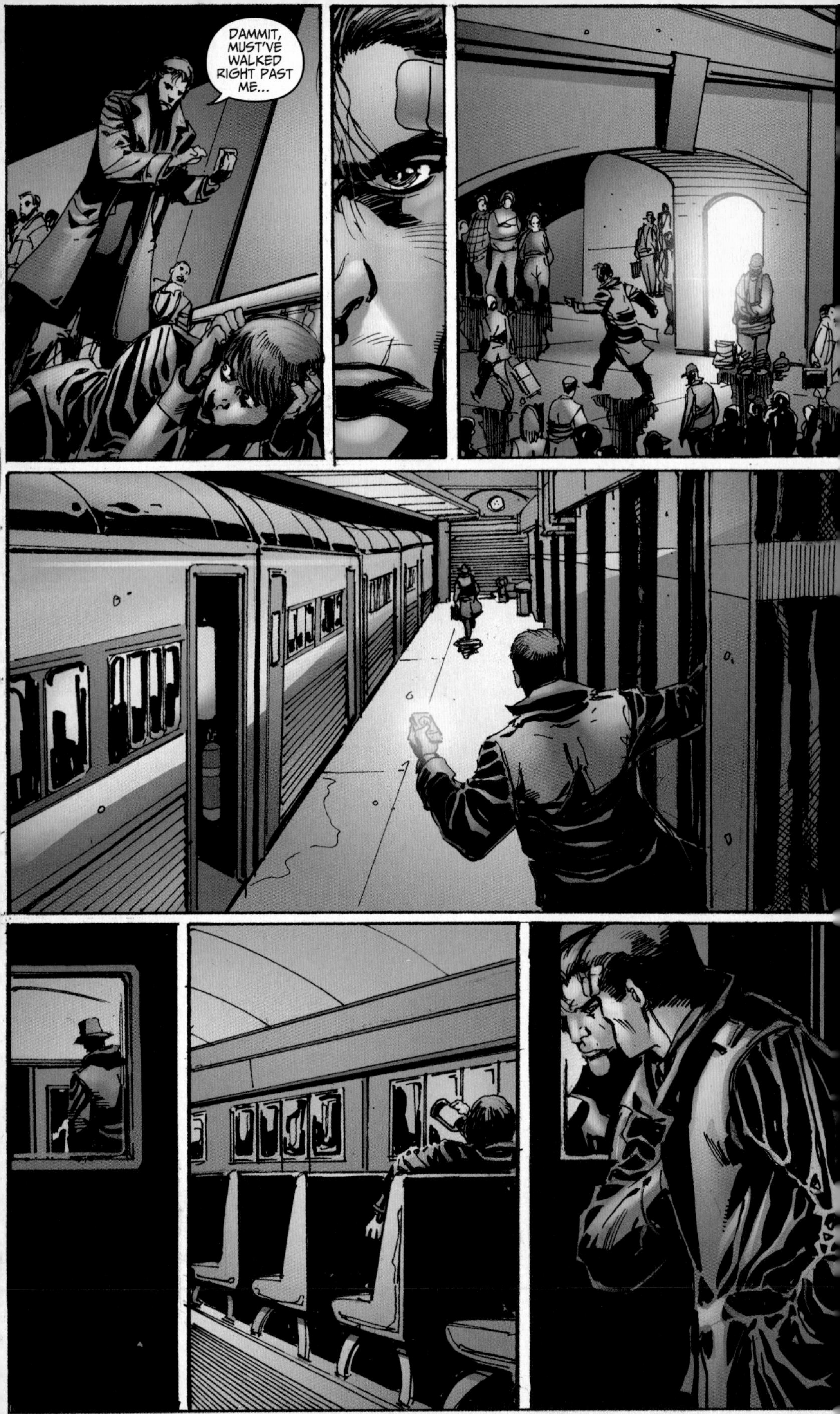
DAMMIT, MUST'VE WALKED RIGHT PAST ME...

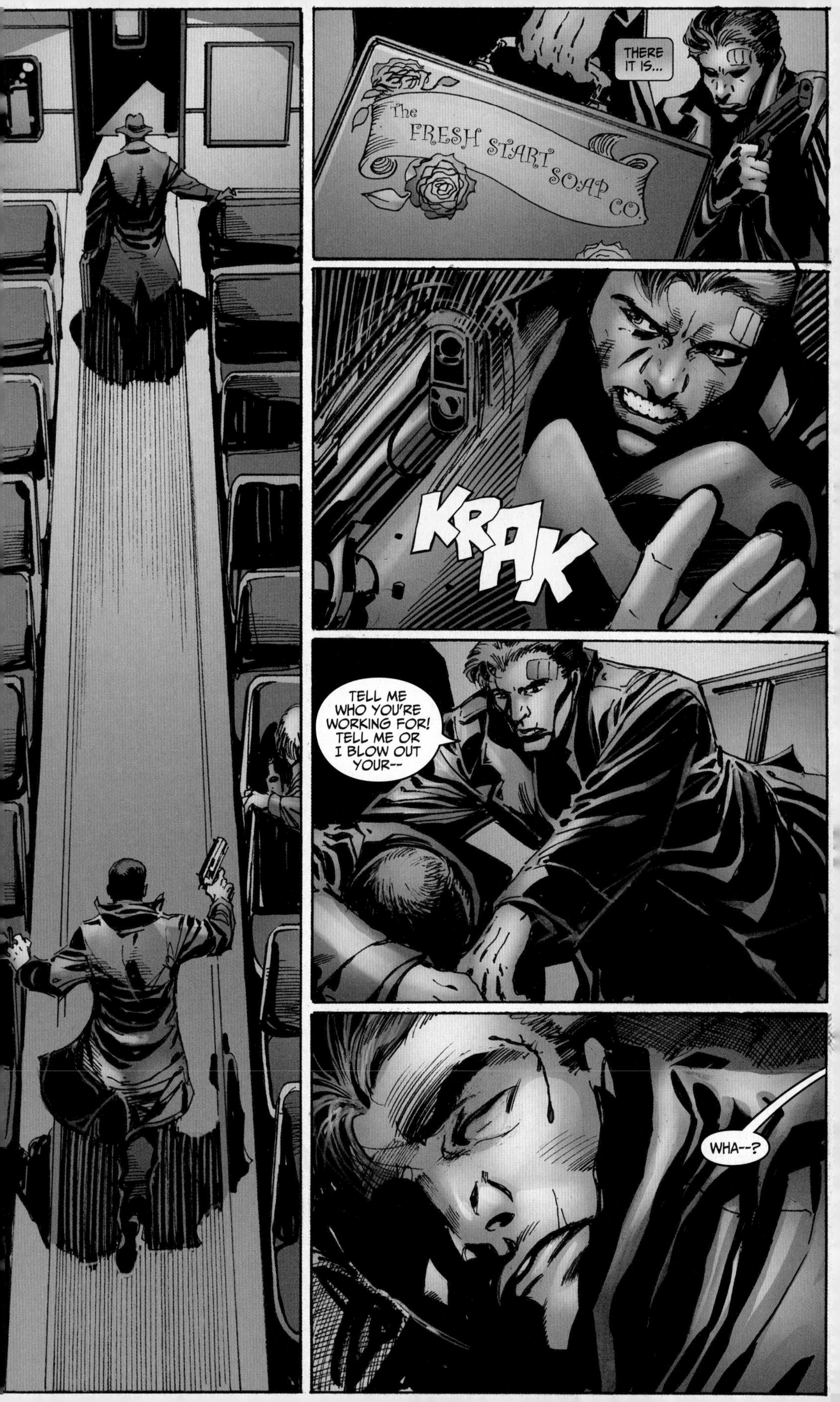

THERE IT IS...
The FRESH START SOAP CO.
KRAK
TELL ME WHO YOU'RE WORKING FOR! TELL ME OR I BLOW OUT YOUR--
WHA--?

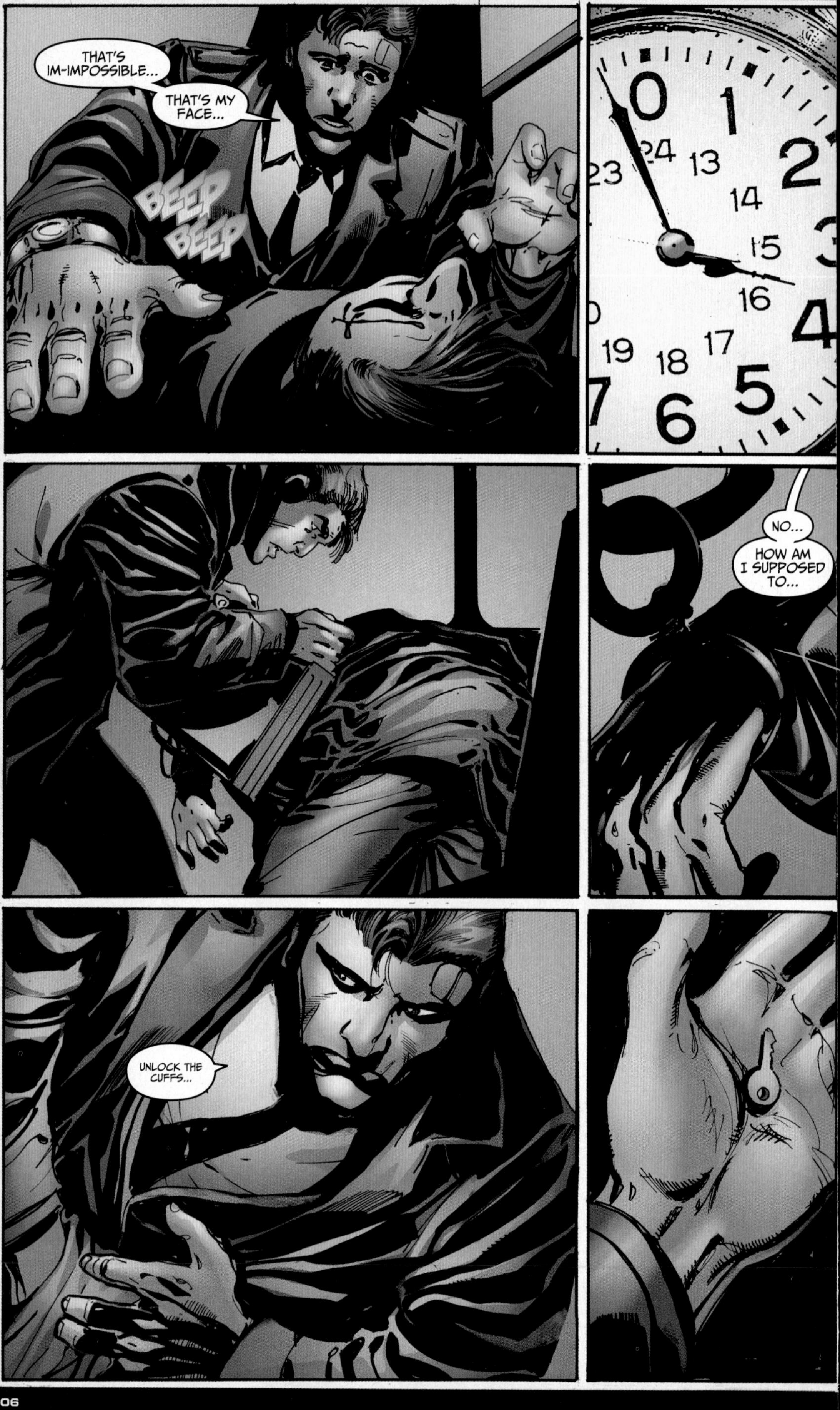
THAT'S IM-IMPOSSIBLE...
THAT'S MY FACE...
BEEP BEEP
NO...
HOW AM I SUPPOSED TO...
UNLOCK THE CUFFS...

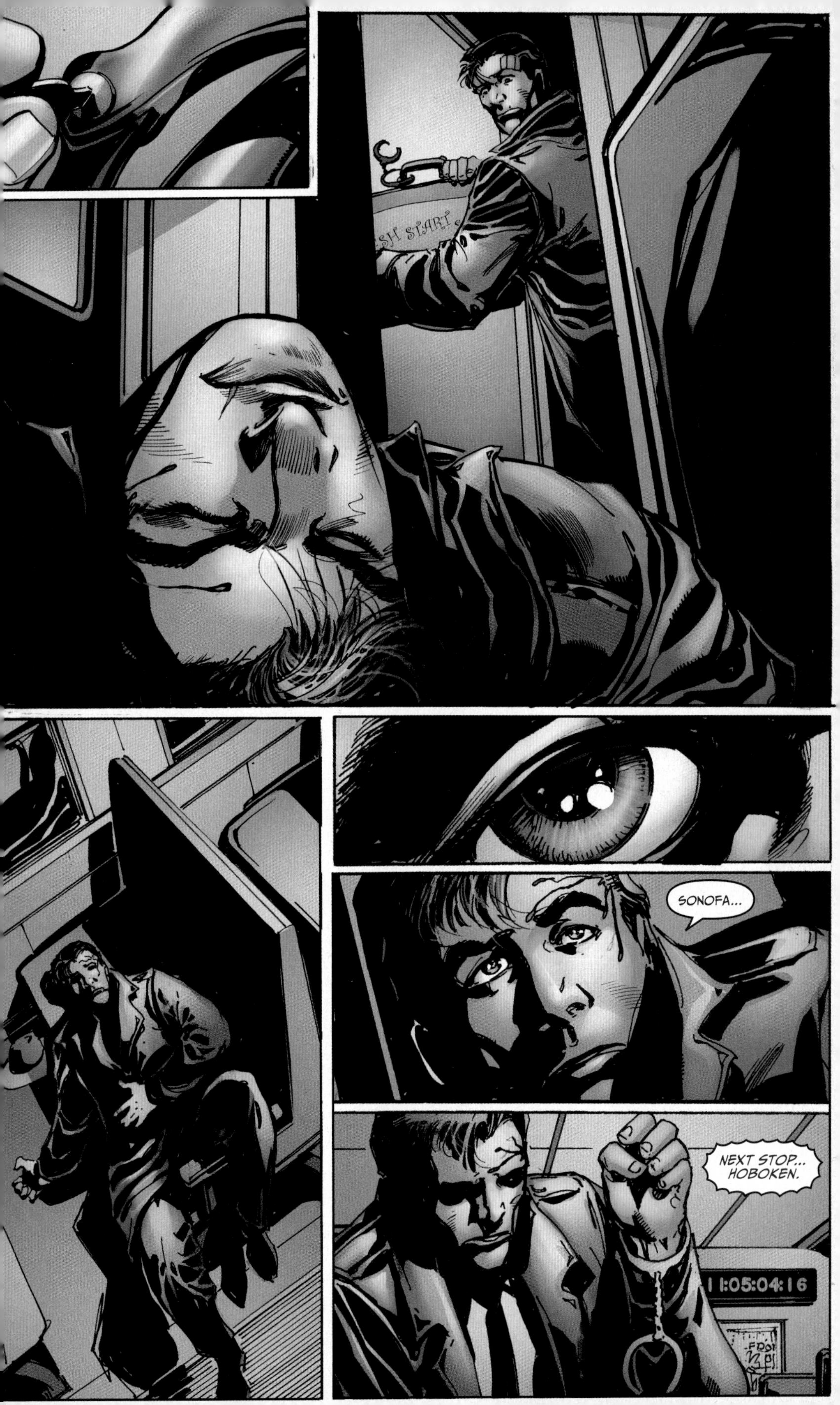
SH START
SONOFA...
NEXT STOP... HOBOKEN.
11:05:04:16

RUN AWAY

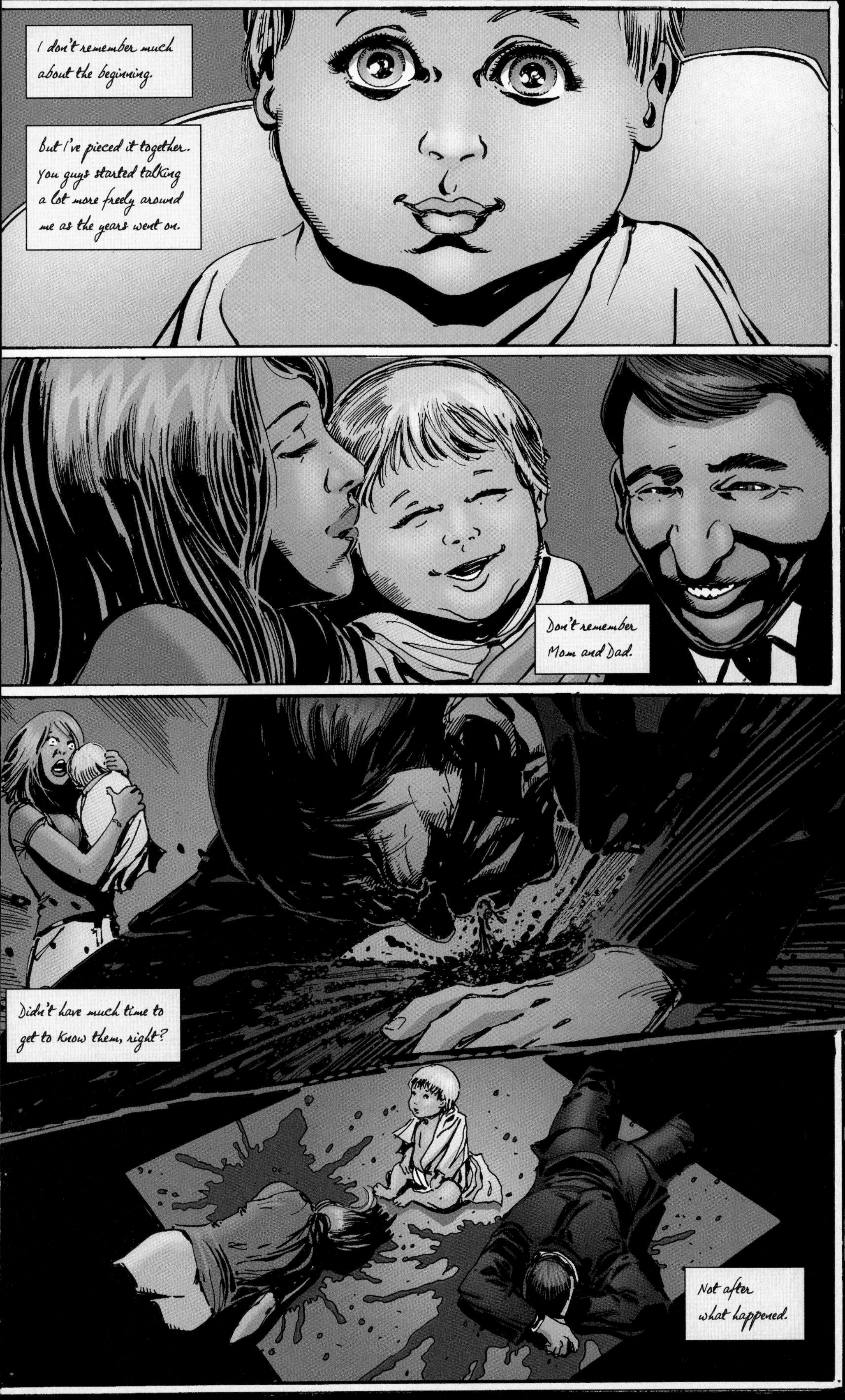
I don't remember much about the beginning.
But I've pieced it together. You guys started talking a lot more freely around me as the years went on.
Don't remember Mom and Dad.
Didn't have much time to get to know them, right?
Not after what happened.

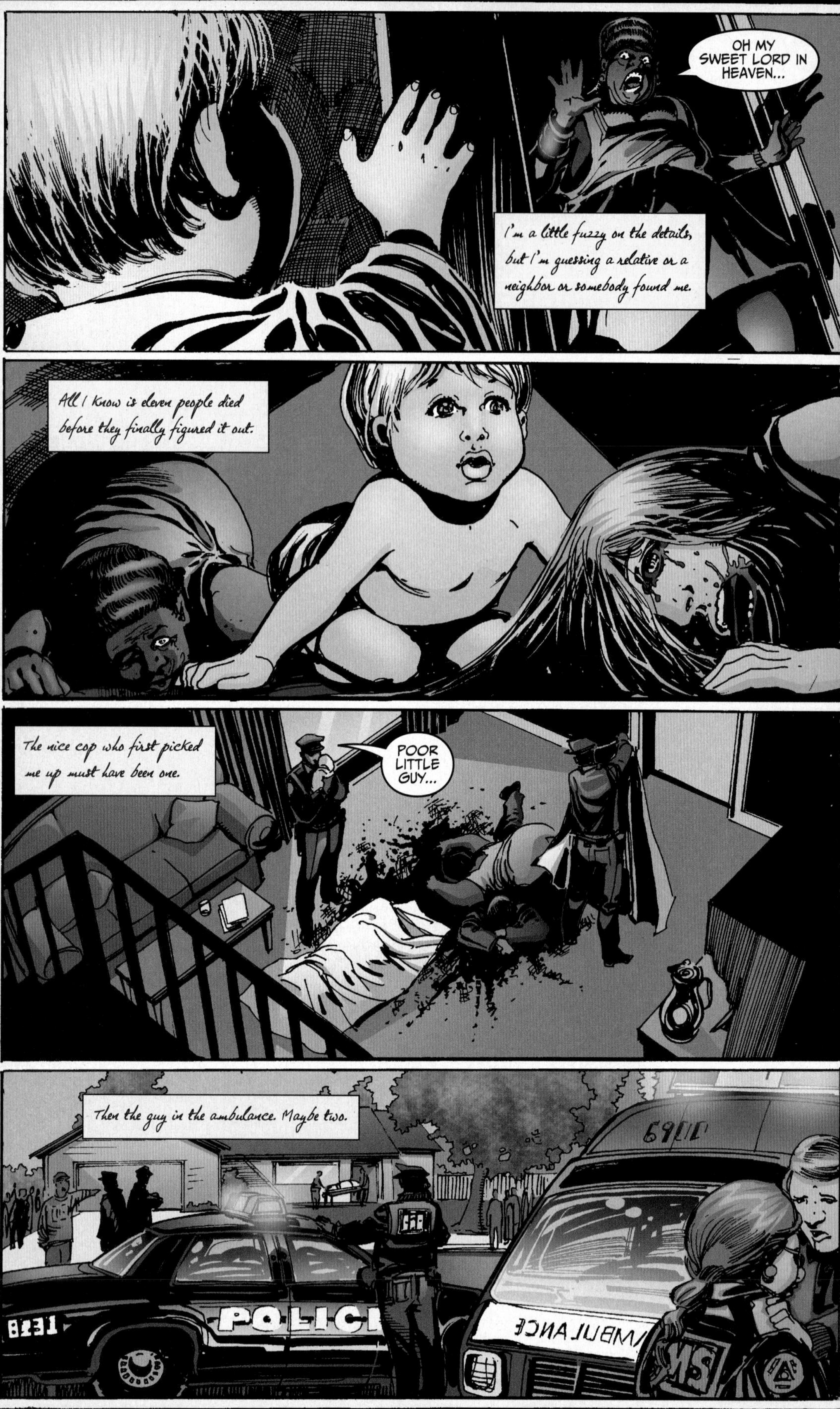
OH MY SWEET LORD IN HEAVEN...
I'm a little fuzzy on the details, but I'm guessing a relative or a neighbor or somebody found me.
All I know is eleven people died before they finally figured it out.
The nice cop who first picked me up must have been one.
POOR LITTLE GUY...
Then the guy in the ambulance. Maybe two.
POLICE
AMBULANCE

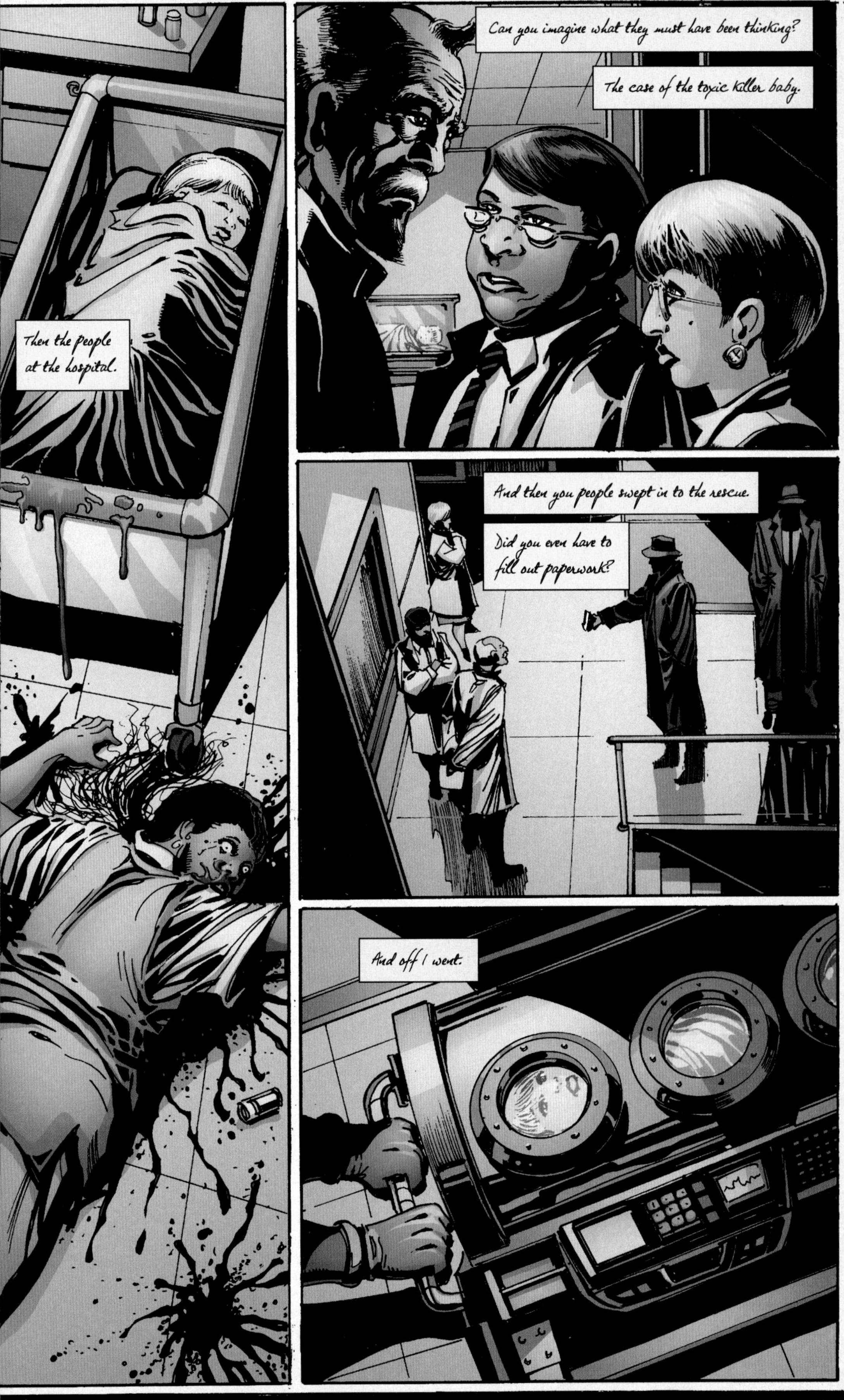
Then the people at the hospital.
Can you imagine what they must have been thinking?
The case of the toxic killer baby.
And then you people swept in to the rescue.
Did you even have to fill out paperwork?
And off I went.

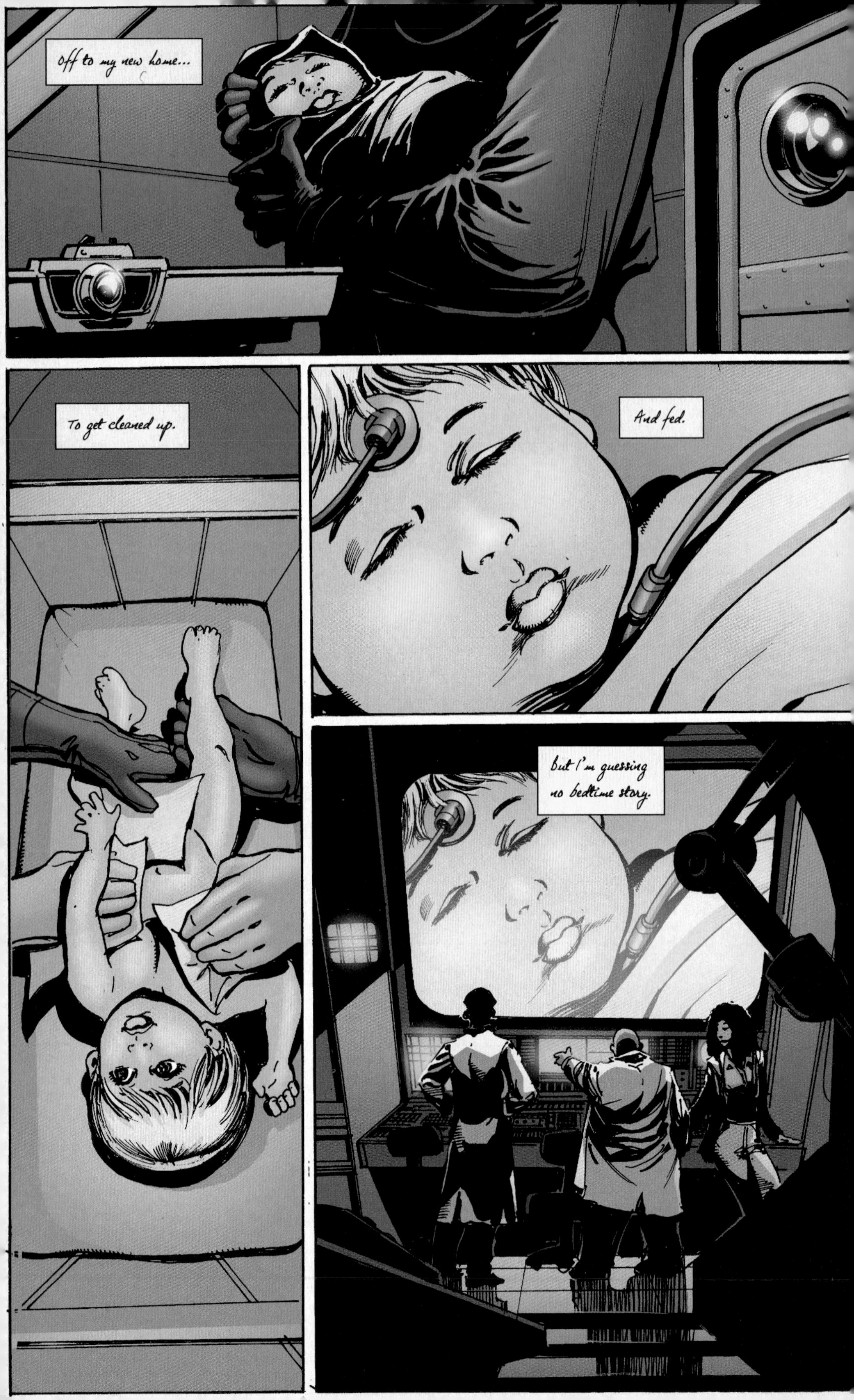
Off to my new home...
To get cleaned up.
And fed.
But I'm guessing
no bedtime story.

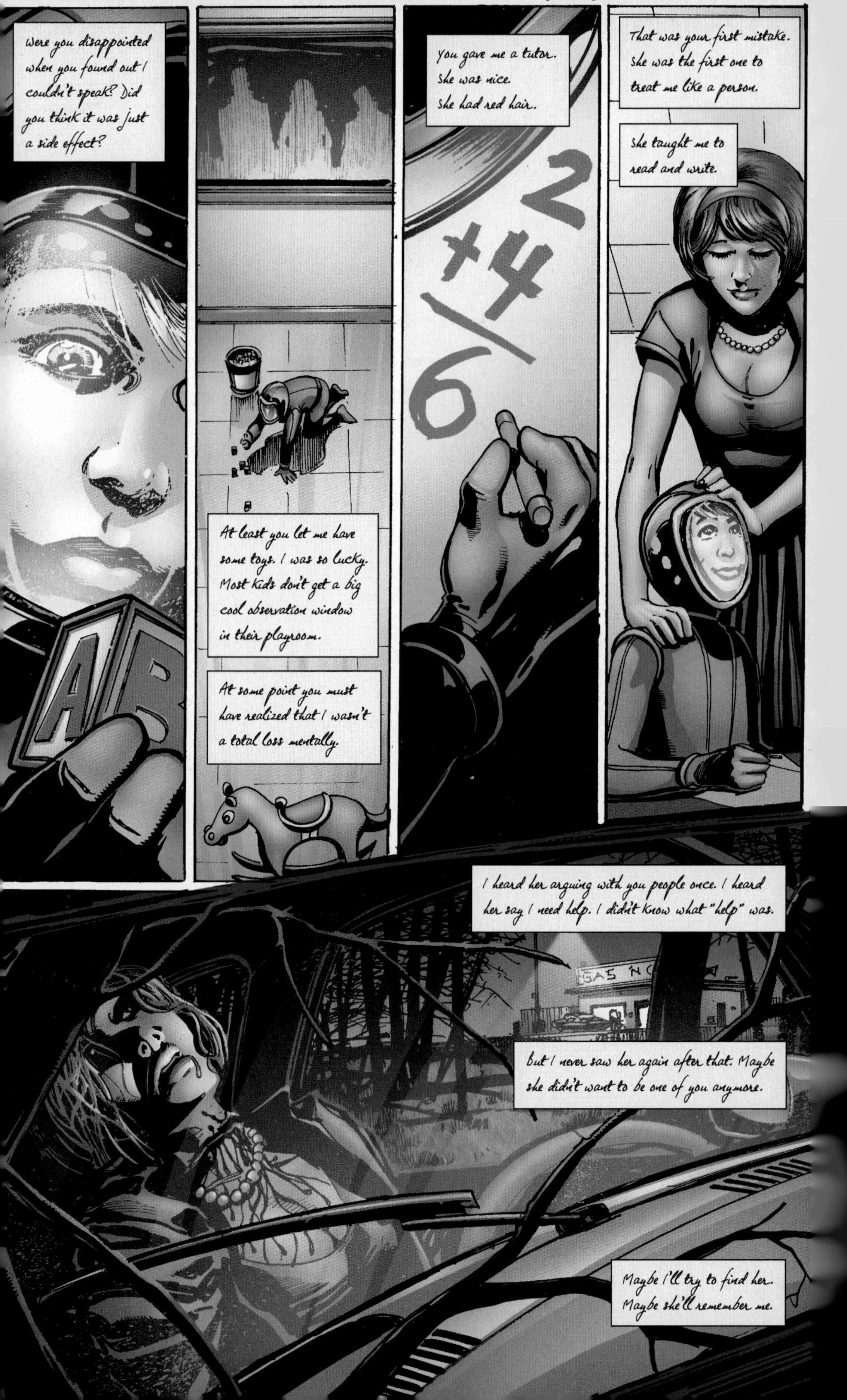
Were you disappointed when you found out I couldn't speak? Did you think it was just a side effect?
At least you let me have some toys. I was so lucky. Most kids don't get a big cool observation window in their playroom.
At some point you must have realized that I wasn't a total loss mentally.
You gave me a tutor. She was nice. She had red hair.
2
+4
6
That was your first mistake. She was the first one to treat me like a person.
She taught me to read and write.
I heard her arguing with you people once. I heard her say I need help. I didn't know what "help" was.
But I never saw her again after that. Maybe she didn't want to be one of you anymore.
Maybe I'll try to find her. Maybe she'll remember me.

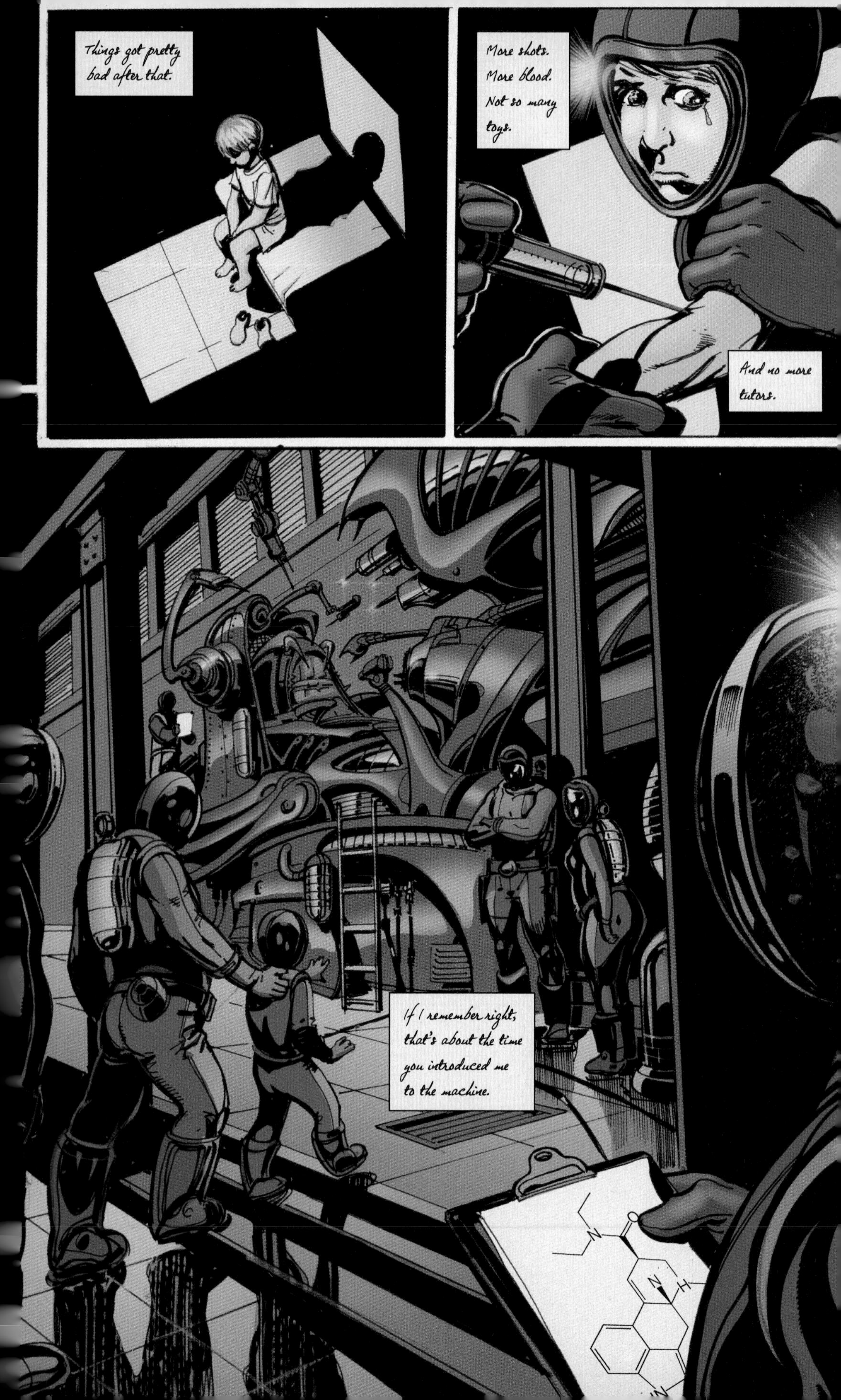
Things got pretty bad after that.
More shots. More blood. Not so many toys.
And no more tutors.
If I remember right, that's about the time you introduced me to the machine.

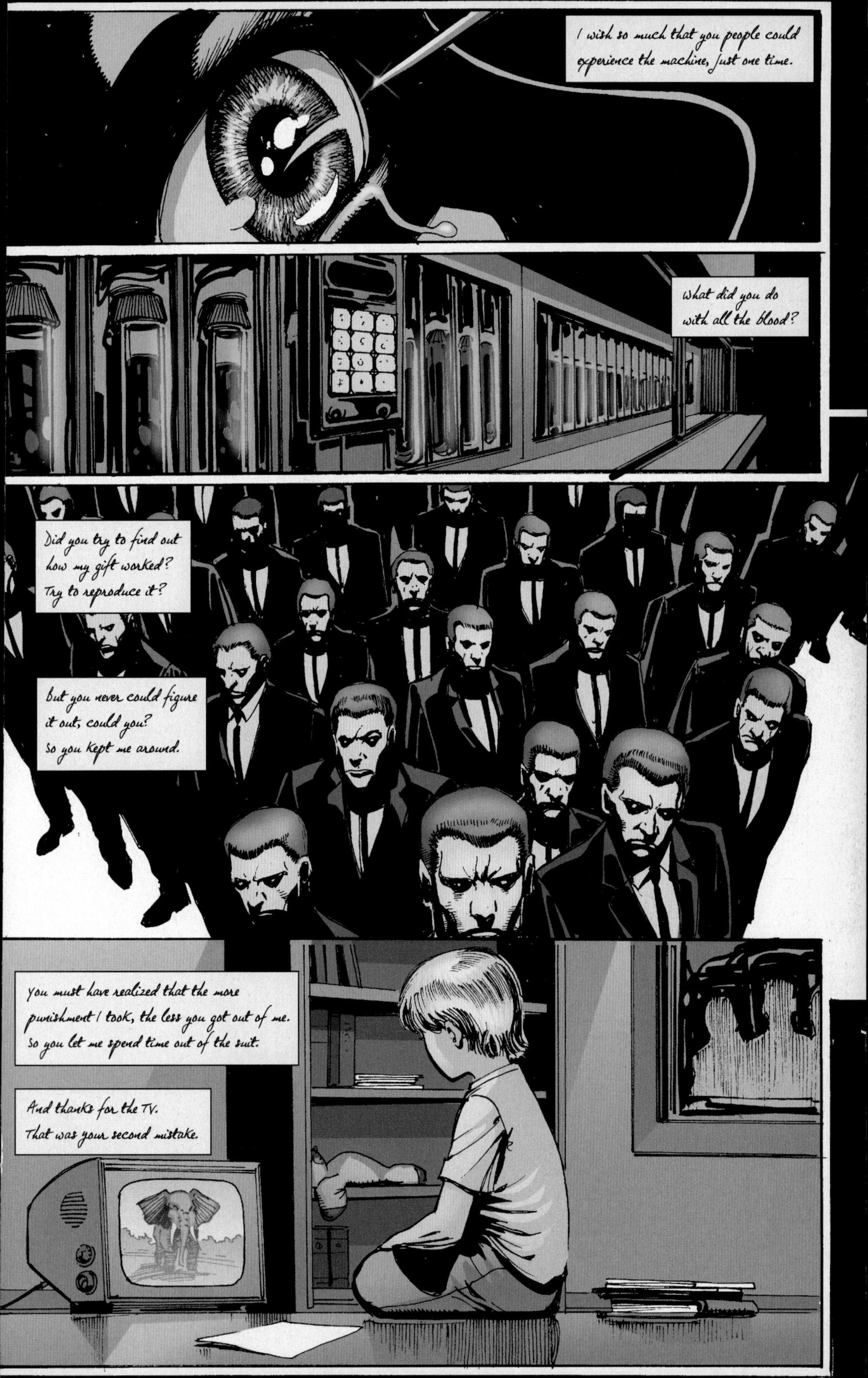
I wish so much that you people could experience the machine, just one time.
What did you do with all the blood?
Did you try to find out how my gift worked? Try to reproduce it?
But you never could figure it out, could you? So you kept me around.
You must have realized that the more punishment I took, the less you got out of me. So you let me spend time out of the suit.
And thanks for the TV. That was your second mistake.

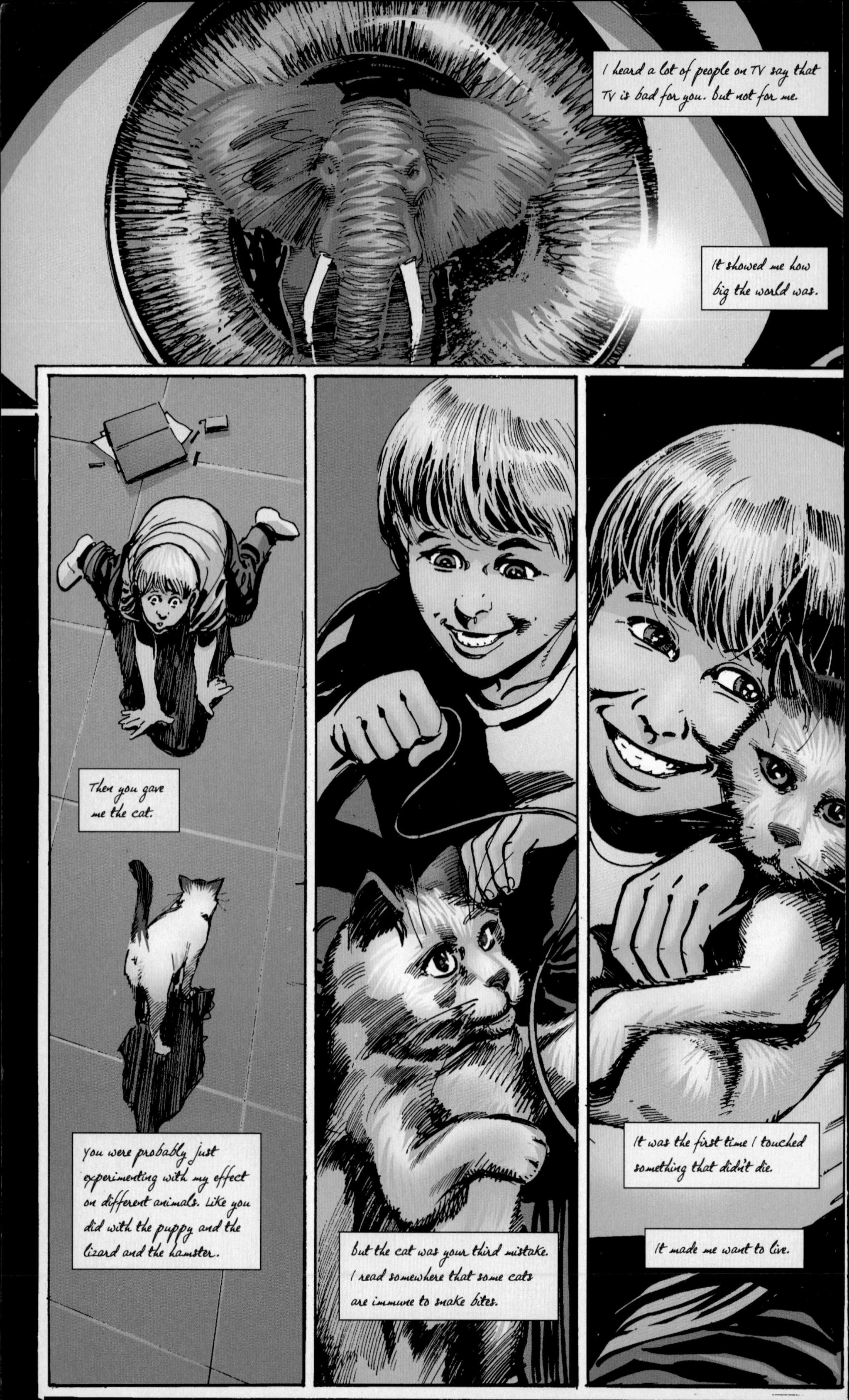
I heard a lot of people on TV say that TV is bad for you. But not for me.
It showed me how big the world was.
Then you gave me the cat.
You were probably just experimenting with my effect on different animals. Like you did with the puppy and the lizard and the hamster.
But the cat was your third mistake. I read somewhere that some cats are immune to snake bites.
It was the first time I touched something that didn't die.
It made me want to live.

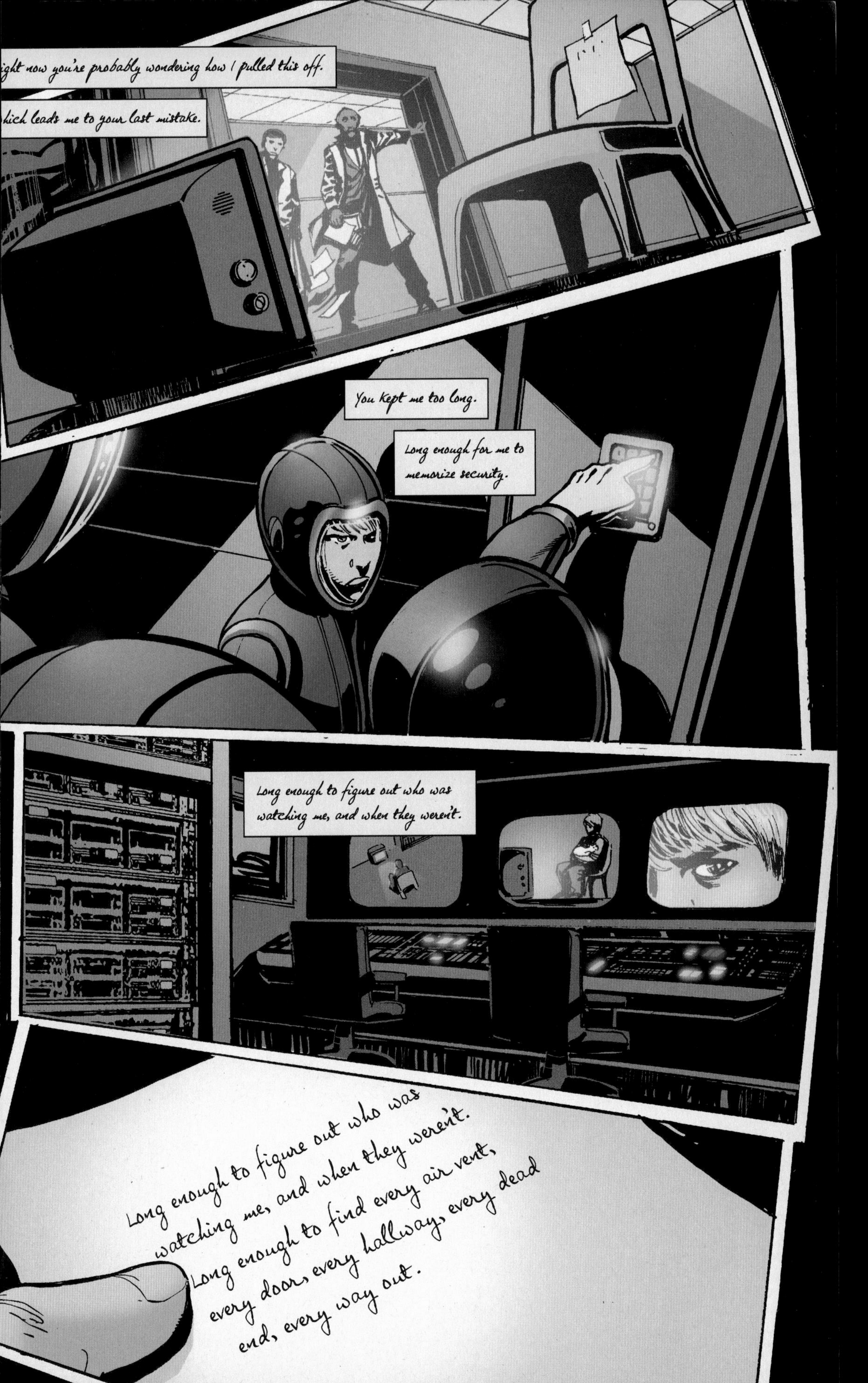
ight now you're probably wondering how I pulled this off.
hich leads me to your last mistake.
You kept me too long.
Long enough for me to memorize security.
Long enough to figure out who was watching me, and when they weren't.
Long enough to figure out who was watching me, and when they weren't. Long enough to find every air vent, every door, every hallway, every dead end, every way out.

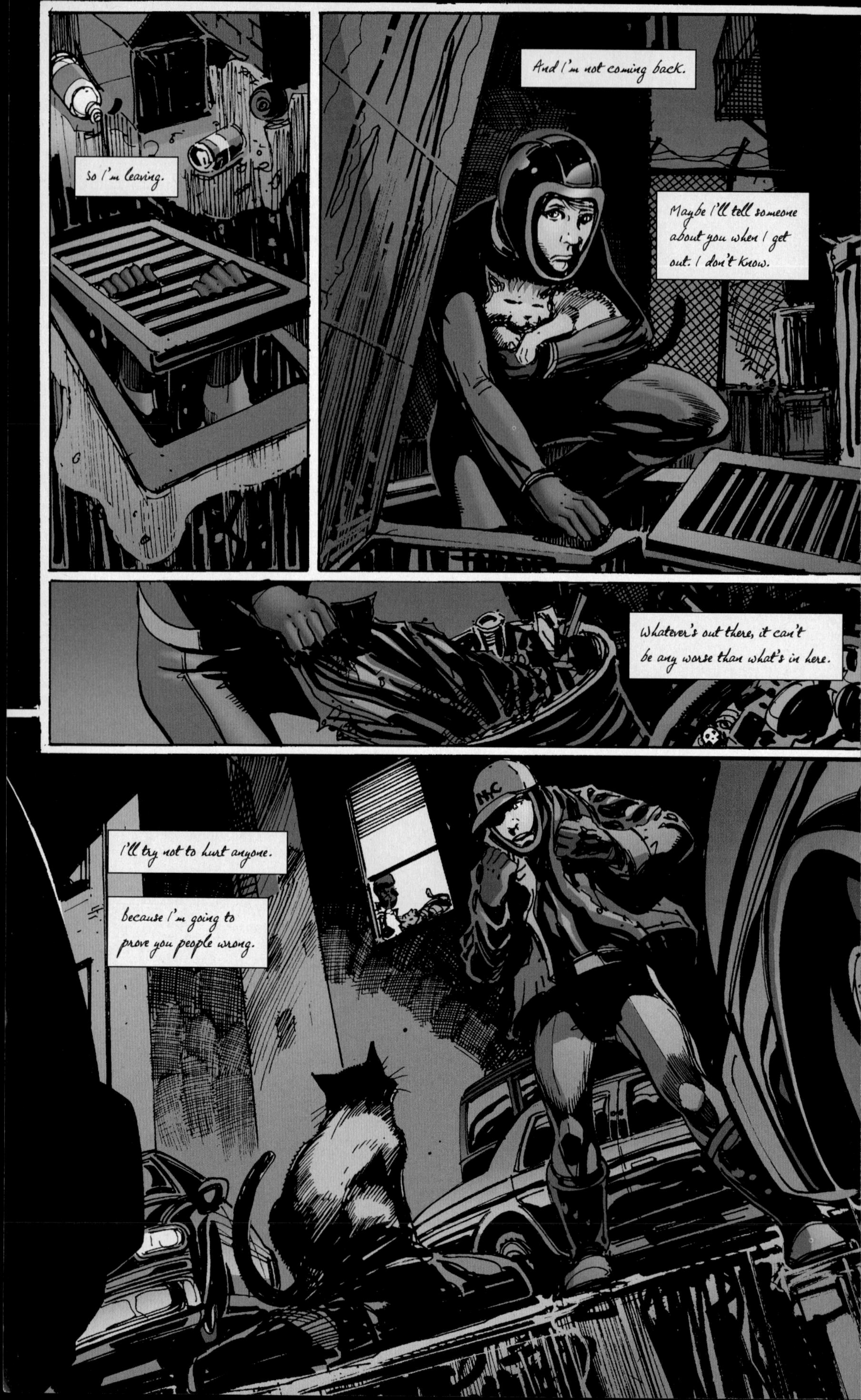

So I'm leaving.
And I'm not coming back.
Maybe I'll tell someone about you when I get out. I don't know.
Whatever's out there, it can't be any worse than what's in here.
I'll try not to hurt anyone.
because I'm going to prove you people wrong.

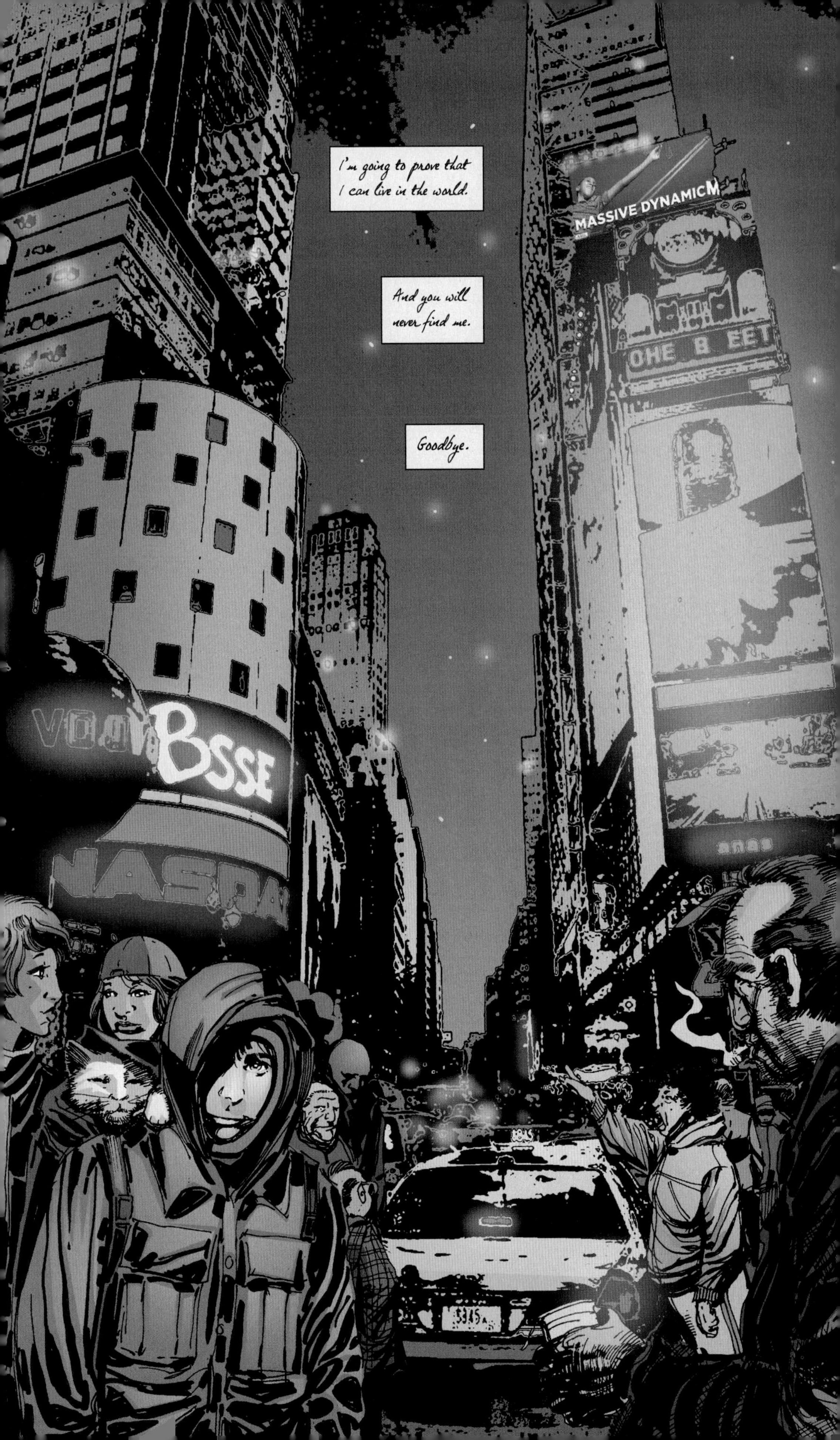
I'm going to prove that I can live in the world.
And you will never find me.
Goodbye.
MASSIVE DYNAMIC

SPACE COWBOY

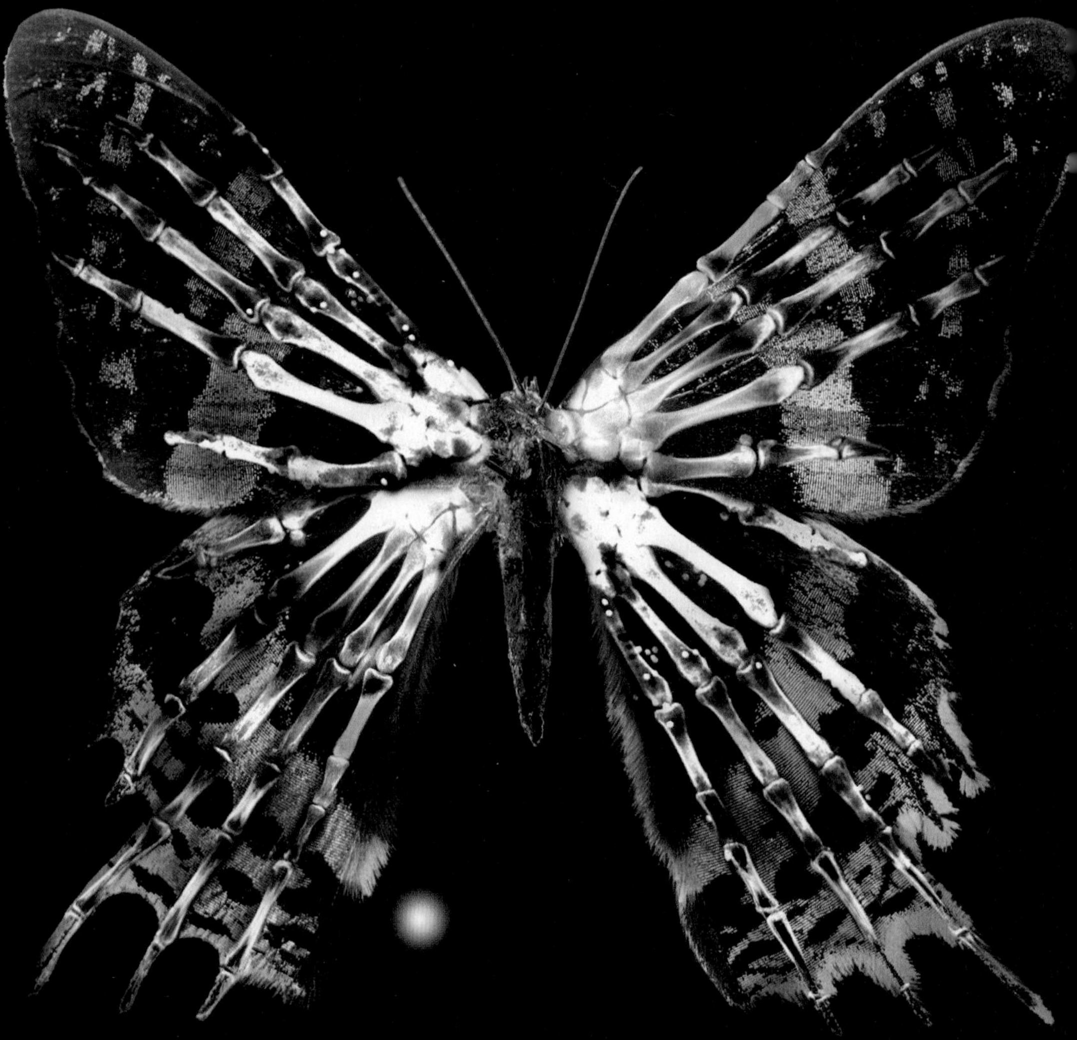

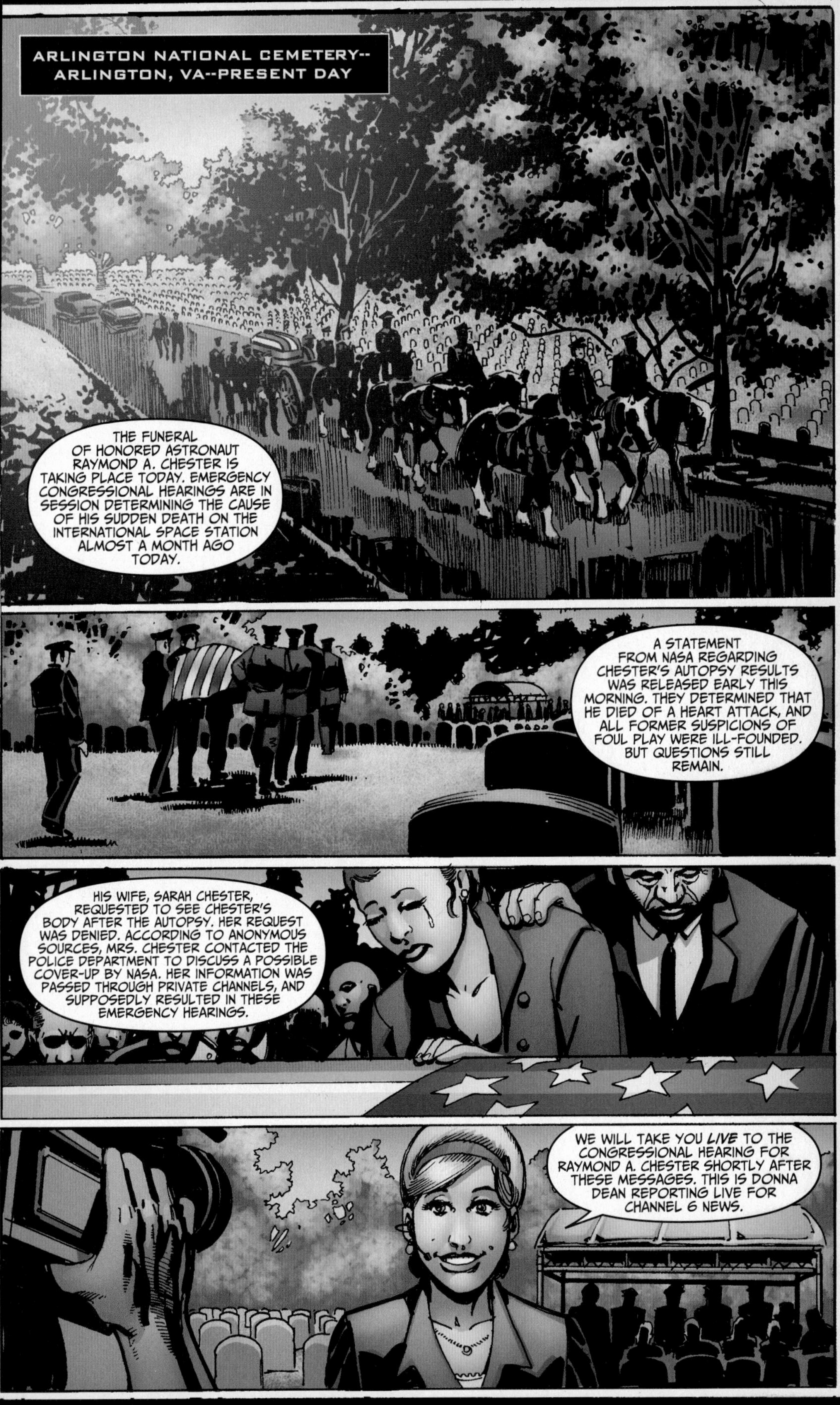
ARLINGTON NATIONAL CEMETERY--ARLINGTON, VA--PRESENT DAY
THE FUNERAL OF HONORED ASTRONAUT RAYMOND A. CHESTER IS TAKING PLACE TODAY. EMERGENCY CONGRESSIONAL HEARINGS ARE IN SESSION DETERMINING THE CAUSE OF HIS SUDDEN DEATH ON THE INTERNATIONAL SPACE STATION ALMOST A MONTH AGO TODAY.
A STATEMENT FROM NASA REGARDING CHESTER'S AUTOPSY RESULTS WAS RELEASED EARLY THIS MORNING. THEY DETERMINED THAT HE DIED OF A HEART ATTACK, AND ALL FORMER SUSPICIONS OF FOUL PLAY WERE ILL-FOUNDED. BUT QUESTIONS STILL REMAIN.
HIS WIFE, SARAH CHESTER, REQUESTED TO SEE CHESTER'S BODY AFTER THE AUTOPSY. HER REQUEST WAS DENIED. ACCORDING TO ANONYMOUS SOURCES, MRS. CHESTER CONTACTED THE POLICE DEPARTMENT TO DISCUSS A POSSIBLE COVER-UP BY NASA. HER INFORMATION WAS PASSED THROUGH PRIVATE CHANNELS, AND SUPPOSEDLY RESULTED IN THESE EMERGENCY HEARINGS.
WE WILL TAKE YOU *LIVE* TO THE CONGRESSIONAL HEARING FOR RAYMOND A. CHESTER SHORTLY AFTER THESE MESSAGES. THIS IS DONNA DEAN REPORTING LIVE FOR CHANNEL 6 NEWS.

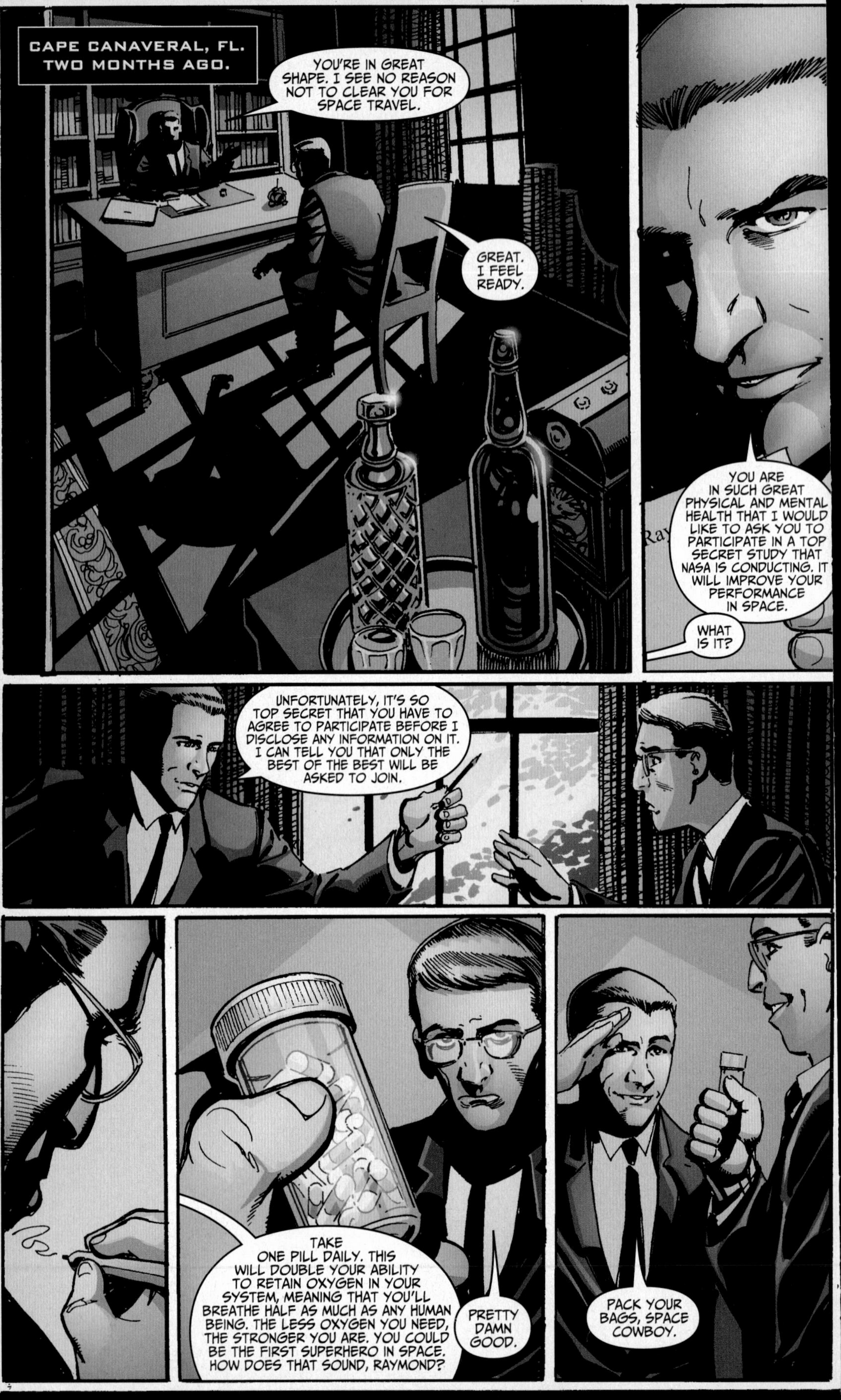
CAPE CANAVERAL, FL. TWO MONTHS AGO.
YOU'RE IN GREAT SHAPE. I SEE NO REASON NOT TO CLEAR YOU FOR SPACE TRAVEL.
GREAT. I FEEL READY.
YOU ARE IN SUCH GREAT PHYSICAL AND MENTAL HEALTH THAT I WOULD LIKE TO ASK YOU TO PARTICIPATE IN A TOP SECRET STUDY THAT NASA IS CONDUCTING. IT WILL IMPROVE YOUR PERFORMANCE IN SPACE.
WHAT IS IT?
UNFORTUNATELY, IT'S SO TOP SECRET THAT YOU HAVE TO AGREE TO PARTICIPATE BEFORE I DISCLOSE ANY INFORMATION ON IT. I CAN TELL YOU THAT ONLY THE BEST OF THE BEST WILL BE ASKED TO JOIN.
TAKE ONE PILL DAILY. THIS WILL DOUBLE YOUR ABILITY TO RETAIN OXYGEN IN YOUR SYSTEM, MEANING THAT YOU'LL BREATHE HALF AS MUCH AS ANY HUMAN BEING. THE LESS OXYGEN YOU NEED, THE STRONGER YOU ARE. YOU COULD BE THE FIRST SUPERHERO IN SPACE. HOW DOES THAT SOUND, RAYMOND?
PRETTY DAMN GOOD.
PACK YOUR BAGS, SPACE COWBOY.

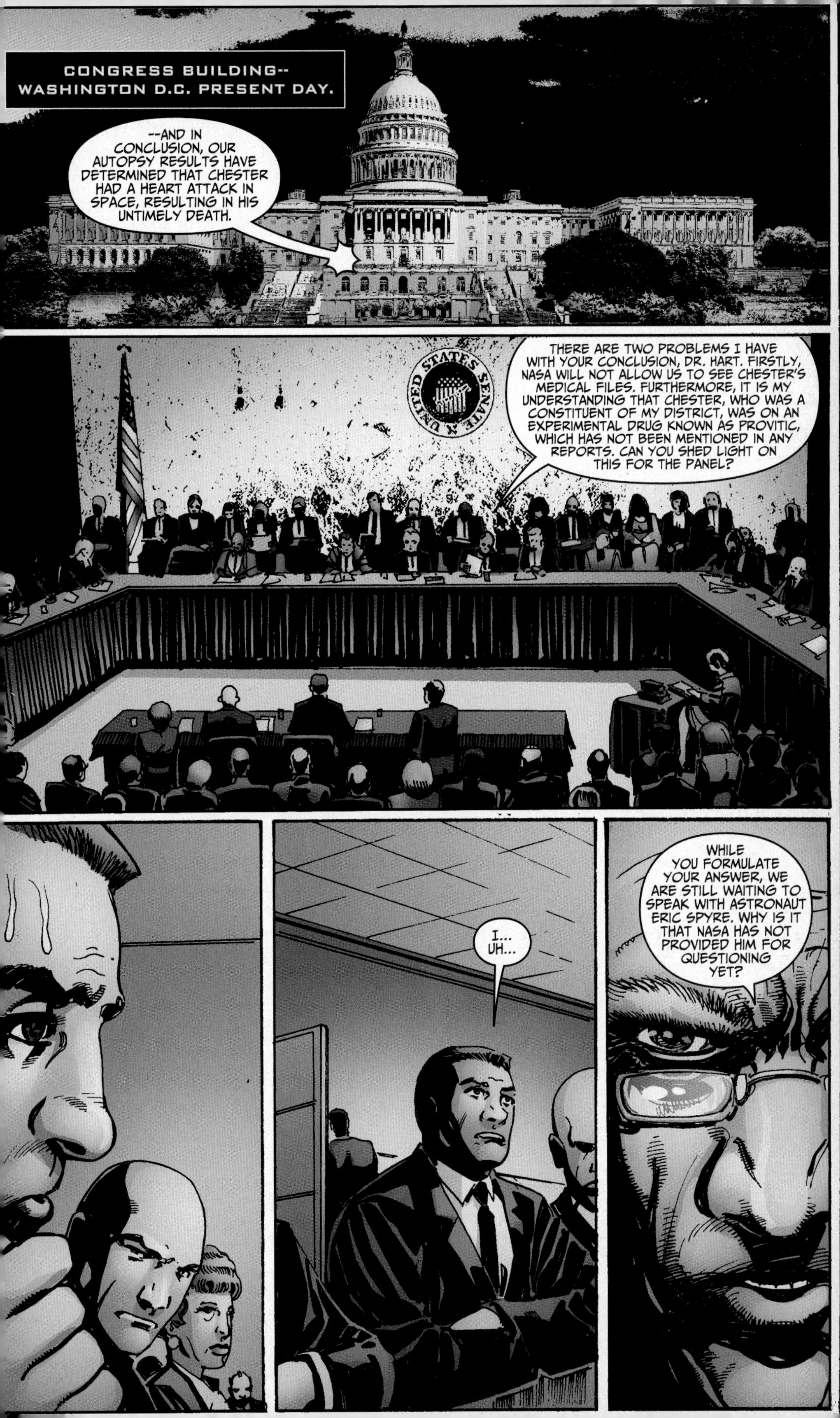

CONGRESS BUILDING--
WASHINGTON D.C. PRESENT DAY.
--AND IN CONCLUSION, OUR AUTOPSY RESULTS HAVE DETERMINED THAT CHESTER HAD A HEART ATTACK IN SPACE, RESULTING IN HIS UNTIMELY DEATH.
UNITED STATES SENATE
THERE ARE TWO PROBLEMS I HAVE WITH YOUR CONCLUSION, DR. HART. FIRSTLY, NASA WILL NOT ALLOW US TO SEE CHESTER'S MEDICAL FILES. FURTHERMORE, IT IS MY UNDERSTANDING THAT CHESTER, WHO WAS A CONSTITUENT OF MY DISTRICT, WAS ON AN EXPERIMENTAL DRUG KNOWN AS PROVITIC, WHICH HAS NOT BEEN MENTIONED IN ANY REPORTS. CAN YOU SHED LIGHT ON THIS FOR THE PANEL?
I... UH...
WHILE YOU FORMULATE YOUR ANSWER, WE ARE STILL WAITING TO SPEAK WITH ASTRONAUT ERIC SPYRE. WHY IS IT THAT NASA HAS NOT PROVIDED HIM FOR QUESTIONING YET?

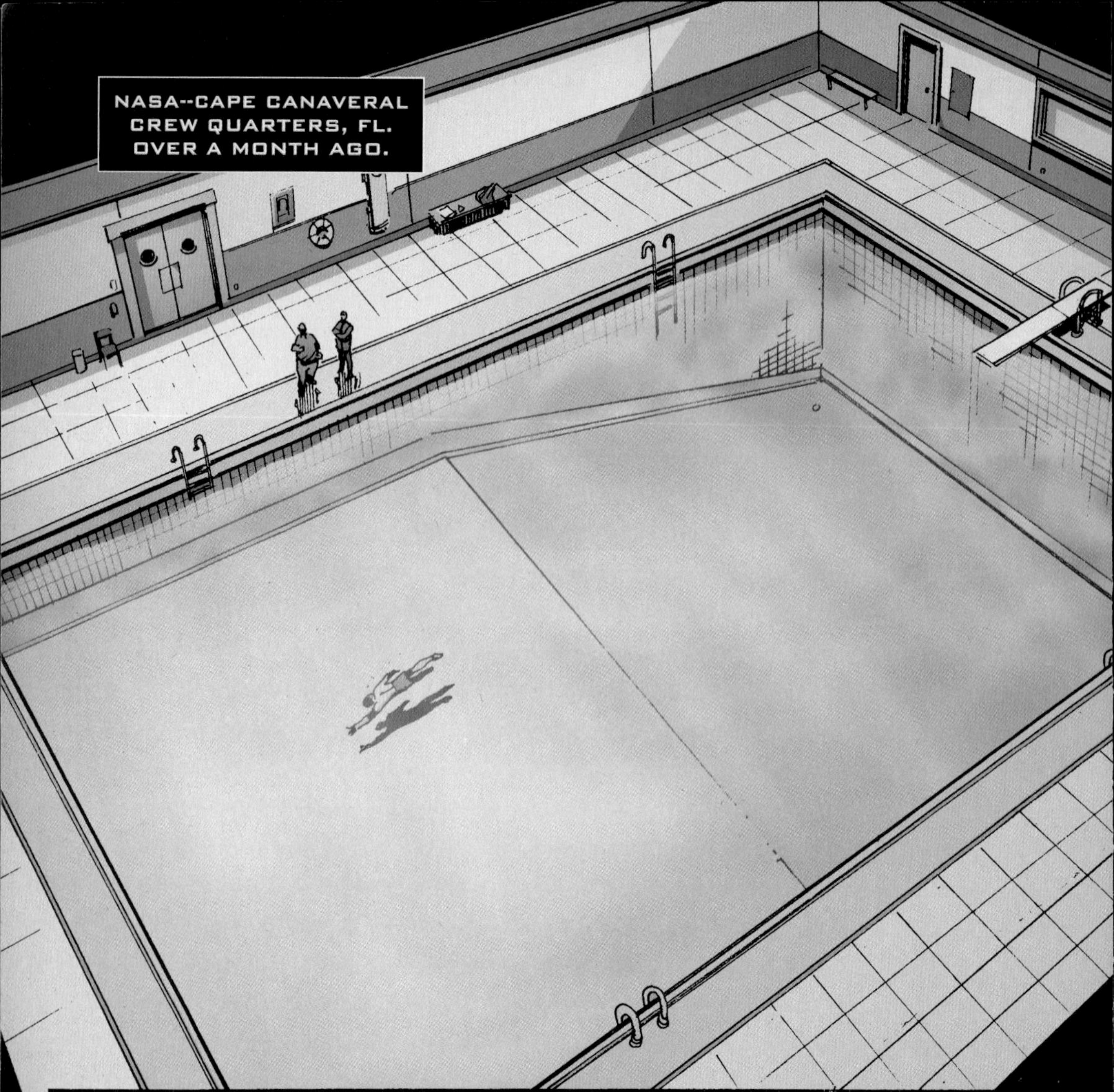
NASA--CAPE CANAVERAL
CREW QUARTERS, FL.
OVER A MONTH AGO.

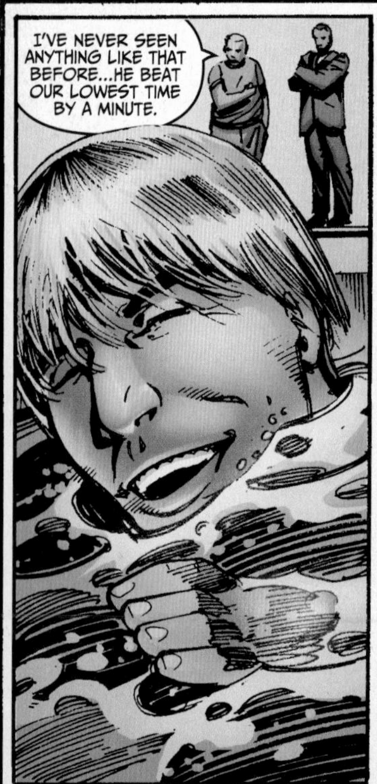
I'VE NEVER SEEN ANYTHING LIKE THAT BEFORE...HE BEAT OUR LOWEST TIME BY A MINUTE.

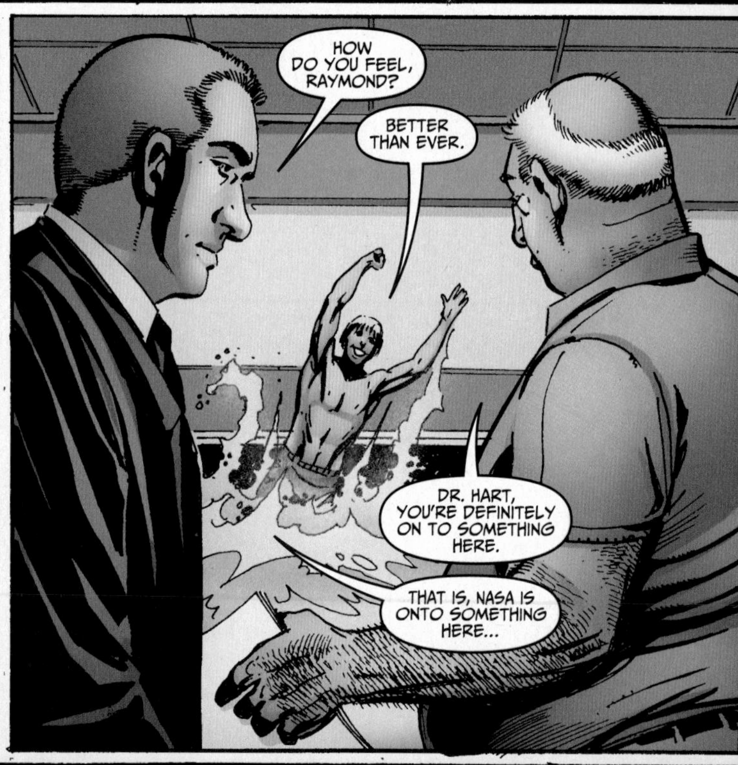
HOW DO YOU FEEL, RAYMOND?
BETTER THAN EVER.
DR. HART, YOU'RE DEFINITELY ON TO SOMETHING HERE.
THAT IS, NASA IS ONTO SOMETHING HERE...

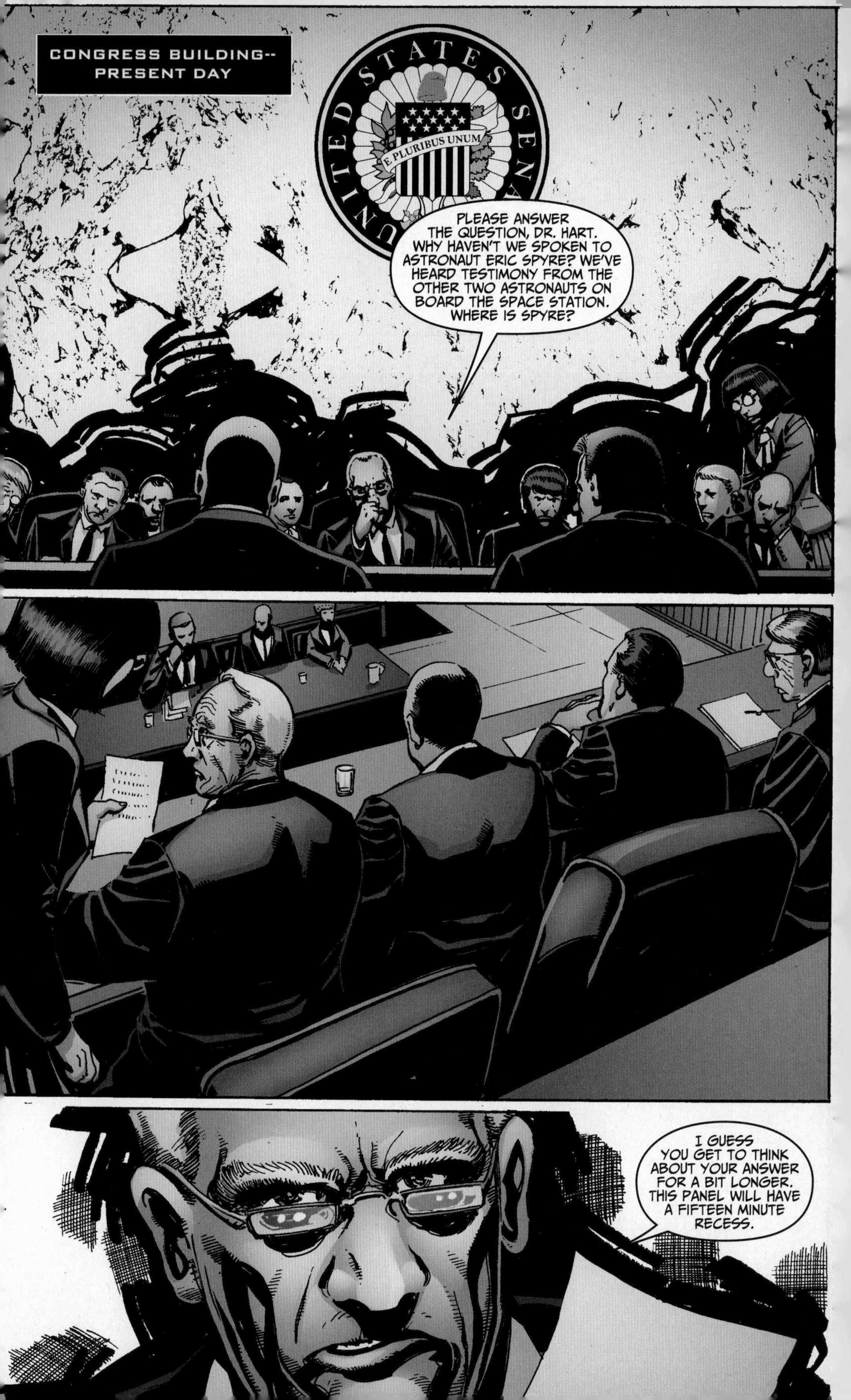
CONGRESS BUILDING--
PRESENT DAY
UNITED STATES SEN
E PLURIBUS UNUM
PLEASE ANSWER THE QUESTION, DR. HART. WHY HAVEN'T WE SPOKEN TO ASTRONAUT ERIC SPYRE? WE'VE HEARD TESTIMONY FROM THE OTHER TWO ASTRONAUTS ON BOARD THE SPACE STATION. WHERE IS SPYRE?
I GUESS YOU GET TO THINK ABOUT YOUR ANSWER FOR A BIT LONGER. THIS PANEL WILL HAVE A FIFTEEN MINUTE RECESS.

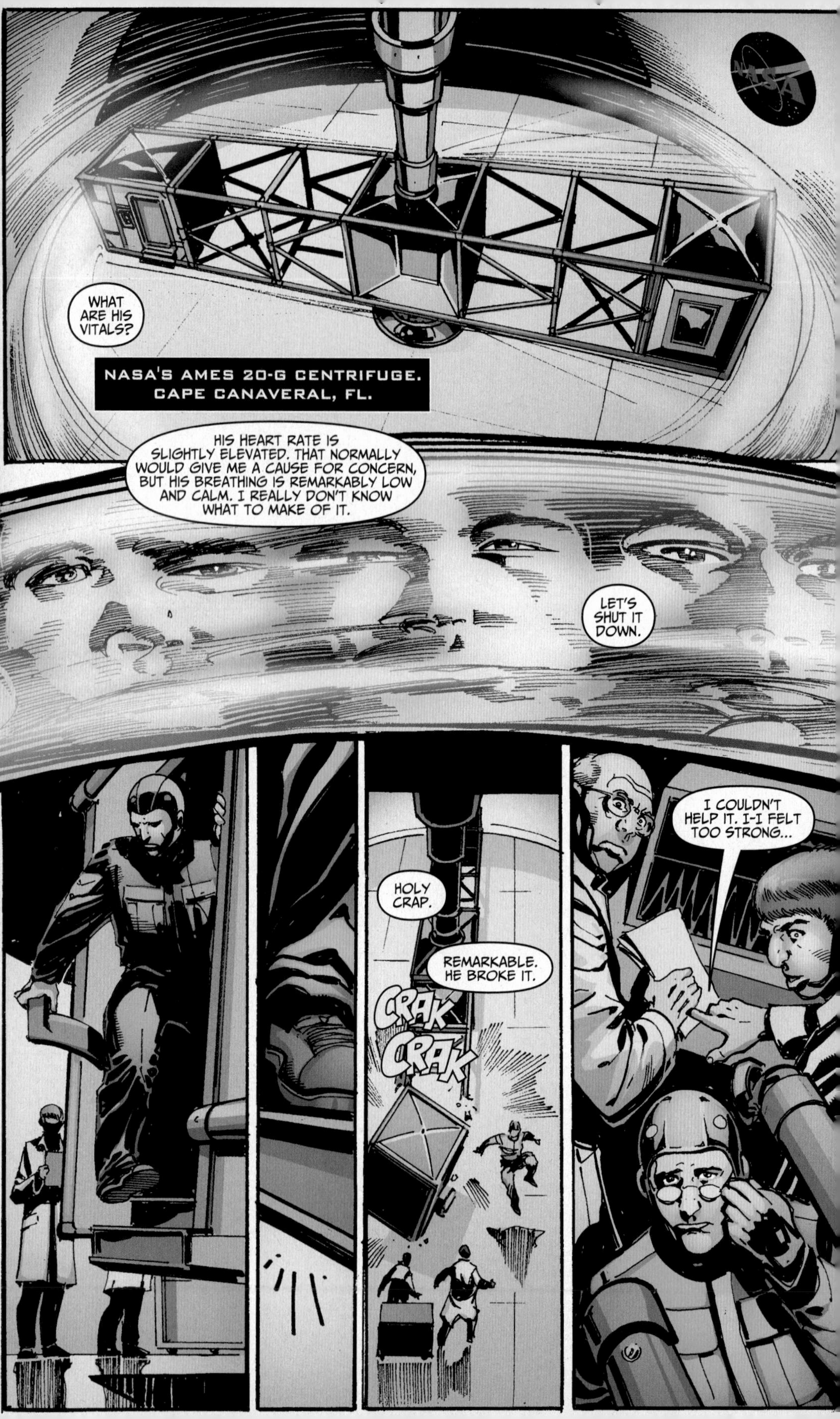
WHAT ARE HIS VITALS?
NASA'S AMES 20-G CENTRIFUGE. CAPE CANAVERAL, FL.
HIS HEART RATE IS SLIGHTLY ELEVATED. THAT NORMALLY WOULD GIVE ME A CAUSE FOR CONCERN, BUT HIS BREATHING IS REMARKABLY LOW AND CALM. I REALLY DON'T KNOW WHAT TO MAKE OF IT.
LET'S SHUT IT DOWN.
HOLY CRAP.
REMARKABLE. HE BROKE IT.
CRAK
CRAK
I COULDN'T HELP IT. I-I FELT TOO STRONG...

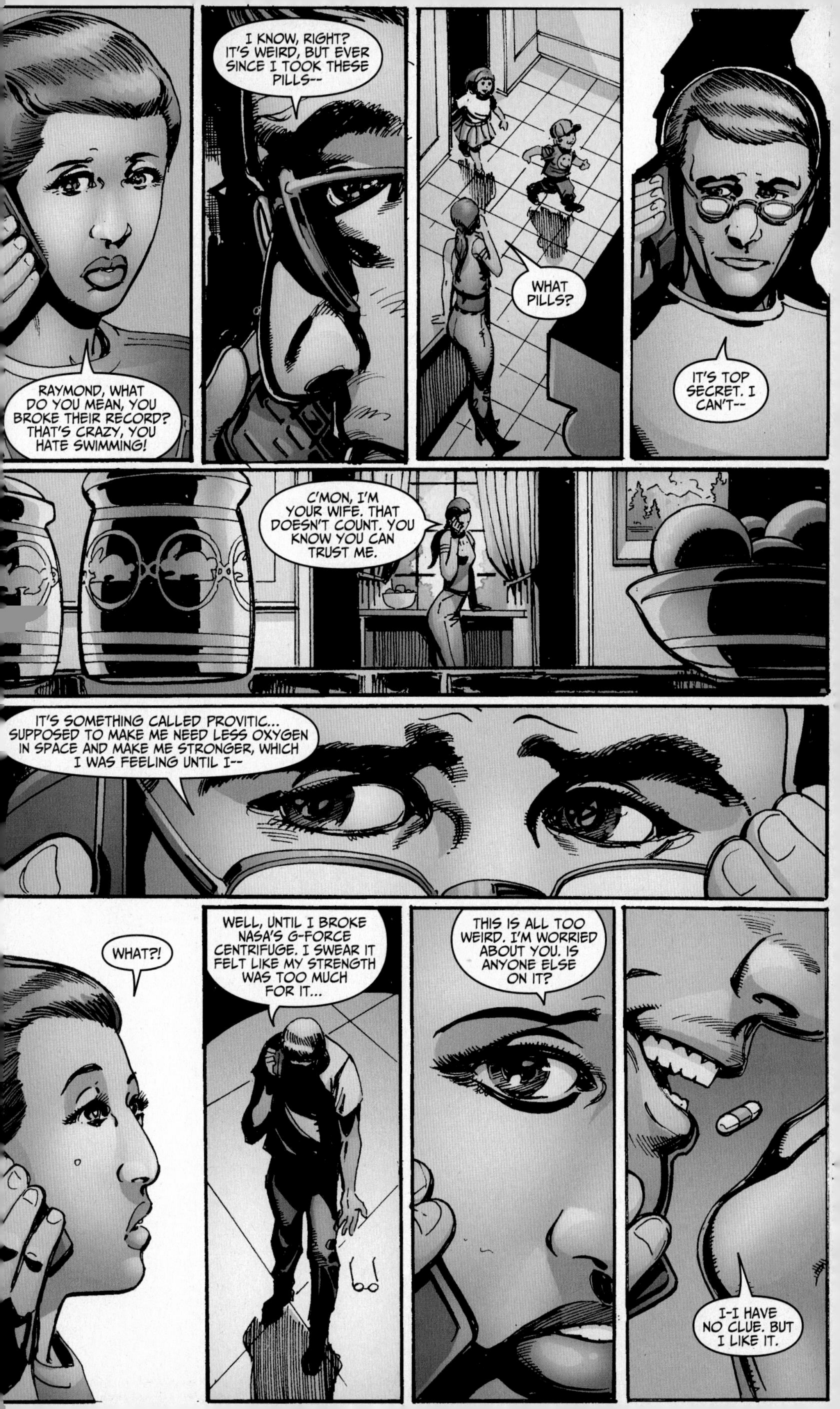
RAYMOND, WHAT DO YOU MEAN, YOU BROKE THEIR RECORD? THAT'S CRAZY, YOU HATE SWIMMING!
I KNOW, RIGHT? IT'S WEIRD, BUT EVER SINCE I TOOK THESE PILLS--
WHAT PILLS?
IT'S TOP SECRET. I CAN'T--
C'MON, I'M YOUR WIFE. THAT DOESN'T COUNT. YOU KNOW YOU CAN TRUST ME.
IT'S SOMETHING CALLED PROVITIC... SUPPOSED TO MAKE ME NEED LESS OXYGEN IN SPACE AND MAKE ME STRONGER, WHICH I WAS FEELING UNTIL I--
WHAT?!
WELL, UNTIL I BROKE NASA'S G-FORCE CENTRIFUGE. I SWEAR IT FELT LIKE MY STRENGTH WAS TOO MUCH FOR IT...
THIS IS ALL TOO WEIRD. I'M WORRIED ABOUT YOU. IS ANYONE ELSE ON IT?
I-I HAVE NO CLUE. BUT I LIKE IT.

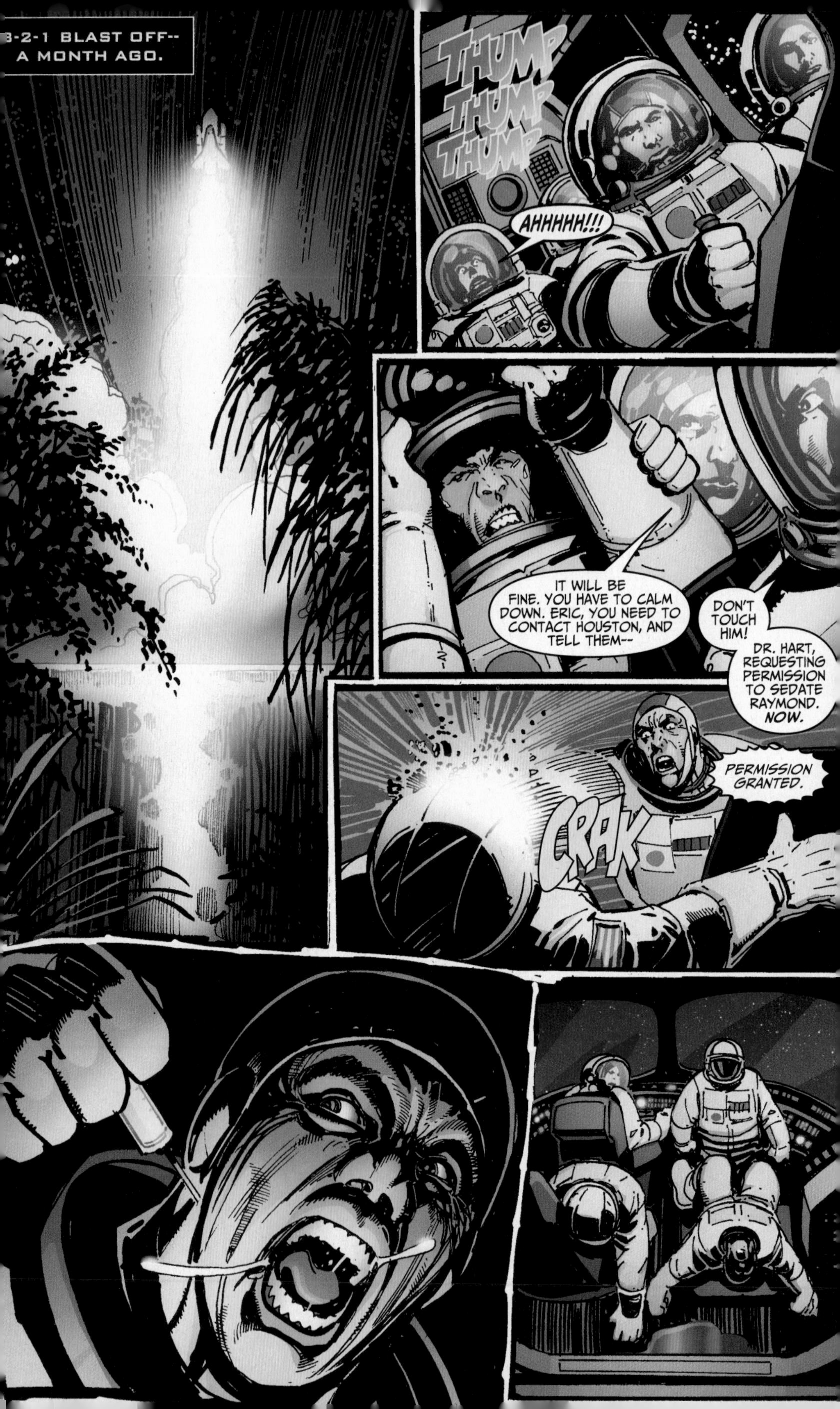
3-2-1 BLAST OFF-- A MONTH AGO.
THUMP THUMP THUMP
AHHHHH!!!
IT WILL BE FINE. YOU HAVE TO CALM DOWN. ERIC, YOU NEED TO CONTACT HOUSTON, AND TELL THEM--
DON'T TOUCH HIM!
DR. HART, REQUESTING PERMISSION TO SEDATE RAYMOND. NOW.
PERMISSION GRANTED.
CRAK

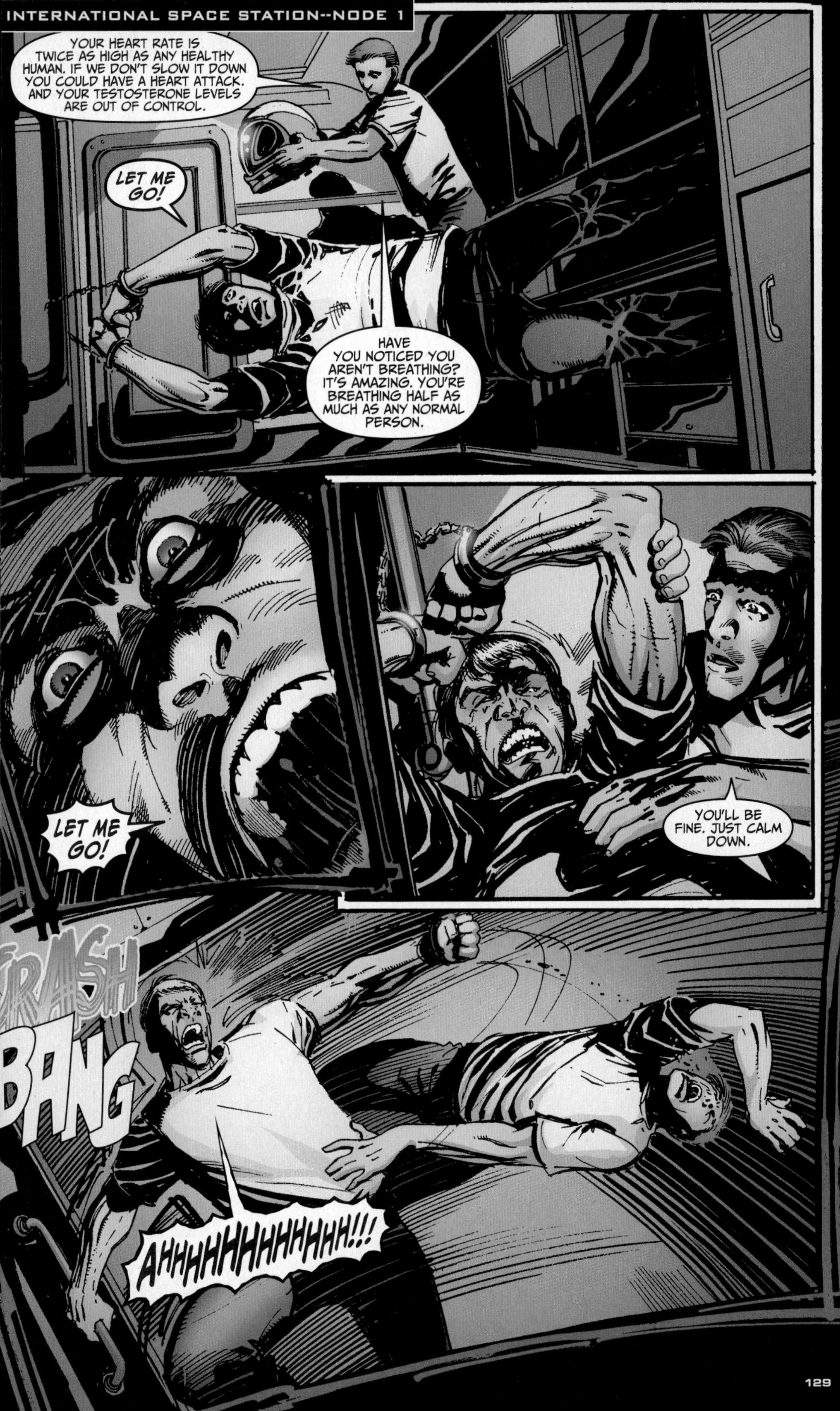

INTERNATIONAL SPACE STATION--NODE 1
YOUR HEART RATE IS TWICE AS HIGH AS ANY HEALTHY HUMAN. IF WE DON'T SLOW IT DOWN YOU COULD HAVE A HEART ATTACK. AND YOUR TESTOSTERONE LEVELS ARE OUT OF CONTROL.
LET ME GO!
HAVE YOU NOTICED YOU AREN'T BREATHING? IT'S AMAZING. YOU'RE BREATHING HALF AS MUCH AS ANY NORMAL PERSON.
LET ME GO!
YOU'LL BE FINE. JUST CALM DOWN.
BANG
AHHHHHHHHHHHH!!!

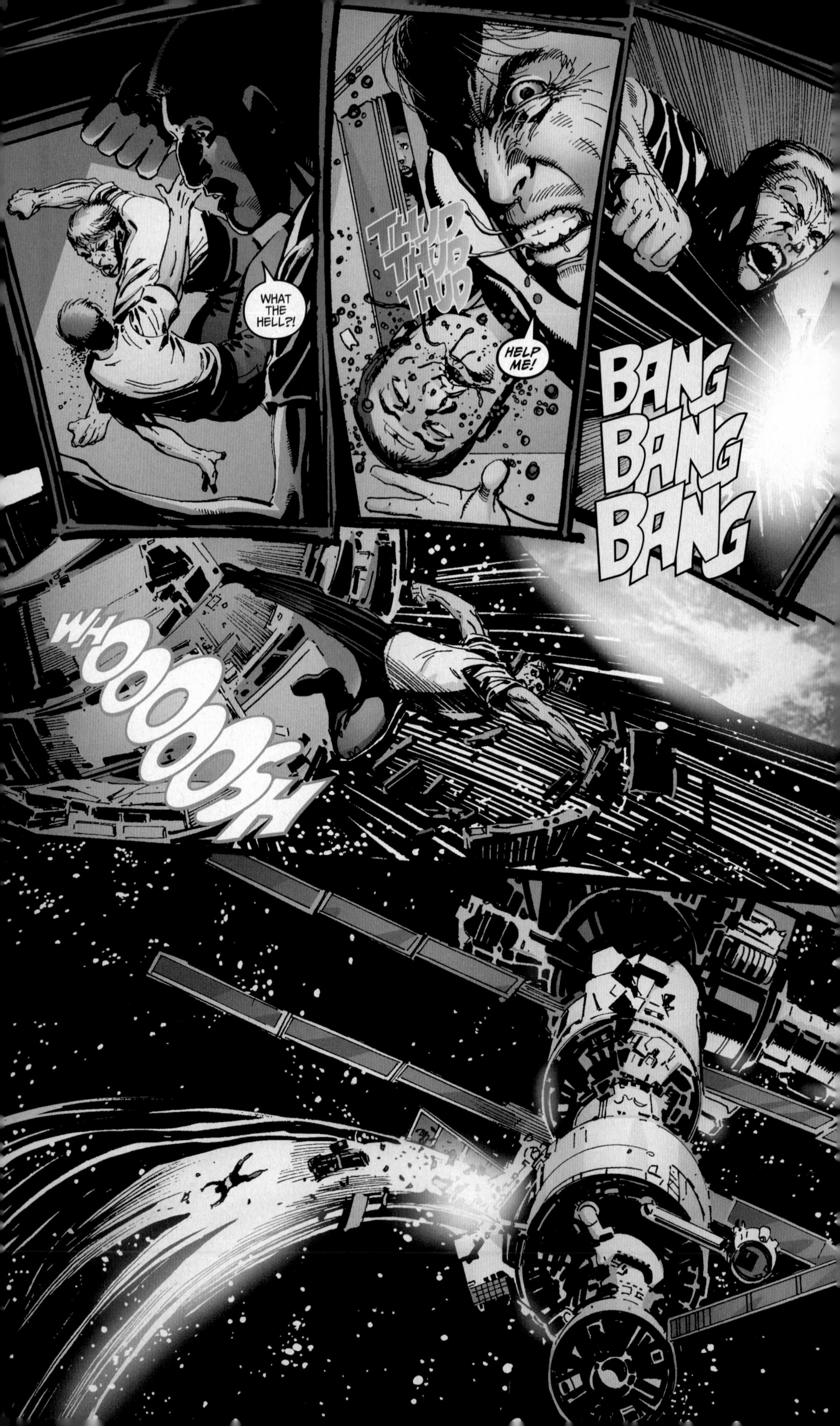
WHAT THE HELL?!
THUD THUD THUD
HELP ME!
BANG BANG BANG
WHOOOOOSH

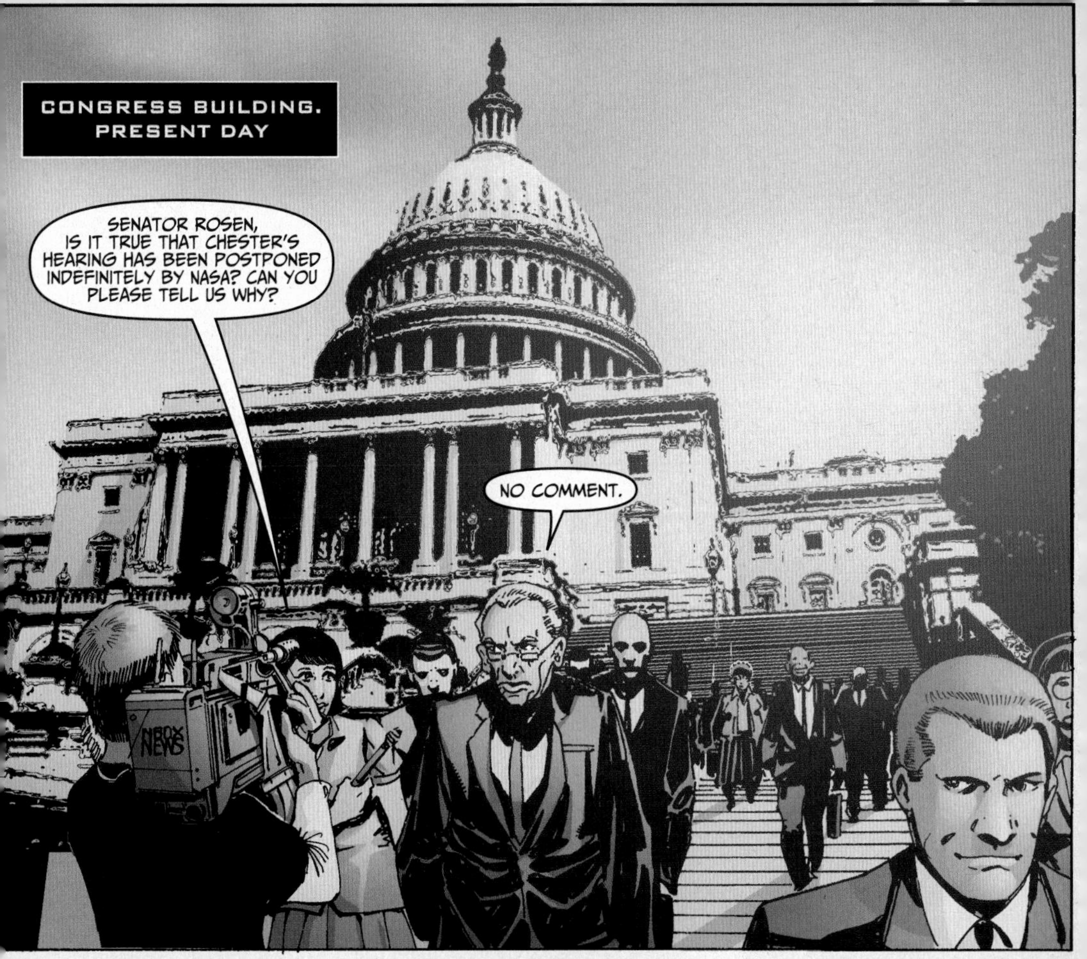
CONGRESS BUILDING. PRESENT DAY
SENATOR ROSEN, IS IT TRUE THAT CHESTER'S HEARING HAS BEEN POSTPONED INDEFINITELY BY NASA? CAN YOU PLEASE TELL US WHY?
NO COMMENT.
NBOX NEWS

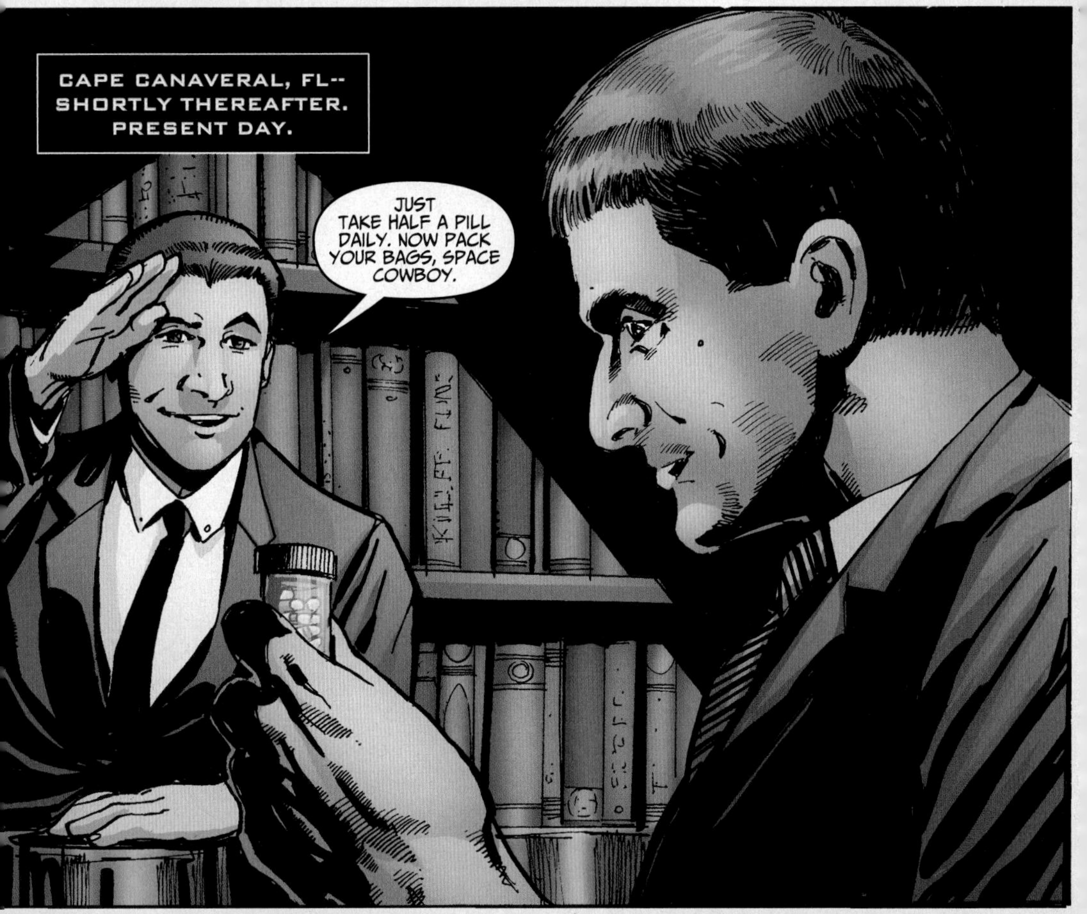
CAPE CANAVERAL, FL-- SHORTLY THEREAFTER. PRESENT DAY.
JUST TAKE HALF A PILL DAILY. NOW PACK YOUR BAGS, SPACE COWBOY.

HARD COPY

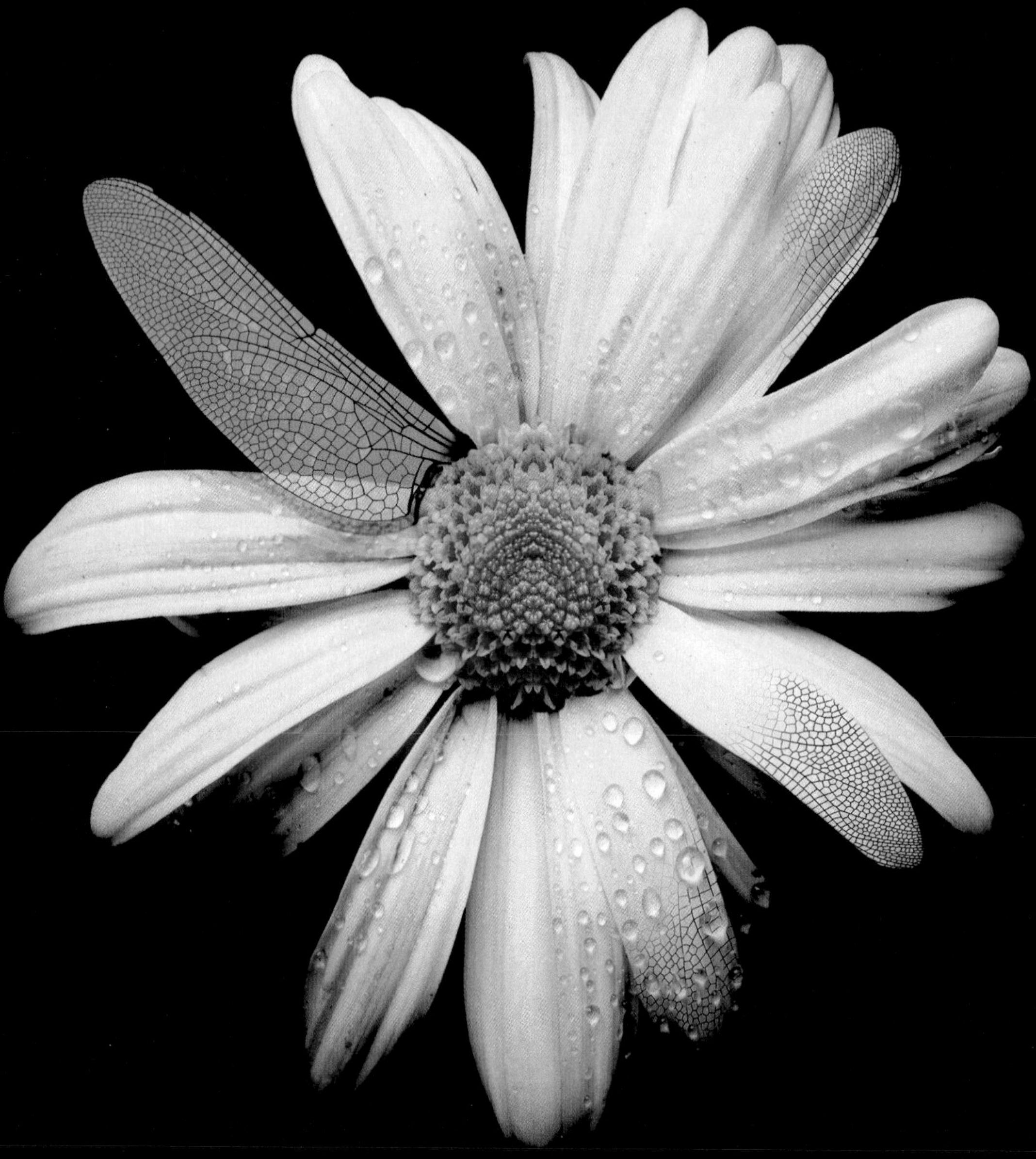

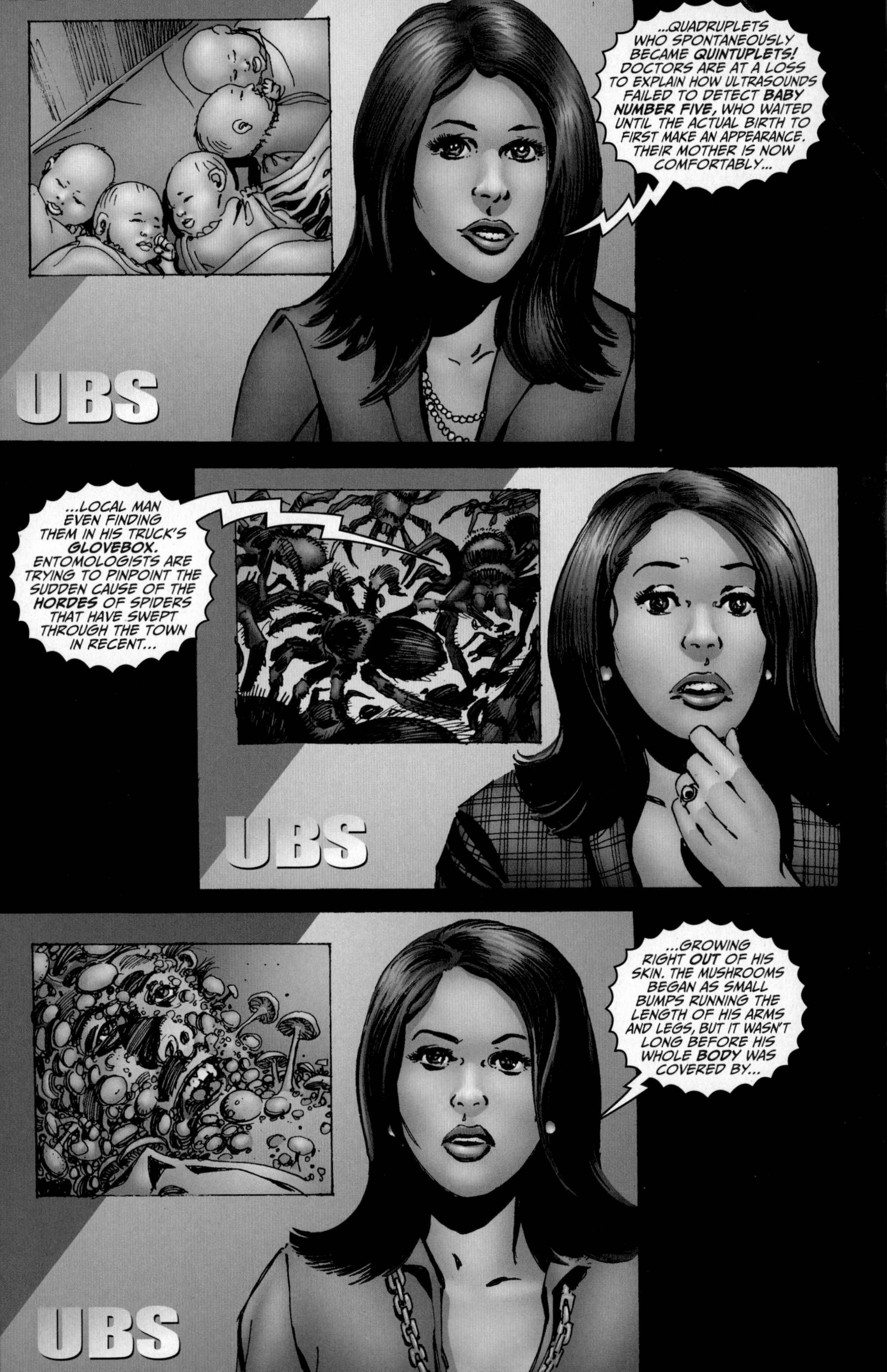
...QUADRUPLETS WHO SPONTANEOUSLY BECAME **QUINTUPLETS!** DOCTORS ARE AT A LOSS TO EXPLAIN HOW ULTRASOUNDS FAILED TO DETECT **BABY NUMBER FIVE,** WHO WAITED UNTIL THE ACTUAL BIRTH TO FIRST MAKE AN APPEARANCE. THEIR MOTHER IS NOW COMFORTABLY...
UBS
...LOCAL MAN EVEN FINDING THEM IN HIS TRUCK'S **GLOVEBOX.** ENTOMOLOGISTS ARE TRYING TO PINPOINT THE SUDDEN CAUSE OF THE **HORDES** OF SPIDERS THAT HAVE SWEPT THROUGH THE TOWN IN RECENT...
UBS
...GROWING RIGHT **OUT** OF HIS SKIN. THE MUSHROOMS BEGAN AS SMALL BUMPS RUNNING THE LENGTH OF HIS ARMS AND LEGS, BUT IT WASN'T LONG BEFORE HIS WHOLE **BODY** WAS COVERED BY...
UBS

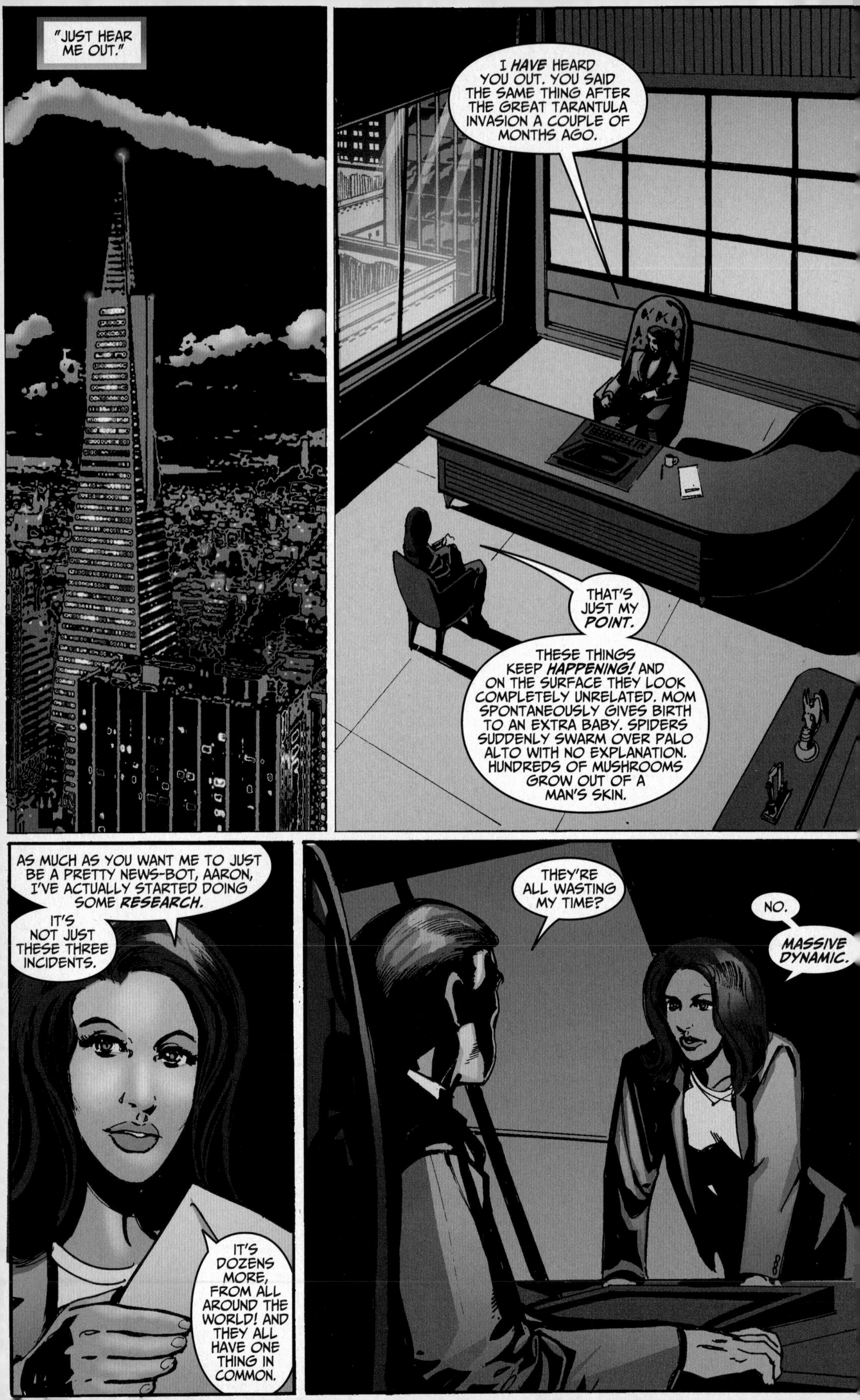
"JUST HEAR ME OUT."
I HAVE HEARD YOU OUT. YOU SAID THE SAME THING AFTER THE GREAT TARANTULA INVASION A COUPLE OF MONTHS AGO.
THAT'S JUST MY POINT.
THESE THINGS KEEP HAPPENING! AND ON THE SURFACE THEY LOOK COMPLETELY UNRELATED. MOM SPONTANEOUSLY GIVES BIRTH TO AN EXTRA BABY. SPIDERS SUDDENLY SWARM OVER PALO ALTO WITH NO EXPLANATION. HUNDREDS OF MUSHROOMS GROW OUT OF A MAN'S SKIN.
AS MUCH AS YOU WANT ME TO JUST BE A PRETTY NEWS-BOT, AARON, I'VE ACTUALLY STARTED DOING SOME RESEARCH.
IT'S NOT JUST THESE THREE INCIDENTS.
IT'S DOZENS MORE, FROM ALL AROUND THE WORLD! AND THEY ALL HAVE ONE THING IN COMMON.
THEY'RE ALL WASTING MY TIME?
NO.
MASSIVE DYNAMIC.

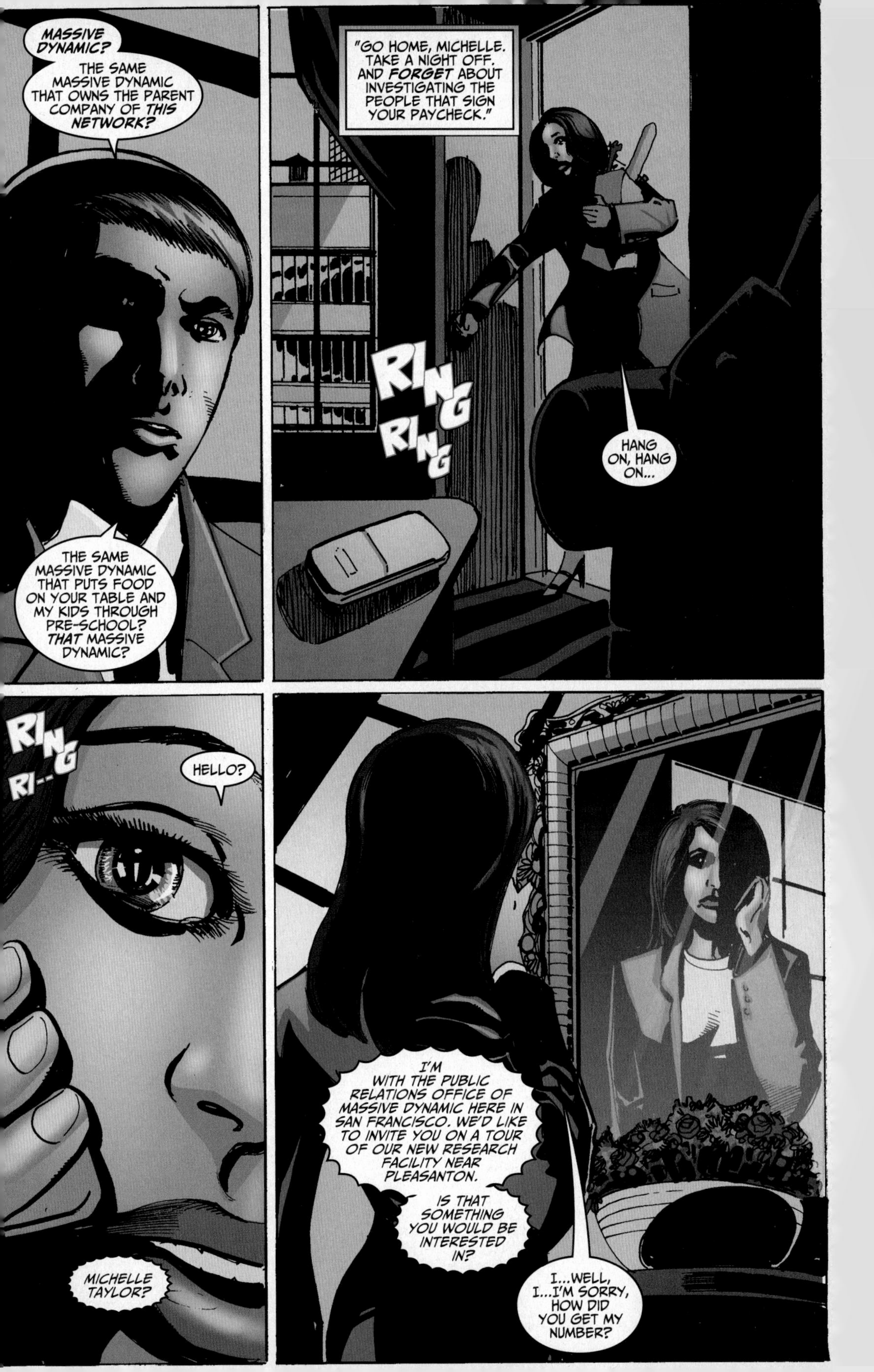
MASSIVE DYNAMIC?
THE SAME MASSIVE DYNAMIC THAT OWNS THE PARENT COMPANY OF THIS NETWORK?
THE SAME MASSIVE DYNAMIC THAT PUTS FOOD ON YOUR TABLE AND MY KIDS THROUGH PRE-SCHOOL? THAT MASSIVE DYNAMIC?
"GO HOME, MICHELLE. TAKE A NIGHT OFF. AND FORGET ABOUT INVESTIGATING THE PEOPLE THAT SIGN YOUR PAYCHECK."
RING RING
HANG ON, HANG ON...
RING RI--
HELLO?
MICHELLE TAYLOR?
I'M WITH THE PUBLIC RELATIONS OFFICE OF MASSIVE DYNAMIC HERE IN SAN FRANCISCO. WE'D LIKE TO INVITE YOU ON A TOUR OF OUR NEW RESEARCH FACILITY NEAR PLEASANTON.
IS THAT SOMETHING YOU WOULD BE INTERESTED IN?
I...WELL, I...I'M SORRY, HOW DID YOU GET MY NUMBER?

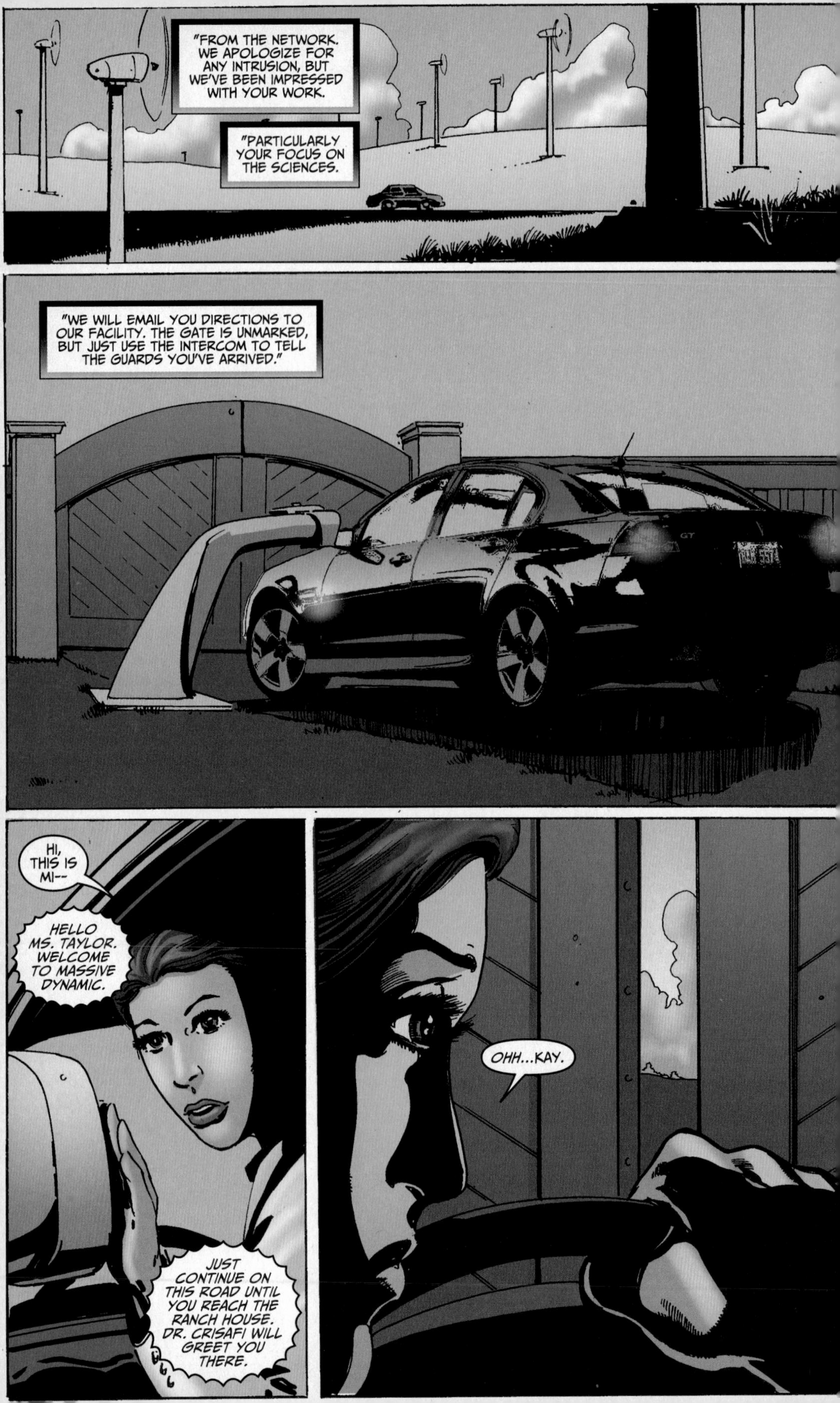

"FROM THE NETWORK. WE APOLOGIZE FOR ANY INTRUSION, BUT WE'VE BEEN IMPRESSED WITH YOUR WORK.
"PARTICULARLY YOUR FOCUS ON THE SCIENCES.
"WE WILL EMAIL YOU DIRECTIONS TO OUR FACILITY. THE GATE IS UNMARKED, BUT JUST USE THE INTERCOM TO TELL THE GUARDS YOU'VE ARRIVED."
HI, THIS IS MI--
HELLO MS. TAYLOR. WELCOME TO MASSIVE DYNAMIC.
JUST CONTINUE ON THIS ROAD UNTIL YOU REACH THE RANCH HOUSE. DR. CRISAFI WILL GREET YOU THERE.
OHH...KAY.

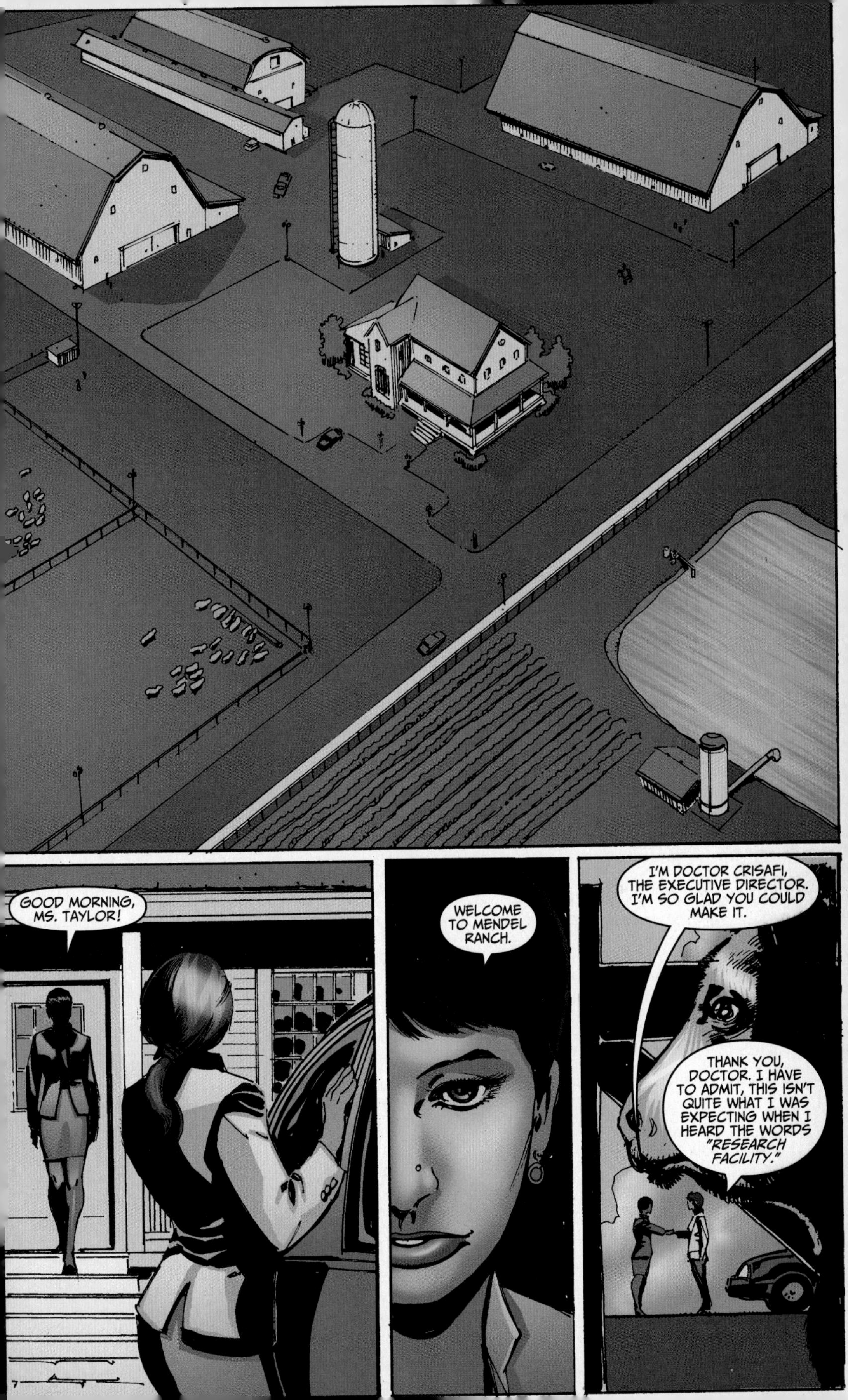
GOOD MORNING, MS. TAYLOR!
WELCOME TO MENDEL RANCH.
I'M DOCTOR CRISAFI, THE EXECUTIVE DIRECTOR. I'M SO GLAD YOU COULD MAKE IT.
THANK YOU, DOCTOR. I HAVE TO ADMIT, THIS ISN'T QUITE WHAT I WAS EXPECTING WHEN I HEARD THE WORDS "RESEARCH FACILITY."

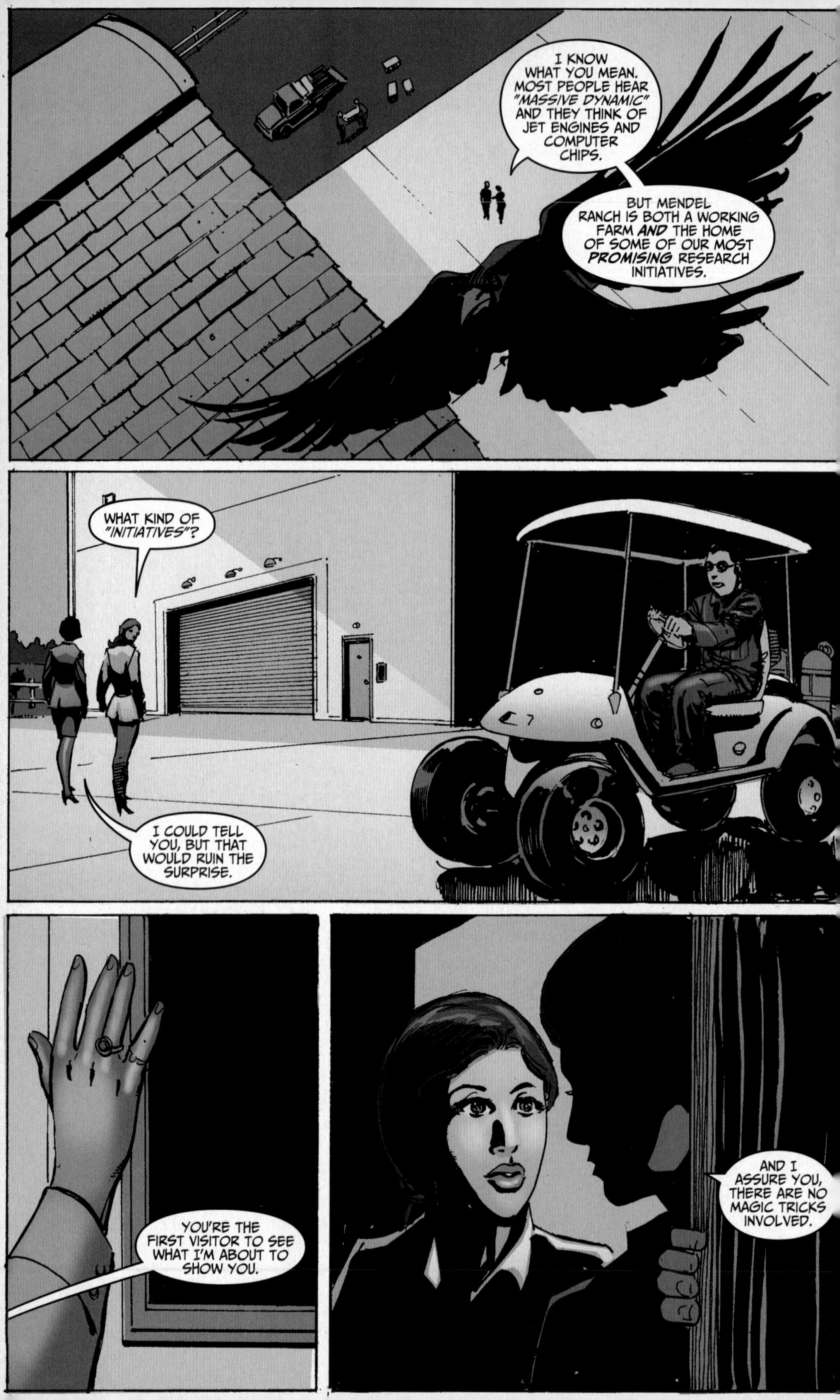
I KNOW WHAT YOU MEAN. MOST PEOPLE HEAR "MASSIVE DYNAMIC" AND THEY THINK OF JET ENGINES AND COMPUTER CHIPS.
BUT MENDEL RANCH IS BOTH A WORKING FARM AND THE HOME OF SOME OF OUR MOST PROMISING RESEARCH INITIATIVES.
WHAT KIND OF "INITIATIVES"?
I COULD TELL YOU, BUT THAT WOULD RUIN THE SURPRISE.
YOU'RE THE FIRST VISITOR TO SEE WHAT I'M ABOUT TO SHOW YOU.
AND I ASSURE YOU, THERE ARE NO MAGIC TRICKS INVOLVED.

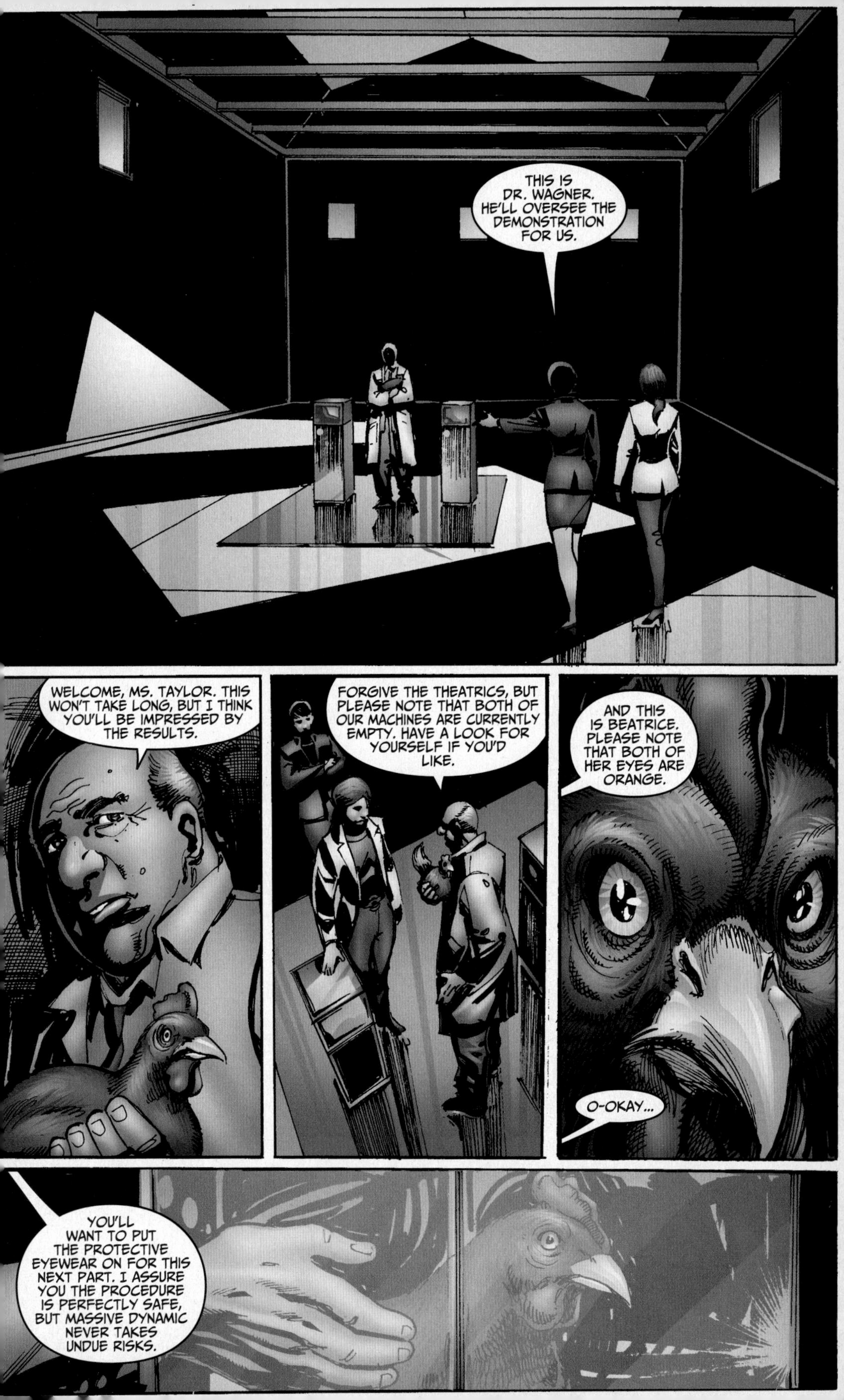
THIS IS DR. WAGNER. HE'LL OVERSEE THE DEMONSTRATION FOR US.
WELCOME, MS. TAYLOR. THIS WON'T TAKE LONG, BUT I THINK YOU'LL BE IMPRESSED BY THE RESULTS.
FORGIVE THE THEATRICS, BUT PLEASE NOTE THAT BOTH OF OUR MACHINES ARE CURRENTLY EMPTY. HAVE A LOOK FOR YOURSELF IF YOU'D LIKE.
AND THIS IS BEATRICE. PLEASE NOTE THAT BOTH OF HER EYES ARE ORANGE.
O-OKAY...
YOU'LL WANT TO PUT THE PROTECTIVE EYEWEAR ON FOR THIS NEXT PART. I ASSURE YOU THE PROCEDURE IS PERFECTLY SAFE, BUT MASSIVE DYNAMIC NEVER TAKES UNDUE RISKS.

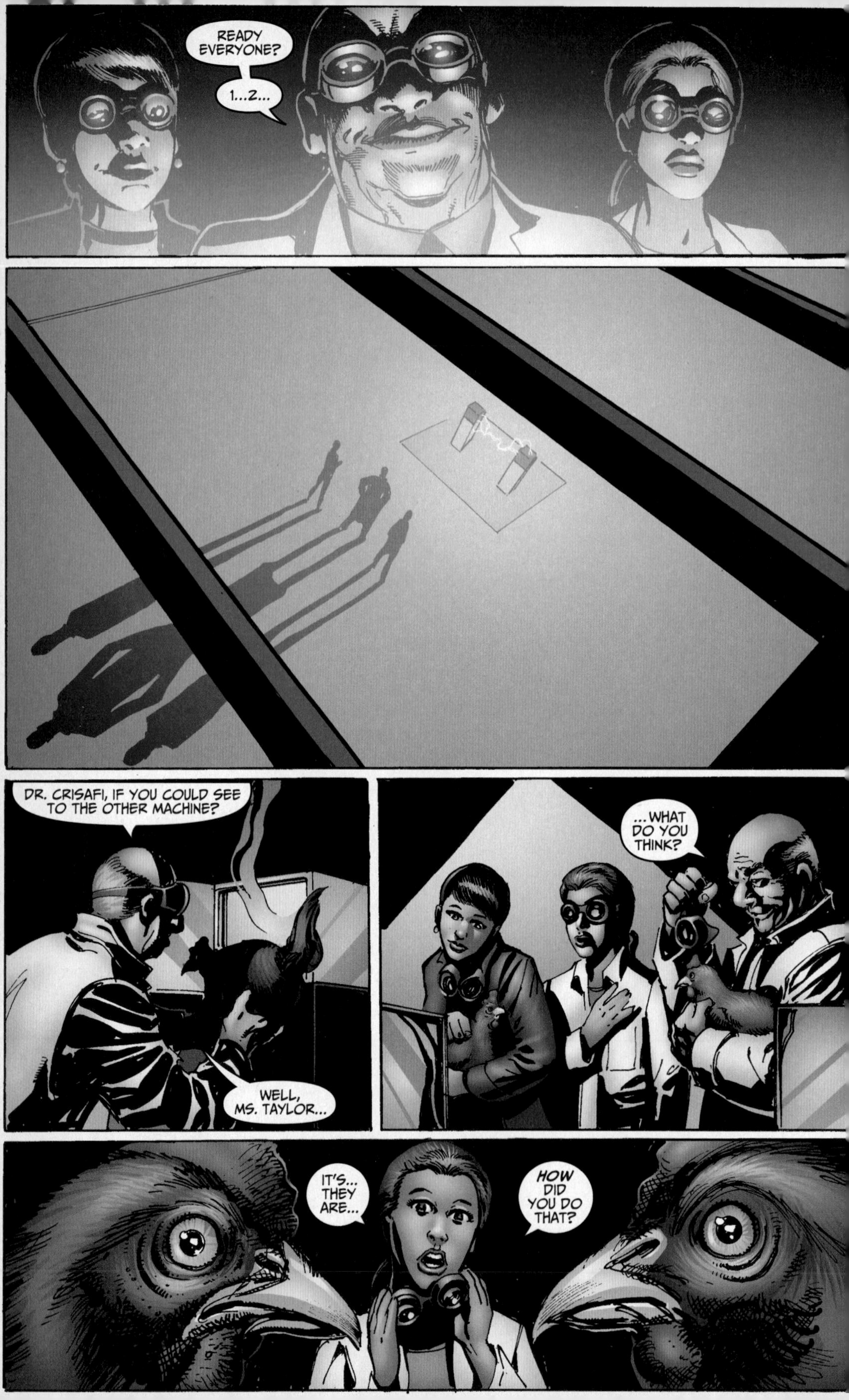
READY EVERYONE?
1...2...
DR. CRISAFI, IF YOU COULD SEE TO THE OTHER MACHINE?
WELL, MS. TAYLOR...
...WHAT DO YOU THINK?
IT'S... THEY ARE...
HOW DID YOU DO THAT?

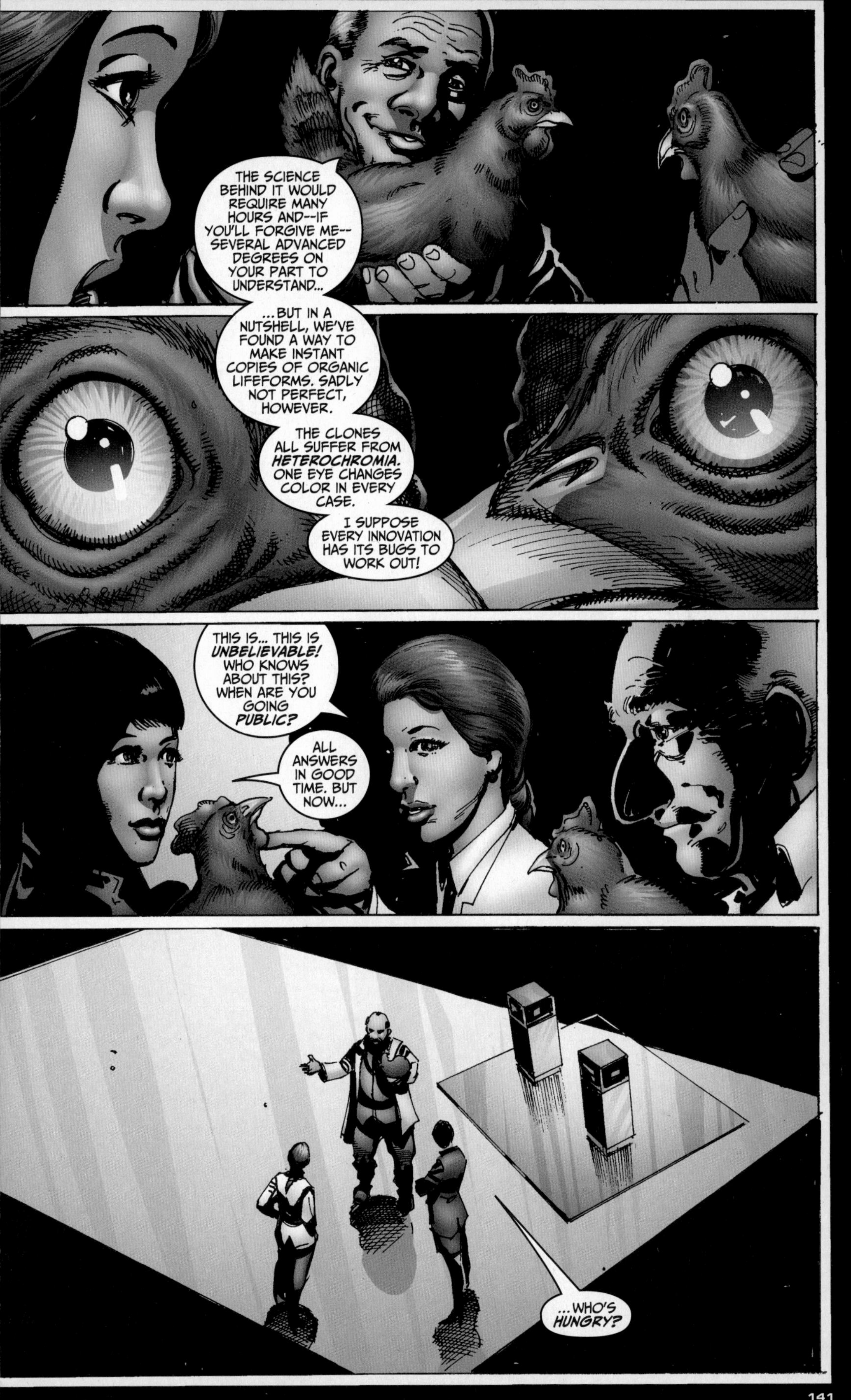
THE SCIENCE BEHIND IT WOULD REQUIRE MANY HOURS AND--IF YOU'LL FORGIVE ME--SEVERAL ADVANCED DEGREES ON YOUR PART TO UNDERSTAND...
...BUT IN A NUTSHELL, WE'VE FOUND A WAY TO MAKE INSTANT COPIES OF ORGANIC LIFEFORMS. SADLY NOT PERFECT, HOWEVER.
THE CLONES ALL SUFFER FROM HETEROCHROMIA. ONE EYE CHANGES COLOR IN EVERY CASE.
I SUPPOSE EVERY INNOVATION HAS ITS BUGS TO WORK OUT!
THIS IS... THIS IS UNBELIEVABLE! WHO KNOWS ABOUT THIS? WHEN ARE YOU GOING PUBLIC?
ALL ANSWERS IN GOOD TIME. BUT NOW...
...WHO'S HUNGRY?

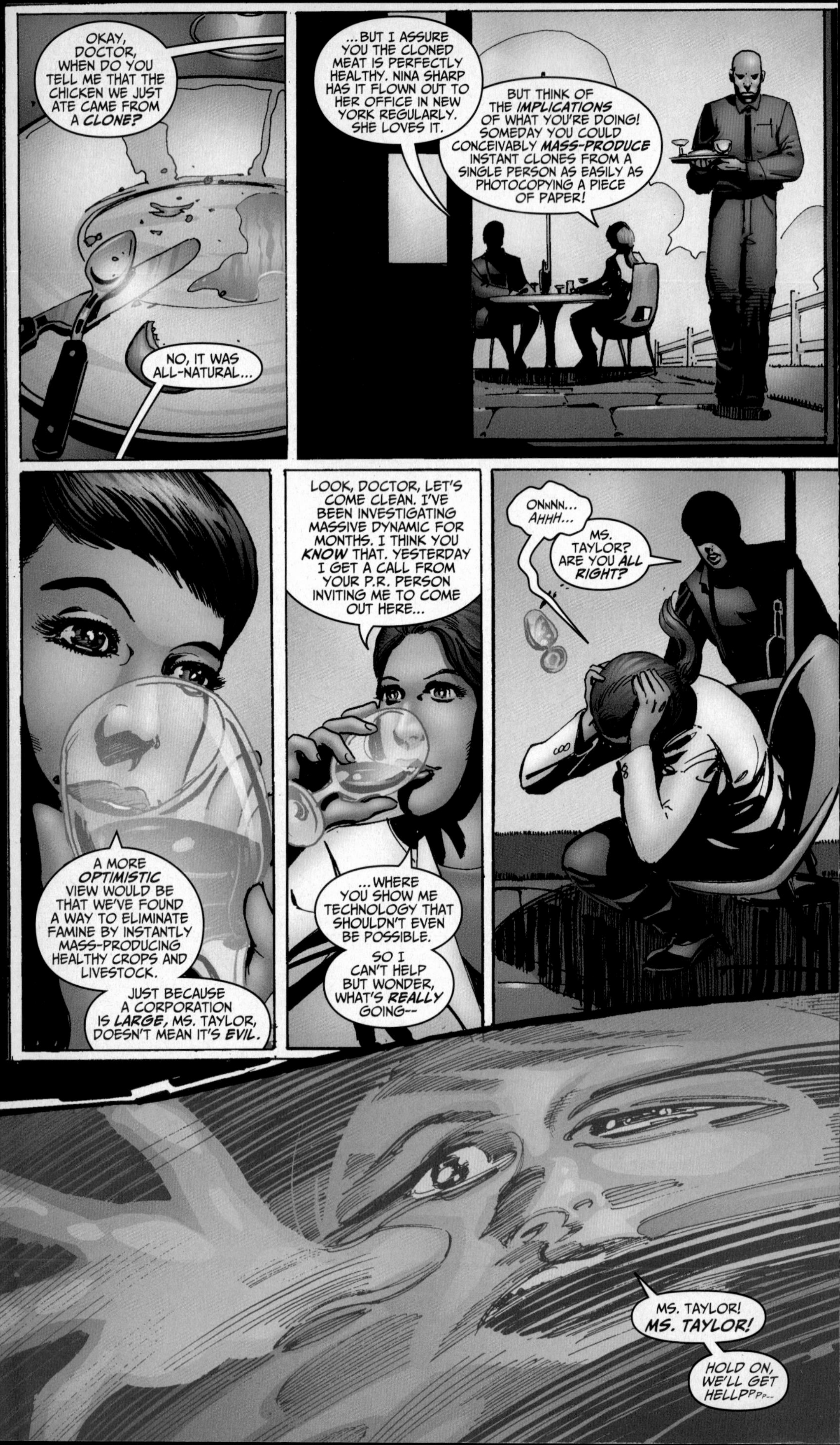

OKAY, DOCTOR, WHEN DO YOU TELL ME THAT THE CHICKEN WE JUST ATE CAME FROM A *CLONE?*
NO, IT WAS ALL-NATURAL...
...BUT I ASSURE YOU THE CLONED MEAT IS PERFECTLY HEALTHY. NINA SHARP HAS IT FLOWN OUT TO HER OFFICE IN NEW YORK REGULARLY. SHE LOVES IT.
BUT THINK OF THE *IMPLICATIONS* OF WHAT YOU'RE DOING! SOMEDAY YOU COULD CONCEIVABLY *MASS-PRODUCE* INSTANT CLONES FROM A SINGLE PERSON AS EASILY AS PHOTOCOPYING A PIECE OF PAPER!
A MORE *OPTIMISTIC* VIEW WOULD BE THAT WE'VE FOUND A WAY TO ELIMINATE FAMINE BY INSTANTLY MASS-PRODUCING HEALTHY CROPS AND LIVESTOCK.
JUST BECAUSE A CORPORATION IS *LARGE*, MS. TAYLOR, DOESN'T MEAN IT'S *EVIL*.
LOOK, DOCTOR, LET'S COME CLEAN. I'VE BEEN INVESTIGATING MASSIVE DYNAMIC FOR MONTHS. I THINK YOU *KNOW* THAT. YESTERDAY I GET A CALL FROM YOUR P.R. PERSON INVITING ME TO COME OUT HERE...
...WHERE YOU SHOW ME TECHNOLOGY THAT SHOULDN'T EVEN BE POSSIBLE.
SO I CAN'T HELP BUT WONDER, WHAT'S *REALLY* GOING--
ONNNN... AHHH...
MS. TAYLOR? ARE YOU *ALL RIGHT?*
MS. TAYLOR! **MS. TAYLOR!**
HOLD ON, WE'LL GET HELLPPP--

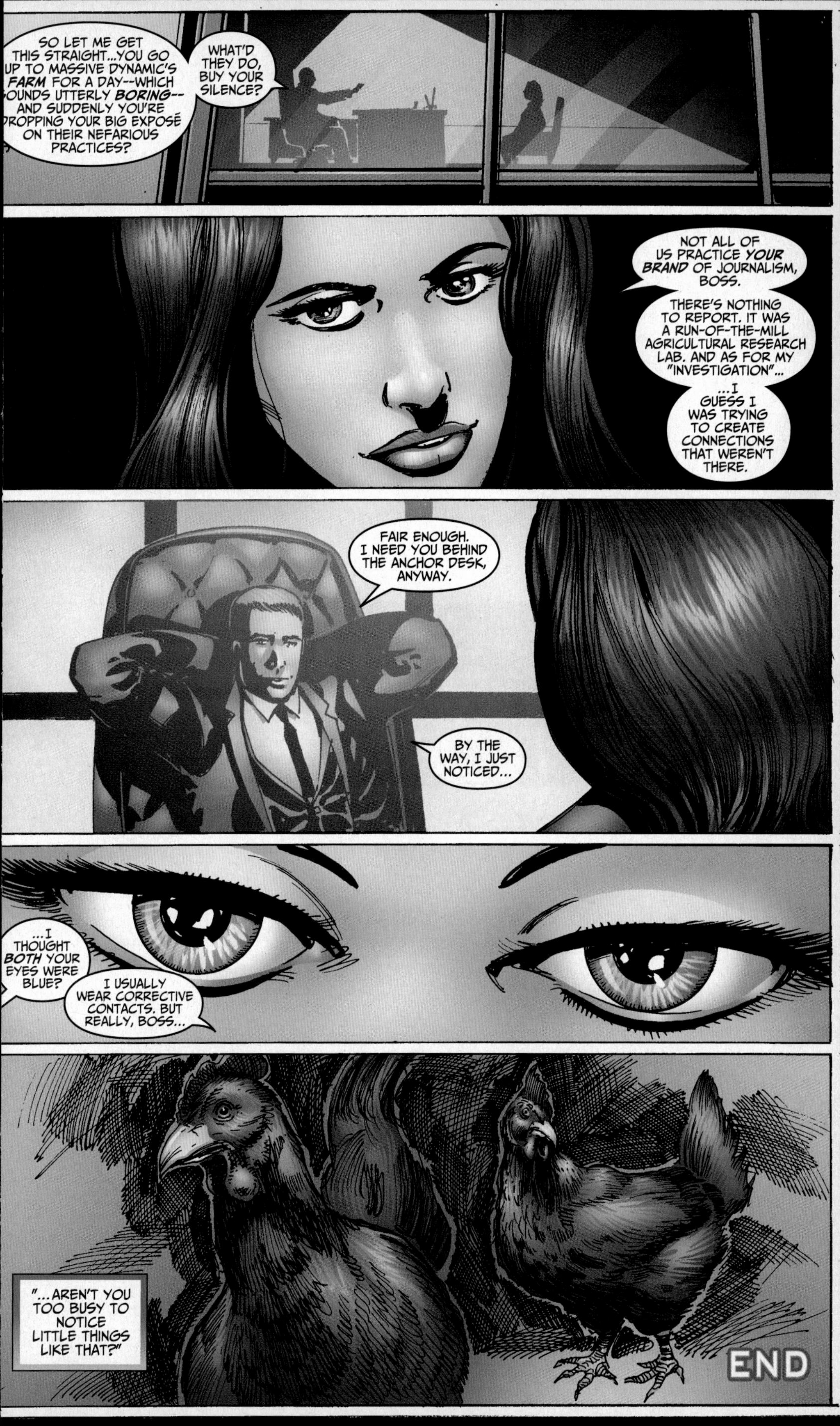
SO LET ME GET THIS STRAIGHT...YOU GO UP TO MASSIVE DYNAMIC'S FARM FOR A DAY--WHICH SOUNDS UTTERLY BORING--AND SUDDENLY YOU'RE DROPPING YOUR BIG EXPOSÉ ON THEIR NEFARIOUS PRACTICES?
WHAT'D THEY DO, BUY YOUR SILENCE?
NOT ALL OF US PRACTICE YOUR BRAND OF JOURNALISM, BOSS.
THERE'S NOTHING TO REPORT. IT WAS A RUN-OF-THE-MILL AGRICULTURAL RESEARCH LAB. AND AS FOR MY "INVESTIGATION"...
...I GUESS I WAS TRYING TO CREATE CONNECTIONS THAT WEREN'T THERE.
FAIR ENOUGH. I NEED YOU BEHIND THE ANCHOR DESK, ANYWAY.
BY THE WAY, I JUST NOTICED...
...I THOUGHT BOTH YOUR EYES WERE BLUE?
I USUALLY WEAR CORRECTIVE CONTACTS. BUT REALLY, BOSS...
"...AREN'T YOU TOO BUSY TO NOTICE LITTLE THINGS LIKE THAT?"
END

"A faithful translation of the beloved '90s TV show." -Under the Radar

THE X-FILES

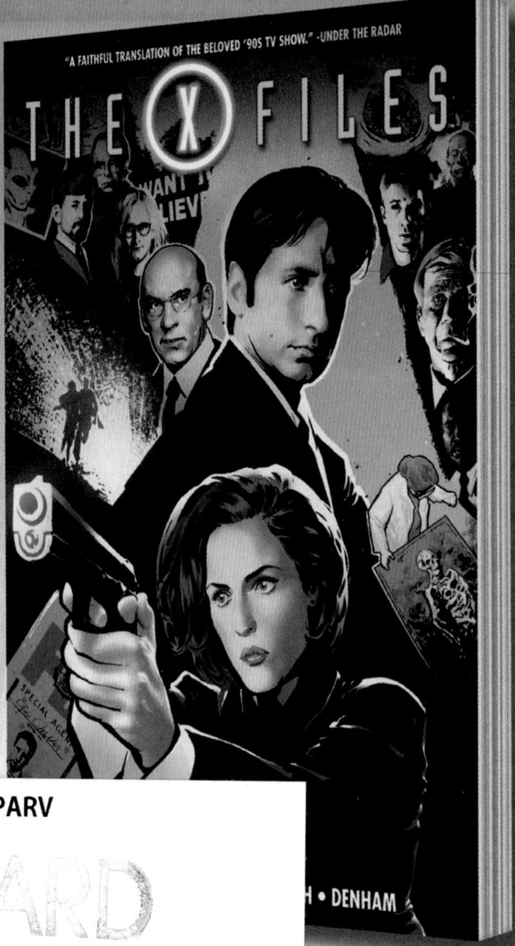
"A FAITHFUL TRANSLATION OF THE BELOVED '90S TV SHOW." -UNDER THE RADAR
THE X FILES
H • DENHAM

AMERICA'S MOST WANTED SPOOKS AND GHOULS TREMBLE IN FEAR AS THE FBI'S (VERY) SPECIAL AGENTS RETURN TO DUTY INVESTIGATING THE STRANGEST CORNERS OF AMERICA. AFTER EXAMINING TWO CASES INVOLVING POSSESSION, MULDER AND SCULLY ARE SENT TO SAN FRANCISCO TO SOLVE A STRING OF MURDERS, BECOMING TARGETS OF THE TONG UNDERWORLD IN THE PROCESS. LATER, A TRIP TO THE MYSTERIOUS BADLANDS TO INVESTIGATE A SERIES OF DISAPPEARANCES LEADS THEM DEEP INTO THE NETHERWORLD.

PRODUCER AND SCREEN
JOINS MARV WOLF
ILLUSTRATOR BRIAN DENHA

Hit shows become

CHUCK

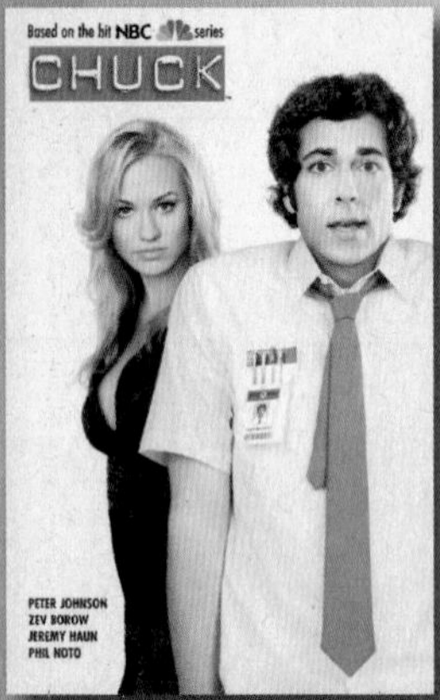
Based on the hit NBC series
CHUCK
PETER JOHNSON
ZEV BOROW
JEREMY HAUN
PHIL NOTO

Johnson • Borow Haun • Noto

HEROES Books 1 & 2

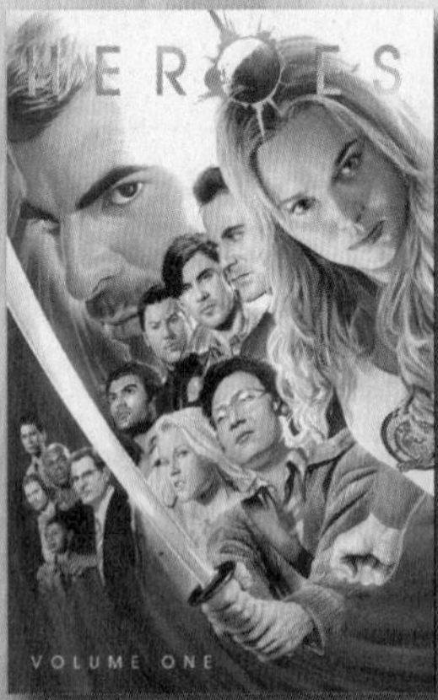
HEROES
VOLUME ONE

Various writers & artists

SUPERNATURAL: ORIGINS

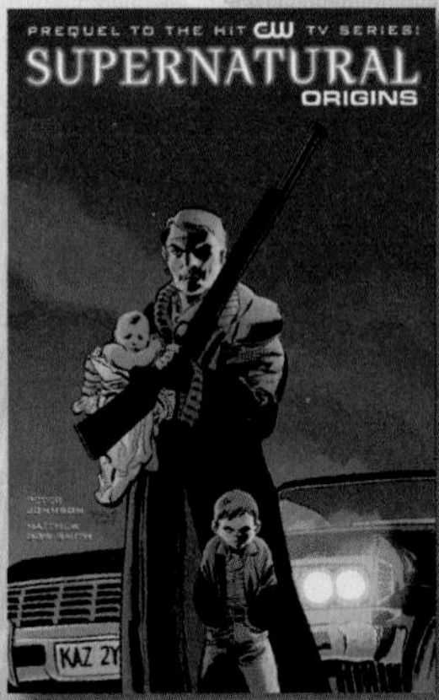
PREQUEL TO THE HIT CW TV SERIES!
SUPERNATURAL
ORIGINS
KAZ 2Y

Johnson • Smith

SUPERNATURAL: RISING SON

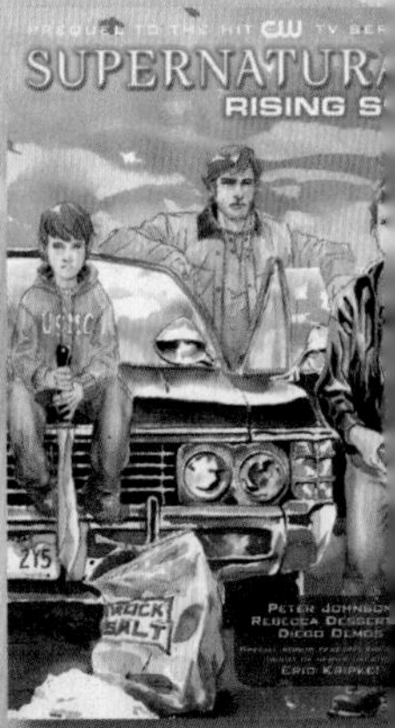
SUPERNATUR
RISING S
PETER JOHNSON
REBECCA DESSERT
DIEGO OLMOS
ERIC KRIPKE

Johnson • Dessert Olmos